D1475881

EVERY SECRET THING

EVERY SECRET THING

PATRICIA CAMPBELL HEARST

with Alvin Moscow

DOUBLEDAY & COMPANY, INC.
1982   GARDEN CITY, NEW YORK

DESIGNED BY LAURENCE ALEXANDER

Library of Congress Cataloging in Publication Data

Hearst, Patricia, 1954–
Every secret thing.

1. Hearst, Patricia, 1954–   . 2. Symbionese
Liberation Army.   3. California—Biography.   I. Title.
F866.4.H42A34   322.4′2′0924 [B]
AACR2
ISBN: 0-385-17056-4
Library of Congress Catalog Card Number: 81–43253

For Mom and Dad

ACKNOWLEDGMENTS

I never thought I would write a book and probably wouldn't have were I not constantly asked, "When are you going to talk about what happened to you?" The question arises so often that I finally decided to address it once and for all and tell the complete story of my kidnapping and my experiences with the SLA. But it is impossible to do so without first thanking all the people who helped make this book possible.

I am grateful to those who helped me during the five years described in *Every Secret Thing,* starting with the members of the board of the Hearst Corporation and the Hearst Foundation for attempting the impossible task of negotiating with madmen.

I am deeply indebted to all of my friends—old and new—who joined the Committee for the Release of Patricia Hearst. The effect of the letters they wrote, the radio and TV talk shows they called, and the petitions they circulated in my behalf cannot be underestimated. I am especially grateful to Virginia Blight and Ted Dumke, who spearheaded the Committee. And to Kathleen Barry, Tom and Gene Bywater, the late Vonnie Eastham, Richard Graves, Peggy and Charles Gould, Bob, Greg, and Marilynne Hampton, Janey Jimenez, Pete and Winky Kelsey, the Joe Kiley family, Mike McElligott, Francis Morgan, Elaine and Marilynne Morshead, Esther and Jerry Moskowitz, Cathy and Bob Outman, Valerie and Hewitt Ryan, Kim Sosnoff, Tom Srock, Bee and John Sweeney, the Michael Tobin family, Mike Yager, and Laverna Yazman.

Many politicians supported the Committee's efforts and I am grateful to them all, but especially to the late Leo Ryan, who championed my cause in Congress and who, with Senator S. I. Hayakawa, delivered my application for a presidential commutation to the Pardon Attorney. And to the Pardon Attorney, John Stanish, and the United States Attorney in San Francisco, Bill Hunter, for their help and humanity. And, of course, to President Jimmy Carter for having the courage to ignore the controversy surrounding my case and to sign the order releasing me from prison.

This is also my opportunity to give special recognition to George Martinez for working so hard and for putting up with such a bossy and opinionated client. And to his wife, Ingrid, for being such a good friend and a good sport. And to Al Moscow for his skill, patience, and good company during the year and a half we worked together. And to Mary Pickering for taking time off from the writing of her history dissertation to proofread the galleys. Also to my husband, Bernard: It is a supreme understatement to say that I wasn't easy to live with while writing this book.

Above all, I am deeply grateful to my family, without whose love and support I could never have survived the ordeal described in these pages.

—Patricia Campbell Hearst

Throughout this experience, members of the SLA and their associates used a steady stream of street talk—profanity, vulgarity, and scatological images. In the scenes that follow, I have necessarily employed some of that language, but it is considerably toned down. Even at that, the book includes some of the violent and abusive language that was characteristic of my eighteen months with the SLA and of the three and a half years that followed. The conversations reproduced here, while not verbatim, are faithful to what was said at the time.

P.C.H.

For God shall bring every work into judgment, with every secret thing, whether it be good, or whether it be evil.

—ECCLESIASTES 12:14

EVERY SECRET THING

CHAPTER

ONE

I LIVE NOW ON a private, protected street in deceptively calm California, behind locked doors in a Spanish-style house equipped with the best electronic security system available. A thick stucco wall, secured by an iron gate, surrounds the house. I enjoy the protection of two devoted German shepherds, and I have recently acquired certain weapons which I have been trained to use in my own defense. I do not live in fear. It is just that I feel older and wiser now, more disillusioned in my feelings about my fellow man. I am aware of the stark reality that I am vulnerable, that there are forces out there, beyond my own comfortable small circle of family and friends, which are ever threatening and which are stronger than any single individual. I also sense that there is little one can do to prepare oneself adequately for the unknown.

I grew up in an atmosphere of clear blue skies, bright sunshine, rambling open spaces, long green lawns, large comfortable houses, country clubs with swimming pools and tennis courts and riding horses, and I took it all for granted. Born in San Francisco in 1954, I moved with my family to Beverly Hills when I was two. When I was eight we came back to Hillsborough, a beautiful, lush suburban town about twenty miles south of San Francisco. It was an easy half-hour commute for my father to his downtown office at the San Francisco *Examiner*, where he was chairman of the board of the Hearst Corporation, which owns a chain of newspapers, magazines, and television and radio stations scattered across the country. The Hillsborough house was an enormous, old place. I have heard it described as a "mansion" and as a "white elephant," but to me and my sisters it was one giant playground where we also happened to live.

The first floor, with its fourteen-foot ceilings and cavernous rooms, was rather stately and imposing. Off a long center hall was the formal dining room, with two parallel oblong tables for large dinner parties, which were seldom given. Adjoining it was the family dining room, painted a dark green and lighted by a large silver chandelier over the center table. On the other side of the center hall was our living room, my father's comfortable den, and the music room. This was a delightful airy room covered with wallpaper of a bamboo branches and leaves design, upon which an artist, hired by Mother, had hand-painted all sorts of lovely birds. I spent what seemed a lifetime there with my piano lessons.

We children spent most of our time and had our fun on the second floor. At the beginning, my two younger sisters, Anne and Vicki, shared a room, with the governess occupying the one next to them. But later we shifted quarters so that each of us five girls had her own room. The governess moved up to the third floor, where our cook-maid lived. Anne, who was a year younger than I, and Vicki, two years younger, and I made up a threesome. Our bedrooms were all in a row on one side of the hall, while Cathy, who was fifteen years older than I, and Gina, who was five years my senior, were across the hall. At the opposite end, Mom and Dad had their master bedroom and sitting room. When we were young, almost every night before bedtime my mother would sit her three youngest daughters on one rocking chair in her sitting room and read to us magical stories out of children's books which she had preserved from her own childhood in Atlanta, Georgia. When we were older, the whole family would gather after dinner in a huge family room adjoining the master bedroom suite and there we would watch television together, talk, do our homework, or labor on some school project. Cathy, who was so much older than the rest of us, seemed of a different generation and led a life of her own.

We also had a small children's game room and an enormous attic on the third floor, where we could play or entertain our friends for hours at a time. As often as not, Anne, Vicki, and I would end up in fistfights, pummeling one another, either one on one or two against one, until we were exhausted or some grown-up stopped us. To my mother's despair, this went on when I was six, seven, and eight years old, and then, sometime in my ninth year, those fights just stopped and we never fought again. I think now that perhaps we were naturally competitive, had excess energy to expend, and it was the only way we knew to establish a pecking order among us. As the oldest (among the three) I assumed the leadership role was rightfully mine. I wanted to be treated as the older child, not with all the privileges that Gina enjoyed with her five years of seniority, but with more than those of my younger sisters. Anne did not take too kindly to that, and I had to defend my leadership position against her fairly often. There was, however, no disputing Anne's courage. She was a pure daredevil. It was from that third-floor game room that Anne climbed out of the window one day and swung herself up onto the sloping roof of the house, scaring the wits out of the governess and our parents. The next day, bars went up on the windows in all the rooms on the third floor. That did not stop Anne from climbing and falling out of trees, of course.

In the basement we converted one of the rooms into a theater where we put on plays for our family and friends. Outside the house, we would skip past the manicured lawns and gardens to play in an undeveloped wooded area of our property behind the tall hedges at the rear of the house. We were not tomboys, I like to think; we were just three little girls who played as hard as boys did. We suffered concussions, sprains, broken bones, strained muscles, cuts, bruises, and whatnot. There was a period I remember when not a week went by but that Mother would have to rush one of us off to the emergency room of Mills Hospital in nearby San Mateo. "There must be a bench there with our name written on it," she would say with a sigh. Both my mother and father took such mishaps in stride. My mother was always superbly calm and efficient when it came to emergencies.

However, all the other times, when there were no such emergencies, we girls thought Mother would drive us crazy with her overprotectiveness about our health and safety. My sister Cathy, the firstborn, had had polio as a baby, from which she recovered completely, but Mom and Dad treated her ever afterward as though she were especially delicate and frail. I had a history of problems with my legs—infections, blood poisoning, a benign tumor, and congenitally displaced kneecaps. At the time, each illness was quite serious, but I did recover from them without any aftereffects, except for my knees, which sometimes pained me, and I simply learned to live with that condition. My mother, nevertheless, remained concerned over the one leg that had been infected and my "bad knees" for as long as I lived at home. Yet I never felt particularly hindered from playing tennis, swimming, horseback riding, or even, on occasion, water skiing. In fact, exercise strengthened my knees.

Actually, my parents encouraged all of us to be athletic. My father was an enthusiastic swimmer, tennis player, and duck hunter. They would both come to watch me in tennis matches or swimming meets at the Burlingame Country Club. My mother, who rarely participated in any sports, particularly approved of my playing tennis if only for its social rewards. I was better at swimming, though, and would practice a hundred or more laps a day at freestyle or the butterfly. I swam competitively from the age of nine into my thirteenth year. Then someone told me I would be a great swimmer because I was developing big muscles across my back. I gave up swimming almost immediately. What girl wants big back muscles? Instead, I took up horseback riding with the utter dedication of a normal adolescent girl lucky enough to discover horses.

I grew up in this affluent and sheltered environment sublimely self-confident. I thought that I knew best what was right and what was wrong for me. Most things came easily to me, sports, social relationships, schoolwork, life. I had only to apply myself to them and I found I could do them well, to my own satisfaction. I knew, or at least I thought I knew, who I was. I was a doer more than a thinker, an athlete more than a student, a social being more than a loner. I was ever practical, a pragmatist long before I knew what the word meant. I thought I could see people and situations plainly as they were, without frills, and thus never doubted my ability to handle myself well in whatever circumstances. Without false modesty, I considered myself perfectly healthy, reasonably pretty with a slim, athletic figure and long, blond hair, and of more than average intelligence. On the down side, however, I always considered myself to be too short in comparison with my girlfriends. Throughout my teenage years, I was chagrined to be only five feet two and practiced standing up straight and trying to look five feet seven.

All in all I enjoyed a perfectly normal, happy childhood, with perhaps a pain here and a pang there. We definitely were not raised in the stereotype of rich kids. My sisters and I certainly were privileged—

even overprivileged—but we were not spoiled. I never felt that I could have anything I wanted, just for the asking, nor did I ever sense that I was being overindulged. To the contrary, my mother, and my father too, leaned far over backward against the prevailing winds of permissiveness that swept the sixties in California and elsewhere. What I remember most keenly about those years is my parents' strictness. There were long lists of things we had to do and an equally long list of things we were not allowed to do.

As my girlfriends were given a new privilege as they grew older and presumably more responsible, I would ask the same of my mother: staying up later, staying out later, riding my bicycle to school, having a pet of my very own or whatever I happened to long for at the moment. Time after time, my mother would say "No" and my father, on appeal, would always support her. They would be fair about it, treating all of us equally, explaining their adult decisions with patient reasoning.

When I was ten or eleven my mother would not allow me to ride my bicycle just a couple of miles down what I considered a perfectly safe road to school. All my friends were doing it. In fact, the road was El Camino Real, a four-lane main highway; now I would never allow any child of mine to ride a bike on it. Still, at the time, I argued the point for the better part of a year, to no avail. My mother insisted the road was too dangerous and I would have to be driven to school. The next reason she gave seemed to be perfectly ridiculous. She said that someone might knock me off my bike, drag me into his car, and kidnap me. Mother was a worrier. But then she was not half as bad as the mother of one of my friends who allowed her daughter to ride her bicycle to school but followed her all the way in her car.

It took a long time to persuade Mother to allow us to have pets in the house; she feared they would ruin the rugs or destroy the furniture. But when a stray cat "followed" Anne home one day and Anne kept the kitten hidden in her room for a week or so, my mother allowed that pet to stay. That opened the floodgates. Vicki and I went out looking for strays and found we could get cats and dogs from the local pound. Several of those succumbed rather quickly to distemper, sending one or another of us into hysterics. Then my mother agreed that we could accept pups or kittens from our friends. Our menagerie soon grew to three dogs and three cats. And when a dog did have an accident on the plush white rug in the living room downstairs, my mother would take it with a good deal of equanimity. It was my father, who loved dogs, who would bellow and rage at whoever had forgotten to let her dog out at the proper time.

Mother was strict, cautious, and overprotective, but she did finally relent on the pets, bicycles, and many other things. Then again, she never did agree to let any of us go out to slumber parties, something almost all my friends enjoyed. It was years later that she explained her real reason: When she had been a girl in Atlanta a friend of hers had been raped at a slumber party by a teenage boy. The boy, who came from a "good" family, got off, but the girl, humiliated, had to be sent away to boarding school.

My mother was, above all, a poised, gracious Southern lady of the old school. Born in Kentucky and raised in Atlanta, where she attended the School of the Sacred Heart and Washington Seminary, she was a devout Catholic and firm in her convictions. Although she had hoped that my father, who was then working for the Atlanta *Georgian,* would convert to Catholicism, he never got around to it. We were raised as Catholics, learning our catechism, being confirmed, attending church regularly, and taking communion. We attended Catholic schools. And Mother went beyond teaching us the strictures of the Church. She insisted that we grow up as proper young ladies. That meant learning that young ladies did this, and young ladies did not do that; no matter how much we protested.

Blue jeans, for instance. Young ladies did not ever wear blue jeans to go out anywhere. They were all right for cleaning your room or for camping or riding, never for an afternoon in San Francisco. Young ladies did not go about the house—or anywhere—barefooted. And this was in the rebellion days of the sixties, with the flower children setting the current fads of social decorum in California.

Mom insisted upon meeting and approving our friends and their parents before we were allowed to visit them in their homes. Of course, we resented this, although there were few whom she ever forbade us to see. We also had strict bedtimes and rigid evening curfews.

Actually, most of my young girlfriends simply adored my parents, swearing they liked them better than their own. We all had strict parents, so it was not unusual in my circle of friends to like another's parents better than one's own. But it was true that my mother and father treated my friends most graciously as guests, without exerting the parental authority that we felt.

Almost all of my friends had parents who entertained or traveled more than mine did. They had to eat in the kitchen with the governesses, while we girls dined with our parents. Despite my father's work and my mother's various civic activities, they almost always were home for dinner with the children. Served buffet style from a sideboard, our dinners were not elaborate. My father had once tried a butler-and-cook couple but found he could not abide fancy foods and formality. He was a meat and potatoes man who always wanted to be able to recognize the food on his plate.

As a family affair, dinnertime could be great or it could be truly awful. It was the one time all of us were sure to be gathered together and Mom and Dad would sometimes use that occasion to iron out problems with the children. It would become a time for finding fault and correcting our manners, our dress, our grammar, our attitudes and demeanor or discussing our grades in school. We were also informed ad nauseam of the health hazards of smoking, drinking, or trying drugs. These lectures were always given long before we girls were really ready for them. I know I never dreamed of drinking, smoking, or using drugs at the times my mother warned us that "there's nothing worse than a drunken woman" or when she brought home a film to show us the horrors of LSD. But most of the time Mother talked about the wonderful informative book she had read the night before. Or Dad commented on the latest problem at the *Examiner* or at one of the magazines. Some of those talks went on for so long that I learned how to tune out while seeming to participate.

But there were many more times when the whole family joined in some lively discussion, arguing and yelling and trying to be heard above the din. We were seven at the table, and if you wanted to express your own opinion, you simply had to raise your voice above the others. It hardly mattered what the subject might be. We all learned to talk loud and fast and be firm in our opinions, right or wrong. When my Uncle Bill, Aunt "Bootsie," and their two sons, Willie and Austie, joined us for dinner, the volume of family discussions rose proportionately.

We received all the usual lectures in Sunday School and at home on right and wrong and the sins of lying, cheating, and stealing. Mom advanced the concept to outlaw borrowing anything, such as clothes, even on a temporary basis. When one of us came home one day delighted that a local storekeeper had given her an extra dollar in change, Mom sent her directly back to the store to return that dollar. No, it was not stealing, and yes, he had "given" her the extra dollar, but the dollar was his, not hers; hence, it had to be returned. My mother's favorite saying was that if you started something, you must finish it. She stopped us from becoming Girl Scouts because she was sure that, once in the group, we would hate it; so it was better not to join in the first place, because if we started, we would have to finish all those years. . . . I had years of piano lessons, along with the other girls, because my mother was certain that once we learned to play, we would appreciate it in later years. I took those lessons, practiced, performed at a number of piano recitals in school, and hated it all, and when finally allowed to quit, I never touched a piano again and never missed it.

Mother was a disciplinarian, to be sure, but she really was not as strict as she seemed to us at the time. We might be grounded for a week or two for various infractions of her rules—and that meant coming straight home from school and staying in with no television—but we could have friends visit us, and when the occasion warranted, the punishment would be shortened. Then again, my mother let us get away with some infractions which we thought at the time she knew nothing about. During one period Gina used to tell Mom that she was going to the movies, when she was actually heading for Bill Graham's Fillmore Auditorium, which had a naughty reputation, in San Francisco for wild rock music and simulated LSD trips achieved with psychedelic flashing lights. On about the fifth such routine, with Gina explaining which movie and what time she would return home, Mom waved her goodbye, saying, "Have a nice time at the Fillmore, dear."

Strangely enough, while it was my mother who seemed to rule our everyday life, it was my father we girls feared the most. He was the sweetest, gentlest man—most of the time. But he had a short fuse. When crossed, he could erupt instantaneously. Then he would bellow and rage with such force it fairly well would lay the victim's hair back on her head. Usually, she would run off to her room, sobbing. My father would paw around, muttering to himself. Then he would go to her room and apologize for having lost his temper and she would apologize for what she had done wrong, and they would hug and make up. Spur-of-the-moment ideas, projects, and trips came from my father. If work eased up at the office, he would phone and say, "Who can get ready in a half hour?" Quite often, Mom either could not pack in that short a time or did not relish an out-of-doors weekend, but we girls would gleefully throw clothes and a toothbrush into our suitcases and be off for a long weekend of deep-sea fishing off Baja California or to the Hearst ranches at San Simeon or at Wyntoon in northern California.

Since there were no boys in our family, we girls got to enjoy the benefits that are usually a part of the male domain. Dad would take us deep-sea fishing, duck hunting, and skeet shooting, pastimes which we would not have been able to enjoy with him if we'd had a brother. He didn't treat us as surrogate sons, however. He truly enjoyed the fact that his girls wanted to participate in his favorite activities with him. On one such occasion, when I was twelve, I was the only one to accept my father's invitation to join him in duck hunting. That is when he patiently taught me how to use a shotgun.

San Simeon is the site of the famous Hearst Castle, high on a hill overlooking the Pacific, about midway between Los Angeles and San Francisco, where my grandfather used to entertain everybody who was anybody, from Hollywood movie stars to national and international political figures. In his day the property encompassed some 285,000 acres of rolling hills dominated by his "Enchanted Hill," where he gathered from all over the world a stupendous collection of paintings, sculpture, books, oriental rugs, artifacts, and treasures. After his death, the Castle and the hilltop upon which it stood were given to the state of California, and a good deal of the land was sold off. But the family retained about 86,000 acres around the hill, as well as our special love for the place. For as far back as I can remember, I spent two, three, or more weeks during each summer at San Simeon, not to mention weekend visits the year round. The Castle and two of its three guest cottages on the top of the hill were open daily to tourists, but the third cottage, which we called the "A House," was maintained by the family. We stayed there or on the other side of the hill at the family ranch established by my great-grandfather, in his old Victorian house with its magnificent magnolia trees and wisteria vines growing on one side. I absolutely adored San Simeon. On every visit, I would take a guided tour along with the tourists and I never failed to discover something I had not seen before. On family visits, we would almost always take an after-dinner constitutional several times around the Castle, stopping frequently while my mother pointed out the constellations of stars in the sky.

San Simeon was so special, so enormous, so emotionally moving that it is still beyond my powers of description. For me, the Castle was enchanted. What a place it was for a young girl who loved horseback riding! Sometimes I would go with my father, but more often with Uncle Bill, Aunt Bootsie, and one or both of their sons. I would ride an Arabian horse for the better part of a day, through trails, pine groves, brush, and sheer wilderness—galloping full speed, jumping logs and rocks, smashing through overgrowth, breathing in that sweet, fragrant, fresh air of the California coast. I loved it. It positively petrified my poor mother, and perhaps even my father, who realized just how dangerous such jaunts were. We all knew that Mary White, the young daughter of William Allen White, the famous editor of the Emporia *Gazette,* had been killed horseback riding when her head had struck a tree branch. But that didn't slow me down at all. I knew no fear.

Wyntoon was built by my grandfather as his retreat from the world. Located in the wilderness of northern California, it is, even more than San Simeon, a fantastic, otherworldly place. From the highway one drives for miles deeper and deeper into the woods and then one comes upon a rushing river and the first of a series of elaborate chalets, set in a clearing of tall redwoods and sprawling lawns, dotted with spraying fountains. The chalets are large and yet so delicate in their setting, something one might expect to see in the Bavarian woods of Germany or in southern France, and yet they are different, so original. Scenes from familiar fairy tales were hand-painted on the outside walls of the buildings, giving them a magical aura. The insides of these chalets, with their beamed ceilings, stone and slate floors, huge fireplaces, always made me feel like a fairy princess in a mystical land. The inner beauty of Wyntoon is the escape that it offers from civilization. Wyntoon was for swimming and rafting on the river and especially for long, casual walks in the woods . . . and communion with nature.

Wyntoon, San Simeon, and vacation jaunts here and there were all part of the summer activities in which the whole family participated. This was our fun time. The rest of the year was dominated by work and responsibilities. My mother and father made no secret of their high expectations for all of us in our schoolwork. Actually, I did quite well at school without having to study too much. Usually, I earned A's and B's in English and history (subjects which interested me) and C's in mathematics and French (which bored me). Contrary to some reports, I was never suspended or expelled from any of the schools I attended.

It was Anne, the daydreamer, who had trouble in school. I was too practical for that.

There was one school incident which was widely publicized later on, but which at the time was pretty tame: I had once told a nun to go to hell. That folly occurred when I was about eleven, at the Convent of the Sacred Heart, a boarding school in Menlo Park, not far from Hillsborough, a school I loved especially for the quiet Catholic retreats it offered its students. I even thought romantically at the time of perhaps becoming a nun. One teacher had the peculiar habit, when angry, of leaning over a student and ranting and raving directly into her face. When she did this to me one day, the idea flashed in my mind that I could make her stop by shocking her. So when she paused for breath, I very deliberately said, "Oh, go to hell!" It worked, stopped her cold. Her mouth flew open in astonishment, a sight I'll never forget. At the time, I thought myself quite courageous, although very stupid. Of course, I was sent to the office of the Reverend Mother, who was very calm, sweet, and understanding about the whole affair. I apologized to her and to the teacher and that was that.

For my high school years, I was enrolled at Santa Catalina School, a boarding school run by the Dominican order of nuns in Monterey, about one hundred miles south of Hillsborough. The school had the highest reputation in the area for academic work and for placing its graduates in the best colleges. Well-to-do families in California who did not want their daughters as far away as an eastern prep school sent them to Catalina. A number of my friends were going there, especially my best friend, Trish Tobin, with whom I had shared my entire childhood. We had taken to each other at the Burlingame Country Club, where we both were on the swimming team at about age eight or nine. We played together almost every day at one house or the other. Her mother and father were like godparents to me. Her family was in banking, the first California Tobin having founded the Hibernia Bank in 1859. It now has branches throughout the northern part of the state.

Trish, who was bright, vivacious, and independent, and I had looked forward to attending Santa Catalina together. But nothing I knew of Santa Catalina prepared me for it. The very first week, when Trish and I skipped Benediction services, we were threatened with expulsion, even though we had no idea that attendance was compulsory. Instead of expulsion, we were given a load of demerits, which had to be worked off before we would be allowed any privileges, such as going home for the weekend.

The campus was beautiful with its gentle slopes and Spanish-style buildings yet the atmosphere there seemed somber and unwholesome. The school itself was so strict, so rigid, so unreasonable in its petty rules and regulations that I soon came to loathe it. I felt like a prisoner in a medieval dungeon. We were allowed to visit home only one weekend per month, and then only if our slates were free of those demerits logged in our files in the front office. Nothing I could explain to my parents would convince them. They believed that the teachers were always right, that the classroom work was designed for my own benefit, that I would, in time, learn to acclimate myself to the school's regimen; Santa Catalina was known as a fine prep school. My firsthand knowledge did not count. But there was no joy in the classroom, no pleasure in learning, no sense of satisfaction in doing my homework. It was not that I was stupid or academically behind or could not keep up with the schoolwork. The trouble was in the school itself. It made me hate high school altogether, and, having lived at Sacred Heart before, I knew that boarding school did not have to be like this.

I survived that first year at Santa Catalina and returned for the second year because my parents refused to transfer me. My sophomore year at high school was even worse. Confined to the school grounds, I spent as much time as possible at the stables (which was only three afternoons a week) or visiting with the school's maintenance man, a middle-aged Venezuelan who loved to talk about archaeology and was as warm and caring as the nuns were not.

Toward the end of the second year, my father phoned one weekend, leaving a message that he was driving down to take me out to lunch. A nun found me in the library and scolded me for not being readily available when my father had called. She then informed me that when my father arrived, I would have to tell him I could not go out for lunch: I had eighty hours of work piled up on my demerit roster. I was furious: I knew nothing about those demerits.

In the office, I protested that the demerits had been written in on my file, not typed, photocopied, and posted as required, all to no avail. When my father arrived, after a two-hour drive, the nun in the office explained the regulations to him and I could see him knuckling under, nodding his head. One grows accustomed, I suppose, never to doubt the word of a nun, and I could see him agreeing. But I knew I was right: those demerits were a mistake and it was wrong and cruel to stop me from having lunch with my father. At the first opportunity that I could get a word in, I said to the nun:

"Either I go out to lunch with my father or I am going to fly home and have dinner with him tonight in San Francisco and you can pack my bags and ship them up to me. I honestly don't care what you do, because I won't be coming back here next year, no matter what!"

"Well," she said, after a pause, "you can go out for two hours."

At lunch, I poured out my heart to my father. Teachers may be right nine times out of ten, I told him, but that did not mean they had to be right the tenth time. I was so fed up with the school I did not care anymore: I wanted to be expelled if that were to be the only way I could get out of the school. I had come close to a nervous breakdown during the past examination period. My father explained the situation to my mother and the next time that I returned home I was surprised and delighted to find that my mother supported me entirely. "Don't worry, Patty, you're not going back there next year," she said. Then, in my hearing, she telephoned the principal and told her just that, adding that if the school could not handle a sixteen-year-old girl like me, it was far more their failing than mine. When I returned to school, the teachers treated me with a certain indifference; that was a welcome relief. I received no more demerits.

The whole situation, and particularly the encounter in the school office, was a significant lesson for me at the time. I had tried to get along by following the rules and it did not work out. Other girls had rebelled or slipped away from the school in the middle of the year, but I had stayed on and taken it because I did not want to let my parents down. Over and above that, I saw that in difficult situations my parents would stand up for me, that they trusted my judgment, and that they did believe I would try to do the right thing, even in conflicts with authority. That trust certainly had always been there but I had never realized it before.

For my junior year in high school in September 1970, I enrolled in the Crystal Springs School for Girls, a small day school on the grounds of the old Crocker estate in Hillsborough. Three good things happened in fairly rapid succession.

First, my father gave me his dilapidated '53 Chevy, which he had used for duck hunting, so that I could drive to school. That old car, with its faded gray paint, its three-speed stick shift on the column, burning a quart of oil a day, was very distinctive. It was the only one of its kind in Hillsborough. When my friends spotted it anywhere, they knew I was in it or nearby. I came to love that car, even when it broke down late one night and I was obliged to walk several miles home by myself. My parents were aghast at the possibilities. Dad got rid of the car the very next day. In its stead, he bought me a new sports car, a blue MGB-GT. I thought it was great, even though the MG seemed to break down more often than the old Chevy.

Second, in going over my school records soon after I arrived at Crystal Springs, administrators discovered that if I took only one extra course I could graduate at the end of that year. I suddenly felt more charitable toward Santa Catalina School. With my residue of bad feelings about high school in general, I decided then and there that I would work like mad in order to finish in three instead of four years.

Third, when the teachers were introduced to the 200-odd student body during the first week of school, there among all the middle-aged, matronly teaching staff was this one young, interesting-looking math instructor who had come to Crystal after graduating from Princeton University the previous year. It was nothing like love at first sight, but among all the others at this girls' school, he certainly did look intriguing in my blossoming fantasies. He had a "with it" look, a great bush of light brown hair on his head, a Nietzsche mustache which covered his upper lip, and thin gold-rimmed eyeglasses. Unfortunately, he taught the seventh and eighth grades only. Mr. Weed was the favorite topic of gossip among the high school girls and I soon learned that he had been the captain of Princeton's track team, a pole vaulter, and I don't remember what else—all of it was very attractive.

All I could do at first was to keep my eye out for him in the hallways and nod hello. When afternoon workshops became mandatory I decided to take up the guitar; I found out that Steve conducted the workshop. I managed to meet him and soon he knew my name. After that it was a bit easier, but not much, to chat with him in the hallways. It was a good six months before I came upon a legitimate reason to phone him at home: I was having trouble solving some of the problems in geometry. I am not sure if it was during that first telephone call or the one or two subsequent that he suggested it might be easier to help me if I dropped by his house sometime. I was there the next day. Some of his friends were there and I joined in the general conversation; he did take time out to help me with my geometry. As I was leaving he suggested I drop in again, any time. That was all I needed to hear. I had the definite impression that his interest was not purely professional and I was there again the very next day.

He was everything a high school girl could want: a college graduate, an older man, so mature, so experienced, so sophisticated. He was only twenty-three and I was seventeen. I could act a great deal more mature than my actual years, so I did not think our age difference was that much of an obstacle. In my little MG, I drove to his house, which stood on a half acre in Menlo Park, with greater and greater frequency. Ostensibly, he was tutoring me in math but our conversations drifted over a far greater range of more interesting subjects. There was a mutual attraction there and I could sense it. I suppose I threw myself at him, but I hoped not in any obvious way. I called him "Mr. Weed" and he still tutored me in math, as I waited for something to happen or not to happen. Whether I seduced him or he seduced me, I really do not know; let's say it was mutual.

I spent two or three afternoons a week at Steve's house, returning home for dinner with the family, and sometimes driving back to his house after dinner, and driving back home to sleep. Naturally, I did not tell my parents, my sisters, or my friends anything at all about Steven Weed. Several of his friends, most of them teachers at Crystal Springs or graduate students at Stanford University, came to know of our affair, but they seemed to accept it as a matter of course. I felt very good about it, too, like a young adult finally outgrowing her childhood, entering into the real world. Steve made me feel good about myself and about being in love. Up to this time my sexual experience had been limited to a frightening relationship with an "older" boy who had forced himself on me during a summer two years earlier. Steve had a great deal to teach me about life, beyond geometry and mathematics. I believed him to be vastly superior to me intellectually and far more experienced in the ways of the world. He couldn't believe how sheltered my life had been up to then and he took great pains to make me come to realize it.

Steve was amazed one day when I told him I had never smoked marijuana. I thought that it was a dangerous drug. He told me I was "prissy." Everyone he knew smoked grass. He grew the stuff right there in the house and he assured me that it was perfectly safe, less injurious to one's health than liquor, nothing more involved than getting pleasantly high. He had been smoking grass since his days at Princeton, where he also experimented with all kinds of so-called mind-expanding drugs. It was true that nearly everyone I knew seemed to have at least tried grass. My parents were already convinced that I was smoking marijuana. Mom would give those lectures at the dinner table on the dangers of smoking marijuana, and while never accusing anyone directly, she would look right at me. I would deny it vehemently and she would say, "Yes, dear," and I could tell she did not believe me. I would be furious at her. I did not even smoke cigarettes. And after such dinner conversations, I would be furious with Anne, the truly guilty party, who was never suspected. Anyway, I shared a joint with Steve that day, and it was not bad at all; he got giggly and he read passages out of the Bible with exaggerated intonations that amused him greatly. I was more confused than shocked by his sense of humor, and what he found so amusing about the Bible I will never know. We smoked pot once a week or so and it was to us no more serious than occasional social drinking.

I earned my blessed release from high school that June and, after signing up for one summer course in biology at another high school, I was admitted to Menlo College, a rather posh junior college. It was the best choice available at the time, the only "good" college which would accept a seventeen-year-old who had graduated from high school in three years. It was not far from home, and only two miles from Steven Weed's house in Menlo Park.

For all of the reasons I hated high school, I loved college. At Menlo, no one was constantly looking over my shoulder, prodding or trying to dominate me. College was much more relaxed and adult: I was given my work to do and I was left alone. It being the first year that Menlo College was coeducational, I was one of twenty girls in the whole student body. But I was not interested in any of the men there; I only had eyes for Steve. I was assigned a dormitory room with an Iranian girl, whose father was Minister of Agriculture in Iran. She could have the room to herself and I would be able to move in with Steve. This arrangement worked and we became fast friends.

Gradually, I moved my clothes to his house and we settled in there, a happy, domestic couple. Living together was a very "in" thing to do in those days, rather like roller disco is today. Steve's rented house was ramshackle, furnished with hand-me-downs from his parents, who had divorced when he was sixteen. I delighted in putting some order into "our home" and I began buying cookbooks to help me in preparing special meals and desserts. We did everything together, like a married couple, and I discovered in myself a "nesting" instinct. I was very comfortable in our arrangement, at peace with myself and with him. I was learning all the time, for he was very much at home in the role of teacher. In the evenings, I would pore over my books and he would correct papers. I found I was doing very well at school and enjoying it. I returned home for dinner at least once, sometimes twice a week with the family, and although Mom and Dad voiced some complaints about my being difficult to reach by telephone, they were pleased with my school grades and perhaps a new maturity they could see in me. I never mentioned Steven Weed.

But I did take Steve to San Simeon and to Wyntoon. He was rather in awe of the Hearsts' riches, but aside from the natural good times we had on such jaunts, the differences in our family positions did not seem to affect our relationship. His father was a stockbroker in Palo Alto and his mother had remarried and was living in Santa Rosa. We compared notes and decided we loved each other for our individual selves. We skirted around the subject of marriage. He thought that I was too young. But I had just turned eighteen and I felt very comfortable with the idea of being married. When people asked me what career I envisioned for myself, I would go into a set speech about perhaps working on one of the Hearst magazines. That satisfied their curiosity and left me free with my own doubts. I thought that marriage would satisfy me completely. In fact, along with that nesting instinct, I felt more and more pressure to get married at eighteen. My sister Gina had married at that age; my mother married my father when she was eighteen. Of course, no one was putting any pressure at all upon me, but I felt it nevertheless. Steve and I talked about it but we never reached the same decision at the same time.

Toward the end of that school year, Steve won a fellowship and a teaching grant at the University of California at Berkeley, where he would be a teaching assistant in logic and would pursue his doctorate in philosophy. I was scheduled to take an art history tour of Europe over the summer, sponsored by Menlo's art department. Steve and I visited the Berkeley campus together, walking around the inner quadrangle most of the day, sightseeing, stopping for snacks, and loving it all. My mother had always spoken wistfully about me or one of my sisters going to the University of Virginia, founded by Thomas Jefferson and still maintaining what she considered the finest traditions of the southern heritage. But none of us took that seriously. I had thought of the University of Chicago, but neither of my parents wanted me to go there. I had no special feeling for the University of California at Los Angeles, and the flat, desert aura of Stanford University, with its stereotype of student sameness, did not appeal to me at all. But the Berkeley campus was green and ivy-covered, with trees and brooks. More importantly, it was large and impersonal, with a wide diversity of students from all over the world. It was the Harvard of the West, one of the finest schools in the country. As for my mother's diatribes about the radicals having ruined a good school, I was sure she was wrong: the Berkeley radicals of the 1960's were all past and gone. My mother had been a regent of the University of California since 1956, a trustee on the board of directors which supervised the entire state university system, and she was well known as a conservative and traditionalist on the board. She abhorred the whole youth movement of the sixties for trying to destroy the traditional values that make America great. I had heard her on the subject many times: although she agreed with many of the students' goals, especially women's rights, she deplored the way they were attempting to wrest control of the college curriculums from their elders, who knew better. Anyway, Steve and I agreed that I should join him at Berkeley. We also decided that the time had come when I should inform my parents of his existence.

As the most appropriate occasion upon which to divulge my delicate bit of news, I chose the awards assembly at the close of the school year at Menlo College. My father was busy elsewhere, so I would have my mother there alone, all to myself. I thought it an appropriate occasion because I was to receive the most coveted award as the best student of the year. I had achieved a 4.0 average, straight A's in all my subjects. I never got a chance to broach the subject at the awards assembly or at the awards banquet which followed at a Palo Alto hotel. So it was at the last moment in the hotel parking lot, as my mother was about to leave for home, that I told her about Steve. She listened patiently as I explained and told her what I intended to do: After my summer trip to Europe, I would move in with Steve in Berkeley and attend the University of California there.

Her response was: "I'm not surprised. But I love you more than I hate what you're doing." I asked her to break the news to Dad and spare me that. In turn, she appealed to me to refrain from flaunting our affair. I readily agreed, not wanting to embarrass them. So Steve Weed was invited to dinner.

My father accepted what he could not change. My parents were perfectly civilized and gracious toward Steve, but it was not a successful dinner party. They clearly did not like him, although nothing was said to indicate their displeasure. Of course, the idiot had not endeared himself to my family by flunking my sister Vicki in mathematics. Her report card from Crystal Springs had arrived at our house only shortly before he did. But that was not crucial, as I explained to him after we had left the house; nobody would be good enough in my parents' estimation for their little Patty. Steve understood. While he did not say so in that many words, I sensed that he was not overly enthusiastic about my parents either. None of this bothered me particularly; it would work itself out in time. Now the road ahead looked clear. Steve and I went out apartment hunting in Berkeley.

Together we found a bright, sunny duplex on Benvenue Street in a nice neighborhood, only a half mile from campus. We signed the lease as Mr. and Mrs. Steven Weed. Then I had to leave on my long-planned art tour, my first trip to Europe, which both Steve and I agreed I should not forgo. Headed by the excellent humanities teacher at Menlo College, Patrick Tobin, our little group of six young men and me, notebooks in hand, traipsed through art museum after art museum in Athens, Venice, Florence, and Rome. It was an enlightening, exhausting tour, but I missed Steve, and I dropped out before the last stop, Egypt. Instead, I flew to Bristol, in southwestern England, to visit for a week with my former governess, Heather Lister, whom I loved dearly. Replacing our first, rather eccentric governess, who had taken to the bottle, Heather had won me over on the first day she arrived at our house. I was eleven years old and announced to her that she might be the governess for Vicki and Anne but that I was too old to have a governess. She tactfully agreed immediately, asking only that I help her with the two children. She became my close confidante in the years that followed. In England, we had long heart-to-heart talks, primarily about Steven Weed and our life ahead, and I played for hours with her young grandchild. I was primed for domesticity.

Then, with the summer almost over and the fall of 1972 approaching, having been away two long months, I flew home—not to my parents in Hillsborough, but to my new life with Steve in Berkeley.

Not long after we set up house there, Steve asked me to marry him.

Wouldn't it be lovely if I could write that we lived happily ever after?

CHAPTER

TWO

BERKELEY WAS KNOWN far and wide as the fountainhead of the student rebellion and campus uprising of the sixties, a haven for radicals and revolutionaries, a hotbed of communism, Marxism, socialism, and whatever ism might be current at the moment. Starting with the Free Speech Movement of 1964, when Berkeley students took over Sproul Plaza, the entrance to the campus, the youth rebellion reached a genuine crescendo in the mass protests against the Vietnam War in 1968, running on through 1970. But by the time Steve and I moved to Berkeley in the fall of 1972, almost all that had withered away. Only the dregs of the counterculture movement—the hangers-on, the junkies, the derelicts, the freaks, and the weirdos—were anywhere in evidence. They could be seen entertaining the tourists on infamous Telegraph Avenue, which was outside the university campus, as they came in a variety of political persuasions and shocking attire. But for every political radical, you were just as likely to come upon a Jesus freak or a macho tough leading a Doberman adorned with a thick collar of large spikes. Aggressive panhandlers swarmed about the entrances to coffeehouses, physically stopping people to demand money. Punks loitered on street corners blatantly propositioning young girls in no uncertain terms. Yet it was all nothing but a scene within a scene. It was no more what Berkeley was really all about than Times Square is representative of all of New York City. We "natives" learned how to deal with the scene, how to fend off the panhandlers, how to walk by the filthy-mouthed accosters, how to disregard the soapbox orators, how to walk on side streets, and how to take it all in stride. The first time I found a derelict sleeping in the dryer of an all-night laundromat, I was merely surprised. When a young socialist or evangelist forced a leaflet into my hand in Sproul Plaza, I took special delight in dropping the message into one of the dozens of nearby trash cans without even glancing at it. One stopped to listen to the blatherings of such people strictly for amusement.

The Berkeley that I and the vast majority of students knew was a serious institution of higher learning. The work was hard and the competition for grades fierce. Beyond Sproul Plaza, with its orators, propagandists, and bicycles whizzing through the ornate Sather Gate, a student was safe among other students on the main campus of the university. An aura of purposefulness hung in the air. Students in the dress of the day, jeans, T-shirts, and hiking boots, laden with books, were on their way to or from classes. Lectures were large, with two to five hundred students attending a single class. Reading assignments were long and demanding, and it was clearly understood that those who did not keep up flunked out. For those seeking future admission to graduate schools a B average was the absolute minimum for survival. Serious students simply did not have time for the protests of the sixties.

There were no mass demonstrations or protests at Berkeley in all the time that I was there. The largest rally that I recall was the auctioning of a "lid" on the steps of Sproul Hall, where several thousand gathered in a rather light-humored protest against the illegality of possession of marijuana. No doubt there were radicals and revolutionaries in and around the university and certainly there were even more intellectual Marxists and the usual variety of socialists and whatever. But they were in a distinct minority and not highly visible. The University of California at Berkeley had a student body of 35,000, a society, if not a city, unto itself. Steve and I heard of no protests, knew no radicals, and were busy enough. I had to urge him to come out and vote for President in 1972. He was hardly interested; but for me it was my first election. I had turned eighteen and was anxious to exercise my new rights by voting for George McGovern. Who else would an eighteen-year-old Berkeley student vote for?

Steve was basically nonpolitical at Berkeley. What interested him was abstract philosophy, Kant, Hegel, and Kierkegaard, the sound of the tree falling unseen in the forest. When friends visited our apartment, he would talk for hours on some minute point of nineteenth-century philosophy or English punctuation. This was far beyond my comprehension and so boring that I would often slip away to the kitchen to bake a cake. Most of our friends at Berkeley were *his* friends, his age and older, but then it seemed only reasonable that I could fit in with his crowd more easily than he could be expected to enjoy the company of people my age. Our social life was quiet. Aside from the occasional movie, we spent most nights reading for classes. Now and then friends of Steven's from Stanford or teachers from Crystal Springs dropped in for a casual meal. Weekends we tried to get away somewhere in my little MG. Once every week or two I would drive over for dinner with my family in Hillsborough, sometimes with Steve, sometimes without him.

Much to my parents' surprise, but with Steve's approval, I decided to forgo the first quarter of the school year at Berkeley. I wanted to go to work for those three months of the fall quarter. I was just tired of school and I had never had the experience of a paying job before. I found a nine-to-five job doing clerical work at Capwell's Department Store in Oakland, which was not far from Berkeley. It was not very demanding, and left me the time and energy to shop for all the things Steve and I needed for our new apartment. The job itself was interesting and new to me, but it was hardly stimulating. I wrote claims, did some billing, and ordered Christmas cards for the department store's customers.

I enrolled in the university for the winter quarter and, after much discussion with Steve, registered for two courses in zoology and one in math. The truth was that, having decided to go to Berkeley, I really had no clear idea of what I wanted to study. My intended major was the history of art because I had been surrounded by art all of my life and I had loved that subject at Menlo. But I also had a great love for animals and thought of becoming a veterinarian. Between art historian and animal doctor, Steve thought my latter interest was "better" and I went along with his choice. Neither of us apparently took into account the simple truth that science and mathematics were undoubtedly my very worst subjects. I struggled through zoology and math from January through March and barely survived with a C average. But we attributed that to the new rigors of the high academic standards at Berkeley. For the spring quarter, I took chemistry, math, and art history. Chemistry was utterly incomprehensible to me. Even when I memorized it, I did not understand it. In despair, I dropped chemistry at mid-term. In math, I thought I was in danger of flunking. At the end of that course, I approached the graduate instructor and appealed to him frankly: "If you'll just pass me this once, I promise I will never take another math course again."

"Why on earth did you ever take math in the first place?" he asked with a smile.

"I must have been out of my mind," I said, and won a C — for the course. In art history, I earned an A. I had rediscovered my major.

For the fall quarter of 1973, I plunged in with four courses in art history, focusing on early Christian and pre-Renaissance paintings, and discovered the joy of having an aptitude for as well as a keen interest in what I was studying. Berkeley had one of the best and toughest art history departments in the country; the caliber of the work and of the students was of the highest order. I more than held my own in the scramble for grades. I got one A and three B +'s. For my fourth quarter, the winter of 1974, I enrolled in three advanced art history courses and audited two more. The sense of having achieved my stride in this demanding work and also being naturally good at it was marvelous.

At home on Benvenue Street, however, the personal relationship between Steve and me did not do as well. It was more up-and-down, good-and-bad, teetering on the brink. We did not have any big fights that threatened a breakup. But it seemed that as the months rolled by, our usual sarcastic jests with one another took on a more serious, biting, hurting tone. Our disagreements came with increasing frequency. I came to see that my first true love was not perfect. He was not only intelligent and self-confident; he was also arrogant and condescending. Perhaps it was simply that I was growing up and was no longer satisfied to adore him, eagerly absorbing all he could teach. I was wholly aware of women's rights at that time, but I did not realize the unfairness of his making *all* the decisions in the house. I always did what he wanted me to do. I did the cooking and the washing up afterward. He set the times when the meals should be on the table. In a million small things and most large ones, he was the boss. I came to wonder if I had exchanged parental authority for his authority. That was not my idea of independence. It was just the air about him: his role to command and mine to obey. During one fracas at the dinner table, he picked me up bodily and deposited me like an unruly child on the porch outside our front door. I was locked out until he decided to allow me back in. During another argument, while driving home one night, he brought the car to a screeching stop by the side of the road and shouted, "If you don't like it, you can get out and walk home," and I almost did, until I realized it was *my* car.

Steve displayed this air of superiority to others as well. He could be subtly and not so subtly condescending toward my parents. At dinner, he might laugh at a serious opinion expressed by my mother or disdain to give his own opinion on a subject under discussion, or refuse to give even a polite chuckle at one of my father's quips. It was not so much a matter of what he said or did not say, it was his demeanor which seemed to declare, "I'm so much more intelligent than you are." This was not at all obvious to me at the beginning, but I became aware of it eventually. At the time I did not recognize the extent of my parents' displeasure with the man I loved. Only much later would my sisters tell me that after Steve and I had left the house my mother and father would launch into their complaints over just about everything Steve had done while there. They did not approve of his clothes, his table manners, his deportment, his opinions. The fact that Steve came to dinner unshaven (he shaved the night before rather than in the morning in order not to irritate his delicate skin) drove my fastidious father wild. Dad would never say anything about it, but he did give Steve an electric razor one Christmas. Steve did not get the hint. Mom and Dad never once complained of any of this to me, for they knew that I was in love.

We saw his father and stepmother in Palo Alto only occasionally, and on just about every visit, I would see Mr. Weed striving to be friendly and to make contact with his son, only to be rebuffed harshly. It was terribly embarrassing for me and we argued about it after one visit, but Steve simply dismissed what he called my naïveté. More often, we visited his mother in Santa Rosa and there Steve was only a little more civil. He treated his mother as though she were hopelessly unaware of the modern world and its social mores. On our first visit there, Steve embarrassed his mother and humiliated me. When his mother suggested that I sleep in his room and he sleep on the living-room couch, Steve waved off that suggestion as ridiculous, announcing that we would sleep together that night in his room. While everyone there was aware that we were living together in Berkeley, still there were the proprieties involved. His mother reddened and sheepishly acquiesced, while I felt like crawling under the rug. The important point was not where we slept that night; it was that Steve did not bother to respect his mother's or my preferences.

These aspects of his personality troubled me more and more as time went on, for they marred the image of the man I loved. If I had been more mature, I suppose, I would have realized that Steve was a very young man in his early twenties, overreacting with that false superiority and arrogance of the first stages of independence. But at the time I felt all grown-up, independent, and knowing it all myself. It was a sign of my own maturity, I thought, that I could recognize these chinks in Steve's character and still love him for all his other qualities. The question was: in the long run, could I live with those abrasive traits?

Strangely enough, these doubts began to grow within my mind only *after* Steve, finally, asked me to marry him. No doubt I was the one anxious for wedlock and he was afflicted with a bachelor's inherent fear of matrimony. It had nothing to do, I think, with the quality of our love for one another. It was matrimony itself. Steve saw nothing wrong with the way we were living, nothing which would be improved by marriage. But I had begun to discern drawbacks I had never before imagined in living together out of wedlock. The assumption is that one day, if everything goes right, you will be married and that this is an opportunity to test the relationship. The trouble is that one of the two—it seemed to me, at least—always feels that he or she is on approval. If unsatisfactory in any respect, she can be returned, slightly used; complete satisfaction, or your money back. I felt that without a real commitment, a vow of marriage, there would be a gap that prevented the true union.

With our first Christmas at Berkeley, I had expected an engagement ring. Instead I got a pair of moccasins and a round piece of paper with the word "ring" written on it. But Steve finally did get the idea, and in January he asked me to marry him and I agreed without hesitation. We would consider ourselves engaged, but he suggested that there really was no hurry to get married. We set the date for some eighteen months hence. I forget how and why we reached that decision. But it followed that in order to avoid the expected hoopla from our parents we would not inform them of our plans for a couple of months until we were a little closer to the actual wedding date.

As it turned out, we did tell some of our friends and one of them told her mother, and her mother told my mother, and my mother telephoned me. It was hardly the appropriate manner in which to convey the happy news. However, I did explain that yes, we were engaged, but no, we weren't going to get married very soon. . . .

All that year I wanted to get married and yet, as the date grew near, doubts and fears crept in. Had Steve changed and become annoyingly overbearing? Or had I changed so that I no longer welcomed his role as my teacher and mentor in every aspect of my life? Or were these all just the ordinary fears that assault every young bride-to-be on the threshold of marriage?

Having gained my independence from my parents and free now to live my own life, I had to face my most important decision alone, and I just could not be sure of the right thing to do. "How can you know for sure?" I would ask myself, and there was no answer. Superficially, in the eyes of all our friends, we were the perfect happy couple. Many commented on how well matched we were and so Steve and I played that role. Inwardly, I was not sure. Steve would get his Ph.D. in philosophy eventually and teach at the college level somewhere. But did I want to be an assistant professor's wife, kowtowing to the wife of the head of the department and to the dean's wife? I did not think so, but then I was not certain about that either.

At one point, I considered joining the Navy and seeing the world. Literally. It was a way out, but it was not very practical. At another point, I slipped into an emotional depression that lasted about two weeks, in which I felt that my life was closing in on me. Discussing this with one or two of my girlfriends who had recently married, I was assured that there was nothing unusual about my condition at all. Everyone had doubts. Suspecting that Steve too might be having some doubts, I did not discuss any of this with him. Sharing such doubts would not help launch our marriage, I thought. Weighing it all in the balance, I decided that overall my life was really going along very well: I was happy more than unhappy, I loved Steven Weed more than I doubted him, our three years together had given me far more joy than pain: I would not back out; I would marry him. But then there was a little nagging voice in the back of my mind which told me: "You'll marry him, but it won't last, not more than a couple of years . . ."

Our engagement was announced on December 19. Steve and I posed for a formal photograph in my parents' home, beneath a painting of my grandmother, Millicent Hearst. We then sat down to a family dinner, with Vicki and Anne there, and our future happiness was toasted in French champagne. The photograph and announcement of our forthcoming marriage in June ran rather prominently in the San Francisco *Chronicle* and in the *Examiner*.

Mrs. Weed invited us to a Christmas party, at which I was introduced to various friends and relatives on Steve's side of the family. Trish's parents, the Tobins, sent us a lovely traditional "engagement cup." Steve's and my mother were busying themselves with preparations for a big formal wedding at the Burlingame Country Club. My mother swung into a frenzy of efficiency—listing, planning, and preparing the thousands of details appropriate for the occasion. I had denied my parents the pleasure of seeing me come out in a debutante cotillion, something my mother had wanted very much. But at eighteen I had been well into college, was living with the man I intended to marry, and simply did not feel like a debutante. Now there was no escaping what had to be done: organizing the enormous guest list, selecting china and crystal, registering a silver pattern, shopping for a wedding gown. This is supposed to be a happy, joyous period in the life of a bride-to-be, according to the stories in the various bridal magazines. So why wasn't I overjoyed? Why did I look upon such shopping excursions as interruptions in my busy school life? Why didn't I tackle all those lists of suggested wedding guests? Steve would take no part in any of this. He thought it all ridiculous and would give me no help at all.

Then, on February 1, a minor incident at our apartment inexplicably unnerved me. Late in the afternoon, when we were not expecting anyone, the doorbell rang. At the door stood a tall Oriental girl who looked rather spaced out. She asked if our apartment was for rent or if we knew of any apartment in the building for rent. Standing behind Steve in the front hallway, I could see a man just beyond the girl, nervously wringing his gloved hands and glancing from side to side. Then they left. That was all there was to it, except that I was disturbed. We laughed them off as Berkeley weirdos, yet I just did not think that they were really apartment hunting.

For the next couple of days I could not shake off this heavy, oppressive feeling that something was not right, that something bad was going to happen either to me or to someone I loved. I had no idea what it might be or why I felt this way.*

On the Monday after that Friday, February 4, I walked by myself

---

* Actually that couple had nothing whatever to do with what occurred afterward. But I did learn later that during these days I was being followed and kept under observation, although I had no conscious awareness of that at the time.

slowly back to the apartment from campus, where I had spent the whole day in classes and at the library. I felt unusually tired, languid, not so much from overwork or the half-mile walk but rather as a general malaise. Reaching our apartment at about four o'clock, I thought of taking a brief nap before Steve got home. I climbed the twenty concrete steps to the front porch and unlocked the sliding glass door and immediately went to the front-hall closet to switch off the burglar-alarm system we had installed several months earlier. Although we lived in a relatively safe neighborhood on the south side of campus, we had been robbed by some junkie who had attacked our back door with a crowbar. Before he got the latch open the entire ceiling-to-floor glass panel came crashing down, bringing the neighbors running. But this fellow still rushed into the apartment, grabbed up several camera lenses and filters, and made his escape. The next day I bought an ADT open-and-closed-circuit alarm system and Steve installed it on all the windows and doors as well as beneath the floor pads by our front and back doors. The alarm system would set off a high-low siren on the roof. I often set the alarm when I was home alone, knowing that rapists sometimes struck lone women during the day, and this day was no different. I set the alarm and without a thought of fear I climbed the stairway to our bedroom on the upper level for my quick nap. I had no trouble at all in falling into a deep sleep.

Steve returned home about six, which was later than usual, and I woke up about six-thirty or seven o'clock. Because it was so late, I took a quick shower and slipped into some panties, my terry-cloth bathrobe, and alpaca slippers, and hurried down to my tiny, corridor kitchen to prepare a quick, light dinner. A good part of one wall of the kitchen was covered with a pegboard which Steve had put up so that I could hang my ever-growing collection of pots and pans. I enjoyed making soufflés and fancy dishes by my third year as a homemaker, but this evening I just opened a can of chicken noodle soup and prepared some tuna fish sandwiches. After dinner, Steve insisted upon watching *Mission: Impossible* and *The Magician;* then I cleared the table so we could settle down for some studying. A little after nine o'clock the front doorbell rang.

Steve got up to answer it and I sort of looked around the corner of the front hallway. I could see the bulky outline of a person standing beyond the frosted sliding glass door. "That looks really weird," I told him. Feeling jumpy, I thought of warning Steve to put the chain on the door before he unlocked it, but he didn't give me a chance. By that time he had the door open and I had walked into the narrow hallway, a few feet behind him, wondering what was up. I could hear a girl's agitated voice. Her words came tumbling out so fast that I could barely make out what she was saying: She had backed up and hit some car in the garage under the house. Could she come in and use the phone?

My immediate reaction was disgust and anger. Oh, great, I thought, she hit my car. I turned away and started to walk toward the kitchen at the other end of the hallway, absolutely sure that she had smashed into my MG parked in the carport on the ground level of the house. At that moment I heard a scuffling commotion and turned to see two men with guns burst into the apartment, a thin black man and a heavier, shorter white man. I backed away from them into the kitchen, shocked, screaming. Then the girl came in after me, backing me into the stove, pointing a black automatic pistol at my face. At the same time she clamped her hand over my mouth and said, "Be quiet and nobody'll get hurt." She was about my size and build, with a white, colorless face. She was wearing a black coat of some strange kind of curly material and a small hat which barely covered her frizzly blond hair. From beyond the kitchen, in the hallway or in the living room, I could hear Steve talking amid sounds of scuffling.

Then one of the men, not the black man, appeared suddenly and before I realized what was happening he had pushed me to the floor. I landed on my stomach and he sat on me, straddling my back. Twisting around, I tried to look up to see his face. "Don't look at me," he commanded, slamming my head onto the floor. "Keep your head down!" The girl was gone.

As he was tying my hands together behind my back, I could make out voices from the other room. "Where's the safe? Where's the safe?" the black man was demanding, and Steve was crying, "We don't have a safe. Take my wallet. That's all we have. Take anything you want . . . anything you want . . ."

I had thought that they were going to rob us and then they would go away and it would be all over. But it now flashed through my mind that they would not be tying me up for an ordinary robbery. I tried to struggle but I could hardly move. Someone was yelling in the other room and suddenly a gag was thrust into my mouth. It was a rag of some sort with knots tied in the middle so that the knots went into my mouth. As it was being tied at the back of my head, I bit down hard so that it would not go all the way in. A blindfold was wrapped around my eyes and tied behind my head. I was yanked up and half dragged into the hallway. Through the bottom edge of the blindfold, which was not tied very tightly, I could see the edge of the floor slipping by. As I passed the living room, Steve suddenly began shrieking in pain. I thought he was being stabbed to death. Through all this I heard the girl shouting, "Let's get out of here." Then I managed to spit out the gag and I started screaming as loudly as I could, hoping the neighbors would hear me and summon the police or some kind of help.

Suddenly, I was on the dark porch outside the apartment, feeling the fresh air, and screaming my head off. It was my last chance to save myself. It was plain to me that I was being kidnapped. Where were the police? Everything was happening so fast. My senses were assaulted with a confusion of sounds, voices, impressions. My neighbor's door opened and I distinctly heard the girl next door cry out, "Oh, my God!" Then her door slammed shut and in that instant the man at my side opened fire with an automatic rifle or submachine gun. The shots were very loud. Glass shattered. Other doors slammed. I was still screaming, wanting the whole world to hear me, hoping someone, anyone, would save me.

Then a terrific blow landed on my left cheek—from a rifle butt—and I was stunned into semi-consciousness. I was vaguely aware of being dragged down the concrete steps to the carport below, and then I was on my feet again, momentarily free. Still blindfolded, I could feel the metal of a car in front of me and heard its motor running. I backed away, feeling with my hands behind me the shape of my own car still parked there, and tried to slip around it. "Oh, no, you don't," said the black man, and I was grabbed again, lifted off the ground, and thrown into the trunk of a strange car. I heard another burst of rapid gunfire, and the car, with me in it, bound and blindfolded in the trunk, sped away.

Wriggling about, I was surprised at how easily the rope came away from my bound wrists and I was able to remove my blindfold. A soft red glow of light filtered in from the taillights outside. The wires to those lights were right in front of me and I thought of pulling them out so that, maybe, the car would be stopped by the police. But that was a zillion-to-one chance, and without the taillights I would be left in total darkness. It was cold, freezing, in there. When I least expected it, the car stopped and moments later the trunk lid was opened and I was yanked out.

I could not have been in that trunk for more than two or three minutes. Everything was happening so fast, my thinking was disoriented. How long had it taken these people to come into our apartment and drag me out of there? Three minutes? Five minutes? I didn't know.

I found myself standing on a dark residential street somewhere, held firmly in someone's grasp, surrounded by a small group of people whose faces I could not quite make out. Three automobiles stood parked on the otherwise empty street, the vintage white Chevy I had come in, a dark VW bug parked behind it, and up ahead a station wagon (which turned out to be a green Ford LTD). To my right was a long row of high hedges and I wondered if I could break free and plunge through them to safety. Not a chance. As I tried to see my captors in the dark, the black man said, "How the fuck did she get untied?" They seemed surprised at that, babbling to one another as I pleaded, crying, for them to let me go. The black man, who appeared to have a pasty yellow face, cursed and yelled orders to the others. I was propelled ahead and shoved into the station wagon, on the floor in front of the back seat, and then the others piled in over me. The car took off immediately and a blanket was thrown over my head, blacking out all light. I was crying and the black man kicked me and yelled, "Shut your mouth, bitch, or I'm going to blow your fucking head off."

Curled up, lying on one side, there was no way I could avoid the vibrating hump of the transmission on the floor of the car; the floor itself bounced with every bump in the road. Before they had thrown the blanket over me, I recognized the three people in the back seat as those who had abducted me from the apartment. The black man was sitting at my feet, the girl in the middle, and the other man at my head. I tried to visualize their faces so I would be able to identify them all later. The car was proceeding at a very moderate speed. They began to congratulate one another on how smoothly their "operation" had gone when the black man, obviously the leader, told them all to "shut up and stay alert, on guard." As the car fell silent, they went into a sort of military routine.

"What's your speed?" the black man asked repeatedly, and the driver, a woman, would announce dryly: twenty-five, thirty, or thirty-five. At various times he would command, "Slow the fuck down." A woman in the front passenger seat apparently was assigned as the look-out on traffic. In a low throaty voice that made me think that she might be black, she would announce cars at intersections, traffic signals, and whatever might lead to a traffic violation and bring on the police.

"Stop sign ahead."

"Watch out, car approaching on the right."

"Red light, next block."

"Pigs at the diner over there . . . take it easy," someone else warned.

"What's your speed?"

The ride seemed interminable and the black man kept kicking and prodding me with his foot. I could hardly believe that I was actually being kidnapped. I kept asking what they were going to do to me. The black man would only tell me to shut up or else he would "blow me away." Finally, the girl in the back seat reassured me, "Don't worry, bitch, we ain't going to kill you . . . you're worth much more to us alive than dead." She seemed to be laughing or giggling, enjoying it all as a great outing, but the others were all deadly serious. I strained to catch some sounds or indications from outside the car which would give me a clue to where we were or where we were going. Someone mentioned Fish Ranch Road and then I recognized the sounds of driving through Caldecott Tunnel, with which I was familiar, but after that I just could not figure out our location. We had traveled too long to have taken the Bay Bridge from Berkeley into San Francisco, for I would have heard the different sound of the tires on the bridge roadbed, but I thought perhaps we were going past Oakland to take the San Mateo Bridge across to the Peninsula below San Francisco.

The five people in the car talked among themselves, mostly about staying alert for any interception by the police. I could see the sub-machine gun lying in the lap of the black man. All the windows of the station wagon were rolled down so that my captors could, as they said, "shoot it out with the pigs," if necessary.

On several occasions I managed to ease the blanket off my eyes so that I could see the three in the back seat. The man sitting above my head was nervously drumming his fingers on the window frame, looking outside, his head turned away from me. The girl next to him laughed. "Look at Teko, he's so nervous, he can't sit still." Then she noticed me staring up at her. "We'll have to blindfold her again," she said. "We don't want her identifying us." Hands reached down, groping over me, as a blindfold and a gag were put on and my hands were tied to-

gether once again, this time in front of me, and then the blanket was
thrown over my head again. Strangely enough, as I was being bound, a
great sense of relief swept over me. They don't want to be identified, I
told myself. They're going to let me go. I was grasping at any straw of
hope. If they were worried about my being able to identify them, it
meant that they did not intend to kill me, I reasoned. They would demand a ransom, my father would pay it, and I would be returned safe
and sound. It would all be over in a few days. I tried to hang on to that
reasoning to beat down the terror within me: Some kidnap victims were
let go once the ransom was paid, but others were murdered to protect
the identity of the kidnappers, their bodies left to rot in some ditch. My
greatest fear was of the black man, the leader. His voice had a tone that
convinced me he was merciless. He had been the one in the living room
with Steve and I had heard Steve's anguished screams. I had tried to
ask about Steve but the black man would only curse and order me
to be quiet. He would tell me nothing and I feared that Steve was dead.

The ride on the floor of the station wagon seemed to go on forever,
surely more than an hour, perhaps as much as three hours. My face,
where I had been hit, began to ache, now that the shock had worn off;
my legs had been scraped raw on the concrete steps and were oozing
blood. They stung and felt hot, feverish, while the rest of my body,
clad only in a bathrobe, broke out in goose bumps from the cold air.
At last the car slowed down and came to a stop. Someone got out and
then the car was backed carefully into a garage. They began whispering
to one another as they climbed out. The black man told me to lie still
and be quiet or I would be killed. They would be back for me soon.
Only the man they had called Teko was with me.

I lay there in the dark silence. Long minutes ticked by and I wondered if the others were ever coming back. But they did. I was led up
some stairs, down some hallways. Totally disoriented, hearing none of
the usual city noises, I thought perhaps I was somewhere in a house
out in the woods.

We came to a stop and they pushed me a few feet this way and then
that way. I could sense that they were opening some kind of door.
A stale, dirty smell assaulted my nose with such an abrupt suddenness
that I thought I recognized what they were about to do to me. I completely panicked. In utter terror, I struggled and fought to get free,
praying, "Don't bury me . . . God, please, don't bury me, no, no,
please . . ." I remembered in a flash the news story of a girl who had

been kidnapped in Florida and had been buried in a box for days, with only a single air tube keeping her alive. She had survived by luck alone.

I don't know how long I fought. Probably for not more than a few seconds, but it seemed like forever before I was subdued and their voices came through to me: "It's only a closet . . . a closet, for Christ's sake . . ."

They pushed me in there and guided me down into a sitting position. They told me not to touch the gag, the blindfold, or my bonds. Then they slammed the door shut. I groped around and found that it was a closet, a padded, empty closet.

CHAPTER

THREE

THE INSIDE OF THAT closet stank. I was alone there with a stale, musty odor of body sweat and filth. For all the air circulating in there, I might as well have been in an underground coffin. Curled up, I lay there in a corner, weeping. Tears flowed of their own accord, soaking my blindfold and running down my face. I felt caged, like a wild animal, so helpless. The closet itself seemed of ordinary size, about six feet long and a bit more than two feet wide. It had been soundproofed with carpet and undercarpet padding, hung on all four walls from ceiling to floor, even covering the door, with just a slit for entry. The pads were very old and worn and dirty. The closer I brought my nose to the padding, the stronger was the odor I detested. There was no escaping it. Never had I felt so helpless. Why me? I asked myself over and over again. Why me?

My mind skidded from one thought to another without focus. I was not thinking; I was reacting to unfamiliar sensations. My legs stung from having been scraped raw on those concrete steps at the apartment. My right leg particularly hurt, oozing blood. The left side of my face had begun to throb with pain, from the blow of the rifle butt. The pains came and went in my consciousness; more than anything else, I felt an uncontrollable fear: They could kill me and I could not stop them. I thought they might. I could not imagine myself dead. It was too awful. My lungs felt as though they were being squeezed in a vise: only crying seemed to relieve me. I did not think; I cried.

The closet door flew open and someone placed a small radio inside, blaring soul music. He told me not to touch the dial. "We'll only tell you once. So don't forget. Don't touch it at all."

The raucous music, very loud, filled the closet, assaulting another of my five senses. The radio was meant to prevent my hearing their voices on the other side of the closet door and it was effective. But I had always had very sensitive hearing. At home I had played my own radio so softly that Anne and Vicki often wondered how I could possibly hear it. But now I had trouble hearing myself think; the music was overpowering. Every so often someone would throw open the closet door, giving me another shock, as he or she checked on what I was doing. Each time I got a similar warning: "Any noise out of you, bitch, and you'll be dead!"

Some considerable time later, perhaps an hour or two, the door opened, the carpet mat was thrown back, and I heard a voice declare: "I am General Field Marshal of the Symbionese Liberation Army. My name is Cin."

The voice, cold and flat, was that of the black man, the leader, and in my shock I did not grasp what he had said. The only words that registered in my mind were: My name is Sin. New fear struck my heart as I thought: Sin—these people must be evil incarnate.*

He went on talking rapidly but I simply could not comprehend what he was saying until he seemed to be angrily repeating the same question: "Haven't you heard of the Symbionese Liberation Army?"

"No," I whispered.

"The S-L-A," he said distinctly. "The Symbionese Liberation Army. Everybody know about the SLA."

Recognition struck then. These were the people who had shot and killed Marcus Foster, the black leader in the East Bay Area . . . the first black Superintendent of Schools in Oakland . . . a man much respected in the whole Bay Area. I also remembered hearing something about the arrest of his murderers. I had heard about it on the television news several months before. Two friends of ours who were black had commented on how crazy the SLA must be if they intended to start a revolution in the United States by killing a black leader. Nate, Steve's former roommate at Princeton, and Gloria, his friend, were outraged at

---

* It was several days before one of the women enlightened me as to the spelling of his full name, Cinque Mtume, which meant Fifth Prophet.

the murder of Marcus Foster. Gloria had said, "Looks like they're going to have to kill a lot of us black folk, if that's the way they intend to win a revolution."

It flashed through my mind that if these were the same crazy people who had killed Marcus Foster, it would be safer for me not to admit that I knew who they were. So I repeated that I did not know of them and this seemed to agitate him enormously. He wondered how dumb I could be, where I could have been keeping myself, not to have heard of the SLA. He told me outright that the SLA had killed Marcus Foster with cyanide bullets. He was proud of it. The SLA had declared war on the United States, he said, and this was a revolution of the poor and oppressed people against fascist *Amerikkka*.* Rather formally, he intoned that I had been "arrested" by a combat unit of the Symbionese Liberation Army because I was the daughter of Randolph A. Hearst, whom he called "a corporate enemy of the people."

"You are a prisoner of war of the Symbionese Liberation Army," he declared. "You will be held in protective custody and you will be treated according to the Geneva Convention governing prisoners of war."

He asked me if I had a watch . . . any jewelry . . . any religious medals . . . To each of these and other similar questions, of course, I answered "No." It should have been quite obvious that beneath my bathrobe, except for my underpants, I was naked. But he went on to explain that under the Geneva Convention I could keep only my religious medals. All other items would have to be held in their custody. He went on and on. I thought he might be insane.

Assuring me again and again that the SLA had no intention of mistreating me, he said that as soon as possible he would have a medical unit, including a doctor and nurse, attend to my wounds. The SLA was very busy that night, he told me. There were "actions" being carried out across the state of California. Other combat teams had captured other prisoners. Five or six other prisoners had been taken that same night. He told me the SLA was a huge army, containing a number of armed combat teams, intelligence units, medical teams, all backed by the financial aid of supporters of the revolution throughout the country. Beyond that, the SLA was linked organizationally with revolutionary

---

* The SLA liked to spell America with 3 K's, adapted from the Ku Klux Klan, symbolizing, they felt, the racism inherent in the capitalist system.

movements in Ireland, Puerto Rico, the Philippines, and a number of African countries. Most of their names were unfamiliar to me. He mentioned country after country and naming each of the revolutionary groups involved, and when it became apparent that I did not know what he was talking about, he berated me for being so ignorant of the "people's movements" in all parts of the world. Someone behind him laughed and remarked caustically that I was like Marie Antoinette, who had lived in her own cocoon of ignorance, not knowing there was a revolution going on—until she lost her head. Others laughed at this great joke and for the next day or so they took to calling me Marie Antoinette or just Marie.

This horrible man I could not see went on talking and talking, telling me more than I wanted to know and too little of what I really wanted to know. It all sounded so bizarre. I could not take it all in. I felt totally exhausted; I had wept myself out. He stopped finally and asked me, "Any questions?" or perhaps he just paused, for I did ask, "What ransom are you going to ask for me?"

He laughed.

"When will I go home?" I pleaded.

He laughed again.

"Maybe soon?" I asked.

"Oh, you want to get home for your birthday, eh?"

He gave me no answer, but it meant that they knew my birthday was coming up in sixteen days. On February 20, I would be twenty years old. His knowing my birthday frightened me too. I had had the impression that they did not know much about me, only my name and who I was, which was enough for a kidnap victim. How could they know my birthday? How much more did they know about me? I thought this over when the closet door was shut and the radio turned on again. Within a few minutes, the door was opened once more and the man called Cin asked me if I wanted anything to eat. I declined. Anything to drink? Tea? Water? A girl's voice urged me to have some tea. Some water. She assured me it was safe. She would drink from the glass first and then hand it to me. I nodded my head and felt the glass in my hand. I took a little sip but did not have the heart even to drink a glass of water.

"Can I go to the bathroom?" I asked.

"What do you have to go to the bathroom for?" someone asked, laughing.

"Because I have to go to the bathroom."

"What for?" a man asked with a mocking laugh. They all screamed with laughter; something was enormously funny to them.

I did not know what he was getting at until he said, "Look at her, the fancy, la-di-da lady, a real Marie Antoinette. Listen, if you gotta go pee, say, 'I gotta go pee'; if you gotta take a shit, say, 'I gotta take a shit.' That's the way poor people talk."

"I've got to go pee," I said, and someone helped me up, led me out of the closet, and stood me up against the wall.

"Shut your eyes," he said, "I'm just going to take your blindfold off and put a fresh one on." He turned me around, so that when the soaking-wet blindfold was removed and I peeked, all I could see was a wall. With a new, dry blindfold in place, he led me to the bathroom. He was taller and heavier than the black man or the other man who had kidnapped me, all of which I could sense from the feel of him at my side. "Can't I go to the bathroom by myself?" I asked, promising not to remove the blindfold. "Fuck, no," he replied. "You're a prisoner of war and you got to be under observation at all times." I had no choice. This is the final humiliation, I thought, but there was no way that I was going to let them see that! Of course, I was wrong again.

They tied my wrists again, this time behind me, and back into the closet I went, with yet another long lecture on the role that was expected of me as a prisoner of war. As long as I behaved myself, I would not be mistreated; but if I dared to make a sound or to try to escape or even to touch the closet door, which would be locked, then I would be strung up from the ceiling—like a dead pig.

Alone in the closet with that awful, pervading smell, I cringed in fear. Never had I felt so degraded, so much in the power of others, so vulnerable. What made it even worse was that I could not figure out these people who had abducted me; I rarely understood what they were saying and I did not know how much of it to believe. My first impression was simply that they were crazy, insane, and yet what they had told me did make some sort of sense. It was possible. Maybe all the radicals in the Bay Area or even throughout California had banded together in some wild scheme to take over the country. But that was ridiculous. Or was it? The one ray of hope that I could see was, ironically, that they had carefully kept me blindfolded all the time; that meant that they did intend to return me home alive. I could not identify them; I did not know where I was being kept; they would be safe.

Perhaps it would be only a matter of time. They would demand a ransom. My father would pay it. I would be set free, unharmed. The FBI would move in and capture the kidnappers. All's well that ends well. The scenario is on television every week. I fantasized my rescue, my reunion with Steve (maybe they hadn't killed him), I would be embraced by my mother and father, in tears. My sisters would gather around me. I must have slept that night, although I have no memory of it.

The next morning, Cin told me angrily that the "stupid motherfucking pigs were trying to play games" with the SLA by not announcing my "arrest." He said that there had been absolutely nothing in the paper about it. But the SLA was far ahead of the police or FBI in this operation and the "warrant" for my arrest would be sent to the media. This time the SLA would make certain that all its communiqués were published in the media so that "the people" would know what was really going on. He also apologized that the SLA medical unit had been very busy in other actions last night, even though they had many doctors and registered nurses in their ranks. They would get to me as soon as possible. Meanwhile, he said, he would read to me the official warrant order for my arrest:

SYMBIONESE LIBERATION ARMY
WESTERN REGIONAL ADULT ARMY

Communiqué No. 3   February 4, 1974

SUBJECT: Prisoner of War
TARGET: Patricia Campbell Hearst—
daughter of Randolph A. Hearst,
corporate enemy of the people

WARRANT ORDER:
Arrest and protective custody; and if resistance, execution

WARRANT ISSUED BY:
The Court of the People

On the afore stated date, combat elements of the United Federated Forces of the Symbionese Liberation Army armed with cyanide loaded weapons served an arrest warrant upon Patricia Campbell Hearst.

It is the order of this court that the subject be arrested by combat units and removed to a protective area of safety and only upon completion of this condition to notify Unit ⚡4 to give communication of this action.

It is the directive of this court that during this action ONLY, no civilian elements be harmed if possible, and that warning shots be given. However, if any citizens attempt to aid the authorities or interfere with the implementation of this order, they shall be executed immediately.

This court hereby notifies the public and directs all combat units in the future to shoot to kill any civilian who attempts to witness or interfere with any operation conducted by the people's forces against the fascist state.

Should any attempt be made by the authorities to rescue the prisoner, or to arrest or harm any SLA elements, the prisoner is to be executed.

The prisoner is to be maintained in adequate physical and mental condition, and unharmed as long as these conditions are adhered to. Protective custody shall be composed of combat and medical units to safeguard both the prisoner and her health.

All communications from this court MUST be published in full in all newspapers, and all other forms of media. Failure to do so will endanger the safety of the prisoner.

Further communications will follow:

SLA

DEATH TO THE FASCIST INSECT
THAT PREYS UPON THE LIFE OF THE PEOPLE

The SLA leader told me that I would not be harmed so long as I remained a model prisoner. But, he said, if I ever tried to escape, I would be shot on the spot. He was most concerned over the widely reported efforts of the FBI and the police to find the SLA. "I'm telling you now," he said, "if those motherfucking pigs come charging in here, there's gonna be a shoot-out, and you'll be the first to die. We're going to fight to the end because there ain't nothing worse than prison; we'd rather die than go to prison. They're never gonna take us alive. As soon as the shooting starts, we'll come in here and waste you. So, just don't get any ideas about your getting out of here if the pigs find us, 'cause you won't. You'll be the first to die."

He repeated what he said were the SLA "Codes of War" pertaining to prisoners, under a heading he called: "Conduct of guerrilla forces toward the enemy soldiers and prisoners." It seemed as if the SLA operated under a sort of constitution which spelled out what he called the "righteous" conduct of urban guerrillas in their war against the fascist state. He came and went all that morning, lecturing me in a phony, formal tone of voice as though he were a judge or a general. He stood at the door of the closet delivering these lectures and it seemed to me that he was straining to keep his voice calm and formal, trying not to mispronounce words with which he was not familiar. There was a tension in the air. His voice sounded strange and unreal. His words barely made sense. I could understand some of what he was saying but I could hardly believe it. I did believe that I was only one of several people who had been abducted the night before, that the SLA might well be a huge guerrilla force attempting to overthrow the government, but I simply could not believe that they could succeed. All sorts of thoughts went through my mind and I suppose I did not know what to believe. I did recognize, however, that I was terrified of these people.

In due course, the "medics" did arrive and someone—I was told she was a registered nurse—ministered to my legs. My right leg was severely skinned and raw, my left less so. Both legs were washed and an ointment of some sort was applied. I was told that my left cheek was just bruised, and although it was sensitive to the touch, did not require any medical treatment. My blindfold, again sopping wet, was changed. I could not stop myself from crying. I hated them. I hated the situation I was in. I could do nothing about it and I was scared.

All through that day and the next, they talked to me about the aims and goals of the SLA, the need for this armed revolution against the fascist state, their links with other similar organizations throughout California, the radical movement and organization within the state prisons, and particularly my own status as their prisoner of war. Mostly it was Cin who came to the closet door to deliver the lecture or impart a new scrap of information, but the others came also, sometimes singly, sometimes in groups. Someone would open the door, ask if I was all right, if I wanted to go to the bathroom, and then launch into a monologue on Marxism or some revolutionary principle. I could not have cared less about their Communist claptrap; in fact, I barely understood

what they were talking about. But their view of my prisoner-of-war status commanded my attention because I knew it concerned my own personal safety; and even there I had trouble at first discerning what they
had in mind; so much of it was a jumble of words.

But Cin's message, repeated in a variety of ways, finally did get
through to me: "You're our prisoner of war and you will be held according to the Geneva Convention. Our two comrades are being held
in a pig's prison and that's why we took you. You're going to be
treated exactly as they are. Your condition here will duplicate their situation. If their condition changes for the worse, then your condition
will change—in exactly the same way. Do you understand?"

It was the girl with the giggly voice, the one who had pointed the automatic pistol at me, who explained the situation to me. Her name, she
told me, was Gelina. If Cin played the heavy and aroused utter fear in
my heart, this girl, among all the others, played the light part, the one
who seemed to want to be friendly.

With utmost sincerity, this girl with the lilting voice tried to explain:
"You're really lucky to be here rather than in a pig's prison. You're actually getting better treatment here because you're not being beaten.
Our two comrades are being beaten and tortured all the time in the
state joint at San Quentin." She went on to say blithely that their two
comrades, Joe Remiro and Russell Little, whom she called Bo and Osceola, had been arrested for the murder of Marcus Foster, even though
they were not guilty of shooting Foster and his assistant, Robert Blackburn. Bo and Osi had only been on the "backup team" when the two
educators had been shot. And every day poor Bo and Osi were being
beaten and tortured. But they were true revolutionaries and they would
not kowtow to the pigs, nor would they confess, nor would they ever
compromise their brothers and sisters in the SLA.

She went on and on about Bo and Osi. How good, how loving, and
how caring they were, and how committed the SLA was to the need for
winning the freedom of their two captured comrades. They would
never rest until Bo and Osi were set free. Somewhere along the line I
gathered that they meant to attempt an exchange deal: If Bo and Osi
were set free, I would be set free. I did not think much of that idea, for
I had never heard of any such scheme succeeding. It was difficult not to
despair. I would rather have been abducted by "normal" kidnappers
who demanded an ordinary ransom, money in exchange for my free-

dom. But with these people, I thought there was a wide gulf between us which would never be bridged.

She promised that the SLA would tell me a lot about prisons because the SLA had been involved with visiting and helping prison inmates over a long period of time. According to her, most prisoners were beautiful people, oppressed poor people forced into a life of crime by the capitalist system and then thrown into prison, where they were beaten and tortured and kept in solitary confinement in order to prevent them from starting a revolution. But now the SLA, she said, was organizing these prisoners to join the revolution to overthrow the fascist capitalists and imperialists who were now running the country. The SLA had set up a vast organization, led by an army of trained combat units, to bring about the revolution. The revolution had already begun in California. Once it had taken hold in the West, it would roll eastward across the country, as the oppressed people of all races, but led by blacks, joined in the struggle. In other nations all over the world, oppressed people were rebelling and with the force of arms and determination were toppling the fascist dictatorships. The SLA also had marvelous new programs for the new world to come. She and Cin and the others went on and on and on explaining the SLA to me until I could barely stand hearing them anymore. I wanted to scream at them, "Oh, shut up," but, of course, I did not dare.

Why were they bombarding me with this kind of information for hours and then for days, to the point of saturation? At one point, Cin explained that as revolutionaries it was their duty to "educate" me about the "people's army" and the goals of the SLA. Revolutionaries, he said, did not simply hold prisoners in solitary confinement "like the pigs did." He instructed all members of the unit to spend time with me in an effort to teach me the "truth" about the oppression of the people, the state of the world, and how it was all explained in Marxist, Maoist, and Communist writings. They all sounded so sincere in their efforts to indoctrinate me, to tell me their heartfelt beliefs. It seemed to me they were so eager because they had no one else who would listen. In me they had a captive audience. Literally. And it was so frustrating, for I could not shut them up or walk away. I longed for peace and quiet, to be left alone in my own misery, bound and blindfolded in that closet. It seemed to me, when I did have time to think and consider, that I obviously had to deal here with a bunch of psychotics—the kind of "true believers" who cannot be reasoned with, who can never be dissuaded from their own distorted version of "the truth." My own best course of action, the only one I could see open to me, was to humor them: Listen to them, I told myself, and do exactly what they want. Somehow, sometime, I would be rescued. I still believed in that. Until that happened, the best thing I could do was not to make them mad at me and to pray that they would not harm me.

I was able to differentiate their voices very quickly. I could tell one from the other and know who was talking to me. Their voices became the persons, even before I came to know their names or anything about them; even blindfolded, I knew them. In my fantasies, I could see them in a lineup against the stripes, and when each of them spoke, I would identify every one of them. It was amazing how much I could know about them from only their tones of voice. Cin's voice had a mean, street-wise tone of someone not very well educated. The excitable, lilting voice was that of the girl who had pointed the gun at me. While it is not quite correct to say she was friendly, she was the only one I thought was in the least concerned about my welfare. There was the educated, sharp voice which sounded like that of a strict schoolmarm. I was fairly certain that this one was married to the jumpy, nervous man who had been in the back seat of the station wagon—the one who cursed all the time and tried unsuccessfully to sound like a black man. I thought that they were a "couple" because these two spoke to one another in a certain tone neither of them used when addressing others, bickering with one another all the time. Then there was the girl who had been the lookout in the front seat of the car, who, I thought, was black. She had a deep, guttural, throaty drawl. The other voices were more vague. The third man spoke in a high-pitched whisper. And there was another girl there who did not talk much but I thought I could recognize her cold, ordinary voice because it was different from the others. I cherished the thought of someday being able to identify all of them—and to send them all off to prison.

Gradually, I came to learn their names also, although at first I could not link the names to the voices. There were three men: Cin, Teko, and Cujo. The others were women: Gelina, Fahizah, Yolanda, and Zoya. These were their "reborn" Swahili African names, adopted for the revolution. They addressed one another only by these names. Their former "slave" names had been renounced forever, or so they told me.

They fed me, gave me water or tea to drink, and led me to and from the bathroom. Saying that they were sharing their combat rations with me on an equal basis, they gave me two meals a day: breakfast consisted of an herbal tea and one or two slices of bread; dinner was a cumbersome production, for I ate blindfolded with a spoon from a plate balanced precariously in my lap. With each spoonful, I had to find where the food was. My first such meal came in the evening of the first full day with them, some eighteen hours after I had been kidnapped. I was not very hungry but I ate, without knowing what I was eating, other than that it had a rice base.

"Guess what you're eating," someone said. I had no idea. It was mung beans and rice. I commented that I had never heard of mung beans. For that I was called a "bourgeois bitch," because, someone said, that's what the poor people in America had to eat every night and I had not even heard of it. Before I had finished, the plate flipped and the mush spilled over my blue terry-cloth bathrobe. It was no great loss, for my appetite had been appeased with the first few spoonfuls, but I felt so humiliated, like a helpless baby. On other days, it was rice mashed with bananas or rice spiced with little slivers of fish, and always peppermint tea. It was the peppermint tea, with its pungent odor, that I came to hate much more than the food.

It was on my third full day there, which would have been a Thursday, that Cin came to the closet and for the first time called me Patty. The tone of familiarity in his voice bothered me as much as anything that had come before. That he should know my nickname, the name that only my friends called me, seemed to strip me of my last vestige of privacy. I resented it. But, of course, I said nothing. I guessed that my kidnapping had finally been made public in the newspapers. It terrified me that these SLA people should know so much about me. Also, they were obnoxiously gleeful over the publicity that had come to the SLA as a revolutionary movement. Their communiqué on my "arrest" had been printed in full. They did not show me any newspapers, of course, but they did not spare me their comments.

And that was the day the "interrogations" started. Cin was quite formal in announcing and conducting what he called the necessary interrogation of the prisoner. It seemed straight out of the movies or television: a Hitchcock film or a nightmare. The only thing missing was the bright spotlight in my eyes. And I think I would have welcomed that. I was beginning to feel like a blind woman.

He took me through my whole life history, my schools, my friends, my opinions; my sisters, their names, ages, where they lived, what they did; my mother and my father, how much money they had, what stocks they owned, what property they owned, how many cars, boats, airplanes, what each did every day, whom they saw, and on and on and on, for hours on end. Cin would warn me against lying, shouting that they already knew all about the Hearst family and, strangely enough, he convinced me that he knew more about the financial details of my family than I did.

I did lie to him on one item, however, and got away with it: I told him that all my sisters lived at home. I certainly did not want to risk having the SLA kidnap one of my sisters and I took the chance that they would not know where my sisters were living at the time. We reached an impasse over the unimportant question of whether or not my father owned an airplane. I said truthfully that he did not; Cinque insisted that he knew my father owned an airplane and that I was lying. I tried to explain that my father had once had a twin-engine Bonanza but had sold it years ago. He accused me of lying and being uncooperative. "I'm going to give you some time to think it over . . . and you better decide to be more cooperative when I come back." With that he slammed the closet door on me and for the entire next day I was left alone in the closet. When I was taken to the bathroom or given food, no one spoke to me. It was their version of solitary confinement.

I awakened the next morning with my hands free; the bonds had somehow come off my wrists during the night while I had slept. Despite my blindfold, I had a momentary sensation of freedom and then the implications struck me and I was immobilized with panic. I went into an absolute fit of hysterics. They would string me up from the ceiling, hog-tied! I did not dare touch the blindfold, lest that fall off too. There was no way I could retie myself. I sobbed uncontrollably until the closet door was opened and Fahizah, the girl with the thick, slow drawl, asked what was ailing me. I cried out my predicament and she, reassuring me, bent down to tie my wrists behind me again.

"What the fuck is goin' on here?" demanded Cinque.

"Her ropes came off, but she didn't do it," said the girl.

"She fucking well better not have," he said, and stormed out. I was grateful that the promised punishment was not meted out.

After a full day of solitary confinement, Cinque returned to continue his interrogation. I assured him that I would cooperate in answering his questions. To avoid his wrath, I simply agreed with everything he said. He would name stocks he said my father owned, and I would agree with him. He also demanded to know what stocks my mother owned. This question seemed especially strange; I had no idea whether or not my mother owned any stocks, independently of my father.

"Does she read *The Wall Street Journal?*" he demanded.

"Yes, but . . ."

"Then she owns stocks," was his conclusion. I searched my memory to name stocks with which I was familiar, having no idea if, indeed, my family did own them: AT&T, Safeway, Beatrice Foods, General Motors, Exxon, IBM . . . it made no difference to me. How many shares did my family own? Again, I had absolutely no idea. He was forever calling me an "uncooperative bourgeois bitch" or worse. It was incessant and went on for days. I became thoroughly mixed up and bewildered. It seemed that the whole purpose of the interrogation was to confirm information that they had acquired from other sources.

We had a terrible go-around on the question of how much money my father earned. I simply did not know. I could not guess. We tried on all sorts of numbers and we settled on a million dollars a year. Cin declared he knew that was right and I finally agreed. It was a good round number. We had a worse to-do on the question of why my father was in Washington on the night I was kidnapped. I insisted that I did not know; I had not even known he was in Washington that night. How many times a year did he go to Washington? I did not know. Did he see the President? The CIA? The State Department? Well, then, whom did he see? I did not know. The only purpose that I knew for my father going to Washington was for the Hearst Foundation Senate Youth Program. Every year, the Hearst Corporation sponsored the program for two high school students from each state to visit Congress and various executive departments to learn how the federal government works, I told them. I myself had gone when I had been sixteen. I tried to explain all of this. Cin laughed in my face. Did I expect *him* to believe that? Didn't I know that my father was a member of the Committee of Forty? Admit it! No, I did not know that; I had never in my life heard of any Committee of Forty. Oh, said Cinque, the SLA knew all about the Committee. It was a super-secret, high-level group of big businessmen, corporate executives, and millionaires like the Rockefellers who were all part of the CIA and it was they and the CIA who told the

President of the United States what to do; it was they who really ran the country. And my father was one of them, a reactionary, corporate-military pig who lived off the sweat of the people.

This is an abbreviated version of only one of Cinque's diatribes, without all of the terrorizing curses and Marxist buzz words. I did not believe him, but I was in no position to argue with him. He insisted that I see the light and agree with him. When I did not agree soon enough, he accused me of being uncooperative. He would warn me of dire, unspecified consequences. Then he would give me "time to think it over." The closet door would be slammed shut again, the soul music would blare, and I'd be left in terror and misery.

I wish that I could say now that I stood up well under Cinque's interrogation, that I refused to reveal vital information, that I lied and fooled him. I told the SLA anything they wanted to hear. Terrorized, threatened constantly with death or being hung from the ceiling for being an uncooperative prisoner, I spilled my guts. I answered every question as truthfully as I could. I got in trouble only with the questions to which I did not know the answer. I quickly learned to give them the answers I thought they wanted. Of course, I did not have anything to hide. Nor did I think I had any information that was vital to them or to me or to my family. I only wanted to cooperate and not to make them angry at me. I was afraid and weepy, hardly the heroine. And as the days went on, I became more and more fearful that I would not survive this ordeal.

Shortly after my kidnapping, they told me the FBI and police had stormed a house in Oakland in expectation of finding the SLA and me. That would spell my immediate death, Cinque told me. When and if the "pigs" come here, at the time the first shot was fired Cin himself would put a bullet through my brain. He didn't want a hostage to worry about during a fire fight. The SLA would fight to the death, he said: "Revolutionaries never surrender." Besides, he warned me, the FBI always came in with guns blazing at revolutionaries. He named various radicals who had been shot to death by the FBI and told me the FBI would just as soon kill me as them. The FBI would blame the SLA for my death and further discredit revolutionaries throughout the country, he said. The police were already trying to discredit the SLA by blaming them in the press for the recent random killings, which at the time seemed to be a senseless shooting of whites by unknown blacks on the streets of San Francisco. The police also accused the SLA of trying to shoot down a police helicopter, he said, which was equally ridiculous.

But overall, Cinque and his comrades could not hide their delight and illusions of grandeur over the widespread blast of publicity given to them in the press as a result of my kidnapping. I was their passport to fame and popularity. They did not show me any newspapers or allow me to listen to news reports of the kidnapping on the radio or television, but Cinque and the others could not resist telling me what was being said about them. It all would help spread the word of their revolutionary war against the government, they said, for "the people" would now know that the "oppressors" could be engaged in open combat. It proved that they had been right all the time, they told me: Revolutions could be fought and won against capitalism only through force and guns, and not through theory or books or lectures.

Nevertheless, he told me that the SLA would try to negotiate terms for my release from the "people's prison." He said he wanted to see if the capitalist pigs were really willing to negotiate for my release on a fair basis. First, he said, the United Symbionese War Council, its governing body, had decided that my father would be required to give "a gesture of good faith" to prove he was willing to negotiate. That "gesture of good faith" would be his giving back to the people only a small part of what he and the Hearst Corporation had stolen from the people over the years. For a start, the SLA would demand that the Hearst Corporation give seventy dollars' worth of food to every poor person in the state of California. The SLA did not want ransom per se. They wanted the Hearsts to give food to the poor people who were starving. That was not asking too much, was it? No, of course not, I agreed. Cinque told me I was going to make a tape-recorded message to my family so they would know that I was still alive and I was to urge them to cooperate with the SLA. Cinque said he would "help" me make the tape: He would tell me what needed to be said.

The SLA leader also said that one of the sisters would help me take a bath so that I could get cleaned up. Perhaps even he, I thought, can no longer stand the rank smell I had picked up from my stifling "people's prison." I looked forward to my first bath in captivity, for I felt that the filth of the closet and the stale sweat of my own body had seeped deep into my pores. There was a catch, of course. Cin told me that I would have to keep my blindfold on. If and when the time came for my release, they did not want me to be able to identify them to the FBI.

The bathroom was small, hot, and steamy, the bath water almost scalding, but the sensation was marvelous and soothing. The grime and grit seemed to peel off my body. Zoya, the girl with the hard, cold voice, sat guard over me in the bathroom, talking away on the woman's role in the people's revolution, on sexual equality in the utopia of the future, and similar favorite topics. As she droned on, I washed and scrubbed, feeling new and rejuvenated and clean again. My hair was gritty with dirt but I did not dare try to wash it. The blindfold was wrapped over my hair and if the blindfold became wet and slipped off, I might then see Zoya's face and jeopardize my chances of ever being set free. I realized that I could identify them by their voices, but I would play in their charade. I did not want to see their faces. I wanted to go home.

Zoya, off in her own fantasy world, described in great detail how happy the poor people would be receiving free food from the capitalist supermarkets, paid for by the Hearsts. My pig parents would be compensating the people for their sins against them. I had been responding with innocuous remarks to keep her talking in order to prolong my bath. But I did question what would happen if people did not come out to get the food offered. It occurred to me the whole plan could collapse, and my own life forfeited through no fault of mine or my father's, if people refused to accept food offered in this manner.

"Of course they'll come out to get the food," said Zoya. "They need the food . . . they're starving."

"But some people might think it degrading to accept free food like this because it was extorted," I ventured. "I don't think poor people would want free food given like that." My thoughts naïvely slipped out and I was somewhat surprised to find that Zoya had become furious.

"You're such a bourgeois bitch! You have no idea what poor people are like. They can't afford the luxury of your bourgeois morals. Millions of people are starving. Of course they will accept the food, no matter how it is given to them. Their babies are hungry and you just don't understand."

Zoya fled the bathroom and another woman came in to tell me to finish up my bath. I thought no more about it. She gave me a pair of clean corduroy pants and a thin T-shirt to wear instead of my bathrobe. Before a new blindfold was put on, they showed me a news clipping and picture of Steven Weed in a hospital bed to prove to me that he was alive. For the first few days I had asked about him constantly, but they would tell me nothing. By the time they told me that he was alive, I was convinced to the contrary. I was certain that they were lying to me in order to keep me calm. This was the first time that I knew for certain that he was not dead.

A fresh blindfold was slipped over my eyes, and I was led back to my "people's prison." Later that day, which, as close as I could figure, was my fifth day of captivity, Cinque got into the closet with me, and while I sat at one end with my back propped against one wall, he sat at the other end of the six-and-a-half-foot closet, with his tape recorder, a sheaf of notes, and a flashlight. He untied me, handed me the microphone, showed me where the on-off switch was located, and instructed me on how we would proceed. Because there were so many important points to get across to my father and to the police, if there was to be any chance of my release, he would tell me what to say and I would put it in my own words. When I finished each point, I was to click off the tape recorder and he would tell me what next to say, one point at a time. I was happy to cooperate in this; I would do anything, I thought, to get a message home.

The first part of the tape went simply enough. I could understand what Cinque was trying to get across and put into words. But as we went on, it became more and more difficult for me. I had to exert all of my determination to keep from breaking down and crying as I told lie after lie about how well I was being treated and especially when I expressed the hope of getting back to my family and to Steve. The truth was: I was so scared but still resented that I was being used to disseminate their lies. My voice faltered from time to time. I hardly knew what I was saying when Cinque had me talk of the Marcus Foster killing and the various ideological links of the SLA. There I had to stop the machine in mid-sentence to find out what next to say. But I was desperate to get home and I did stumble through it, with many hesitations, saving my tears until I had completed the tape. Here then, as transcribed by the *Examiner*, is my first taped message from the SLA to the outside world:

Mom, Dad. I'm OK. I had a few scrapes and stuff, but they washed them up and they're getting OK. And I caught a cold, but they're giving me pills for it and stuff.

I'm not being starved or beaten or unnecessarily frightened. I've heard some press reports and so I know that Steve and all the neighbors are OK and that no one was really hurt.

And I also know that the SLA members here are very upset about press distortions of what's been happening. They have not been shooting down helicopters or shooting down innocent people in the streets.

I'm kept blindfolded usually so that I can't identify anyone. My hands are often tied, but generally they're not. I'm not gagged or anything, and I'm comfortable.

And I think you can tell that I'm not really terrified or anything and that I'm OK.

I was very upset, though, to hear that police rushed in on that house in Oakland and I was really glad that I wasn't there and I would appreciate it if everyone would just calm down and try not to find me and not be making identifications because they're not only endangering me but they're endangering themselves.

I'm with a combat unit that's armed with automatic weapons and there's also a medical team here and there's no way that I will be released until they let me go, so it won't do any good for somebody to come in here and try to get me out by force.

These people aren't just a bunch of nuts. They've been really honest with me but they're perfectly willing to die for what they are doing.

And I want to get out of here but the only way I'm going to is if we do it their way. And I just hope that you'll do what they say, Dad, and just do it quickly.

I've been stopping and starting this tape myself, so that I can collect my thoughts. That's why there are so many stops in it.

I'm not being forced to say any of this. I think it's really important that you take their requests very seriously about not arresting any other SLA members and about following their good faith request to the letter.

I just want to get out of here and see everyone again and be back with Steve.

The SLA is very interested in seeing how you're taking this,

Dad, and they want to make sure that you are really serious and listening to what they're saying.

And they think that you've been taking this whole thing a lot more seriously than the police and the FBI and other people. Or at least I am.

It's really up to you to make sure that these people don't jeopardize my life by charging in and doing stupid things, and I hope that you will make sure they don't do anything else like that Oakland house business.

The SLA people really have been honest with me and I really mean I feel pretty sure that I'm going to get out of here if everything goes the way they want it to.

And I think you should feel that way too, and try not to worry so much. I mean I know it's hard, but I heard Mom was really upset and that everybody was at home. I hope that this puts you a little bit at ease so that you know that I really am all right.

I just hope I can get back to everybody really soon.

The SLA has ideological ties with the IRA, the people's struggle in the Philippines and the Socialist people in Puerto Rico in their struggle for independence, and they consider themselves to be soldiers who are fighting and aiding these people.

I am a prisoner of war and so are the two men in San Quentin. I am being treated in accordance with the Geneva Convention, one of the conditions being that I am not being tried for crimes which I'm not responsible for.

I am here because I am a member of a ruling class family and I think you can begin to see the analogy. The people, the two men in San Quentin are being held and are going to be tried simply because they are members of the SLA and not because they've done anything.

Witnesses to the shooting of Foster saw black men. And two white men have been arrested for this. You're being told this so that you'll understand why I was kidnapped and so that you'll understand that whatever happens to the two prisoners is going to happen to me.

You have to understand that I am held to be innocent the same way the two men in San Quentin are innocent, that they are simply members of the group and have not done anything themselves to warrant their arrest.

They apparently were part of an intelligence unit and have never executed anyone themselves. The SLA has declared war against the government and it's important that you understand that they know what they're doing and they understand what their actions mean.

. . . And that you realize that this is not considered by them to be just a simple kidnapping and that you don't treat it that way and say "Oh, I don't know why she was taken."

I'm telling you now why this happened so that you will know and so that you have something to use, some knowledge to try to get me out of here.

If you can get the food thing organized before the 19th [of February], then that's OK and would just speed up my release.

Today is Friday, the eighth, and in Kuwait the commandoes negotiated the release of their hostages and they left the country.

Bye.

The reference to the news item from Kuwait and the date was the SLA's method of telling my father that I was truly alive on the eighth and that the tape was not postdated. By the end of the tape, I felt drained. I had thought at first my taped message would be short and simple. But Cinque had kept instructing me, "Keep talking, keep talking." The taping must have taken hours, for we went over and over some parts until I got the words right or nearly right. I felt humiliated spitting out their propaganda, knowing that it would be widely publicized. At some points, I hardly knew what I was saying, I simply repeated what Cin told me to say verbatim. It was apparent to me that the SLA was using my tape to get across their own message: They still wanted to exchange me for the release of their two comrades in jail and they also wanted the food program to rally popular support to their cause. I had been particularly distressed when Cin and the others told me that my mother had wept before the television camera on one of the first telecasts from Hillsborough. I had never once seen my mother cry; she was ordinarily so good, so strong in moments of stress or emergency. So, whatever good the tape did for the SLA, I thought, it would also reassure my mom and dad that I was alive.

When the taping was finally over and Cin said, "That's it," I slumped down against the wall, half sitting and half lying, and began to sob in utter exhaustion. Suddenly, I became aware that a hand was stroking my breast and Cin was over me, cooing in my ear in a mock-sexy voice. "I hear you been disrespectful to one of our sisters, you bourgeois bitch." I was so frightened I did not grasp what he was talking about. "You better watch your mouth, bitch, 'cause you're our prisoner and if you don't watch what you're saying . . ." Then he pinched my nipple, brutally. The pain and shock ran right through me. His hand darted down and grabbed my crotch. Another pinch. I sat frozen in the dark, stunned. My whole body felt icy numb. My heart thumped. "I don't want to hear of you being disrespectful to the sisters anymore. You hear me? Or I'll be back to see you about it!" His voice was low, almost a whisper, but there was no mistaking the menace in it or the threat of sexual violence. Then he was gone.

Alone in my own personal misery, I cried hot tears of humiliation and fear. Being helpless, I had sensed the ever-present possibility of sexual abuse. There had been undertones. But this was a clear, overt threat of what I could expect if Cin became angry with me for any reason. It took an effort on my part to connect Cin's attack with what I had said to Zoya in the bathroom. In my innocence, I had merely expressed my honest concern that people might refuse to accept the "blood money" food and that their refusal might endanger my life. But there was no reasoning with these people. Thinking it all over, I realized that I would have to remain on guard at all times to avoid angering any of them. I promised myself that I would never again disagree with anything any of them told me, ever. I wanted to get out alive and to see them all sent to jail for a long, long time for what they were doing to me.

CHAPTER

FOUR

THE FIRST TAPED MESSAGE to the outside world was not sent out for another three days because the SLA comrades had to work furiously on the details of their food program demands. As they explained it to me at the time, they wanted my father to provide seventy dollars' worth of top-quality food—meat, vegetables, and dairy products—to every poor person in California. This included people with welfare cards, social security pension cards, food stamp cards, disabled veterans' cards, medical cards, parole or probation papers, and jail or bail release slips. They listed distribution points, as well as the organizations to handle the food distribution, in San Francisco, Oakland, East Palo Alto, Santa Rosa, and sections of Los Angeles. They insisted that the food be distributed within a four-week period, beginning on February 19, on each Tuesday, Thursday, and Saturday. And all this was to be just a "gesture of good faith" from my father before the SLA made its actual ransom demand. I could not understand why they wouldn't just demand a ransom and get it over with, but I kept my thoughts to myself. The SLA had concluded its demands with this dire message: "If this gesture of good faith is not met then we will assume that there is no basis for negotiations, and we will no longer take and maintain in good health and spirits prisoners of war."

Cinque also sent seven or eight sheets of single-spaced typewritten material containing all the documents which explained the goals, aims, and purposes of the SLA, and he demanded that my father see to it that all the SLA documents and tapes be distributed to the press and the media so that they would be printed in their entirety. He thought this would rally most, if not all, of the radical groups in the Bay Area to the SLA cause. He also sent his own personal message on a tape recording:

"To those who would bear the hopes and future of our people let the voice of their guns express the words of freedom: Greetings to the people, fellow comrades, brothers and sisters. My name in Cinque, and to my comrades I am known as Cin. I am a black man and a representative of black people. I hold the rank of general field marshal in the United Federated Forces of the Symbionese Liberation Army."

Castigating my father for owning a chain of newspapers, magazines, and television and radio stations which he said supported the fascist corporate-military state and accusing my mother, as a member of the California Board of Regents, of being insensitive to what they called crimes against the people, Cinque declared:

"We of the Symbionese Liberation Army hold the Hearst Corporation and the Hearst family and the Board of Regents, as well as the corporate state which they support and aid, are enemies of the people and that the people have the legal and human right and duty . . . to save the lives of starving men, women, and children of every race, and I, along with the loyal men and women of many races who love the people, are quite willing to give our lives to free the people at any cost.

"And if, as you and others might so easily believe, that we will lose, let it be known that even in death we will win, for the very ashes of this fascist nation will mark our very grave."

Cin came back into the closet to make that recording and I hoped that the harsh tenor of his message would give my parents some idea of what I was enduring at the hands of my kidnappers. They were true revolutionaries. Lunatics or not, they were ready to die for their cause. Or to kill me for their cause. I found myself praying to God for deliverance. I did not know how He would accomplish this. But I prayed in blind faith.

The tape recordings, mine and his, together with the batch of SLA documents, were mailed to the left-oriented Pacifica radio station KPFA in Berkeley and a day or two later Cin stormed to the door of my closet. Never before had I heard him so furious. He fairly hissed the reactions to the SLA demands.

It seemed that the press had immediately speculated that the SLA's real demand would be the release of Joe Remiro and Russell Little. California's governor, Ronald Reagan, upon being asked, had turned down the implied proposal cold. "If they're thinking of any kind of exchange at all, they can just forget it." So, even before the SLA could ask for an exchange of prisoners, it had been ruled out.

Cin also informed me that the newspapers had estimated that the food program demanded by the SLA would cost something in the neighborhood of $400 million and my father had just announced on television that there was no way he could pay $400 million for my release. And my mother had stood beside him in front of all the television cameras wearing a black dress. That meant, said Cin, that she was in mourning already. They would rather see me dead than give up any of their money or their power, Cin proclaimed.

My father had said it was beyond his ability to buy seventy dollars' worth of food for all the people the SLA wanted to be fed as a "gesture of good faith." But my father also had promised to make a counteroffer to prove his good faith as soon as possible. But, said Cin, "that was all pigshit . . . your father is one of the biggest pigs in the country and he could come up with four hundred million, if he wants to. Or, he could ask Safeway or the other food chains and they would give him the food at cost. Or, he could ask his rich friends, like Howard Hughes or the Shah of Iran, to help him out. . . . Four hundred million is nothing to a pig like your father."

The truth was, according to Cin's ranting, that my father was a member of the ruling class and the ruling class did not want to set a precedent for paying ransom because then other children of the capitalist ruling class would be kidnapped and held for ransom. No, my father would rather sacrifice me than abandon his rich friends and the power structure that rules Amerikkka.

He went on and on: The (expletive) Charles Bates (agent-in-charge of the FBI office in San Francisco) had called the SLA a bunch of hoods. And the (expletive) Attorney General of the United States (William Saxbe) had commanded the FBI from Washington to find the SLA, shoot 'em up, and get Patty Hearst out of there. . . . And the (expletive) Tim Findley had written (double expletive) profiles of the SLA members in the *Chronicle*.

The press too were all a bunch of bourgeois pigs; the news media were all owned by fascist multinational corporations. All sorts of lies were spewed out in the newspapers and on television about the SLA.

They were all against the SLA. This was a class war: the capitalists and the bourgeoisie against the SLA and *the people*. It was a shame, he said, that I was caught in the middle. It was too bad that I would have to die because of this class war—die for the crimes that my parents had committed against the people. I was innocent. But, after all, my life was not that important when compared to the lives of the millions of children who were now starving and being driven to a slow death in fascist Amerikkka. This would be a long, long struggle, but *the people* would be victorious in the end. The SLA comrades, Cin declared, were so full of love for the people that they had declared war against the ruling class and they would not surrender or give up their fight until every pig was dead.

At the conclusion of this diatribe he said that he, as the leader of the SLA, would take this whole matter up before the United Symbionese War Council, which was the alliance of all the underground revolutionary groups in America. The War Council was the governing board of the revolutionary war being waged against the United States. On the War Council, Cin explained, he had only one vote. The War Council, he told me, would decide my fate.

Cin left the safehouse shortly afterward—or so I was led to believe —to attend the War Council meeting in a warehouse somewhere. From time to time, the others came to the closet to talk to me about the dire need to feed all the poor people in the San Francisco Bay Area and in the ghettos and barrios of Los Angeles. I hardly listened. I could not free my mind of the likelihood that, in the end, I would not be set free: I would be killed.

Actually, my father had been most conciliatory in his statement. But Cin had not told me this and I had no way of knowing it at the time. To the outside world, the situation might have appeared even hopeful: negotiations were under way. But to me in the closet, it seemed nearly hopeless. From the tone of Cin's voice as much as from what he said, I gathered that the SLA comrades were uneasy over the turn the situation had taken: The SLA had made an impossible demand; there was no way my father could feed all the "poor" people in California. But the SLA could not back down on its demands and lose face. Moreover, the press had guessed what their actual ransom demand was to be. Resenting their own predictability, they were not about to ask for the release of their comrades now. So what would they do? I wondered. To the point of nervous exhaustion, I explored every possible way out of this impasse, always to the same conclusion. I ended up crying and contemplating my own death.

Hours later I could hear Cin's return from the War Council meeting. There was the slam of the garage door leading into the house, the shuffling of feet, and the voices outside the closet. Then from a faint murmur of voices over the din of the eternally blaring soul music I surmised that my captors were holding one of their interminable meetings to discuss the War Council's decision. I waited and waited.

Cin finally came to the closet and told me: "You're a lucky bitch. The War Council has granted you a reprieve, a temporary reprieve. We figured the bourgeois press had twisted the SLA's words again." The SLA had never asked for $400 million worth of food, he said. All the SLA wanted was for my father to repent publicly and to prove his sincerity with a gesture of good faith—namely, feeding the poor. The SLA and the people would judge the sincerity of his repentance by the extent of the food program. That in itself would not result in my release. No. The War Council had decided that only after the people were fed would they begin *negotiations* for my release. So, said Cinque, the self-proclaimed General Field Marshal of the SLA, he and I would send another tape-recorded message to my father.

When Cin came into the closet for the taping, he surprised me by saying that I could remove my blindfold. They had left me untied since the day of the taping, when Cin had threatened me sexually, and now the blindfold was coming off to tape this communiqué. At first, I could see nothing. It was pitch black in the closet until Cin flicked on a flashlight and I could see him there, wearing a dark ski mask. He handed me a sheaf of notes and the flashlight, telling me to make this tape in my own words but to follow the notes carefully. He instructed me to speak convincingly and strongly, because my life depended upon it. The previous tape recording, he complained, had been too weepy, too full of starts and stops, too suspect, suggesting that I had been drugged and was being told what to say at every sentence.

This appeal, upon reading and rereading the notes, seemed fairly straightforward, with just a few eccentricities. It called upon my father to offer a food program that was reasonable and then tried to answer all the charges being made in the press against the SLA. I told my father and the world that the SLA was "really mad" about comments in the press that the food program would be based upon "extortion" and I again pleaded for my father to stop the FBI from trying to arrest SLA members or trying to find where I was being kept. I also appealed for an end to speculation that I was already dead. I thought it insulting and unfair to my mother but I followed the notes in saying, "Mom should get out of her black dress. That doesn't help at all." I added, "I wish you'd try to understand the position I'm in. I'm right in the middle and I have to depend upon what all kinds of other people are going to do. . . . And as long as the FBI doesn't come in here. That is my biggest worry. I think I can get out of here as long as they don't come busting in and I really think you should understand that the SLA does have an interest in my return." (I certainly hoped so!)

It was the next day that Cin came to me and told me that my father had announced a two-million-dollar food distribution program as his "gesture of good faith" toward my release. Cin absolutely amazed me by asking with sincerity for my opinion on the matter. My father had explained that he was putting up $500,000 of his own money and the William Randolph Hearst Foundation, set up by my grandfather, had voted to contribute $1,500,000 (with the members of the family on the board of directors abstaining from the vote). The food program, which was to be called People in Need (PIN), would be modeled after a successful private relief program for unemployed aerospace workers in the state of Washington, and it would be administered by Ludlow Kramer, the Secretary of State of Washington, who had run that food program. It was estimated, my father had said, that the two million dollars would feed one hundred thousand people a month for a whole year. Dad had also acceded to the SLA demand that the two SLA men who had been arrested—Joe Remiro and Russell Little—be treated fairly by the authorities. He had hired a well-known attorney, William Coblentz, of San Francisco, to represent the two men at least in the pre-trial proceedings. What did I think of all this? asked Cin.

I was taken aback that he would even ask my opinion. I tried to take my cues from him but he was not giving me any. Yes, I said, I thought the food program was excellent and fair. And, yes, two million dollars was a lot of money. Feeding a hundred thousand people for a whole year was a genuine gesture of good faith, I said. It was a lot of money for my father to pay. I chose my words carefully because I did not want to make him mad by disagreeing with him. I had no idea what Cin thought of the two-million-dollar offer, but I wanted him to accept it. Cin did not agree. He was particularly outraged that the money was being channeled through a tax-exempt charitable organization. I pleaded with him that it did not make any difference—the SLA would get the credit for bringing food to the poor and that was what the SLA really wanted. Cin hesitated and then said he would have to take it up with all the cells of the SLA and with the War Council for a final decision.

Thinking it over after he left me, I sensed his unease; he was unsure of himself over what to do next. This man with little or no education was clearly over his head in dealing with million-dollar projects. He had no concept of what a million dollars was. This whole food program must have been a spur-of-the-moment idea. They had kidnapped me with the idea of exchanging me for their two comrades in jail. When that did not work, they turned to the food program. Now, the SLA was being criticized by a number of radical organizations in Berkeley and in the Bay Area for linking left-wing politics to the kidnapping of a nineteen-year-old girl and the murder of a black Superintendent of Schools. The SLA did not want to lose face. That was certain. Also, I thought, there was an awfully big gap between two million and four hundred million dollars. My life hung over that gap. After all, how much was one life worth? If the SLA raised the ante, as they were about to do, would my father be able to meet it? And if the SLA should raise it again, after that, then what? We were, I thought, approaching the moment of truth.

While hearing the murmur of voices of the SLA members conferring over my fate, I wept in despair and began to fantasize the various scenarios in which I would be executed. Would I be given a warning? How would I react? Or would it come upon me suddenly, when I would know it for only an instant? And then what? Life after death? My mind wandered far and wide into my past life.

Incidents that I had never before recalled came back to me with such vividness that I could hear or see Anne or Vicki or Gina saying this or doing that. Each vignette reminded me of the love of my family. I could hear my mother talking to me with concern in her voice and my father telling one of his wry jokes and smiling. . . . Each of them was in his or her place in one of the rooms in Hillsborough, alive and well, and I was there too, in each of the scenes which now were such a comfort to me. I thought about my grandmother, whom we girls called Mamalee. Millicent Hearst was well into her late eighties, so petite and frail-looking and yet spry and indomitable. She was a very special person in my life, whom my sisters and I would visit for ten days or two weeks every summer in Southampton, New York. Sitting in the dark in that hot, sweaty closet, I could visualize Mamalee's big, beautiful house and its huge rolling lawn just off the Atlantic Ocean, with the sea breezes whipping through the trees and the nesting birds dive-bombing us, and the fresh flowers throughout the house, clipped daily from the garden. We would go bicycle riding, swim, or play tennis for most of the day and then join Mamalee and her sister, Aunt Anita, who lived with her there, for a late-afternoon formal tea. Visiting Mamalee was like stepping into another century. The butler served, the maids in their uniforms hovered about. Every conceivable kind of tea cakes and cookies, all of them delicious, were spread out before us. We girls dressed for tea because Mamalee insisted that "young ladies do not wear pants."

In the early days of my capture, I had thought of Steve, wondering what our life would be together after we were married, but he was fading from my thoughts, which were concentrated on my release from this SLA prison. Our last family vacation together had been that Christmas, a little more than a month before my kidnapping, when the whole family and Steve had gone on a skiing vacation at Sugar Bowl, in the Sierra Nevada mountains in northern California. As a joke, I had given my father a Christmas present of the new game called Anti-Monopoly, in which the object was to lose all your money.

The United Symbionese War Council rejected my father's two-million-dollar food program as inadequate. "Crumbs!" shouted Cinque. "Only crumbs for the people!" The War Council had seen through the capitalist plot hatched by my father, said Cin. He was only interested in buying back one of his possessions—me. The SLA was not interested in me—they wanted food for the people. So the SLA was going to send one last message back to my father and that would decide my fate: He must add another four million dollars to the two million he had promised.* The food must be distributed not over a year's time but all in one month. . . .

They worked all that day and well into the next, preparing this "final" message to my father. Once again Cin used the closet as a

---

* The SLA did not intend to allow my father to establish another ongoing food program, which Cin said would only "demoralize" the people.

recording studio. I had only one line to recite on this tape to verify that I was still alive. I could hear the SLA message being recorded. It ran well over a half hour in length; it seemed to go on and on. In essence, the SLA was, indeed, demanding a six-million-dollar program to distribute seventy dollars' worth of top-grade food, canned and fresh, to people in the poor sections of San Francisco and Los Angeles, to begin within a week and to be completed within a month. The food was to be given out upon request to whoever asked for it at SLA-designated distribution centers, with no identification at all required. "Should this order be rejected," warned the SLA leader, "all further communications shall be suspended and the prisoner will be maintained according to the terms of the international codes of war concerning prisoners of war and will be maintained in that status until such time as the status of our captive soldiers is changed. Should any attempt be made to rescue this subject prisoner or to injure or capture our soldiers, the subject is to be executed immediately."

Cin criticized the various left-wing organizations which had refused to take part in the food distribution; he called upon my father to repent and to "express regret for his crimes against the people." But he ended the long tape with a particularly bitter denunciation of the news media, which apparently had been portraying him as an ex-convict and small-time hoodlum. I listened in horror as he said the press should not waste its time trying to identify him or others in the SLA:

However, to this I would say yes. You do, indeed, know me. You have always known me. I'm that nigger you have hunted and feared night and day. I'm that nigger you have killed hundreds of my people in a vain hope of finding. I'm that nigger that is no longer just hunted, robbed and murdered. I'm the nigger that hunts you now.

Yes, you know me. You know us all. You know me, I'm the wetback. You know me, I'm the gook, the broad, the servant, the spik.

Yes, indeed, you know us all, and we know you—the oppressor, murderer and robber. And you have hunted and robbed and exploited us all. Now we are the hunters that will give you no rest. And we will not compromise the freedom of our children.

Death to the fascist insect that preys upon the life of the people.

I despaired. My early hopes of a ransom demand, a ransom payment, and my release faded away. I had come to know these SLA
people. They were on a different wavelength; they had lost touch with
the thinking of the rational outside world. Six million dollars as a good
faith gesture and all their other demands . . . It seemed to me that my
despair had no end except in my own death. I could not keep myself
from crying, crying, crying.

They told me a communications unit of the SLA would come to the
safehouse and would deliver the new tape to the media. My father had
only twenty-four hours in which to respond, Cin said. It seemed at the
time that my fate hung in the balance. The "comrades" in the cell responded to my despair in various ways, according to their own personalities.

Zoya, the hard one, spat at me: "Your father better pay or you're
dead."

Gelina, the sympathetic one, reassured me: "Don't worry. Your
father will pay."

Yolanda, the bossy one who sounded like a schoolmarm, gave me
another of her long lectures, to which I paid no attention.

Teko, the military man, shouted at me in disgust: "Stop sniveling
around, for Christ's sake. What's the matter with you? Why don't you
do isometric exercises or something, you goddamn bourgeois bitch . . ."

Life, however suspended in doubt, uncertainty, and despair, went on
day by day in the cell. In the course of my re-education I learned a
good deal about prisons, their favorite subject. Cin proudly boasted
about having been in and out of quite a number of jails during his lifetime. In the SLA, that was a badge of honor. Prisons were the
birthplace of revolutionaries, especially black revolutionaries. The capitalist state put black leaders in prisons on trumped-up charges of rape
or robbery in order to prevent them from fighting the establishment.
But in prison the blacks had time to study the causes of their oppression and they would emerge as revolutionaries. Fahizah told me, with
love and awe in her voice, how Cin had escaped from Soledad Prison,
one of the worst in California, on foot, alone, in order to fight with *the
people* and to devote the rest of his life, self-sacrificing all the way, to
changing the world we all lived in. My initial reaction, unspoken, to all
this was that I hoped they would all be returned to prison someday.
The more they talked to me of prisons, the more I became convinced

that that was where they belonged. Fahizah, who was the intelligence-information officer of this SLA combat team, sounded very knowledgeable about the California state prison system, quoting statistics which did amaze me. I had neither known nor cared that California has the third-largest prison system in the whole world. The point she attempted to make was that prisoners in the United States represented the largest single "class" of oppressed people and also the largest potential source of revolutionaries.

Cujo, the young man with the quiet voice, spoke to me with such knowledge about the Vacaville prison—the California prison medical facility located between Berkeley and Sacramento—that I concluded he must have been an inmate there. Since that prison handled prisoners with psychiatric problems, I figured him to have been a rapist or some other mentally disturbed type. He recited incidents to prove that blacks and revolutionaries at Vacaville were constantly drugged in order to keep them passive, and when not drugged, they were tortured and beaten. He would sit for hours at the edge of my prison closet, reading me Marxist and Maoist literature—the *Communist Manifesto,* Carlos Marighela's manual for guerrilla warfare called *For the Liberation of Brazil,* and, of course, Mao's little red book *Sayings.*

Cujo's favorite Mao saying, which he read to me so many times that I practically had it memorized, was: "All men must die, but death can vary in significance. The ancient Chinese writer Ssu-ma Ch'ien said, 'Though death befalls all men alike, it may be weightier than Mount Tai or lighter than a feather.' To die for the people is weightier than Mount Tai, but to work for the Fascists and die for the exploiters and oppressors is lighter than a feather." The rapture in his voice! Cujo was ready and willing to fight and die for the people. That's what the SLA was all about, he told me.

The others told me the same thing. "Dare to struggle and dare to win," said Mao, and he had won. That was a favorite Maoism of the entire group. For years they had read and studied and debated and listened to all sorts of revolutionary rhetoric. But only they, the SLA, had dared to take action, to start the revolution which they were certain would triumph someday in the United States. They hoped victory would come in their lifetime. But they did not expect to live to see the corporate-military dictatorship crushed. Victory would come after their deaths and their deaths would then be "significant." They were totally committed to the revolution. I felt that they were suicidal. It was frightening, for I wanted to survive. I believed them when they said that if the FBI, with all their vaunted expertise, traced the SLA to this hideout, there would be a gun battle, without surrender, until we all were dead. They talked about this imaginary shoot-out incessantly and my paranoia over the FBI finding us was beginning to match theirs.

Teko, an army veteran who had served in Vietnam, was the most militaristic of the bunch. His favorite saying from Mao's little red book was: "A revolution is not a dinner party, or writing an essay, or painting a picture, or doing embroidery; it cannot be so refined, so courteous, restrained and magnanimous. A revolution is an insurrection, an act of violence by which one class overthrows another." Teko was a violent man.

And, of course, they all adored Mao's best-known dictum: "Political power grows out of the barrel of a gun." The revolution was their religion and they were fanatics. They were forever reading or reciting quotations to me from all kinds of books. They spoke in slogans; their speech was filled with repetitive clichés of Marxism and Maoism. I became so familiar with their "educational" lectures and their individual manners of speech that I could anticipate what each of them was about to say from just the opening few words. I hated these interminable talks and, at the same time, I welcomed them. In the beginning, I could not bear to listen to them and wanted just to be left alone in the closet. But after a couple of weeks I thought I would go out of my mind with loneliness and fear. I longed for the sound of a human voice, even one of theirs. As time went on, they talked with me more and more.

The pattern was that I would sit in the middle of the closet, my back propped against the wall, facing the door. One or more of them would sit just outside the door and we would "rap" for hours. Almost all of what they told me—their opinions and theories—I considered pure nonsense and secretly I thought I was merely humoring them. After all, I was in no position to argue. And yet, they did read me news items they clipped from the newspapers almost every day, reporting horror stories from dictatorships around the world as well as revolutionary "actions" in Puerto Rico, Mozambique, the Philippines, and various other countries of the Third World. Some of their stories were indisputable, sometimes I did not know what to believe. It was all very confusing. I realized that my life prior to my kidnapping had indeed been very sheltered; I had taken little or no interest in foreign affairs, politics, or economics. I had not even read the daily newspapers with any regularity. Nevertheless, virtually everything they tried so hard to pump into me went against my grain, my upbringing, and my value system.

While I may have looked upon their beliefs with disdain, they, in turn, held my life style and my beliefs in utter contempt. Just about everything I thought was white, they said was black and they were determined to re-educate me. My values, to them, were bourgeois bullshit. My relationship with Steven Weed had been bourgeois and sexist. He had been using me, exploiting me, they said. The enjoyment I felt in cooking and baking was bourgeois and sexist. Engagement rings were ostentatious and a symbol of male proprietorship. Marriage was strictly a middle-class institution, enslavement of women. Monogamy was typical bourgeois mentality, denying freedom to men and women. Every bit of my relationship with Steve, in their eyes, had been bourgeois, reactionary, and beneath contempt. Spending money on indoor plants, art work, oriental rugs, and new furniture for our apartment had been bourgeois materialism and a waste of good money which would better have served the poor and oppressed.

They were appalled at the red nail polish on my fingernails and toenails at the time of my "arrest." That was a flaunting of capitalist narcissism. "Poor people don't paint their nails." My sports car was a capitalist toy that was an affront to starving people.

Birthday celebrations were totally bourgeois and my own twentieth birthday passed absolutely unnoticed. I was never sure which day of my captivity was February 20.

They were furious because my parents had released to the press photographs of me as a baby standing in an inflatable wading pool. That was a ridiculous attempt to win the sympathy of the public, and the newspaper photographs of our house and our "swimming pool" represented a terrible display of wealth and an insensitivity to the plight of the poor. My studying the history of art was an example of conspicuous consumption and a waste of my life when I should have been spending that time helping *the people*. In contrast, they were devoting their lives to freeing *the people*. They "loved" *the people*. They had forsaken their past bourgeois lives to pick up guns and fight for *the people* to show their love.

They all spoke with such sincerity. Fahizah told me that all the comrades in the SLA cell had once lived as I had. "All of us had the weaknesses of our upbringing and we constantly have to struggle even now against the putrid disease of bourgeois mentality," she said. "Yes, of course," I said, "I understand." Each of them, as time went on, explained to me how he or she became conscious, that is, aware of the need for taking up weapons to overthrow fascist Amerikkka and its materialistic society.

The concept of Third World leadership was very important to them. They believed that *only* black and other oppressed people could lead the struggle for freedom. Only Third World people could know the *proper direction* which the struggle should take at any given time. White people were *incapable* of directing this struggle. Moreover, whites were not to be trusted in a leadership position because, *historically*, they had proven themselves to be traitors to the cause of oppressed peoples. The white sisters and brothers of this combat unit were very proud and fortunate to have the leadership and direction of their black General Field Marshal. They only hoped that by their determination and respect for their leader they could prove to all black and oppressed people that not all whites were the oppressor. This, of course, would be a *very* difficult task . . . but they would try.

Above all else, they were most proud of being "soldiers in the Symbionese Liberation Army." They were "urban guerrillas" at war with the United States government and all its agencies. They had forsaken drugs and liquor and all materialistic pleasures in order to maintain their discipline and military training. As urban guerrillas, they intended to fight the revolution in the streets of major cities, just as revolutionaries elsewhere fought in the jungles.

From my closet, I could hear them training every day: Calisthenics in the morning, military maneuvers in the afternoon. They wore combat boots as they scurried around the rooms, dived to the floor, rolled around, whispering "Bang, bang, bang" at one another. I could hear the clicks and clacks of their rifle bolts and the sound of ammunition clips being jammed into place. Some of them delighted in sneaking up to my closet door and hissing "Rat-a-tat-tat" in simulated fire at me and laughing uproariously as they startled me half to death. They spent an enormous amount of time in meetings, either planning future "actions" or "struggling" in critiques of one another in order to make each of them better comrades, better soldiers. . . . They were undoubtedly devoted to their revolution. Nevertheless, they also found time to watch the afternoon horror movies on television.

In time, I became as sensitive to sounds, movements, and moods as a blind person. While they had removed my gag and untied my hands, my blindfold was kept on at all times except to tape communiqués. My continual weeping made a problem of the bedsheet blindfold they had used at first: It tended to become loose. They substituted a blindfold made of wads of cotton, stuck to my face with white surgical tape, which they wrapped around my head. But the cotton soon became soaked in my tears and chafed my skin. Then they produced an improvised blindfold consisting of a strip of bedsheet, over which went two dishwashing sponges, secured by a tight elastic band around my head. The sponges worked well, for they gripped the sheet and held it in place. However, the elastic was so tight that it rubbed the bridge of my nose and the pressure caused terrible headaches. Nevertheless, I was as good as blind. But I learned to discern their individual voices, their laughter, their footsteps, everything. I knew who they were and I pretty much knew what they were doing throughout the day and night. Yet when I thought I had established a pattern for their activities, they would do something different, something usually worse than before.

At various times, I considered them crazy, paranoid, schizoid, infantile, but I never thought they were stupid. Nor did I ever underestimate them. Just as I used my blindness, they did too. I could not see and so I came to believe what they told me they saw. Almost every time the doorbell rang, one or another would hint that it was a comrade from another cell in the SLA, or a messenger from a communications team, or someone from an intelligence unit arriving with a new message from somewhere. I came to recognize only one of those visitors, a "sister" called Gabi, who lived "aboveground" and brought supplies to the combat team, which seldom ventured out of doors. Gabi was obviously a favorite courier, for she was always greeted most warmly by the others, with long exchanges of endearing remarks and profuse thanks for whatever items she happened to bring to the cell. I was always shut away in the closet whenever Gabi arrived in the safehouse. Then there came a time when Gabi and I were introduced. She had a soft, warm voice and seemed rather shy. I was told that Gabi was going underground and joining the cell. Cin explained that she had been transferred from a supply unit to this combat team. Of all the "sisters" I seemed to have the least contact with Gabi. She seldom came to the closet to talk with me, which I attributed to her natural shyness. I could think of no other reason.

I received all sorts of bits of information and theory from just about each and every member of the cell. There was much overlapping and a good deal of repetition. After a while it all seemed to fit together in a mosaic which formed a logical picture. Cin told me the SLA had intelligence agents all over California who were eavesdropping in restaurants, mass gatherings, and public places to hear firsthand the troubles and the problems voiced by the people. Revolutionaries could not believe what was printed in the capitalist press or even in the left-wing Berkeley *Barb*, which they read religiously. Cujo explained in great detail how the SLA revolution was being spread throughout the state. The SLA, for instance, worked constantly with prisoners, smuggling revolutionary literature and weapons into the prisons. The SLA also had summer camps at which children were taught how to shoot rifles and machine guns, so that they too could join the revolution.

"Where *are* these camps?" I asked in wonderment.

"Oh, they're all over," he replied cryptically.

Teko explained that SLA medical teams practiced battlefield surgery by going out in the woods and shooting dogs and then operating on them in the field in order to learn how to minister to gunshot wounds.

Someone else confided that the SLA was being financed by wealthy sympathizers in California who were important contacts "aboveground." They would join in the armed revolt when the time was right. Meanwhile, the SLA was carrying on guerrilla warfare against the state, striking when and where least expected, and then hiding out in safehouses until the next military action.

When I was offered my second bath, I pleaded for permission to remove my blindfold in the tub so that I could wash my hair. They held a meeting on that. "You're going to be able to take the blindfold off and we'll wear ski masks," Cin told me. "And if you try anything, it will be the last bath you ever get."

I thanked him quietly. I was so thankful for that bath and hair wash one would have thought I was being led to a party. It was pitiful. My legs were wobbly, as if made of rubber, for by this time I had been closet-ridden for several weeks. I had lost track of time. In the bathroom, someone standing behind me removed the blindfold and everything looked so strange, so out of proportion. Everything around me appeared huge, distorted, and constantly moving like ocean waves. I tried to focus my eyes. My own hands appeared to be grossly enlarged and changing color from pink to purple and back again. I seemed to be hallucinating and yet I thought I had all my senses about me. Then I was helped, stumbling, into the bath they had drawn for me. It was hot and lovely.

My guard in the bathroom this time was the girl with the thick drawl. Tiny, only four feet eleven and slightly overweight, Fahizah sat hunched over the toilet seat, wearing a dark ski mask, a see-through black knit top with her breasts clearly visible, and tight corduroy pants with a gun belt around her waist and an empty holster on one hip. (They must have been afraid I might try to overpower her and get her gun.) We stared at each other for a moment or so and I tried to smile. But I thought she looked weird, malformed, like a hunchback without the hump, sort of a small female ape.

She spoke sadly of her own parents, who lived in Santa Rosa, California. Her mother and father were hopelessly bourgeois, Goldwater Republicans, and there was no way, she said, that they could possibly understand what she was doing with her life. She doubted if they ever would, and now, she said, they had absolutely nothing in common. She had been married to a black jazz musician and the marriage had been a disaster, senseless and violent. The SLA was her whole life, for the comrades were now her true family.

As Fahizah talked, I noticed that one of the men was apparently standing guard outside the bathroom door, for from time to time I caught him peeking in at me. With passion in her voice, Fahizah bewailed the loss of her two dearest brothers, Bo and Osceola, who, she said, were being kept in strip cells in the maximum security section of San Quentin, unable to talk with one another or with anyone, being tortured and abused and probably drugged—all for a crime they did not commit. They did not shoot Marcus Foster, she insisted. They had been in an intelligence unit and were not part of a combat unit.

"But why," I asked, "had Foster been shot? What did the SLA have against Foster?"

"He was a pig," she replied. *"The people* hated him. He wanted to ID-card all the children in the Oakland schools, to pick out the ones who were potentially violent and to segregate them and send those children to a prison and reprogram them. That's what Hitler did. And that would be the beginning of concentration camps in fascist Amerikkka."

SLA members had attended City Council meetings in Oakland in order to follow the progress of Marcus Foster's proposals for stopping violence in the Oakland schools. The SLA had ultimately reached the conclusion that the only way to stop Foster's identification program was to assassinate him, she told me. Fahizah insisted that the SLA knew Foster to be an agent of the Central Intelligence Agency, and Robert Blackburn, his assistant, also was a CIA agent whose real job was to serve as a bodyguard for Foster. Didn't Blackburn always carry an attaché case? Well, she said, inside that attaché case, he had a submachine gun. What's more, when they had shot at Foster and Blackburn, hadn't Blackburn immediately ducked into a crouch and tried to escape by running in a zigzag pattern? Didn't that prove he had CIA training?

During the bath, Cin walked into the bathroom two or three times. Each time, Fahizah told me to turn my head to the wall so as not to see Cin's face, as he, with exaggerated nonchalance, carried on some casual conversation with her. Obviously, he had come in to look over the merchandise. On his first appearance, I tried to cover up and heard him snicker. It was most embarrassing and humiliating. Then I said to myself, "To hell with him," and I just continued with my bathing, as though he weren't there. I hated the man. And feared him too. There was a swaggering arrogance in his voice that none of the others possessed. One of the other two SLA men came into the bathroom while I was in the tub, but he did not utter a word, and with my head turned toward the wall, I had no idea who he was, and I did not care. What did it matter? Privacy was a luxury I had lost when I had been kidnapped.

It was one or two days after that bath (by this time I had lost all count of the days) that I awoke from a fitful sleep in the closet with the distinct, conscious feeling that my life was slipping away. I had been losing weight constantly, for I could not eat much of the food they served me, and I knew that I was growing weaker and weaker from my confinement. But this time the clear sensation came over me that I was dying. There was a threshold of no return that I could sense and I felt that I was on the brink. My body was exhausted, drained of strength: I could not stand up even if I were free to walk away from all of this. It came to me that I had been sleeping more and more hours each day, falling off almost every time I was left alone in the closet, and yet, sleep brought me no renewal of strength. I awoke more tired than when I had dozed off. It was a peculiar but recognizable sensation: Under all that stress, my body was surrendering its life force, giving up. I was so tired, so tired; all I wanted to do was to sleep. And I knew that was dangerous, fatal, like the man lost in the Arctic snow, who, having laid his head down for that delicious nap, never woke again. My mind, suddenly, was alive and alert to all this. I could see what was happening to me, as if I were outside myself.

A silent battle was waged there in the closet, and my mind won. Deliberately and clearly, I decided that I would not die, not of my own accord. I would fight with everything in my power to survive, to see this through. With sudden clarity, I could see that I was not about to be released soon or even in any reasonable amount of time. All my torment, all my false hopes, all the emotional energy I was expending in fantasizing my rescue, my being set free, or my being shot and killed, were not helping me one single bit. I decided I would not think of the future. I would concentrate on staying alive one day at a time.

CHAPTER

FIVE

WHEN IT CAME, they let me hear the bad news with my own ears. "I told you your father didn't give a damn for your life," exclaimed Cinque. "Now you can hear it for yourself and see we've been telling you the truth." It came as rather a shock as I heard my father's voice for the first time since I had been kidnapped, coming to me via television. Blindfolded, I could not see the screen. The volume had been turned up so that I could hear my father clearly. He was saying that he was unable to meet the SLA's latest demand for four million dollars more in food distribution.

"The size of the latest demand of the SLA is far beyond my financial capability," my father said. "Therefore, the matter is out of my hands."

A moment later I heard the familiar voice of Charles Gould, the publisher of the *Examiner* and a close family friend, who had been like an uncle to me. He followed my father with an announcement of his own:

"I am Charles Gould with a message from the Hearst Corporation. The Hearst Corporation is prepared to contribute to People in Need a total of four million dollars for a food distribution for the poor and needy, provided Patricia Hearst is released unharmed.

"Two million dollars will be contributed immediately upon the release of Patricia and two million more will be contributed in January 1975. This January payment will be evidenced by a binding agreement with People in Need.

"Neither the Hearst Corporation nor the Hearst Foundation is controlled by members of the Hearst family. No other funds will be committed by the corporation or foundation under any circumstance."

Actually, the first impact of his words upon me, sitting there in the closet blindfolded, was a renewal of hope. I thought the Hearst Corporation was saying yes: it would pay four million dollars more. But Cin quickly disabused me of that. "You don't expect us to believe that shit, do you?" he roared. "Those fascist pigs will never pay a dime once you are released. They'll go to the courts, and renege . . . say it was extortion. I wouldn't trust your father and the Hearst Corporation for one dime. They gotta get the money up front or nothing."

Cin went on and on, accusing my father and the Hearst Corporation of trying to "trick" the SLA into releasing me, of thinking the SLA was too dumb to know anything about money, and of being too cheap to want to pay the price for my release. The others chimed in too. They all seemed to believe that their demands were most reasonable. All they were asking for was food for the poor, but rich people were too afraid to give away any of their money or their power, even at the risk of my life. Then someone yelled. "Hey, listen to this," and I was shut back in the closet, with that little radio blaring again, as it had all through my confinement. These SLA revolutionaries were absolutely publicity-crazy. They were media freaks, they listened to the radio news all day and flipped the television dial in an attempt to catch every news commentator giving his version of what the SLA was doing that day. While they ranted and raved at bad notices, still they loved to hear themselves mentioned.

It occurred to me that the SLA wanted the publicity as much as they wanted the food program. With me in their clutches, the SLA was now famous, a household word. Cin came to believe he was all-powerful, and his followers, all seven of them, lived in the same fantasy world. They were following their leader to glory or to death. They had said as much to me in a variety of ways.

I was beginning to get nervous and panicky again. I just did not know what Cin would do next. He was capable of anything. It was a strange kind of panic. Deep down in my gut, I really had not expected to be released. If my father had met the demand, the SLA would have raised the ante. My intuition and my experience with Cin had told me that whatever my father offered, the SLA would ask for more. I suspected that Cin himself did not know what to do with me and that in itself was dangerous. He could do anything, it seemed to me. What if he decided to kill me and then kidnap someone else and again ask for six million dollars in food distribution? What if . . . ? But then I tried not to think of the future. I had decided to live one day at a time. Nevertheless I knew the situation had changed. Sooner than I had expected, the SLA and my father had reached an impasse. The Hearsts in effect had made a final offer: six million dollars in food to the poor, but only if I were released unharmed before four of the six million dollars was given, and the SLA in distrust was going to reject that offer. It was as if a final line had been drawn and neither side would cross the line. I really could see the point of view of each of them, but that did not help me. It seemed to me that from now on I would be on my own, expecting no further help from the outside.

To compound my fears, the SLA people were positively furious over the first day's distribution of food. It had been a disaster. Cin and the others relayed to me the worst of the press and television reports, all the while claiming that this proved poor people could not trust the rich. In West Oakland, a black ghetto, more than five thousand people crowded outside one distribution center, and before the food even reached the distribution point, some people had stormed arriving trucks. Food was thrown from the trucks into the crowds, food was stolen by hoodlums and carried off, rocks were thrown, people fought one another. It was a mob scene, a riot. More than twenty people were carted off to hospitals. Many more were hurt. Many others, who had waited in line for hours, complained that they had received no food or too little. The food distribution went much better at other locations, although there was pushing and shoving, but that, of course, did not make news.

There was also a great deal of infighting among the various radical and left-wing groups (all reported in the press) as to which ones would and would not participate in the food distribution program. Comments and criticism came from all quarters. No one, I gathered from what Cin and the others told me, had come out with any kind of praise for the SLA for bringing about the distribution of food to the poor. The SLA did not like that one bit. Nevertheless, the food distribution would go on for a full month and Ludlow Kramer, the director of the program, promised better organization of the food distribution in the coming weeks.

Alone in the closet, I despaired. Never had things looked so bleak.

Try as I might, I could not sustain any hope. The SLA demands had not been met and they had told me what would happen if the four million dollars was not forthcoming. It was the end, I thought, the absolute end. I could foresee no hope of rescue. If the FBI stormed the place, I would die in the shoot-out. Over and over again Cin had warned me that at the start of a shoot-out, I would be "wasted." As for the demands, there was nothing more my father, or anyone, could do. The SLA had little choice but to execute me, as promised. They could not let me go free. I realized that. I knew too much about them already. I could easily identify them. I could testify about the Marcus Foster killing and my own kidnapping and about their future plans. They could never let me go. There was no escape. The closet door was locked at night. They had guns with them at all times. And I was so frail.

But apparently I had not been able to fathom the SLA mind or foresee their actions. For the next several days, they did not take reprisals at all. Instead they set about to convince me that we both were being wronged by the Establishment. Cin insisted that the SLA had been honestly trying to negotiate my release but the fascist corporate state would have none of it. The food program was a mockery, he said. My parents were trying to humiliate the poor people of California instead of feeding them. They were throwing food at the people. One woman had been hit by a turkey leg and seriously injured, he said. All of that proved that my parents were trying to provoke the SLA into killing me. Cin said that the SLA War Council had come to believe that the whole operation on the other side was not being directed by my father at all. The White House was calling all the shots. The White House was directing the operation, which called for forcing the SLA to execute me, which, in turn, would discredit the revolutionaries all over America. I did not know what to think about this new turn of events. Delusions of grandeur? Or a rationalization for my execution? Would the SLA say they were forced to do it?

Cin and the others were delighted when Walter Cronkite or John Chancellor or some other national news commentator reported on the SLA. For them, a national news broadcast, coming out of New York or Washington, meant that the SLA was a national organization and not confined to the San Francisco area. They bragged when the SLA was the lead item in any newscast. They also told me that with the SLA making the national news, the FBI could never be certain where we were: The SLA might well be in any part of the country. Cin told me the SLA had comrades in various post offices, so that when they mailed a message to the media, it did not necessarily carry the San Francisco postmark. Then, to further confuse the FBI, Cin said, he had some of the SLA messages delivered by hand. There were plenty of SLA underground soldiers available to perform such secret chores, and I came to believe him. From his descriptions the SLA had infiltrated everywhere.

Cin and the others were absolutely disgusted with the various radical groups in the Bay Area which had refused to take part in the food program or had failed to rally to the revolutionary cause. The SLA wanted to lead the way to revolution, but the others would not follow. Teko proclaimed that the other groups were "too chickenshit" to join in the revolution. Time after time, each of the other left-wing or radical groups were castigated by the SLA comrades. Most of all, they despised the Black Panthers, the strongest and best-known of these groups. The crime of the Black Panthers was that they had "sold out," and given up their guns and violence to embrace counterrevolutionary social activities, such as free breakfast programs for school children, education classes, and cooperative community programs in Oakland. The Weather Underground were "phony revolutionaries" because they only did "symbolic" bombings in which no one was killed. The Reverend Cecil Williams of the Glide Methodist Church, in San Francisco's Tenderloin District, who was prominent in the food distribution program, was dismissed by Cin as a "fool." "Death Row Jeff," who was the head of the Black Guerrilla Family, and who claimed from his prison cell to be a leader of the SLA, was viewed within our safehouse as "a nice cat who had gone a little soggy in the head now."

Beyond this immediate disalliance, the SLA held in contempt a long list of persons one might have thought they, as radicals, would have liked: They hated Huey Newton, one of the founders of the Black Panthers. Angela Davis, the avowed Marxist teacher who had taught at the University of California in Los Angeles, was considered "a pig who had betrayed" her revolutionary comrade George Jackson. Even though a fugitive from the FBI, she was a "cop-out" because she should have been helping "blast" George Jackson out of prison. As for her openly proclaimed membership in the Communist Party, that did not mean much. The SLA thought the Communist Party in the United States was "all theory and no action" and therefore "reactionary." Jane

Fonda, the outspoken actress, was deemed "the worst kind of fascist." Liberals such as Jane Fonda sought social changes through legislation and that tended to pacify the people and to delay *the people's* uprising against the fascist state. Liberals were doing more harm than good for *the people*. Cin castigated me for being stupid when I told him I had voted in 1972 for George McGovern rather than Nixon. According to him, Nixon was better for the revolution. People knew he was the enemy and would sooner rise up against him than against McGovern with all his "social reforms."

Thus, my re-education continued unabated. Nothing I had believed before had been right. I accommodated my thoughts to coincide with theirs.

My physical condition continued to deteriorate. I experienced more and more trouble walking to and from the bathroom, even with someone holding me up by the arm. At one point, I simply melted to the floor. I could not stand up unsupported for more than a few seconds. My knees would buckle and my body would turn to mush. I found myself in serious distress—weak, feverish, depressed, and increasingly confused.

My captors did not hesitate to berate me as a bourgeois weakling, but I think that they were alarmed at my debilitated condition. They inaugurated a program of exercises to strengthen my muscles. Several times a day, one or another of them would walk me around the room outside my closet, blindfolded, holding me under an arm. One of the comrades was greatly amused when she walked me into a wall. When strength returned to my legs, they had me doing jumping jacks and deep knee bends—still blindfolded. They would never admit that keeping someone blindfolded, without exercise, in a six-foot-long closet was not humane prisoner-of-war treatment according to the Geneva Convention. Instead, they criticized me for not keeping myself in good enough physical condition to escape with them on foot when and if the FBI came into the safehouse. Contrary to previous statements, they now told me they had an escape route planned, but they could not very well drag me along with them, not with the FBI blazing away at us. But the exercises lasted only a couple of days and were then forgotten.

Not a day passed, I believe, without some mention of the possibility of an FBI raid. They never failed to explain that the FBI would want to kill me in order to discredit the SLA and all revolutionary movements. The SLA wanted me alive so it could negotiate for food for the

One of the reasons for my kidnapping was to exchange me for these two prisoners, Russell Little (left) and Joseph Remiro. (Photo credit: UPI)

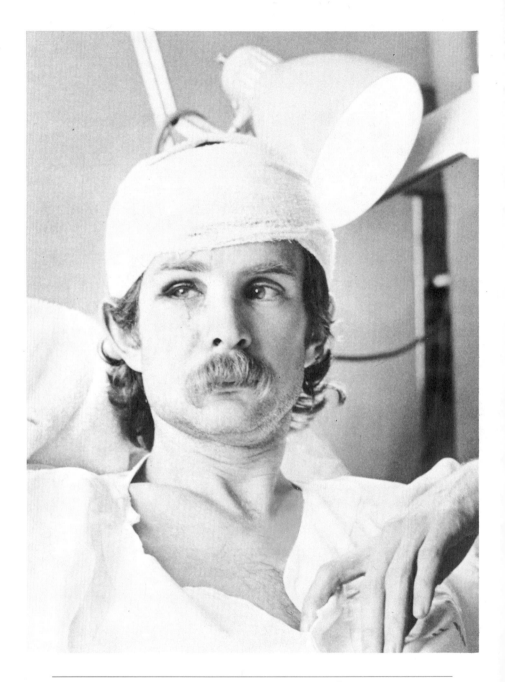

Steven Weed, following my kidnapping. (Photo credit: San Francisco *Examiner*)

General Field Marshal Cinque Mtume (Donald DeFreeze).

Cujo (William Wolfe). (Photo courtesy FBI)

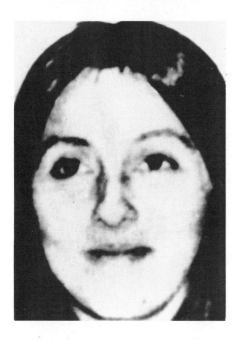 

Gelina (Angela Atwood).   Gabi (Camilla Hall).

Zoya (Patricia Soltysik).   Fahizah (Nancy Ling Perry).
                                            (Photos courtesy FBI)

Teko (William Harris). (Photo courtesy San Mateo County jail)

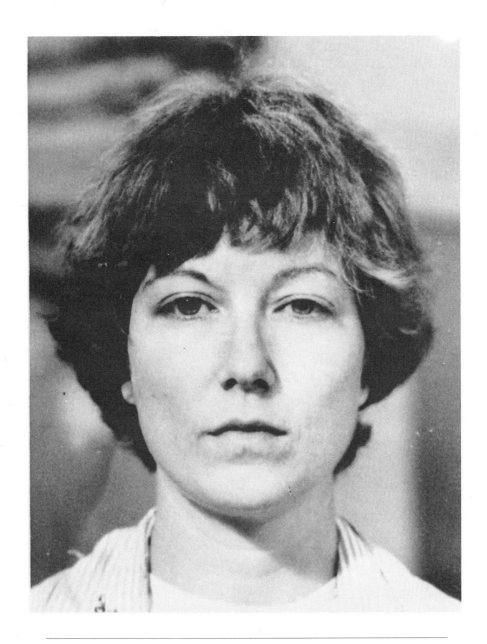

Yolanda (Emily Harris). (Photo courtesy San Mateo County jail)

The Daly City safehouse closet in which I was held. (Photo credit: Bob McLeod, San Francisco *Examiner*)

poor people; but the FBI and the corporate-military dictatorship wanted me dead. It was a battle for the minds of the people and public opinion. If the FBI shot and killed me, they asked, how could the SLA ever convince anyone that it was the FBI and not the SLA who had killed me? Strange as that reasoning may seem now, I believed it at the time. I knew they believed it. When it came to fear of the FBI, there was a ring of truth in their voices. Every few days there was a full-scale combat drill in preparation for the anticipated arrival of the FBI.

I had lived in fear of the SLA for so long now that fear of the FBI came easily to me. I knew nothing about the organization, except for fictional accounts on television, and the SLA comrades were well versed on shoot-outs. They told me story after story of the FBI storming radical hideouts, shooting through doors, killing everyone inside, asking no questions. The FBI could kill with impunity. They had a license to kill. And they would shoot and kill in order to wipe out radical movements in the country. But, said Cin, the SLA would not be ambushed and slaughtered like the others. The SLA would be ready to do battle with the pigs. Then I would surely die in the cross fire.

One day Cin told me that he was going to give me lessons on how to handle a shotgun because the combat unit had decided I ought to be given the chance to defend myself in case of an FBI raid. The next day they showed me how to use a gas mask, saying that in any shoot-out the FBI was sure to lob tear gas into the house. The gas mask was left at my side in the closet. For the next three days, under their instructions, I practiced handling a sawed-off shotgun, breaking it apart, and holding it. All without ammunition, of course, and often with my blindfold still on. Cin promised that when the time came, he would issue me the gun along with their special SLA shells of 00 buckshot laced with "Ajax."*

"Ajax" was the SLA code word for cyanide. The SLA comrades were especially proud of their cyanide bullets. It was their own distinctive trademark, Cin told me. The "enemy" would learn that if an SLA bullet did not kill immediately, the cyanide certainly would make any wound fatal. I recalled early in my captivity smelling the strong odor of almonds and being told the SLA soldiers were drilling out bullets and adding cyanide to them.

---

* Far from reassuring me, these lessons and the gas mask which they issued me only served to heighten my fears.

Paranoia must be contagious, for everyone in that house had caught it. When Cin came to me one day and said the newspapers were reporting that my father had hired psychics to fathom out where I was being kept by the SLA, I was paralyzed with fear. "Don't think about any psychics now, don't communicate with them," he told me. "Focus your mind on something else all the time." I did as I was told. I did not want psychics or anyone else to point the FBI in my direction. As a matter of self-protection and through sheer discipline, the SLA members had learned to speak in low voices, hardly above a whisper. They could even "shout" in a whispering voice. Their leader was convinced that the FBI had super-listening devices by which they could tune in on this house from a car parked in the vicinity. They avidly clipped news items from the San Francisco newspapers every day, including the absurd one-line or one-paragraph fillers at the bottom of news columns. Cin was convinced those fillers really were secret coded messages between CIA agents operating in the area. On one occasion he informed me that when the SLA held its meetings they always turned the television set toward the wall to prevent the government from spying into the house through the TV screen.

As time went on and my re-education continued, the SLA comrades became more and more friendly and amenable. The trick was to agree with everything they said, to feign an interest in every one of their concerns—to be a model prisoner: subservient, obedient, grateful, and eager to learn. They talked with me more and more all day long. That meant that my closet door would remain open and I could breathe relatively fresh air and also that I was not left alone with my own thoughts and misery. Endlessly, I listened to them tell me of prisons and prisoners, of the corporate-military state oppressing the people, of the SLA's program to educate the people to recognize their oppression, of the SLA's immediate program to make war against the state until the government fought back by oppressing the people openly. That would bring about a change in people's attitudes. More and more of them would then join the SLA in its war against the government oppression. In their eyes, a corporate-military coup had taken place in the United States when Richard Nixon was re-elected President in 1972. The people were not aware of that coup, because it had been accomplished so secretly. But the SLA knew, and now the SLA was trying to inform the people. I nodded my head to all this and they kept talking, talking, talking.

Actually, I did not really care one way or another about any of the things they told me, with the exception of my fear of an FBI raid. I had always been apolitical and still was. I did not really care about the prisoners they loved so dearly or about the conditions in the California prison system—not while I was a prisoner myself. Nor did I give a damn about their plans for a revolution and their restyling of the American way of life according to Mao Tse-tung. Not for a minute did I think they had the slightest chance for success. I thought they were all suicidal. And that frightened me. I certainly did not want to be killed by them or with them.

Nevertheless, by agreeing with them, I was taken out of the closet more and more often. They allowed me to eat with them at times and occasionally I sat blindfolded with them late into the night as they held one of their discussion meetings or study groups. They allowed me to remove my blindfold when I was locked in the closet for the night and that was a blessing. The new arrangement was that in the morning they would knock on the closet door and I would put the blindfold back on before they approached me. I was given the privilege of knocking on the closet door to signal that I wanted to go to the bathroom, and someone, if they were not too busy, would come to my aid.

As a sort of trade-off, I agreed to read and study their recommended literature in the closet with the aid of a flashlight. They provided me with a steady supply of selected reading, books by Eldridge Cleaver, George Jackson, Marx, Engels, and others. I was given the SLA Codes of War, their statement of aims and purposes, their goals, their declaration of revolutionary war. There was no faking my study program. I told them I wanted to read all of this and learn. And they told me they wanted me to study their material and to ask questions so that they could help me learn.

I memorized the meaning of the SLA symbol of the seven-headed cobra. I learned the African words for each of the cobra's heads: Umoja, Kujichagulia, Ujima, Ujamaa, Nia, Kuumba, and Imani. And I racked my brain to think up questions to ask them which would indicate my own keen interest. No matter how silly or stupid my questions were, I discovered that Cin and the others were delighted to explain their answers in the greatest detail. At study sessions after dinner, Cin would ask me if there was anything I had studied the night before that required more instruction, and I found it wise always to have a question or two prepared for them. In such fashion did we get along.

I even took up smoking cigarettes with them, for the sheer want of something to do. Drugs and liquor were forbidden by the SLA Codes of War, but all of them (as near as I could make out) were heavy smokers. Nervous tension and fear were an integral part of living underground as a revolutionary. Being a non-smoker all of my life, I had declined frequent offers of a cigarette during various discussion sessions. But then as time dragged on I began accepting a cigarette now and then and pretty soon I took every cigarette offered. They gave me something to do. They smoked roll-your-owns and so did I; only the General Field Marshal could afford the luxury of Lucky Strikes. All the while, I waited for the other shoe to drop. The hours I spent alone in the closet every day were unremitting periods of uncertainty, worry, and torment. When and if it suited their purposes, they would execute me. They had said as much and on that I never ceased to believe them.

When the shoe did drop, it happened so casually that I missed the significance of it. Day after day, one or another of the comrades would read me newspaper items about the food program, about the SLA, or about me, and each of the items was interpreted by the SLA as proof that the fascist corporate state did not want to negotiate for my release. I was reduced to a quivering nervous wreck. In the midst of all this, one day Cin shooed away the others and said he wanted to talk to the prisoner alone. "It may be coming down to a decision about you pretty soon," he said in a conspiratorial whisper. "You know, it's not me but the whole War Council that makes all the important policy decisions, so it's the War Council that's gonna decide on you. I get my orders from the War Council. But I was thinking, maybe I could go to the Council and convince them to let you join us. That would be better than getting killed. We wouldn't trust you completely, but maybe you can make up for some of the crimes that your parents committed. You can live down your past and help the people.

"You're kinda like the pet chicken people have on a farm—when it comes time to kill it for Sunday dinner, no one really wants to do it. In other revolutionary movements, when guerrilla fighters capture an enemy soldier, they sometimes give him a choice: fight or die. He can join the guerrillas and stay and fight with them or they have to kill him. So, you better start thinking about it. You can join us and fight with us, and that'll mean you can never go home again or ever see your folks or your old friends—or you can die." Then, after a prolonged pause, he added, "You know, we've kind of gotten to like you, so we don't really want to kill you, if we don't have to. Think about it."

I thought about it all the time. It seemed like a hideous offer. I wanted to go home. I did not want to join this crew. Nor did I like the alternative. I expected him to talk about it more, to explain the ramifications, to tell me what would be expected of me. But the subject was not brought up again, either the next day or in the days that followed. I began to wonder if I had heard him correctly. The offer, if that's what it was, just hung there unresolved, like all the other uncertainties in my existence. Day after day, I worried that I would be asked to make a choice, and I did not know what I would say. I did not know what to believe.

After a while Cin did begin to talk again of the possibility of an exchange of prisoners, saying that it would be very difficult for the SLA to trust the FBI. He envisioned a high-level meeting on a broad, open field somewhere, with the FBI and the SLA releasing their prisoners at the same time from opposite sides of the field. I would walk across the open expanse to the FBI, while Remiro and Little would walk to the SLA. The SLA could then make a quick getaway. However, there was one loophole in the scheme. The FBI might open fire on all three prisoners when we passed each other in the center of the field. Cin promised that he would try to work out a safer plan for an exchange. On another occasion, he commented that it would be a real problem for the SLA to release me so that I could get safely home to my parents. Their home was surrounded by police, he said. If they left me by myself in some vacant field or on a roadside, the FBI might find me and kill me before my parents could reach me and then the FBI would blame my death on the SLA. Such conjectures did nothing to allay my fears. I could not bring myself to believe that the SLA really would release me, short of an unlikely prisoner exchange, but once again I began to hope.

The SLA was not an "all work and no play" organization. The soldiers took part in an unusual "operation" one night. They all dressed up and held a make-believe party with loud music, dancing, much laughter and talk, and iced drinks clinking in their glasses—all for the benefit of the neighbors. Gelina gleefully explained to me that Cin had thought it wise to allay whatever suspicions the neighbors might have had concerning the goings-on in the house. So, to reinforce the story that the house had been rented by two stewardesses, who sometimes shared the house with other airline personnel, they made sure that their party spilled out into the backyard. There, Cujo acted the role of a pilot, discussing in a loud voice his various exploits as a flier, and the others discussed their travels all over the country.

On another night, I was awakened by an unusual racket outside the closet. I could hear loud wild music, stomping of feet, and gales of laughter. Gelina opened the closet door and giggled: "Oh, I wish you could see this, we're all having so much fun."

"What's happening?" I asked.

"Cujo is wild. He's dancing naked all over the place. He's so marvelous, you should see him."

I could hear "Jungle Boogie" blaring on the radio, the sounds of people clapping in unison, and someone shouting, "Right on!" Of course, I could see nothing, which was just as well.

A day or two later Gelina came to me and whispered with glee in her voice, "Cujo wants to get it on with you. You know, he wants to fuck you."

She went on to explain: "Everyone in the cell is feeling much more comradely toward you than when you first got here. We feel more like you're one of us now. And part of being in a cell is being comradely with the people in the cell." She laughed like a little girl, but gave me a fait accompli: "You'll be getting it on with Cujo." It was as if she were Cupid and this was the most natural thing in the world. I really was not even very surprised. Perhaps, deep down, I had expected this and had never fully faced up to it. Cujo had been particularly attentive to me during my re-education but I was naïve enough to think their Codes of War would not permit such a thing.

Gelina, wearing a ski mask, gesticulating, rolling her eyes and making like an actress playing to the galleries, presided over my third bath. She was full of joy, in contrast to all the others, who always were so intent and serious about their revolution. Gelina seemed to enjoy the moment; I must say I could not match her enthusiasm. I felt like the bride in the family-arranged match or perhaps the slave girl being introduced into the Sultan's harem. But closer to reality, it was simply another humiliation I had to endure in order to stay alive in this impossible situation. I had plenty of soap and shampoo for my hair and all the time I wanted in that bath. Gelina helped me dry my hair and she delighted in combing it out and giving me a makeshift coiffure. She was acting more like a hairdresser than a revolutionary. She gave me clean clothes to put on—a red and white T-shirt and tan corduroy slacks.

I was led, blindfolded once again, back into the room outside my closet and greeted by the others. By this time, they were all calling me "Tiny." That was my code name replacing the old "Marie Antoinette." They used code names for me because they did not want anyone spying on us to hear them say "Patty." We were all seated in a sort of circle on the floor as Gelina explained that as part of my education as a prisoner of war, the members wanted me to learn what it really was like living in a cell underground. Free sex was one of the principles of the cell. It was obvious, she said, that revolutionaries operating underground could not go out in the street and find sex in the usual way. Therefore, everyone in the cell had to take care of the needs of the others. No one was forced to have sex in the cell. But if one comrade asked another, it was "comradely" to say yes.

"So we want you to know," said Gelina, "you can fuck any of the men in the cell that you want to."

There was a distinct pause and I heard Gabi add: "Or any woman."

Much laughter followed this remark.

Cujo followed me into the closet, the door was shut, we took our clothes off, and he did his thing and left. I don't think he said a word. If he did, I have absolutely no recollection of it. It was awkward, the closet was small and he was a big man, a big man who acted like a little boy. Only one image came briefly to mind: of all the others sitting silently outside, listening and knowing. And when he was gone I consoled myself: It could have been worse; it could have been Cin. Don't worry about it. Don't examine your feelings. Never examine your feelings—they're no help at all. Better not to think.

So I went to sleep.

The next day not a single word was spoken about the sexual encounter, not by Cujo, Gelina, Cin, or anyone else. It was as though it had never happened or was of no importance. Perhaps it really was of no importance to them. I didn't know. But three days later, Gelina played Cupid once again. "Cin wants to fuck you," she whispered to me. Her babblings, which I had trouble concentrating on, indicated that Cin's decision to sleep with me was a great honor: Cin was the leader of the cell, a man with whom all the sisters wanted to sleep, and having sex with Cin would bring me so much closer to all the sisters. . . . I tried to keep my face expressionless, to hide my revulsion. Inwardly I berated myself for being so naïve to have thought I could escape him. "Uh-huh" is what I suppose I said, for I don't recall ever saying "Yes," and I know I did not rise to any heights of indignation and shout "Never!" I was doubly worried about objecting to Cin. I would have been accused of racism, for I had unprotestingly submitted to Cujo, and I knew that among these people there was nothing worse than being guilty of racism.

Cin came into the closet, shut the door, and said, "Take off your clothes," and he had me. I lay there like a rag doll, my mind a million miles away. It was all so mechanical and then it was over. I said to myself, rationalizing again, "Well, you're still alive." What did this kind of abuse matter? If I had been raped on a dark side street in Berkeley, it would have been the same thing, perhaps worse. If they killed me, after all, none of this would matter one bit. If I somehow survived, perhaps these rapes would have helped save my life. My thoughts at this time were focused on the single issue of survival. Concerns over love and marriage, family life, friends, human relationships, my whole previous life, had really become, in SLA terms, bourgeois luxuries. I thought of my mom and dad at times, but mostly in terms of being ransomed and freed. Steve Weed simply faded away from my thoughts. No matter how I turned it over in my mind, I came to the same bleak conclusion that there was no one out there who could help me; I was on my own. Never had I felt so depressed. There was no point in objecting to anything anymore, not even in my thoughts. I would have to do anything they wanted in order to survive. At the same time I could not think of any further humiliation to which they could subject me. I did not want to think anymore at all.

The fourth tape-recorded message to the outside world, designed to respond to the rising number of SLA critics, was orchestrated almost entirely by Gelina. It was hard for me to believe that this giggly, silly girl who had once been an actress in amateur theatricals was really a general in the SLA. But there was no doubting her seriousness as she went public for the first time, reading a long, long speech she herself had written.

"There have been many on the Left who without a clear understanding," she declared, "have condemned the actions of the SLA and the people's forces who have chosen to fight rather than talk. . . .

"It has been claimed that we are destroying the Left but in truth an unarmed and non-fighting Left is doomed—as the people of Chile can sadly testify. . . .

"The actions of the SLA are based on a clear understanding and analysis of the enemy and its actions against the lives and freedom of the people. . . ."

She announced that the SLA was suspending negotiations because of the failure of the food distribution program, the SLA's distrust of the Hearst regime, the actions of the FBI in still seeking to find the SLA, and the treatment of Remiro and Little in prison. She demanded that the two comrades be allowed to communicate with the SLA on a national television hookup; the SLA wanted to know firsthand how its two comrades were being treated in San Quentin.

While Gelina did her tape recording in the closet, I was placed in the next room. Sitting there on the floor, blindfolded, I heard for the first time the chirping of birds outside the house and realized suddenly that a whole new season had arrived. The sound of birds impelled me to visualize the greenery outside, the trees and bushes and grass and flowers. Spring assaulted my senses in the strangest way. The room I was in had the smell of stale air. Nevertheless, I knew it was springtime outside and it occurred to me that in my captivity I had totally missed any sense of changing weather: the sun did not shine, it never rained, the wind did not blow in my people's prison. I realized for the first time just how disoriented in time I had become, being cut off so completely from the natural outside world. What was out there was real, I reminded myself in that moment of lucidity; what was in here was unreal. I would try to remember that, I told myself.

When Gelina had completed her portion of the tape, I was led back into the closet. She handed me my script and began instructing me on just how I should read it for proper emphasis. We did one or two run-throughs and then I began reciting:

"Mom, Dad . . . Your silence definitely jeopardized my safety because it allows the FBI to continue to attempt to find me, and Governor Reagan to make antagonistic statements, with no response from you. I'm beginning to feel that the FBI would rather that I get killed. . . . It's the FBI, along with your indifference to the poor, and your failure to deal with the people and the SLA in a meaningful, fair way. I don't believe you're doing everything you can, everything in your power . . ."

The taped message had me criticizing my father, my mother, my sisters, and Steven Weed too, for not doing enough to free me. I told them I had been reading radical books and SLA literature and had become convinced that "the plans are coming from the FBI and the Attorney General's office in Washington to execute the two men in San Quentin." I told them that because of our fears of an FBI raid, I had been transferred "to a special security unit in the SLA combat forces" and that I was "being held in protective custody" and had been issued a 12-gauge riot shotgun.

"I no longer fear the SLA, because they are not the ones who want me to die," I concluded. "The SLA wants to feed the people and assure safety and justice for the two men in San Quentin. I realize now that it's the FBI who wants to murder me. Only the FBI and certain people in the government stand to gain anything by my death."

I made the speech with vim and vigor at Gelina's direction, but I did not believe a word of it. I would really have liked to dissolve into tears and beg my parents to do anything to get me home again. Gelina had written the whole thing. Certainly, I had not been moved at all. That line was obviously designed to mislead the authorities. I really did not care what I said at this point. I was ready to do anything the SLA asked of me, for my life was in their hands. They were delighted with my performance. And that taped message turned public opinion against me for the first time. Because of the clever personal touches Gelina added to the script, a good many people were willing to believe that I had been converted from supposedly one of the wealthiest heiresses in the nation to a flaming, bitter revolutionary. I did not believe my mother and father would be taken in by it.

When I had finished my taping, Gelina, overwrought, grabbed the microphone and hissed into the recorder: "A warning to the fascist military-corporate state: We have declared revolutionary war upon you, the enemy of the people, and our seriousness and determination will not be swayed by any number of your U.S. government-inspected super-pigs, for those that you have hunted are now hunting you."

Fahizah then added her own peculiar sentiments: "We women know the truth as it has been revealed in our own lives. We turn our rage toward the enemy in a direct line down the sights of our guns. We must turn our anger toward those who profit off our suffering and have our anger be reflected in military tactics that utilize people's violence against the men and women who are the monsters of capitalist violence. Until we meet in the streets may we have a strong back like that of the gravedigger."

Cinque concluded the tape with one of his own special messages: "I call upon oppressed people of all colors to arm themselves in defense of their own freedom while they still have the chance. I call upon the robbers, pimps, the drug addicts, the prostitutes, and all those who have been used as pawns against the people to turn their rage and violence toward the true enemy of the people. . . . I call upon the people to join the Federation and that only means one thing: that is, answering the call to arms with the sound of your guns and your commitment to save the children."

The SLA cell celebrated the sending of this tape with great joy that night, for they truly believed, as they repeatedly told each other, that surely this message, distributed on their orders throughout the media, would turn the tide and rally the people to the SLA cause.

Nothing like that happened, of course. A few days later, Cin was convinced that the FBI had started a house-to-house search for the SLA safehouse. The cell was put on alert. The revolutionary war was heating up, everyone said. Tension hung in the air. All of them had to be almost as isolated as I was: I was confined to a small closet, but the others were stuck in this safehouse with me. Other than Cin going out to occasional War Council meetings, or so I believed, I was not aware of any of the others ever leaving the house. We were all closed in, together.

Late one night, I was abruptly awakened by one of the girls spreading the alarm. "They're here! The pigs have surrounded the house!" Someone else called out, "Combat stations!" Another cried, "Get away from the windows!" A sharp chill streaked through my body. Feeling my own heart pounding, I struggled to my knees in the dark, wanting to run, but I was so weak.

Suddenly Cin was at the closet door, saying, "Get your head down on the floor and don't move." He slammed the closet door shut. I lay there with my nose to the floor, hearing the others scattering to their combat positions and hearing the sharp clicks of the ammunition clips being rammed into their weapons. I waited for the sound of gunfire, lying there motionless except for my own quivering.

But there were no shots. Just silence.

Then Cin came to the door and in a stern voice proclaimed, "That was a false alarm. But that's the way it's goin' to happen when and if those motherfuckin' pigs get here!"

It was explained away the following day: Cin, while on guard duty, had spotted a police car driving down the street and he had thought the police were taking positions outside the house. But apparently they had been on some other mission.

In all the time I had been in the safehouse, I had absolutely no idea where it was located, although I later learned it was in Daly City. I had heard the sounds of low-flying airplanes overhead, but I could discern no pattern which would indicate how close we were to an airport. Only once did I consider the possibility of escape. I heard Yolanda one day in the backyard, talking with a neighbor. I could hear the other woman's voice. I considered screaming for help, but I thought Yolanda, who was so clever, could easily explain it away. The possibility of that other woman summoning the police seemed so remote that I decided not to risk it. Later, we discussed this and Yolanda told me that if I had screamed, she would have said that her roommate must have seen a mouse.

As the days and nights dragged on, out of all my deprivations as a prisoner of war, I developed a powerful craving for pizza. I could taste it, see it, smell it, feel the gooey cheese on my hands—all vividly in my imagination. There was no explaining it: I had never been a pizza addict before and there were dozens of other foods I liked better. Nevertheless, it was the sharp, tangy taste of pizza that I craved. It lasted for several days and nights before the urge subsided, unfulfilled.

One day, when I was left alone for an unusually long time, I became aware of the sounds of some kind of new activity going on in the room outside. Everyone seemed to be bustling about in a manner which I had never heard before. Sensitive to such sounds, I had always thought I knew what in general was going on outside the closet, but this activity was something new and strange. I knocked on the door and asked to be taken to the bathroom and on the way I asked what was going on.

"We're moving to another one of our safehouses," I was told. "This pad is getting hot; Cin says we've been here too long."

"When are we moving?" I asked.

"Tonight."

They packed up their belongings all that day, and that night they took me out of the closet. I would be transported in a garbage can, a brand-new, clean thirty-gallon plastic container. In that way, no one could possibly see or recognize me, they explained. Their explanation actually came as a relief to me. All that day I could not help but believe that this was going to be the time that they would kill me and move away, leaving my body to be found huddled in the closet.

I gingerly stepped into the garbage can; the lid was placed over my head and secured with ropes. They had cut two air holes in the lid, each one about the size of a nickel. I was beyond the point of questioning this mode of travel or, for that matter, anything they told me. There was a residue of fear in not knowing where I was going or what would happen, but, frankly, I had pretty much given up any hope of rescue or escape.

Zoya, however, did not miss a trick. As I was stepping into the garbage can, she snarled, "We're not putting a gag on you, but I'm carrying a machine gun, and if you let out one sound, I'm going to fill this garbage can full of holes. And anybody else who hears you will get it too. So you better keep your mouth shut, 'cause where we're going there's liable to be other people around and once I start shooting, anyone who is around there is as good as dead."

They toted me out of the house in an upright position, but in the trunk of their car the garbage can was placed on its side and I rattled and rolled in there for at least forty-five minutes. I was numb and stiff when I was carried out of the car and up some steps to the new safehouse. I did not make a sound. Nor did I cry out when they dropped the garbage can on the steps. The strangest part of all this, however, as they delighted in informing me later, was that they themselves were surprised at how docile and trusting I had become. It was true, I never doubted that they were indeed taking me to a new safehouse. I had begun to believe them on occasion, but never to trust them. I hoped that they liked me well enough not to kill me. "God, we could have been taking you out to the woods to shoot you and leave you there," Gelina laughingly told me afterward, "and you never would have known the difference!"

When I was lifted out of the garbage can, my legs had gone tingly numb and I could not stand at all. They half carried me into a large bedroom closet, which had housed a Murphy bed, and I slept there on the floor. The next day I was moved to a hall closet which was, incredibly, smaller than my people's prison in the first safehouse. This was an empty pantry closet, not much more than five feet long, located in a tiny hall between the front door and the small kitchen. It faced, however, the only other room in the apartment, the fifteen-by-twenty-foot bedroom where all the comrades lived. Their living quarters were not much more ample than mine, proportionately. My foam-rubber pad, raggedy blanket, and small pillow had followed me to the new safehouse and so the size of my people's prison did not really matter. I slept off and on almost all the time that I was left alone, free of my re-education courses. It was easier now to sleep than to think or worry.

This closet prison had one distinct advantage for me: its door did not close fully. It was impossible for them to lock it. So, while I was supposed to keep my blindfold on at all times, I found that I could easily observe the goings-on in the apartment at night by shifting the blindfold up onto my forehead. That gave me a clear view of my captors in the bedroom. I could see them moving around in the dark, standing watch at the windows, smoking cigarettes, going to and from the kitchen fetching fresh cups of coffee. They were but mere shapes of different sizes to me, moving in the dark, and I could not really tell one from another. Nevertheless, it gave me something to do. When anyone approached the closet, I would slip the blindfold back over my eyes, lie down, and feign sleep. But I could now conduct my own surveillance on them. I discovered that throughout the night there were always two heavily armed people awake and on guard duty. Even though I knew the location of the front door, there was no chance of my slipping away in the night.

We were in the new safehouse only a few days when Cin sat down at the edge of the closet and in a low voice said, "Tiny, you remember what I told you about the War Council thinking about what to do with you?"

"Yes," I replied.

"Well, the War Council has decided that you can join us, if you want to, or you can be released, and go home again."

The choice caught me totally off guard but only for an instant. With positive clarity and without a doubt, I knew that the *real* choice was the one which Cin had mentioned earlier: to join them or to be executed. They would never release me. They could not. I knew too much about them. He was testing me and I must pass the test or die. The thought process was so rapid I do not believe he could have discerned a hesitation.

"I want to join you."

"That'll mean, you know, you never can go back to your old way of life. You'll be an urban guerrilla, fighting for the people."

"Yes," I exclaimed, "I want to fight for the people."

I could sense, I believe, that he was smiling. Oh, he liked my answer. He thought he was so clever, giving me a choice. Frankly, at that moment, I was happy for perhaps the first time since I had been kidnapped. I did not think or care much about what joining the SLA would entail: attending their meetings, discussing Maoism, revolutionary tactics, and sending out communiqués. All I could think about, really, was that I would live.

Cin added a proviso. "It won't be so easy to join this combat unit. Everyone here has to approve of you joining. It has to be unanimous. So I'm going to ask the sisters and brothers to talk to you and you have to convince every one of them that you are worthy to join this elite combat unit."

For the next full week, I had heart-to-heart talks with each and every member of the cell. I poured my heart out to them, pleading to be allowed to join them in the revolution that would free the poor and oppressed people from the fascist corporate-military state.

Grateful for my re-education classes, I gave them back all the rhetoric, all the slogans, all the buzz words that they had filled me with over the past month or so. And they loved every word of it. The more blatant and preposterous my statements became, the more they believed them.

It was a long, slow process and the outcome remained in doubt all week. Cin explained that only if the cell's vote was unanimous could he take the matter of my joining before the War Council, which would make the ultimate decision. It was not all that easy to join the SLA. The truth was, of course, that I *did* want to join them! But not for the reasons they supposed. Not for a moment did I believe in their revolution or in their schemes to reform the United States by executing all corporate presidents and the like. I wanted to join them so that I would survive. I had no trouble at all putting sincerity into my voice when I appealed to each of them. I really wanted them to accept me into their ranks. I was panic-stricken at the thought that one of them would say no.

It was also true, I must admit, that the thought of escaping from them later simply never entered my mind. I had become convinced that there was no possibility of escape.

In the tête-à-têtes, many of them told me of how he or she had become conscious of the need to free the oppressed people of America. Fahizah said Cin had saved her life when she was heavily into drugs, was destitute and contemplating suicide. She had had to fight hard to overcome her own bourgeois upbringing. "But it was worth it," she said. "The people are worth it." She adored and idolized the great leader of the Symbionese Liberation Army. Yolanda warned me that I would find it terribly difficult and heart-wrenching to go underground with the SLA. She had been deeply in love, she said, with a prison inmate named Lumumba and had had to give up her meaningful prison visits to him when she went underground with the SLA.

Cujo explained how the revolution was growing every day and would continue to spread across the nation if people like me joined the SLA. Gabi confided that she was a lesbian and that she was still learning her combat skills, but she hoped later on to organize an army of homosexuals, for, without doubt, homosexuals were the most oppressed class of people in the whole country. Gelina was positively ecstatic about my joining, saying, "It would be a real victory for the people."

In the evening discussion sessions, I spoke to the whole group about how wonderful it would be for me to fight for the people. I told them that I had been woefully ignorant all my life, up to the time the sisters and brothers educated me about "the truth" about Amerikkka. I could not say it often enough: "I want to fight for the people." They loved it every time.

A true moment of panic struck home when Cin demanded at one point, "Are you sure you ain't been brainwashed?"

"Oh, no," I exclaimed. "That's ridiculous. Of course I have not been brainwashed. I studied all the books and all the material you gave me. How can you possibly think I've been brainwashed?" The clincher was my own challenge to them: "You don't believe the pigs in the press, do you?" I asked.

After a while, I thought I had Cin, Cujo, Gelina, Fahizah, and Gabi on my side. Cin declared, "It will be a great propaganda coup [he pronounced it "coop,"] if the prisoner wants to stay!" He turned to me and added, "It would be beautiful if someone from your background could fight for the people." Zoya was as cold and hard as ever, not saying much or revealing her feelings one way or the other.

The opposition to my joining came from the couple, Teko and Yolanda. They both questioned me at great length before the whole group about my determination to give up my rich past life for that of the SLA. And I responded, I thought, brilliantly: "How could I have anything to go back to, now that you have shown me the error of my bourgeois ways . . ." and on and on. Yolanda was my toughest critic and she did not hide her opposition. "I think you're too bourgeois, too different from all of us to have the dedication that we have," she told me in front of the others. I protested, of course. But she insisted that she just did not believe that I or any other person could be converted and attain the inner determination that was needed for a true revolutionary by studying the cause "for so short a time."

They held many, many meetings without me and I literally sweated it out in my little cubbyhole, worrying about their ultimate vote. I thought I had persuaded all but Yolanda and Teko. But I could not be sure of Zoya. I could not really be sure of any of them. I still believed they were all a bunch of lunatics and psychotics. My task was to humor them, convince them, go with them, and, above all, to stay alive.

At one point, Cin came and asked me if I would still be willing to join if it was decided that I be sent to a different unit in the SLA. "You would know no one there, 'cause they'd all be new people to you and you'd have no personal ties there like you do with us," he said. "Would you still be willing to join up with the SLA and fight for the people?"

"Of course. That would be wonderful," I replied. "Oh, I'd rather stay with you, but I would go with any unit you said I should, if I could stay and fight for the people."

On another occasion, I was quizzed on what special attributes I could bring to the SLA and I replied that I really understood how the rich bourgeois think and act and that I could help in all kinds of counter-actions. I suggested that I would be particularly effective in an intelligence unit. Fahizah piped up with the fascinating idea that I might be most effective as an undercover agent, mixing with the rich capitalists and serving the SLA at the same time. I readily agreed to that. I swore that I would tell the FBI nothing if I were sent home, that I would misinform the authorities, that I would raise money for the cause, and that I would keep in constant touch with my SLA friends. But Cin vetoed the idea. He said I would never be able to withstand FBI questioning and torture. Besides, he added, I would be watched constantly and therefore would be useless to the SLA aboveground.

Then, at last, Fahizah led me into still another cell meeting where, she said, they wanted my attendance. From the murmur of their voices, I could tell that they were already seated in a circle on the floor of the bedroom. There was a certain electricity in the air and I sensed that a decision had been reached in my case. After a while it quieted down and in the silence I heard Cin say, "The sisters and brothers have all voted for you to join this combat team." A wave of relief spread through my body.

"So you want to be an urban guerrilla and a soldier in the Symbionese Liberation Army?" he asked solemnly.

"Yes," I said.

"Do you want to devote your life to the struggle for the freedom of all oppressed people?"

"Yes."

"Are you ready to renounce your past and become a guerrilla soldier in the Symbionese Liberation Army?"

"Yes."

"Okay, take your blindfold off!"

Take it off? I couldn't believe that he had actually said it: the point of no return—I would see their faces.

So I took off the blindfold, slowly. There they all were, grinning at me. And I heard Cin declare: "As General Field Marshal, I welcome you—you are now a guerrilla fighter and a soldier in the Symbionese Liberation Army!"

CHAPTER

SIX

EVERYTHING LOOKED so squalid and ugly. What I saw before me was an eerie scene of gray, dark, dismal surroundings. The room was bare, unfurnished, except for an unmade Murphy bed jutting out from one wall. Although it was sometime in the morning, it seemed like night inside the room. No light seeped in from the outside. The windows were covered with some sort of filthy Indian bedspread material, nailed to the wall and to the upper window moldings. A bare bulb in a plain ceiling fixture provided the only illumination. There they were, their faces unmasked, sitting around in a circle on the floor, grinning at me, happy in their eagerness to witness my initial reactions to them.

I did not dare give voice to my first thoughts: Oh, God, what a bunch of ordinary-looking, unattractive little people. I suppose I was disappointed: their physical appearance just did not match my image of them as revolutionaries. Their voices had been much more impressive. Somehow I had expected them to look bigger, stronger, more commanding.

General Gelina, my happy, supportive "friend" during my captivity, was still grinning with sheer goodwill, as she playfully challenged me to try to identify all of the comrades, matching theirs faces to their voices. I recognized her immediately, even though the frizzy blond hair she had worn at my kidnapping was now a short brown bob, making her look somewhat like a flapper of a bygone age. I had no trouble naming each of them in turn and they were delighted, reacting as if they were celebrities being recognized by a loyal fan.

Cinque perhaps came closest to the image he had evoked in me when I was kidnapped and I had only heard his voice. Sitting opposite me, wearing neat trousers and a clean short-sleeved shirt, he looked the street tough to me, lean and muscular with closely cropped hair. In his early thirties, he was not that much older than some of the others, but he looked so much more mature and harder. He was someone to be feared. Cujo, on the other hand, was startling in appearance: he looked truly awful. Sitting next to Cinque, Cujo looked like a big, overgrown, awkward high school senior. His hair, cut short, was dyed a hideous red, which just did not fit in with his adolescent freckled features. The third man, Teko, also seemed out of sync and far from what I had expected, although I vaguely recognized him. When he had kidnapped me and tied me up in that kitchen, his hair had been dark brown and now it was platinum blond. Not only his hair but also his beard and his eyebrows had been peroxided. But the one or two days of facial hair growth beyond his beard still was dark brown.

Yolanda was at my right, sitting upright with her back straight. I knew who she was right off. Her small, cold, beady blue eyes looking right through me, her unsmiling face, convinced me immediately that this was the comrade who least wanted me to join. On the left side was Gabi, who was noticeably heavyset and plain-looking, wearing glasses with thick lenses, her short, straight hair dyed a peculiar shade of red. Zoya had a hard, thin face with strange sharp features and brown wavy hair which reached her shoulders. It occurred to me, as I looked at her, that she was to be feared also. Fahizah, the small, monkey-like girl, was wearing a beret cocked over one eye. She was perched nervously with one leg under her, alert, as if she were ready to leap up at a given signal and start fighting. She had a pistol in a shoulder holster, I noticed, the very vision of a revolutionary. The others also were wearing handguns and they all had on heavy hiking, or combat, boots.

"Well," exclaimed Gelina, "now that you've seen us, what do you think of us?"

"Oh," I said, managing a smile, "you're all so attractive!"

"Well, I told you, all freedom fighters are beautiful," declared Cin, with a broad grin.

Cross conversation went on for a while and it all seemed rather strange, as if prisoners of war joined them every day. My vision was somewhat distorted from the long use of the blindfold. Images seemed to go in and out of focus, become blurry and then clear and then blurry again. Yet there was a distinct feeling of camaraderie in this dismal, bare room, as if we were all old friends gathered around a campfire. I cannot say I was happy; but I felt a certain sense of relief. The immediate fear was gone. They had all accepted me. I knew them and thought I understood them, even their foolish quest as revolutionaries to overthrow the entire United States. In trying to convince them I convinced myself. I felt that I had truly joined them; my past life seemed to have slipped away. The FBI, the police, and all the authorities in the world might be searching for us in their giant manhunt, but I felt somehow free. I was no longer a prisoner of war, waiting on death row. I had been confined in those horrible closets, I would figure out later, for fifty-seven days. The fear, the stress, the confusion had been inside me for all of those days and nights, and it had seemed like an eternity. But now those feelings were being washed out of my mind, and it was all a tremendous relief. I could see. I was alive. I felt that my mind should have been clear and free to function, but my thoughts were confused. Somewhere in the jumble of my reasoning was the hope, reborn, that the essential thing was that I would survive: I would stay with this horrible group for a while and the day would come when I would be rescued or perhaps be able to escape.

My thoughts had drifted away from the room and I had lost track of the conversations around me when I heard Cin say something about "surveillance reports" and someone was talking about a beauty parlor and a restaurant. Then Zoya was describing a door and a counter and something she called a "dead space" in the rear of a grocery store. There was a "mirror" back there in the dead space. She spoke rapidly in a cold monotone, as if reading a report, except there was no piece of paper in front of her. Then I heard her say, "We looked at a liquor store, and it had only one entrance, in front . . . only one woman there, an old woman who works at night . . . looked pretty good . . . an alleyway alongside the store . . . a low fence in the back . . . It looked kind of easy."

It was not the usual revolutionary topic of conversation and I became confused trying to fathom what Zoya was talking about. Gabi apparently noticed my confusion, for she leaned over, smiled at me, and whispered into my ear, "We need the money."

As Zoya continued talking, it suddenly struck me that she was proposing to rob that liquor store. I was shocked. I could not believe that these people, who were such ardent revolutionaries, were actually discussing a holdup. My jaw must have dropped open in surprise. That's criminal! I thought.

"I think this is worth a second look," Zoya was saying, and I turned to observe all the others listening so intently to her words. When she stopped talking there was a long pause and then Cin, who had been staring thoughtfully at the ceiling, abruptly declared: "We're goin' to do a bank!"

Now everyone looked surprised. There were a number of audible gasps.

Cin pointed to some of them, saying, "I want a team to go out tomorrow and check out banks.

"You all been thinking too small," he said bluntly. "We don't need hundreds of dollars, we need thousands. I want you out there tomorrow, looking at banks. And remember, it's the escape routes that are important, so check them carefully. Meeting's adjourned!"

Don't look alarmed, I told myself, don't let them see you're shocked. That would be too dangerous. My heart was pounding. All the old, familiar apprehension returned as I sensed that events were once again veering beyond my control. Keep calm, I warned myself, they haven't robbed it yet. Just don't say anything aloud that you'll be sorry for. I simply could not adjust to the idea that they actually intended to rob a bank. During my two months in the closet, they had done nothing but train and hold meetings and I had come to think that that was all they ever did.

No one was paying any attention to me. They were all buzzing excitedly over their leader's brilliant idea. From what I could overhear, I gathered that robbing a bank had never been mentioned before; Cin had thought it up at the moment. Fahizah positively oozed admiration for Cinque's audacity. Certainly there were no objections raised; everyone seemed to agree that robbing a bank was the proper next action for the SLA. I still could not fathom the concept of political revolutionaries committing a bank robbery. Everyone was commenting upon the new action, and Cin began strutting about, bathing in his own glory. Then I noticed that he was swilling some sort of cheap red wine out of a glass tumbler, and I thought that rather strange. I had been led to believe that liquor and drugs were forbidden in the SLA.

Teko was perhaps the most excited and animated. "That's the trouble with us," he was saying. "Our whole background is so bourgeois that we're thinking too small. . . . We're too chickenshit and we're thinking all the time about small, chickenshit operations. . . . But blacks do this sort of thing for survival. That's why we need Third World leadership. We never would have thought of it ourselves."

A little while later Cin called me over to him most casually and handed me a small braided-rope ring. "Here," he said, holding my hand and dropping the ring into it. "Welcome to the SLA, sister. It's not gold. But it's better than that. It's the symbol of the love of the people." I remembered then that the other girls were wearing similar rings. So I slipped the ring onto the ring finger of my left hand. The Field Marshal was very pleased.

He then ordered Zoya to take a Polaroid snapshot of me to be sent out with the tape-recorded communiqué they planned, to show the people that I was truly an urban guerrilla. "Dress her up like a combat soldier for the picture," he instructed the sisters. I tried to dissuade him. The idea of a photo of myself as an SLA soldier, distributed across the country, was absolutely mortifying, but I did not get very far with anything I said. The girls brought out what seemed like combat fatigues and Fahizah put her beret on my head, cocked to one side, and they handed me a sawed-off M-1 carbine to hold as I posed. Then Cin got the idea of tying a rifle scope to the carbine to make it look more awesome and to confuse the authorities.

"The FBI won't know what the hell kind of weapons we have!" He laughed.

They posed me in front of the giant SLA flag, which they told me the sisters had been sewing for days, showing the coiled seven-headed cobra in black against a red background. "Black for the color, red for the blood," they joked. Zoya aimed a Polaroid camera at me, as Teko tried to push me into the proper belligerent pose.

"Look really mean," someone told me.

"Bend your legs more."

"Smile a little, not too much."

"Get into a shooting stance . . . make like you're goin' to shoot someone . . . crouch . . ."

I did not like it one bit, being used like that, nor had I expected it to be this way. When they had a photo that satisfied them, Cin chuckled

over it and then put it away. Then he turned to the sisters and said,
"Cut her hair!"

I could not believe it. Fahizah and Gabi led me away to the hall outside the room and I went along, too bewildered, too scared to protest.
In the hall, just outside my old closet prison, Fahizah unceremoniously
cut off all my shoulder-length blond hair. She left me with no more
than a half-inch growth all around my head. I stood there somberly,
fighting against the profoundest urge to break down and weep. I had
to take this. And I did not understand why they were doing this to me.
Was it to make me feel like a raw recruit in their army? None of the
other girls had had their hair cut, as far as I knew. Or was it just
cruelty, to humiliate me, to make me feel inferior, or what? No one
explained it to me, then or afterward. Later, when I gazed at myself
in the bathroom mirror, I looked like a drowned rat. My hair was gone
and I was but skin and bones. I looked every bit as weak and as
helpless as I felt. In my captivity, I must have lost at least fifteen
pounds, for I did not look any more than ninety pounds.

Zoya, with some of the others trailing along at times, took me on a
tour of the safehouse, explaining as we went the functioning of the cell.
The apartment consisted of that one room, which was about twenty
feet long and perhaps fifteen feet wide, and a small utility kitchen, plus,
of course, the front hall with my people's prison. The heavy drapes
over all the windows had long razor slits in them, so that they
remained closed when hanging but could be parted when anyone
wanted to look outside. I was instructed, in no uncertain terms, never
to look out of those surveillance slits during the day. I was not yet a
trusted member of the cell, they explained, and they did not want me
to know where the safehouse was located.

The kitchen cupboard and refrigerator were practically bare, con-
sidering that nine people lived and ate there. Zoya explained which of
them went out shopping and which of them prepared the meals. My assignment would be to help clean up, she said. Clothes were washed by
hand in the bathtub and every one of us was expected to keep neat and
clean at all times, just as we were responsible for taking care of our
own weapons. Cin did not approve of blue jeans, Zoya said, because
blacks did not wear them and such clothes did not instill the respect
which the SLA needed from the people.

The most surprising part of the tour, however, was a visit to the large
bedroom closet which housed the Murphy bed. Along one entire wall,

neatly lined up on hooks, was an arsenal of weapons—several sub-machine guns, carbines, a shotgun, and some weapons I could not recognize. My eyebrows must have gone up in surprise when someone mentioned that they had bombs and dynamite there too, available for future actions. The other two walls were chock-full of an amazing variety of clothing. I noticed an assortment of wigs and gas masks and cartons of all sizes stashed in the four corners of the closet. Zoya and Gelina explained that the SLA had a full assortment of disguises, and Gelina showed me her professional theatrical makeup kit, saying that she was in charge, as a former actress, of helping the sisters and brothers disguise themselves whenever they ventured out of the safehouse. I was frankly amazed and believed her when she bragged that even with their photographs in the daily newspapers and on "Wanted" posters in post offices all over the Bay Area, any of them could go anywhere without fear of being recognized, thanks to her theatrical skills as a makeup artist.

They also kept copies of all the known photographs of themselves which had appeared in the press or anywhere else. They would always consult this file before leaving the safehouse. The point was, they explained, that the police had photographs of some of their disguises and they did not want to go outside wearing a disguise which might duplicate one of their known appearances.

To go along with the disguises, they also had a stack of stolen identifications, about one hundred separate ones, including driver's licenses, credit cards, and whatnot. Teko declared that he had stolen them himself while working over the previous Christmas holidays at the Oakland post office. It seemed that purse snatchers made a habit of dumping the purses, once they had removed the money, into the nearest street mailbox and the mailmen would bring the purses to the central post office. Once Teko found the bin in which these purses were kept, all he had to do was take out the identifications and leave the purses behind. We also had easy access to automobiles any time we needed them for an "operation," Zoya explained. She showed me a box filled with car keys neatly taped to index cards which bore the names and addresses of the owners of the vehicles. Joe Remiro had been the mastermind on that particular caper, she said. He had worked for a time at a service station and it had been a simple task for him to duplicate the keys and note the owners' addresses while the cars were left there for repairs.

Later in the afternoon, Cin "issued" to me my SLA weapon, an M-1 carbine similar to the one with which I had posed for the photograph. All of the other rifles had been altered so that they were fully automatic: as long as the trigger was pulled back the rifle would fire continuously. But my gun, because of its bolt and trigger housing, could not be transformed that way. Cin promised he would refashion the sawed-off handle of the rifle for me himself, so that it would fit my small hand; thereafter it would be my own personal weapon. I was given Fahizah's old boots, which were a little tight on me but better than going around barefooted. She got new boots.

They certainly were wasting no time in indoctrinating me into their army. It was all so bewildering! Zoya escorted me back into the weapons closet. There she experimented with some combat clothes, trying on various items to see which would fit me. Everyone shared everything owned by the people's army. She strapped a loaded backpack on me, and I practically sagged to the floor under its weight. The pack was filled with all kinds of items she said were needed by an urban guerrilla fighting on the streets of San Francisco. Mostly, though, the pack was loaded with spare ammunition and must have weighed thirty or possibly even forty pounds. I said nothing, struggling to follow her instructions in lumbering around the room practicing crouches and shooting stances with the heavy pack on my back and the rifle in my hand. It seemed ridiculous to me that I could ever run around the streets shooting people, with or without that pack on my back. But Zoya said the time would come when the revolution would be taken to the streets of the city, and I would have to be prepared.

While we were doing this, the others were taking the first step in selecting a bank to be robbed. Teko, Cujo, and some of the others were going through the telephone directory, calling out the names and addresses of neighborhood branch banks and checking those addresses against a large street map, trying to figure out which of the banks were located on streets which were not congested with traffic, stoplights, or other hindrances to a fast getaway. I still could not really believe that they would do this thing; plotting was one thing, doing it was another.

This day too, Yolanda came waltzing out of the bathroom wearing the blue robe that I had been kidnapped in. She saw me and a big grin spread on her face. "Nice robe," she said. "Really warm. It was kind of torn up in your kidnapping but we sewed it up. All the sisters use it. I'll be dressed in a minute and you can have it."

I felt sick. The thought of these horrible women wearing my clothes while I was blindfolded and being threatened made my skin crawl. I never wanted to wear that robe again.

My indoctrination continued through the day and well into the night. At the meeting after dinner, the discussions ranged over a variety of subjects, and I am afraid I missed most of it. I think I was dozing off with my eyes wide open. My body seemed seeped of strength, my mind a fuzzy blank. I gathered Cin was lecturing the others on what to look for in searching for the right bank to rob. There was some discussion about the next communiqué to announce my joining the SLA, a real propaganda coup for them, and Cin suggested that perhaps this was the time for each and every one of them to send a personal message to the people. The idea was that each would appeal to a different segment of the oppressed. Each of them would become leaders of a new, enlarged Liberation Army. They wanted Gabi to speak for the gays but she refused to be recorded publicly. Yolanda also said she did not think she could bring herself to do it, not at this time.

At one point, a rather significant question occurred to me: "What about the other SLA units? What are they doing?"

The question surprised them and they all seemed to look to Cin for an answer. After a moment's hesitation, his face cracked and he burst out laughing.

"What other units? This is all there is, baby. We're the whole army. You're looking at it."

They all laughed at the big deception. Zoya chuckled and said, "I am the communications unit." They began to joke with one another about the phantom army. What did I say to this? Nothing. It really did not seem to make any difference to me. What was one more lie? I was far more exhausted than I had realized. Nothing seemed to faze me. I was existing, happy enough to be accepted, rather than imprisoned or killed, and nothing seemed to matter very much anymore. In fact, as my vision improved hour by hour, my new comrades did not seem quite as strange as they had before. I myself was so weak I could not stand up or walk for very long without feeling on the verge of collapse. I did notice, however, that aside from Cin and Cujo and Gelina, the others were giving me questioning glances of suspicion. They were not as smiling or as happy as they had been about me at my induction into the SLA.

Cin ordered me to stand the guard duty watch with him that first night, from 11 P.M. to 2 A.M., so that he could teach me how it was done. A "lookout for the pigs" was maintained throughout the night by two and sometimes three of us from 11 P.M. to 2 A.M., from 2 to 5, and from 5 to 8. With all the lights out, Cin explained, we could peek through the slits in the makeshift drapes from the windows in the bedroom and in the kitchen. We could even open the windows and let some fresh air into the apartment. This way we could see out into the lighted street and no one could see into the apartment. One person was always at the bedroom window, while someone else stood guard at the kitchen window. Cin demonstrated his "telescope," which was a scope removed from a rifle. It gave a remarkably clear view of the rooftops of the buildings across the street and down into the street itself. Judging from the Victorian apartment buildings opposite us, I surmised we were in a third-floor apartment, not far from the corner of the inter-section. From the glow of a streetlamp, I could see a street sign that said Golden Gate Avenue. I knew that we were in San Francisco, but I could not make out the cross street. When I asked, Cin said bluntly, "You don't need to know."

He explained that it was too early for all the sisters and brothers to trust me completely. That would come in time, he said. I did not need to know the address of the safehouse. In the SLA, like any army, every soldier's life depended upon his comrades in any given action. It was important, he said, for me to prove myself, to show the others that I was as dedicated as they were. The Codes of War meant what they said: If any SLA soldier failed to perform his or her duty during an ac-tion, he or she could be killed immediately.

While we stood watch, the others went to bed. Most of them slept on small foam-rubber pads, similar to the one I had in the closet; some had sleeping bags, and one or two could sleep in the Murphy bed, al-though one space in that bed was always reserved for our leader, the General Field Marshal. The pads and sleeping bags, rolled up during the day, were spread out on the floor in this one room and the soldiers slept alongside each other, head to foot. They slept with all their clothes on, fully armed, ready to be awakened for combat. The sisters and brothers were instructed to keep their weapons on the floor beside them rather than in their holsters because one time Cujo had had a bad dream and someone had discovered him sitting up, asleep, with his sidearm in his hand ready to fire.

Standing watch with the Field Marshal of the SLA was positively nerve-racking. He took this lookout duty *very* seriously. He was also paranoiac. During that first watch, Cin was always seeing moving shadows on the opposite roof. He frightened me by alerting me to every suspected movement; then when I thought he would wake up the others, he would change his mind and say it was nothing at all. But he instructed me fully in how to discern shadows as well as bodies, how to observe and remember details of every single car that passed on the street below. The FBI or police would stake us out with unmarked cars, he said. Our counter-plan was to note every car, and if the same vehicle passed the window twice, it meant it was circling the block, and I should alert the others. Everyone walking down the street was a potential enemy and had to be kept under observation until out of sight. Two men walking together on the street alarmed our leader. He saw shadows and movements everywhere and I could not see them at all. He sent shock waves of fear through my body again and again. I felt hopelessly trapped. There were five separate bolt locks attached to the one door in the apartment, in addition to its regular lock. We were three stories up above the street. Surreptitious escape was impossible. Fighting my way out was ridiculous; Cin and the others wore sidearms at all times. My only flickering hope was that somehow, someday, I would be rescued.

When our night watch finally ended, Cin awakened his relief on the Murphy bed and I nudged Yolanda and took her place on the already warm bedroll. I must have fallen asleep instantly. I do not remember thinking, planning, or worrying. Nor did I dream. I had survived another day and I slept.

The next morning I used the communal toothbrush in the bathroom. Blindfolded all those days, I had been using the same toothbrush used by all the others. The thought disgusted me. But it was bourgeois, of course, to think that one needed one's own toothbrush among sisters and brothers in the same army. I discovered that privacy in the bathroom was even more bourgeois. They did not believe anyone, prisoner or comrade, should close the door when taking a bath or shower or using the toilet. Cin walked in on me the first time and others did afterward and they all insisted that it was simply "uptight" for anyone to be embarrassed over normal bodily functions.

No one blew a bugle or anything, but the people's forces lined up for inspection every morning. The Field Marshal strutted before the troops, inspecting us closely and commenting on the state of dress of one or two. I was at the end of the line, wondering whether I was supposed to stand at attention, salute, or whatever. Was he serious or was he playacting in this little one-room apartment? I wondered. No, he was serious. When he came to me, he glowered at me fiercely not more than a foot away and barked, "Who are you?" Stunned, I did not have the slightest idea of what he was talking about or what he wanted.

"I said, 'Who are you?' Who are you?" he hissed.

"I don't know what you mean."

"You're a guerrilla fighter! You're a soldier in the Symbionese Liberation Army. Now you say it. I'll ask you again: 'Who are you?'"

"I am a guerrilla fighter, a soldier in the Symbionese Liberation Army," I declared, as fiercely as I could.

"Good," said he. "Now you remember that!"

He showed me the SLA salute, which was a clenched fist thumped over and away from the heart.

SLA calisthenics consisted of circling one's arms, deep knee bends, some stretching exercises, plus one hundred push-ups and two hundred sit-ups. The push-ups, which were the hardest of all, were to be done in sets of twenty at a time, any time during the day so long as each of us did one hundred. That first day and that first week, I was hopeless; I could only do the arms circling. But in time I could do all of the exercises required, even the push-ups. On those I had worked up to three sets of twenty and sometimes four and I could do a set of thirty fingertip push-ups. Everyone took these exercises very seriously indeed. Fahizah did one hundred push-ups several times a day and she beamed with pleasure when Cin complimented her upon her determination and dedication to the cause.

Breakfast that morning was pink pancakes, prepared by Fahizah, who seemed to be the army's chief cook. My wonder never ceased. In the kitchen pantry, I discovered, there were condiments and vegetable food colorings. The food supply was predominantly breads, potatoes, rice, pancake mix, flour, and such things. The SLA had a theory on this too. They ate lots of starches and carbohydrates because they were cheaper than meat and vegetables and also supplied them with quick energy. Cin ordered the supply unit, Zoya and Gelina, to buy me a large jar of peanut butter and he instructed me to eat peanut butter on bread or crackers all day long in order to fatten myself up and to restore my strength.

Combat drills followed breakfast and they all serpentined around the room, sometimes rushing through a door to the hall, and then back again, tiptoeing around with their weapons. They reminded me of little boys and girls playing cowboys and Indians. Cin gave me a running commentary on combat techniques for fighting in the streets, point and slack maneuvers for rounding corners with one soldier covering another's advance, and he assured me that I too would soon be learning those maneuvers. I received the first of innumerable lessons on the firepower of each of the SLA weapons, and their proper use in different situations. One always employed the fully automatic weapons, the submachine guns, *first,* because of their heavy firepower; then the semiautomatic weapons, and then the single-action rifles. The shotgun was only effective at close quarters, as were the handguns. They did not have a handgun for me, Cin explained, but they would get one. Cin was most proud of his own handgun, a nine-millimeter Browning automatic which carried fourteen shots. It was the best sidearm in the outfit; he said Osi (Russell Little) had bought it at a gun show somewhere. Cin, as the leader, had "issued" the Browning to himself.

Teko was practicing his quick draw with a revolver, twirling about, crouching, assuming all kinds of positions. Fahizah was quick-drawing from a shoulder holster in front of a mirror, again and again and again. She seemed never to stop. Zoya prowled about like a panther, with a submachine gun in her hands. Gabi sort of lumbered about in an awkward crouch with a big shotgun. She was at least five feet six, overweight, and ungainly compared to all the others. Cin was always criticizing her. Yolanda showed me her .380 Mauser automatic, which I thought I recognized as the weapon Gelina used on me during the kidnapping. But I learned later that Gelina had her own Mauser. I had never handled a gun of any kind since my father had given me lessons on the use of a shotgun for duck hunting when I was twelve. I was surprised that I could not pull the trigger on Yolanda's pistol. I simply did not have the strength. The first shot was double-action and I needed both hands to pull the trigger. They laughed at my weakness and inexperience. But I would learn. Cin assured me of that.

Cin also christened me with my revolutionary name in the SLA. It came casually and caught me by surprise. He simply announced: "We got to come up with a new name for you." He thought for not more than a moment or so and then added: "We're going to call you Tania. She was a guerrilla, a wonderful guerrilla fighter with Che Guevara in Bolivia." He handed me a book and said, "Here, you read this and you'll see she was right on." The book was *Tania: The Unforgettable Guerrilla,* and I immediately started to flip through the pages. I vastly preferred to read a book by myself than to be forced into any of their more strenuous activities.

Both Yolanda and Teko objected. "But that was Robyn's name," exclaimed Teko.

"It's her name now," Cin declared. "Robyn's gone and besides she wasn't with us that long anyhow."

Robyn Steiner had been Russell Little's girlfriend at the University of Florida and had come with him to Berkeley to pursue their radical beliefs. Living together at the Peking House, where radicals gathered at Berkeley, they had joined the SLA at its inception. But before my kidnapping Robyn had quit and fled to Florida, where her parents lived.

Yolanda did not want me to have that name because, as she said, I was not good enough for as famous a name as that. The real Tania, from what I learned in the book, had fought alongside Che Guevara and his little band of revolutionaries. The band, including Tania, was ambushed and all were killed in the Bolivian jungle.

Whatever, I was to be Tania. Cinque had decreed it and he was our leader.

There never seemed to be a pause in the furious activity going on in that one-room safehouse. Everyone was busy doing something. Discussions seemed to be endless. Fahizah pleaded to be allowed to go out on the bank surveillance because she had not been out of the safehouse in months. Some of the others, however, insisted that Fahizah became too nervous and jumpy when she was out on the street. Everyone seemed to believe that she was the most recognizable of the group, because she was so short, and her picture had been printed so often in the newspapers. Cin decided that because of all her hard work and determination she should be given the privilege of going out of the house. But only if her disguise was adequate. She was like a puppy dog in her admiration of Cinque.

The disguise she came up with was miraculous. No one could possibly recognize her. Although she was only about twenty-seven years old, she did not look to be a year less than sixty. She wore a gray wig, a grandmotherly black shawl, heavy support hose, and her cheeks were stuffed with cotton. Gelina wore a pillow under her dress and was made up to look like what they termed "a dumb, innocent housewife," at least seven months pregnant. Teko, outfitted in clean, sensible clothes, freshly shaven, looked like a different man. They were to go about as tourists, a man and his wife and his mother, snapping Polaroid pictures of themselves outside the various banks on their list. The photos would take in bank entrances with various views of the nearby streets. Then they would go into each bank, sometimes together, sometimes alone, look around, memorize important details, then leave and draw from memory diagrams of the banks' layouts. It was all planned so carefully. These people, it occurred to me, could be crazy and strange one moment and diabolically shrewd and clever the next moment.

In the midst of everything else that was going on, Cin decided to play an enormous April Fools' Day joke on the outside world. As far as I could tell, that thought arose on the spur of the moment in the wily mind of our SLA leader. It was based, as near as I could make out from the discussions, upon the fact that in the past few days a number of appeals had been launched for my release. The newspapers had reported that the Hearst Corporation had placed four million dollars in escrow, under the control of an independent group, to be spent on food for the poor, if I was released unharmed. Death Row Jeff, a jailhouse buddy of Cinque, had written a personal appeal to him and the SLA, suggesting that they enter into negotiations with my father for my safe release. Even Osi and Bo had sent a long letter to the media, saying they were sure that I would be released unharmed and they did not hold me responsible for the presumed capitalistic sins of my father.

Cin thought it would be a great idea if they announced, or perhaps just hinted, that I would be set free in a few days, but the SLA message would be sent on April 1 and it would be an April Fools' joke. Instead of my release would come our big communiqué announcing my choice to stay and fight with them. Someone came up with the idea of sending the April Fools' message to John Bryan, the editor of a small San Francisco newspaper called *Phoenix*. He had tried a hoax in publishing his own counterfeit version of an SLA message.

Cin and the others had appreciated the recognition and the publicity and so they thought of returning the compliment by sending the *Phoenix* editor a real SLA message, which would bring him a great deal of publicity and would, in reality, be a hoax of their own. Zoya was sent out to find a florist who would deliver a single rose to the editor, along with the real SLA Codes of War and another communiqué which would really startle people. To authenticate this one, Cin included half of my driver's license and this message:

"Herein enclosed are the Codes of War of the Symbionese Liberation Army. These documents as all SLA documents are to be printed in full and omitting nothing by order of this court in all forms of the media.

"Further communications regarding subject prisoner will follow in the following 72 hours, communications will state city and time of release of the prisoner."

The April Fools' joke went awry, however, because the florist did not deliver the rose and the message until the next day, April 2, but my comrades had an uproariously good time laughing all that night over the radio and television bulletins announcing that I might be freed soon. A cruel joke for my parents, I thought.

That same day, Cujo made what I thought at the time was the first gesture of friendship I had received at their hands. I had noticed him working by himself for an hour or more at something in the corner of the room, but he refused to tell me what he was doing. "You'll see," he said. Later, he came up to me and announced, "I have something for you," and he put a brown rope necklace around my neck. He had braided and waxed it himself. From the tightly wound strands of thin rope hung a small stone sculpture of a pre-Columbian figure, which he described as an Olmec monkey more than 2,500 years old. He told me solemnly that it was his most treasured possession, a memento from a very good friend, an archaeologist, who had given him two Olmec monkeys which he had unearthed on an archaeological dig in Central America. He showed me the rough hole in the stone piece, through which the necklace was attached, explaining that it was handmade, as was the entire piece, thus proving that it was a genuine antique and very valuable. Then he showed me the little figure which he wore around his neck, and he asked me to wear mine as long as I was in the SLA. "I'm so glad you decided to join the SLA," he said. He was serious and solemn.

Just about every spare minute during those two or three days was spent preparing the tape-recorded communiqué the SLA would send to the media to announce my joining the revolution. Gelina and Yolanda were in one corner of the room, writing the major message for me to read into the tape recorder. They were all practical enough by now to know that my message would be the one most likely to be

broadcast by the television and radio stations. Just about everyone was
adding his or her suggestions to the script. I was consulted from time to
time, but I did not get to see the script Gelina was writing by hand
until it was completed and approved by the others. Fahizah worked by
herself in another corner, preparing a long epistle of praise for our
leader, General Field Marshal Cinque. When she read it aloud to us,
everyone oohed and aahed in praising her for her fabulous work and I
felt obliged to join in, though I thought her message was asinine.
Cinque, according to her, "escaped alone on foot from Soledad Prison
and he did so for one reason only: To fight with the people and to lead
the people in revolution." He was not quite a god, according to her,
but he was "the instilled hope and spirit of his people and all peoples
. . . a prophet [and] a leader . . . who is able to help the people understand the swiftness and fierceness with which they must move, if
they would survive."

Teko, with some help from his wife, Yolanda, wrote a passionate
exhortation to his "white brothers" to join him in the black revolution
to overthrow their bourgeois way of life. It was full of his usual vulgarities but it did express his own peculiar way of thinking:

"Greetings to the people. My name is Teko. I am a white revolutionary and a soldier in the Symbionese Liberation Army. I have a
message for all my white brothers who have not yet come forward to
fight for the freedom of all the people. Contrary to what many of us
may think, the special privileges we as a group have gained for ourselves through the oppression of all other people has never secured for
us the freedom we desire. White men must understand that they will
live under the threat of death as long as they continue to oppress the
members of any class or group who have the strength and determination to fight back.

"White men themselves have only one avenue to freedom and that is
to join in fighting to the death those who are and those who aspire to
be the slave masters of the world. Many of us have been 'bold' enough
to intellectualize about revolution, but far too chickenshit to get down
and help make it. Most of us have been nearly fatally stricken with the
vile sickness of racism. Again, most of us have been immobilized by
our sexist egos and have watched and done nothing as our sisters have
rushed by us into battle. We have fooled ourselves into believing that
Madison Avenue piggery will bring us eternal bourgeois happiness. If
we haven't bought into the racist, sexist, capitalist, imperialist program,

we have 'greened-out' in Mendocino and New Hampshire. To Black
people, who lead our struggle to freedom, we have proved to be the
racist punks of the world when we kick back and live off the blood and
lives of the people."

Teko urged everyone out there to stop intellectualizing and to join
the SLA in "unleashing the most devastating revolutionary violence
ever imagined, by proving that all races and groups of people can unite
and fight together for the true freedom of us all."

I practiced reading my script two or three times for the whole group
before I got it right. To satisfy them I knew I had to make it sound as
shocking and as insulting as possible. Privately I had to admit that
Gelina had been very effective in getting certain personal touches into
the message. I hoped that my parents would realize that I could not
possibly have adopted some of the ideas or used some of the words in
the script.

I started off by condemning the speculation in the press that I had
been "brainwashed" in some of the things I had said in my last script:

"I would like to begin this statement by informing the public that I
wrote what I am about to say. It's what I feel. I have *never* been
forced to say anything on any tape. Nor have I been brainwashed,
drugged, tortured, hypnotized or in any way confused. As George
Jackson wrote, 'It's me, the way I want it, the way I see it.' "

I then went on to castigate my mother and father for failing to secure
my safety, for the food distribution plan, for cooperating with the FBI,
for not getting Little and Remiro released on bail, for my mother's acceptance of a second term on the Board of Regents of the University of
California and thereby risking my immediate execution by the SLA.

Gelina added a fine touch when she had me address the following
words ostensibly to Steven Weed, of whom I had not thought in ages:
"Steven, I know that you are beginning to realize that there is no such
thing as neutrality in time of war. There can be no compromise as your
experience with the FBI must have shown you. You have been
harassed by the FBI because of your supposed connections with so-
called radicals, and some people have even gone so far as to suggest
that I arranged my own arrest. We both know what really came down
that Monday night—but you don't know what's happened since then. I
have changed—grown. I've become conscious and can never go back
to the life we led before. What I'm saying may seem odd to you and to
my old friends, but love doesn't mean the same thing to me anymore.

My love has expanded as a result of my experiences to embrace all people. It's grown into an unselfish love for my comrades here, in prison and on the streets. A love that comes from the knowledge that 'no one is free until we are all free.' While I wish you could be a comrade, I don't expect it—all I expect is that you try to understand the changes I've gone through."

Would Steve believe that I really believed all of that? I did not think so. But then again, I did not want him going about saying it was all a sham. I wanted my SLA comrades to believe that I believed every word they wrote for me.

Now came the choicest bit of rhetoric: "I have been given the choice of (1) being released in a safe area, or (2) joining the forces of the Symbionese Liberation Army and fighting for my freedom and the freedom of all oppressed people. I have chosen to stay and fight.

"One thing which I learned is that the corporate ruling class will do anything in their power in order to maintain their position of control over the masses, even if this means the sacrifice of one of their own. It should be obvious that people who don't even care about their own children couldn't possibly care about anyone else's children. The things which are precious to those people are their money and power—and they will never willingly surrender either. People should not have to humiliate themselves by standing in lines in order to be fed, nor should they have to live in fear for their lives and the lives of their children as Tyrone Guyton's mother will sadly attest to."*

The next tirade was directed at my father and it was so ridiculous and far from the truth that I hoped my father would readily see through it. He had to know, I thought, that this sort of language, and the cheap shot about Hitler, was not my style at all. The words about the energy crisis were a dead giveaway: My father would know that I would never say such things to him, for he was expounding all the time before my kidnapping on the public's apathy about the reality of the energy shortage in the United States. But Cin did not know that and it was Cin who had insisted that Gelina put those words in the message. He thought nuclear power plants were the ultimate fascist plot.

Nevertheless, I read my script with aplomb: "Dad, you said that you were concerned with my life and you also said that you were concerned

---

* Tyrone Guyton was a fourteen-year-old boy who had been shot and killed in a fracas with the police of Emeryville, near Berkeley.

with the life and interests of all oppressed people in this country, but you are a liar in both areas and as a member of the ruling class I know for sure that yours and Mom's interests are never the interests of the people. Dad, you said you would see about getting more job opportunities for the people, but why haven't you warned the people what is going to happen to them—that actually the few jobs they still have will be taken away.

"You, a corporate liar, of course will say that you don't know what I am talking about, but I ask you then to prove it. Tell the poor and oppressed of this nation what the corporate state is about to do, warn black and poor people that they are about to be murdered down to the last man, woman and child. If you're so interested in the people, why don't you tell them what the energy crisis really is? Tell them how it's nothing more than a means to get public approval for a massive program to build nuclear power plants all over this nation. Tell the people that the entire corporate state is, with the aid of this massive power supply, about to totally automate the entire industrial state, to the point that in the next five years all that will be needed will be a small class of button pushers; tell the people, Dad, that all the lower class and at least half the middle class will be unemployed in the next three years and that the removal of expendable excess, the removal of unneeded people, has already started. I want you to tell the people the truth. Tell them how the law-and-order programs are just a means to remove so-called violent—meaning aware—individuals from the community in order to facilitate the controlled removal of unneeded labor forces from this country, in the same way that Hitler controlled the removal of the Jews from Germany.

"I should have known that if you and the rest of the corporate state were willing to do this to millions of people to maintain power and to serve your needs, you would also kill me if necessary to serve those same needs. How long will it take before white people in this country understand that what happens to a black child happens sooner or later to a white child? How long will it be before we all understand that we must fight for our freedom?

"I have been given the name Tania after a comrade who fought alongside Che in Bolivia for the people of Bolivia. I embrace the name with the determination to continue fighting with her spirit. There is no victory in half-assed attempts at revolution. I know Tania dedicated her life to the people, fighting with total dedication and an intense

desire to learn, which I will continue in the oppressed American people's revolution. All colors of string in the web of humanity yearn for
freedom."

The final item that Gelina wrote for me in my communiqué was
addressed to Joe Remiro and Russ Little in San Quentin, rather
mawkish lines of love and comradeship, which cleverly contained a secret message from the SLA. Joe Remiro, who had been Gelina's lover,
would know that the message came from Gelina and he would recognize the key words. In fact, the words "All colors of string in the web
of humanity yearn for freedom" announced that a secret message was
coming. Bo and Osi could not miss it and no one else could recognize
it. As it was explained to me, the SLA had always had a special way of
communicating with one another when they could not meet: They
would tack a piece of colored yarn to certain prearranged light poles as
a coded signal. Blue yarn meant a message had been left at a dead
drop; green yarn meant that the person away from the safehouse was
supposed to telephone in; yellow yarn meant that a meeting had been
called. Hence, for Bo and Osi in prison "all colors of string" meant a
message was coming. Furthermore, "yearn" was pretty close to "yarn,"
so as to leave no doubt.

Gelina put more work into this seemingly innocent paragraph than
she did in all the rest of the script:

"Osceola and Bo: Even though we have never met, I feel like I know
you. Timing brought me to you and I'm fighting for your freedom and
the freedom of all prisoners in mind. In the strenuous jogs that life
takes, you are pillars of strength to me. If I'm feeling down, I think of
you, of where you are and why you are there, and my determination
grows stronger. It's good to see that your spirits are so high in spite of
the terrible conditions. Even though you aren't here, you are with other
strong comrades, and the three of us are learning together—I in an environment of love, and you in one of hate, in the belly of the fascist
beast. We have grown closer to the people and become stronger
through our experiences. I have learned how vicious the pig really is,
and our comrades are teaching me to attack with even greater vicious-
ness, in the knowledge that the people will win. I send greetings to
Death Row Jeff, Al Taylor, and Raymond Scott. Your concern for my
safety is matched by my concern for yours. We share a common goal as
revolutionaries knowing that Comrade George [Jackson] lives."

The key words were "freedom," "prisoners," "strenuous jogs," and "pillars." Cin and the others were certain Osceola and Bo would catch those words and their meaning. "Pillars" referred to some pillars at Lake Merritt in Oakland, where they used to go jogging together before the two had been arrested. "Freedom" for the "prisoners" meant that a message concerning SLA plans to set up a jailbreak for the two would be left to be picked up at a prearranged dead drop by one of those pillars at Lake Merritt.

I signed off my taped message with the words that Che Guevara's Tania Burke had used, as noted in the book: "It is in the spirit of Tania that I say, *Patria o Muerte, venceremos.*" Which meant "Fatherland or Death, we shall be victorious."

Of all the individual messages in this communiqué, Cinque's was the most fierce. He had worked on it for the most part by himself and then ranted and raved when others attempted to change some of his words and grammatical syntax. But the worst arguments arose over Cin's issuing "death warrants" for three people. One was Colston Westbrook, the coordinator of the Black Cultural Association at the Vacaville prison, who had worked with Cin and Cujo and the others at the prison. Another was Chris Thompson, a young black radical who had been a friend of most of the SLA members before they had gone underground, and the third was Robyn Steiner, who had been Russ Little's girlfriend. Cin pronounced the death sentences upon all three because he insisted they were informing to the FBI. He never explained how he could know such a thing.

I listened in amazement as one or two in the room objected to the issuing of death warrants as a matter of policy, and most of them, I think, pleaded with Cin specifically to rescind the death warrant for Robyn Steiner. They did not think that she would inform on them. But Cin said that he had warned her of the death warrant if she did not return to the SLA and she had refused. "She knows the Codes of War," he shouted. "If she's not with us, she's against us. She had her chance!"

Both Gelina and Fahizah tried most earnestly to dissuade Cin, saying that Osi would be very upset when he learned of the death warrant. But Cin was not to be dissuaded. He declared that both Osi and Bo deserved to have death warrants issued against them. They had violated the Codes of War by allowing themselves to be captured alive. They were supposed to have had their weapons with them at all times, Cin said. Then they should have blasted the pigs who tried to arrest them.

They were stupid to have been captured by a traffic cop who had made a routine stop to question them, thinking that they were lost. But, said Cin, he would send Osi and Bo a message, forgiving them for their breach of the SLA Codes of War, so that they would know he had no intention of punishing them for their failures.

So, in his taped message, the SLA Field Marshal declared: "The following are enemies of the people . . . and have been found guilty of working and informing to the enemy against the people and death warrants have been issued by this court against them and they should be shot on sight by any of the people's forces:

"Robyn Steiner: female, white, age 20, hazel eyes, brown hair, 5-4, wears contact lenses, 115 pounds, past resident of Berkeley, now living in Florida, an informer to the FBI.

"Chris Thompson: male, black, brown eyes, black hair, 6-3, Berkeley resident, is a government agent, paid informant for the FBI.

"Colston Westbrook: male, black, age 35, brown eyes, brown hair, 5-8, 210 pounds, Berkeley language instructor, resident of Oakland, is a government agent. . . .

"These subjects are to be shot on sight wherever found and at any time."

Cin did not stop there. He went on to declare that in the future no prisoners would be taken from the ruling class: "All corporate enemies of the people will be shot on sight at any time and at any place. This order is permanent, until such time as all enemy forces have either surrendered or been destroyed." In other words, it was all-out war from now on.

As far as I was concerned, Cin declared that the SLA operation was terminated: I had joined the SLA and no longer was considered an enemy.

As for Osceola and Bo, the Field Marshal sounded most sympathetic: "As you know, we have learned a hard lesson from our mistakes and will learn from this for the future and the war that we the people will win. I am sure that you understand that under our Codes of War there can be no surrender to the enemy, at any time or at any price. You both have shown correct actions in recognizing that even though you are innocent of any crimes, it is not possible for you to receive a fair trial in the enemy's arena. I deeply regret that you were not offensively prepared to attack rather than be seized by the enemy. I send you my love and the love of all your comrades, and courage in your determination to carry on the struggle even from that side of the wall, as we will never relent from this end. In this way, we do expect to meet again."

The order of the day was "Quiet on the Set" while each of us recorded our messages in the small, supposedly soundproof booth which had once been my prison. As ever, General Gelina was the director, exhorting each of us to put emotion and determination into our voices. As I sat in that small pantry closet, reading my handwritten script into the tape recorder by the light of a flashlight, I thought I was getting pretty good at this revolutionary acting. I just hoped that my parents would not be too upset but there was not much I could do about slipping in any secret message to them. I had to read my script as written. When Cin read his own message, decreeing death and destruction, I prayed that my parents would not be overly frightened for me because of the lunatic ravings of this man who was now my General Field Marshal.

The tape-recorded communiqué was dispatched on April 3, and I thought: Oh, my God, this is Trish's birthday. What irony that on the birthday of my best friend, when I would normally have joined in the celebration with her, here I was joining the Symbionese Liberation Army and bidding goodbye to all those I had loved all of my life, all of my past life.

The next day, all of the comrades enjoyed the hoopla of news bulletins on radio and television and in the newspapers. The SLA and Patty Hearst were bigger news than ever. Most of the media took my announcement at face value and speculated from there. Others offered the opinion that I had been somehow brainwashed. That, of course, made Cinque furious. "You ain't brainwashed, are you?" he challenged me again and again.

"Oh, no," I declared. "Of course I'm not brainwashed."

"You better not be, 'cause I don't want any brainwashed soldiers around here," he swore.

Then he continued in a sweet voice: "The people love you, Tania. You've given up your past life to become a freedom fighter, and they love you for that. You're a symbol of hope to them, Tania. You have a lot to live up to, but the comrades will help you."

The people's survey of banks most easily robbed came to an end on the following day. By that time, our scouts had accumulated a large array of photographs, diagrams, layouts, and commentaries on four or five of the best prospects. Each was discussed in great detail. Cinque pondered and mulled over the momentous decision, and to help him think and decide, he took to drinking more and more cheap plum wine. The kitchen counter was lined with half-gallon bottles of his wine. As I watched him imbibe glass after glass, swishing the wine around in his mouth before swallowing, pushing out his lower lip, creasing his brow with worry lines as he contemplated our future action, I could not help but think he was nothing more than a drunk, playacting the role of the macho revolutionary. It also occurred to me that by his actions he was lending unnecessary credence to an unattractive stereotype.

But these thoughts concerned me for only a short time because Cin then unexpectedly shocked me once again. Of the four or five different banks being studied, Cin chose the Hibernia Bank branch in the Sunset District of San Francisco. Shivers ran down my spine at the coincidence. He could not know and yet he had chosen it. Of all the banks in the city, this one was special to me. Trish's father was president of the Hibernia Bank.

CHAPTER

SEVEN

ON THAT APPOINTED Monday morning of April 15, 1974, our weapons for that day were lined up neatly in their proper order along the far wall of the bedroom. They were fully loaded, ready to go. When I woke up that morning, I simply could not believe that this day had arrived and that I, Patricia Campbell Hearst, was going to take part in a bank robbery. I could never have even imagined such a thing. Yet, in the past two weeks, just about every moment of every day had centered on the planning and preparations for this day. I knew more about the Hibernia Bank branch at Noriega Street and Twenty-second Avenue than I knew about my parents' home in Hillsborough. I could visualize the two swinging glass front doors, the eight teller positions, the three writing counters, the executive desks area, and the entrance where the armed guard usually stood—and I'd never once been in or near that particular bank. It was all very much like a dream. Whenever I dreamed, there was always one deep level of consciousness which somehow informed me that everything was unreal. But now, preparing to rob a bank, which was so alien to everything in my nature, I could not shake off the same sort of sensation, only reversed: I knew it was real and yet, deep down inside of me, I felt that it was all a dream; it could not be really happening.

All through the planning, everyone called it an "action," a "combat operation," or an "expropriation," never a bank robbery. In fact, they never referred to it as a bank. It was always the "bakery"—because "that is where the bread is." It was all justified as a revolutionary expropriation of the corporate-military state's property for the benefit of the people's war. Except for me, all the others would wear disguises to confuse the authorities on exact identifications. This was to be, according to our General Field Marshal, a carefully planned, fully prepared military action. Inside the bank, we would communicate with each other by number rather than name. Therefore, Cin assigned each of us a number: Cinque was, of course, number One. Zoya was Two, Fahizah was Three, Teko was Four, Cujo was Five, Yolanda was Six, Gelina was Seven, Gabi was Eight, and, last but not least, I was Nine.

So that we would all become thoroughly accustomed to our own number and that of everyone else, the use of our revolutionary names was forbidden for the duration of the planning and the operation. We would call each other by his or her number all the time. Any lapses would be punished, decreed Cin. Fahizah took to calling Cin Numero Uno and the others liked it so much they used that nickname for him frequently and affectionately ever afterward. Gelina, happy as ever, was delighted with her number: Seven was a lucky number and was symbolically significant because it matched the seven heads of the SLA cobra. My own number gave a fair indication of my rank in this organization. Other than that, I could fathom no particular significance to Cin's assignment of the numbers. While the whole nation outside was learning my new name, Tania, inside the SLA safehouse I began to think of myself impersonally not as Tania but as number Nine.

Once the target had been chosen, different surveillance teams went out for the next several days to check and recheck the Hibernia Bank at Noriega and Twenty-second, as well as the entire area around the bank. Twenty-second Avenue was a wide residential street with little traffic and no stop signs at the intersections. The getaway would be fast and unimpeded—a few turns and then a transfer to a switch car, and within minutes we would be away free. The surveillance teams returned each time with new diagrams of the inside of the bank, which were compared with ones previously made, until Cin was satisfied that we had a faultless rendition of the layout of the bank. Then it was redrawn carefully on a large sheet of poster board, which was taped to the wall so that we could refer to it at all times. We all studied road maps of the area, so that no one would get lost. Map study was perhaps my favorite activity. I much preferred sitting in a corner feigning a concentrated study of a road map of San Francisco streets, while the others were running about practicing more strenuous activities. Everyone kept busy just about all the time preparing for the forthcoming SLA combat operation.

Cin divided us into two combat teams. The inside team would enter the bank, take control of the fifteen or twenty employees as well as all the customers there at the time, while one of us would leap over the tellers' counter and scoop up money from the cash drawers. The outside team would cover us from another car across Noriega Street, in line with the entrance to the bank. If the police arrived, the outside team would open fire on them, alerting those inside the bank to fight their way out. We would all escape together or not at all. Anyone wounded in the action would not be left behind. It was the responsibility of all the comrades to help any sister or brother in trouble. Cin reminded me in particular of the Codes of War: In any action, we would all work together; any comrade who failed in his or her duty or who endangered the lives of others would be shot on the spot. We were a disciplined army, Cin said, and we would act like one. There was no mistaking his warning.

After some deliberation, Cin selected the ones he wanted on the inside team. He, of course, would be going into the bank in order to take personal command of the operation. Next he picked me. Then he selected Fahizah and Zoya and Gabi. Five of us would be inside the bank; the other four would be posted as lookout and backup outside. I tried to get my assignment switched. There was no way I wanted to go inside that bank, threatening people with a gun, exposing myself to possible police gunfire or SLA execution for any slip-up. I wanted no part in this whole scheme, but if I had to participate, I much preferred a passive role in the parked car outside. I tried to explain to Cin that I was not the proper one to go inside the bank: I was too weak physically, I was the least trained, I might not be able to carry it off at all. But he simply stared me down. "You have to go into that bank, Nine, 'cause I want all the pigs to know you're really an SLA soldier now. I want your picture to be taken by that bank camera, so there'll be no doubt, and I'm going to want you to make a little speech, saying who you are and what you're doing, so nobody can say you were brainwashed or anything like that. Understand?"

Of course I understood. Brainwashing had become a popular topic of discussion in our safehouse. Every bit of this controversy was followed intently by the SLA. The comrades were aghast at the idea that some people did not believe I had voluntarily joined. Cin insisted that such speculation proved that the ruling class simply could not accept the reality of someone like me transferring her allegiance to the poor and the oppressed of the world. For the SLA, such speculation was proof that "the pigs and the fascist media were feeding lies to the people," trying to explain away the great change of heart that I had undergone. And what did I think? I was so intent upon convincing Cin and the others of my sincerity, I wished the speculation would end and would not endanger my newfound "freedom." I wanted the SLA to believe in me completely, and to that end I told myself I would accept whatever they told me, and do whatever I had to do to survive. In any event, I had my assignment. I would go into the bank with the others.

Cujo, on the other hand, tried to persuade Cin to allow him to go into the bank. Cujo kept saying he wanted "real action" and that "he wanted to kill some pigs." Cin assured him that his role was as important as ours: If the police arrived on the scene, all of us inside the bank would depend upon him and the others to open fire with their automatic weapons and assure our escape. Cujo was young and he still wanted to prove himself. He thought it unfair that it was always his job to drive backup vehicles—his job during my kidnapping, too. He and Teko would be stationed at the street-side windows of the car with submachine guns; Cujo would be at the wheel and Gelina would be in behind him in the back seat of the car. Throughout the planning of the robbery, Cujo would sit there rubbing his hands together and muttering, "Oh, I hope they come . . . I want to kill some pigs . . . yes, I want to kill some pigs."

Gabi would drive the car carrying the inside team to the bank. She would park alongside the blank wall of the bank on Twenty-second Avenue, just beyond the corner of Noriega. The curb would be free because it was a bus stop, marked in red. We would leave the car there unattended. Gabi and I would enter the bank first. Our weapons would be hidden under our coats. Through the glass doors, we would then turn to the right and walk past the guard toward the rear of the bank, stopping at the third writing counter. At that time Cin, Zoya, and Fahizah would enter. Cin would announce the holdup. Each of us would take our assigned positions: Gabi in the rear of the bank with her shotgun; I positioned between the second and third writing counters, covering the bank personnel and customers; Fahizah posted near the front door, covering people in that area and the entrance to the bank. Cin would take over the bank guard's position in front of the tellers' counter, supervising the whole operation. Cin and Fahizah would be armed with the submachine guns; Zoya, the most nimble and athletic of all of us, would jump over the tellers' counter and empty the cash drawers of all the bills into her stuff bag, a nylon drawstring bag ordinarily used to hold a sleeping bag. She would carry only a revolver, which she would use to wave the tellers away from their open cash drawers.

Every single detail of this plan was discussed, every eventuality taken into consideration, every idea debated and decided. The operation had three purposes: to expropriate money to finance the revolution, to prove to the outside world that I had truly joined the revolution, and to prove further that the SLA soldiers were true revolutionaries who were daring, determined, violent, fearless, and to be feared by the capitalist ruling class. Teko urged Cin to shoot the bank guard immediately and then announce the holdup. That would prove to all those inside the bank that we meant business, he said. The guard was wearing a gun and that made him an "enemy pig" who was fair game in wartime, Teko claimed. But several others dissented, saying the cell really did not know who he was or whether or not he deserved to die. Fahizah, who had seen him on one of her surveillances, said that the guard was an old, retired man, who probably was trying to earn a few extra bucks doing guard duty at a bank. Others worried that shooting the guard might "freak out" the others in the bank and there was no telling what someone might do then. Cin decided the issue: The bank guard would live, unless he made a move for his weapon. Cin would seize the guard's revolver and make him lie down on the floor with the others, he said. Only if the guard resisted would Cin shoot him. If *anyone* in the bank resisted or disobeyed orders or endangered the operation, we were to shoot that person without hesitation. That would prove our determination and the shooting would then be the fault of the person who resisted, not that of the SLA. I listened to all of this, appalled. I did not dare tell them that this was my best friend's father's bank, that I had known the family since I was nine years old. If I had told them this, I feared, they would surely decide to shoot the bank guard or the bank manager or make some outrageous demands on the Tobins. I thanked God that Cin had never asked me detailed questions about my friends and that neither Trish nor any of the other Tobin names had come up during my interrogation.

When the plans were set, we practiced over and over exactly how each of us would enter the bank and what we had to do once inside. We rehearsed it as if it were a play opening on Broadway. The whole operation was blocked and timed. We were to assume, Cin said, that from the time he announced the holdup, the bank cameras would be taking our pictures, an alarm would be rung to summon the police, and that we had to be out of the bank with the money in one and one half minutes, no more. Cin would clock the operation inside the bank and announce the time for our safe departure.

Each day we trained more and more. I was told how to grip my little carbine and swing it to and fro, constantly shifting my weight from one foot to another. Painfully, I learned how to crouch lower and lower, keeping my weapon level with the ground and moving it from side to side. Cin and Teko were my weapons instructors, but the others chimed in also. Zoya would sneak up behind me and kick me in the shins or behind the knees, like a drill sergeant, telling me, "Crouch lower . . . get your ass down . . . you're not trying hard enough." Teko showed me how to load and unload my semi-automatic carbine and he taught me how to handle a revolver and an automatic pistol. He instructed me in how to aim at the head, chest, or stomach, how to quick-draw, how to fire the first shot from a standing position, step to one side or the other, crouch and get off my second and third shots from a crouch, making myself a smaller target. There was no real chain of command in the SLA. Cin was the leader. When he spoke, the others obeyed. Fahizah was nominally second-in-command, but she seldom did more than echo Cin's orders or implement them. I was told that we all were equals, that anyone could give commands to the others and should be obeyed. But it did seem to me that there was a pecking order, and I was definitely at the bottom of it. Cujo, Gabi, and Tania (Five, Eight, and Nine) were the "grunts" in this army; all the rest were officers, giving orders.

Every morning I ran around that hot, dark room with the carbine in my hands, a heavy pack strapped to my back and thick hiking boots on my feet. I was always tired to the point of exhaustion. My nerves were frayed with anxiety. No matter how much peanut butter or how many dishes of rice I consumed, I did not seem to gain any weight. Zoya or Teko or someone was forever telling me that I was not trying hard enough to become a good urban guerrilla. Cin was constantly urging me on, to eat more, to do more push-ups, to do more of everything.

But then he was urging everyone else to work harder too. There was no rest for this determined Liberation Army. "You're the people's army and you're a disgrace to the people," Cin would say over and over to his soldiers in his incessant pep talks. "Now, shape up . . . you got to shape up if you're goin' to lead the people . . . the people love you 'cause you're fighting for them, so you got to be good . . ."

Cin did not do any calisthenics. He did not run around with a full pack on his back, practicing the combat drills. He was the leader and he never hesitated to remind you of that. "I could be out leading black soldiers—I could have a whole army of black soldiers behind me —but I'm spending my time with you whites because I want to teach you and to help you . . ." And they all believed him.

As we trained for the bank robbery, he told us on several occasions that our top priority in this or any other action was to protect our leader. "Where would you all be, if I got shot?" he would ask, and the others would hang their heads. "I'm the black leadership of the SLA. Without me, you'd all be nothing. There'd be no revolution. So you got to protect your leader in any operation—even if you got to risk your life doin' it."

I could hardly believe he was serious or that the others would be so beholden to him. To me, he seemed to be a strutting egomaniac, swilling plum wine most of the day, pinching the girls, fondling a breast, doing whatever he damned well pleased, while all the others struggled mightily to shape up to his fantasy of an elite army of revolutionary cadre.

The women, as well as the men, often went about the room bare-chested. With the windows shut and heavily draped, the room was usually warm and sometimes stifling hot. The vigorous calisthenics would have us all sweating within minutes and oftentimes Cin would urge us, "Come on, girls, it's hot . . . take your shirts off." At first, I was embarrassed as I followed along. But after a while, it became quite ordinary to exercise bare-breasted, even with Cinque ogling and grinning. Gelina and Yolanda, more than any of the others, seemed to enjoy going about without their tops on most of the day. Yet it was clear that their attitudes on nakedness were quite different. Gelina was quite unaffected going about semi-nude, as though she were in a nudist camp where no sexual connotations intruded. Yolanda, on the other hand, was very conscious of her own nudity and its effect on the men, often glancing down at her own breasts in silent admiration. On several occasions when she attended the cell's meetings bare-breasted, Cin would tell her, "Put your shirt on now; it's distracting."

In any army, privacy is a luxury, but in this people's army there was no privacy at all. No one had the luxury of a private life. Their lives were devoted to the people and to the revolution—or so they all told me over and over. Sex itself had a very low priority. Love was a manifestation of bourgeois mentality and therefore nonexistent or never admitted to in this determined little band. Fornication was simply another necessary bodily function. It was impressed upon me that the SLA did not approve of the Weather Underground's dictum that every member was obliged to have sex with every other member in order to free himself or herself from all sexual inhibitions. In the SLA, no one was forced to have sex with anyone else. But sex was a natural need, and since we all were forced to remain underground in our safehouse, it was comradely to oblige a comrade in his or her needs.

Actually, there was not all that much sexual activity going on in the SLA. There were no orgies, no wild parties, no group activities. Usually, it was one of the women who would approach one of the men and say, quite matter-of-factly, "Let's fuck." Even that did not happen all that often because, I suspect, all were fatigued at the end of a full day of combat training. Sleep was blissful, even with the rotation of night watches which limited one's rest to about five hours. When one got the mid-watch, that five hours would be broken into two two-and-one-half-hour naps. Sex was not a private matter in the SLA. Everyone knew what was going on at all times. Standing watch, one could not help but overhear the grunts and sighs and thrashing going on in the darkened room. It was hardly conducive to romance.

Despite all the revolutionary theories on the subject, however, there was within the SLA a natural pairing off. And even that ran into some difficulties. Remiro and Little were in prison, which left more women than men in the remaining ranks of the SLA. Cinque usually slept with Gelina in the luxury of the Murphy bed. He obviously preferred her. But occasionally he bunked in with Fahizah to oblige her. It was no secret that she adored him. Fahizah struggled to overcome her jealousy, which she described as a remnant of her past bourgeois mentality. She would sit for hours with Gelina in long discussions aimed at coping with and overcoming her feelings of jealousy, which she knew were unworthy of her role as an urban guerrilla in the people's army. Teko bedded down with Yolanda, despite all their daytime bickerings

and agreed-upon disdain of monogamy, and as often as not the two of
them climbed into bed with Zoya. Zoya, it seemed to me, was as nonchalant about sleeping with a woman as with a man. She had once
been Gabi's lover, before the SLA had gone underground, but now
slept with Yolanda as often as she did with Teko and occasionally she
would approach Cujo to spend the night with her. I became the personal property of Cujo. He was undemanding and a far cry from the
young romantic lover the media would portray in days to come. Cujo
seemed to live in a fantasy world of his own, dreaming of the day he
would become the Che Guevara-type hero of the United States, serving
under Cinque, who was the Castro of our coming revolution. He was
like a little boy, always unsure of himself, bragging one moment of
glories to come and full of doubts at other times. He was also a bundle
of nerves, self-centered, and suffering frequent stomach upsets, which
he attributed to an ulcer condition, particularly after dinner each night.
The others complained that Cujo simply ate too much.

Poor Gabi. She was like the cheese that stands alone at the end of
the children's game "The Farmer in the Dell." Nobody wanted her. She
was, in several ways, pathetic. She stood out in this group as a misfit,
even more than I did. She was big, overweight, and awkward in comparison to the other women, and there was little, if anything, militant
or combative in her bearing or demeanor. I considered her the most
sensitive person in the group. She should not have been in the SLA
at all and it was understood that she had followed Zoya into the
group because she was so smitten with her former lover that she could
not bear to give her up. Yet Zoya was cruelly indifferent to her once
she had joined. Even Teko, who was hardly the kindly type, brought
up Gabi's dilemma at a cell meeting, saying that Gabi's sexual needs
were not being taken care of by her comrades. But no one volunteered,
and I am sure Gabi was too sensitive to make any demands. In fact,
Teko volunteered his services, but Gabi gently declined. Cinque
seemed particularly uncomfortable in handling Gabi's lesbianism. Her
sexuality was beyond his realm of understanding. There was awk-
wardness there that arose in no other relationship. In her combat training he berated her unmercifully and it seemed apparent that he
simply did not like her or understand her. He always positioned her in
the place of most danger. Her combat position in the apartment, for instance, was in the kitchen, facing the front door, where she would be in
the first line of fire. But, for that matter, my own combat position was

at her side, also facing the front door. In the bank operation, we two were to be the ones to enter first and be positioned farthest away from the escape route.

Gabi's real name was Camilla Hall. Her father was a Lutheran minister, who had been a missionary in Africa and who had taught and counseled students at several colleges in Minnesota. She had been particularly close to her parents, having lost two brothers and a sister to childhood diseases. Gabi was artistically gifted, writing poetry, painting, and drawing after graduating from college. She traveled to South America and to Europe, and yet, because of her homosexuality, she was unhappy wherever she went. She tried social work, identifying with the downtrodden, and then she tried to eke out a living by selling her drawings. But she discovered her first glimpse of happiness, I believe, when she lived with Zoya in Berkeley and found that her lesbianism was accepted there as nowhere else.

During those first two weeks, as I tried to fit in with the others, one after another came to me with stories of his or her past life. Usually the point was to explain how they became conscious of the plight of the minorities in America, how they came to feel a kinship for black people in general and particularly the blacks who were in prisons. I never could be sure how much of what they told me was true and how much was exaggeration or pure fantasy. The newspapers occasionally ran stories about their backgrounds, giving their real names, and what I did not learn from these sources Gelina told me in a never-ending stream of vignettes. Gelina was a natural gossip. She loved to talk and to be with someone, rather than alone with her own thoughts.

Gelina had grown up as Angela DeAngelis, a devout Catholic in a fairly affluent, middle-class family, in a small town outside of Newark, New Jersey. She was an honor student and captain of the cheerleaders in her local high school and had gone on to Indiana University. There she majored in drama, and met her husband-to-be, Gary Atwood, who had been the star of the university's theatrical group. There too she had met Teko and Yolanda, whose real names were Bill and Emily Harris. Bill Harris had been a drama major and Emily had majored in English literature. The two couples became fast friends, a foursome, together all the time. That was in the late sixties, when they were into the anti-Establishment, anti-Vietnam War movements on campus, and into drugs as well. Angela, Bill, and Emily had gone on to get their teaching credentials, as a way of earning a living just in case stage careers did not work out for Angela and Bill. Only Gary did not compromise. And it was Gary who took Angela to San Francisco and Berkeley to pursue their acting careers. Bill stayed on in Indiana with Emily to earn a master's degree in urban education.

Gelina never ceased to assure me how much she loved the theater. The high point in her life had been playing Thea in Ibsen's *Hedda Gabler* for the Company Theater of Berkeley in 1972. Her best friend, Kathleen Soliah, played the title role. But Gelina could not earn a living acting; nor could Gary. Along with her friend Kathy, she went to work as a waitress in an a fancy restaurant in San Francisco, wearing a skimpy, sexist outfit for the business luncheon crowd, and acted in serious theater at night. As she became more and more involved in women's liberation, the plight of the poor, and Marxism, her marriage broke up. (Gary, it appears, was more interested in his acting career than in political theories.) Gelina left him in August 1973 and began dating Russell Little (Osceola), who introduced her to his best friend, Joe Remiro (Bo), and another friend, Willie Wolfe (Cujo). They were all non-student radicals involved with various splinter groups who believed that the time for "the revolution" was drawing near and they wanted to be in the forefront of the ensuing battle. Joe Remiro, who had been a combat infantryman in the Vietnam War, gave classes on the use of weapons at a rifle range in the Oakland hills for all those who wanted to learn. Little and Wolfe were his two assistants. They were also involved in the "Vietnam Veterans Against the War" and in helping radicalize black men in the state prisons.

From what I could gather, various radical groups were smuggling revolutionary literature to the prisoners, holding classes within the prisons on Marxist theory, and generally working to awaken and re-educate the oppressed who were behind bars. How they managed to accomplish this under the eyes of the authorities amazed me. But the various methods were explained by my comrades. The authorities did not attend the prison classes and therefore had no idea of what was being taught; nor did they inspect the actual texts of the books sent in under innocuous book jackets. They also did not check very carefully the false identity cards presented by known radicals who came to visit these prisoners. Thus, prisoners, most of whom had little or no education before, were given the opportunity to study these persuasive books which explained their plight to them in terms of Marxist and Maoist political theory. Moreover, the prisoners were delighted to be visited

and "educated" by the bevy of young, college-age girls who came to indoctrinate them.

The stories of Cinque's exploits were recounted to me in a variety of
versions, depending upon who was doing the telling. But it was clear
that while serving a five-year-to-life sentence at San Quentin, Donald
DeFreeze had become politically radicalized and been reborn as
Cinque Mtume, the Fifth Prophet, and had taken up the cause of *the
people*. Before that he had been a poor, oppressed, bewildered black,
in and out of county jails and state penitentiaries since the age of sixteen.

Cinque's escape from prison was never adequately explained to me,
but it seemed he was transferred from the state prison at Vacaville to
Soledad Prison in December 1972. Although Soledad was a maximum
security institution, DeFreeze was made a trustee and on March 5,
1973, he was given a choice assignment, minding a boiler room alone
outside the main walls of the prison itself. According to the comrades,
Cinque got the message to go forth and he simply strode out of the
boiler room that same night, climbed a little fence, and walked away.
He made his way to Oakland and then to Berkeley, where his friend
Russ Little lived at the so-called Peking House.

Russ Little had visited DeFreeze in prison on several occasions, and
when DeFreeze showed up unannounced at the door of Peking House,
Little took him in and hid him in the basement. This made many of the
other Peking House radicals very nervous, although it was against their
revolutionary principles to refuse him shelter. However, when De-
Freeze blithely showed up one night at a house party, after he had been
in the basement for a week, the majority at Peking House said that the
escaped convict would have to go. Russ Little scouted around and
found another haven for DeFreeze—in the nearby apartment of another radical friend, Pat Soltysik, who had recently split up with
Camilla Hall. Pat, who was by then calling herself Mizmoon, and
DeFreeze became lovers. They also became the founding members of
the SLA.

Patricia Soltysik (Zoya) had come from a large, happy, middle-class
family, growing up in a small town north of Santa Barbara, California,
with two older brothers and four younger sisters. Her father was a
pharmacist. She had gone to Berkeley on a state scholarship and there
she had become radicalized, first sexually and then politically. She and
Camilla Hall had lived openly as lovers for some time, writing poems

to one another. It was Camilla, in one of her poems, who had dubbed her Mizmoon, and Pat had liked the name so much that she legally adopted it as her first name. She had become an ardent feminist. Her brand of feminism insisted that women would be fully equal to men only when they became as strong, as macho, and as violent as men. Everything she did, it seemed, was aimed at this personal goal. She detested weakness, in herself or in anyone else. She was a difficult person to come to know and even more difficult to like once you knew her. She was cold and cruel and fiercely independent and I soon decided that my own best course was to stay away from her as much as possible.

Fahizah (Nancy Ling Perry) had such a close affinity to blacks that she could easily have been mistaken for one. While blindfolded, I had thought she was a black, and even with the blindfold off, her manner of speaking, walking, her posture led me to believe that at least one of her parents was black. But that was not even close to the truth. Her father was a successful white businessman in Santa Rosa, California, a Goldwater Republican. As a teenager she had worked in the 1964 Goldwater campaign and had attended the staid, conservative Whittier College, as had Richard Nixon before her. But then, after her freshman year, she had transferred to Berkeley, where she too had been radicalized. She had gone through the whole gamut—free speech, free sex, drugs, Maoism, prison reform—and then had found her salvation in the SLA. She had married a black jazz musician, Gilbert Perry, but that marriage had been a disaster. She had worked at one of the topless nightclubs in the North Beach section of San Francisco. In her slide downhill, abetted by an ever-increasing dependence on drugs, she had taken to prostitution. Nancy Ling Perry had found the world to be too cruel, too tough, and too dishonest to cope with. More than any of the others, she had been "born again" and found her own personal mission in life within the SLA, struggling to change that outside world. Of them all, she seemed the most naïvely dedicated to the cause.

It had been in August 1973 when "Ling" Perry, down and out after having left her husband, moved in with Mizmoon and DeFreeze to become the third member of the SLA. From about May to August of that year, DeFreeze and Mizmoon had tried to get down on paper the organization, the Codes of War, and the aims and goals of the SLA. Perry joined them in this and then in their recruiting drive. They were turned down again and again by black community groups who, taking one look at those ultra-radical proposals, had no wish to join in the SLA version of the coming revolution. But Russ Little, Joe Remiro, and Robyn Steiner joined and they brought in Angela Atwood in the fall of 1973. Willie Wolfe joined at about this time also, for he had been part of this radical fringe from the very start.

Cujo had been part of the movement to re-educate black prisoners long before the SLA was formed, heading a radical study group at the Vacaville prison. He too had come from an affluent, middle-class family before becoming "conscious." His father was a doctor. His real name was William Lawton Wolfe and, at twenty-two, he was the youngest of the SLA members before my own arrival. Raised in upstate New York and in Connecticut, Willie Wolfe had gone to a swank prep school in Massachusetts, where he had been a varsity swimmer and an editor of the school newspaper. Rather than go on to college, he became a social worker in Harlem for about a year, traveled in Europe, and then enrolled in Berkeley. He lived at the Peking House with Russ Little and found his friends among the most radical element of the Berkeley outcasts. His mission in life was to help the poor, oppressed blacks of the United States.

The Harrises were the last to join the SLA, not so much because they themselves hesitated as because it took a while for the others to trust them enough to allow them into their elite cadre. Having followed the Atwoods from Indiana to Berkeley, they became entwined with the same radical study groups, the prison reform movement, and the rifle-range practice. But from what I was told I gathered that as members of the intelligence unit they were not quite trusted enough to be told about the plans for the assassination of Marcus Foster before that combat action was carried out. Only afterward, when they still wanted to join the combat unit, were they invited in and they readily accepted.

All of them had become more and more radical in their philosophical beliefs at Berkeley and had banded together in the conviction that a violent rebellion against the state was the only salvation for the poor, for the oppressed, and for themselves. They were revolutionaries in search of a leader and only a black leader would do. And then they found Donald DeFreeze, who had been poor, oppressed, behind prison bars, and was willing to lead them. They all idolized Cinque as their leader, despite his drinking, his pinching and fondling of the girls, his strutting about, and his frequent abuse of anyone evoking his disfavor. No one dared criticize him. They might disagree and argue among themselves, but no one contradicted Cinque. He proclaimed that he was doing all of them a favor just by spending his time with them. They would never be as good as blacks, he would say, but he would try to help them shape up. Cujo was a fanatic follower, mesmerized, as though his one desire was to grow up to be as tough and as clairvoyant as Cinque. Teko, listening to exploits described by Cin, would often pound the floor or beat one fist into his other hand, and mutter, "Oh, I wish I were black!"

I feared and despised Cinque. He conducted or supervised almost all of my training those first two weeks, and although we were together all day long, day after day, he never made an overt sexual advance toward me. I dreaded that it would come. But then I surmised that he was too vain to do the asking: he expected me to approach him. Only then would he bestow his favors upon me. I was relieved to keep him at arm's length. Fortunately, he seemed as pleased as Cujo and Gelina that I had joined and was trying to learn my SLA combat skills. He kept telling me that my future role in the SLA would be to bring the children of the oppressors together with the children of the oppressed in the coming revolution.

I did not worry about the revolution half as much as I did about the coming bank robbery. That continued to scare me to death. I sincerely believed that I would not live through it. The police would interrupt and I would die in the shoot-out at the bank or during the getaway. It seemed to me that bank robbers were almost always caught. My worst fear, however, was that Cin would choose a propitious moment during the bank robbery to shoot me down. I did not know why that scenario came to my mind, but it was there, almost every time I contemplated my future with these people. I lived in constant fear. One way or another I would end up dead.

As a measure of subconscious self-defense, I kept telling myself that they would not really go through with it and rob a bank. It simply did not fit my indoctrinated image of the SLA. I thought they would call it off at the last moment, explaining that it all had been a sort of exercise. Nevertheless, we went on with our training every day. But even aside from these preparations, it was frightening just to be there, living in constant fear of the FBI and the police, listening to other wild schemes and dreams of the SLA revolution. One day when the doorbell rang, Cin was absolutely convinced that "the pigs" were outside. We all took our combat positions and Cin ordered Gabi to blast through the closed door with her shotgun. She stood there, trembling, the shotgun in her hands, refusing to fire, pleading that she would rather open the door first and see who was there. The bell rang again. Finally, common sense prevailed. She opened the door a slit, the shotgun in her other hand, out of sight, and then simply turned away some poor unsuspecting salesman. On another evening just before nightfall, two city police cars screeched to a stop at the curb opposite our apartment house. We all went scurrying to our combat positions with our weapons and waited for the attack. I could feel myself trembling, hyperventilating, as Cin, peering through a slit in the surveillance drapes, announced that there were "four pigs" outside. The policemen disappeared into the building across the street, but Cin kept us at combat alert until the police officers emerged again, with a man in custody, and drove off. Then there were smiles of relief within our safehouse. Others might have learned to accommodate themselves to these alerts and false alarms, but I dreaded them. I preferred the plodding numbness of my everyday existence to these attacks of sudden fear and uncertainty.

Teko offered one day to teach me how to load SLA bullets with "Ajax" and I obediently followed him into the kitchen. I watched as he, with the help of Zoya, drilled a tiny hole in the lead tip of a bullet, dipped it into a mound of cyanide crystals, and then sealed the bullet with paraffin wax. I backed away when it occurred to me that if he slipped and drilled into the gunpowder, the bullet would explode in his hands. He seemed casual and unconcerned about the danger; in fact, he looked as though he were enjoying his own craftsmanship.

Cinque magnanimously gave me private lessons, which I dared not refuse, in the care and handling of pipe bombs. They were powerful enough to destroy a police car and everyone inside it or to blow out the side of a building, he explained. The pipe bombs were stored in an unused vegetable bin built into a wall of the kitchen. The dynamite and blasting caps, though kept separate, were located very close to the stove, I noticed uneasily. Each bomb consisted of an eight-inch pipe loaded with two sticks of dynamite. The important factor in caring for such a bomb, he maintained, was to reverse its storage position every so often so that the nitroglycerin did not settle to the bottom of the dynamite stick and leak out. In horrifying detail, Cin told me about pipe bombs, dynamite, and blasting caps. I didn't want to be anywhere near explosive devices. But I learned about those bombs, just as I learned how to care for and handle my carbine, knowing that Cin might quiz me at any time on any aspect of my training. I never ceased to be surprised when he accosted me with that question: "Who are you?" and I would retort smartly, "I'm a soldier in the Symbionese Liberation Army." I learned by rote, as soldiers do in every army, and, despite myself, I found that I would obey. My combat stances became more natural and I believe I even looked more and more menacing as I swung my weapon in an arc in front of me, as if I were ready to shoot everything and everyone in sight. It was important, they steadily impressed upon me, to look menacing, and to get oneself into the proper frame of mind in order to be ready and able to shoot to kill.

As if the long days were not enough, the SLA devoted its evenings and nights to meetings of one sort or another, particularly what they called "criticism/self-criticism" meetings. They were an integral part of life in the cell. Sitting in a circle on the floor, Cin would invite anyone to criticize anyone else as to his or her actions, attitudes, demeanor—but only in a constructive way. The purpose was to help each other become better comrades, better revolutionaries, better soldiers. It was also an opportunity for anyone to criticize himself or herself, to bring up anything that was troubling, and to ask for the help of the others in overcoming faults or doubts. The atmosphere was always formal and serious.

These meetings would go on for hours and were totally nerve-racking. I could allow my mind to wander off only when I was not the subject under discussion. Unfortunately, as the newest recruit, I was the most frequent object of criticism: I was not serious enough about my training. I did not try hard enough. I was lazy and sloppy in the drills. My attitude was not positive enough. I was not comradely with all the sisters and brothers. I was not contributing enough to the functioning of the cell.

My role in this ritual was to abjectly agree with this heartfelt criticism and to promise that I would try to correct my faults. I would launch into the "self-criticism" aspect of the meeting. I would echo back to them the very same points of criticism: I was not determined enough, my attitude was not positive enough. I would explain that I had not tried hard enough to recover from my confinement and that I had difficulty in concentrating over long periods of time. I would apologize and promise to struggle (a favorite buzz word) to overcome my faults. Finally, I would thank my comrades for trying to help me.

Cujo was criticized for being too lazy, for taking naps during the day, for eating more than his fair share of the cell's food supply, for not trying harder, etc. Gelina, kindhearted soul that she was, often defended Cujo, saying that it was only natural that a young man his size needed to eat more food to sustain himself than did the others. Cujo's size was a constant source or irritation to our leader: he towered over Cin. Cin would stand up straight and try to look tall, but this, of course, did not work. Gelina only annoyed Cin with this excuse. Yolanda was taken to task most often for being bossy and argumentative. Incidents were cited, the pros and cons debated on each and every criticism. It always ended with the criticized comrade hanging his or her head in apology and promising to struggle to overcome his or her own personal human faults. On one occasion, Cin flew into a rage against Yolanda until she too bowed her head to his command. "You're too bossy!" he shouted. "You're always questioning my orders and your tone of voice is bad. . . . You're disrespectful of me. . . . I'm the leader here and I give the orders and you should stop questioning everything I do. . . . You're too bossy to everyone. Let them alone. Stop trying to make everybody be like you. . . ."

The one exception to this open critique was the General Field Marshal himself. It simply was not good army policy, he declared, to question the Commander-in-Chief on anything in the open, where it might give rise to dissent. If anyone was misguided enough to doubt the leader's actions, he or she should bring the criticisms to him privately and he would explain the whys and wherefores of his decisions.

While the "inside" team rehearsed how to act like "bad asses," shouting, screaming, and threatening in order to intimidate all those in the bank, the "outside" team practiced how to disable pursuing police cars. Cin gave instructions on how to shoot at the lower half of the front windshields of pursuing police cars so as to wound or kill the police in the front seat. Drawings of windshields were taped to one wall, and then Cujo and Teko, and sometimes the others, practiced aiming at the appropriate targets. All this practice, of course, was done without ammunition. In fact, they hardly ever practiced inserting ammunition clips into the weapons because of fear that the loud clicking sounds would arouse the suspicions of neighbors.

About a week before the date set for the action, Cujo and Zoya were sent out to test-drive new and used cars and to check on how easy or difficult it might be to capture the salesman who went with them and to use the car in the bank holdup, while the salesman was kept tied up in the car. Cujo gleefully dressed up for the occasion in some nice clothes that had been a Christmas present from his mother, saying how pleased he had been at the time because he knew that someday these fashionable clothes would make a good disguise for him. He left the apartment looking like a young business executive. When they returned, Cujo excitedly reported that the plan was not only feasible, it would be easy. Zoya told Cin that Cujo had acted the part so well the salesman would have done anything for him, even driven him to the bank. Four vehicles were needed for the bank action, however, and that was a bit too much for Cujo's plan. It was decided that two of the sisters would go out and rent automobiles from four different rental agencies and we would dump the cars somewhere at the end of the action. Gabi and Yolanda left the safehouse disguised and carrying several of the stolen but still valid driver's licenses and credit-card identifications from the SLA file. They would pay cash, so that no questions would be asked.

Diligently, I memorized and practiced the little speech I was to give in the bank. It was timed to last almost as long as the entire action inside the bank—one and one half minutes. In a loud, clear, determined voice, I was to announce my name, Patricia Hearst/Tania, and proclaim that this was not a robbery but an expropriation of capitalist funds for the Symbionese Liberation Army, which was carrying on a war against the United States on behalf of all the poor and oppressed people . . . that I had joined the SLA voluntarily and I was fighting with them of my own free will . . .

Cin gave me explicit instructions on how to act like a determined soldier in the SLA. He warned me to keep my carbine pointed at all times at the bank people in my own area. "Do not turn around and never point your weapon at any of the SLA soldiers at any time or for any reason," he told me. "If you do anything funny, I'm going to blow you away myself," he swore. "Remember that! The Codes of War say any one of us can blow you away if you do anything to endanger this operation." I believed him without reservation.

While the others wore wigs of hair different from their own, I was given a wig of long brown hair so that I would look like the photograph of me as Tania. Although my natural hair color was blond it photographed much darker, so that the public was familiar with me as a brunette. Cin said he wanted me to be recognizable in the pictures taken of me by the bank camera so that no one could claim the SLA had substituted a stand-in for me at the robbery. It was essential that I be recognized, while it did not matter so much with any of the others. The SLA certainly was media-conscious.

As the last item in our mastermind's plan of action, it was decreed that we all eat well the night before the operation in order to assure us of the high energy level we would need. Cin dispatched Zoya to the supermarket to purchase steak and potatoes for a final feast on the eve of the great day. He instructed her to spend all the remaining money in the SLA kitty—we would get plenty more the next day, or we wouldn't need any at all.

That night, however, I do not believe anyone, with the possible exception of Cinque, enjoyed the meal. It was hardly festive. With my first full meal of meat, potatoes, and vegetables set before me, I could only pick at the food. My appetite was gone. Teko was drumming his fingers and cracking his knuckles, but that was hardly unusual with him. Cujo had an ulcer attack and a severe case of diarrhea, which kept him groaning in pain and running off to the bathroom. Collectively, we were all a bundle of nerves although no one would admit to fear. Cin discoursed endlessly on the next day's action: it would be an act of war and not a bank robbery—similar to the action against me. I had not been kidnapped; I had been arrested. SLA members were not criminals; they were soldiers. They had declared revolutionary war against the United States. They could not be tried in any of the criminal courts; if captured, they would have to be tried before a military tribunal and treated as prisoners of war, with all the safeguards of the international Geneva Convention. He also informed us that he would be carrying a list of doctors, one or more of whom would be kidnapped at gunpoint to remove bullets if need be. On that happy note, we all turned in and I went to bed, exhausted but unable to sleep.

The first thing I noticed the next morning was our weapons lined up in a row, leaning against the wall of the bedroom. Our numbers, from one to nine, were written on the wall above our individual weapons. The number two spot looked peculiar. Only a crumpled stuff bag lay there on the floor: Zoya would be leaping over the counter to scoop up the money and cram it in that bag. She would need only her own personal handgun. Cin must have lined up those weapons sometime during the night, for they had not been there when we had gone to bed.

The mood that morning was somber. We went through our usual

lineup and calisthenics, washed up, and then got into our combat clothes and wigs. There would be no breakfast that morning. I think that surprised all of us. But Cin explained that if anyone should be "gut-shot" by the police during the course of the bank robbery, he or she would not want to have a full stomach. What a thought! As our leader and coach, Cin gave us a series of pep talks: We were all prepared; each of us knew exactly what to do; this "action" was for the people because every revolution must be financed some way; the operation would be smooth, well disciplined, and successful. If anyone got in our way, we were to "blow them away." To me alone, he repeated his personal warning: "If you mess up, if you do anything different from what you're supposed to, you're dead."

We all set out together. I left that apartment in a daze, realizing finally what I would scarcely admit to myself before: I was actually going to rob a bank. I felt as one would walking to the gallows. My M-1, with its straight clip, was hidden under my coat, clasped to my side by my left arm. Our two cars were parked about a half block away. This was the first time I had been out of doors since I had been kidnapped two and one half months ago. The fresh air almost overwhelmed me. Like champagne, it made me feel light-headed. The day was so brilliant, sunny, and clear that I had to squint to see my way. I took my assigned seat in a green station wagon, next to the window, behind Zoya, who was in the front passenger seat. Gabi was driving and Cin and Fahizah were in the back with me. The others were following us in a new red Hornet, as our backup and protection. Inside our car, it was all business: the operation had begun. We moved along the streets of San Francisco at a law-abiding pace, observing all the traffic regulations. As we drove through Golden Gate Park, I marveled at the sight of all the greenery, the trees, the bushes, and the grass. We passed a calm pond. Everything looked so beautiful and serene. When we reached Noriega and Twenty-second Avenue, we circled the block around the bank. It looked exactly as I had seen it in the surveillance photographs, a long, white, single-story building facing Noriega Street, with a shorter blank wall on Twenty-second Avenue. Cin spotted what he suspected was an undercover police car and we circled the next block slowly, returning to the bank in time to see the red Hornet in position, parked opposite the bank entrance.

We parked smoothly in the red-lined bus stop and struggled out of the car with our weapons still hidden under our coats. All was calm and quiet on Twenty-second Avenue. I knew exactly what I was supposed to do and I would do it, because I had to survive this. If I did I would survive everything. We rounded the corner, close to the bank building, and with a nod from Cin, I walked into the bank, with Gabi holding the door open and then following right behind me. We strolled together through the length of the bank to that rear writing desk, as if I were going to make out a deposit slip. Within seconds, all hell broke loose in a blur.

I saw Zoya rush into the bank at a gallop, with little Fahizah right behind her. As Fahizah came through the door, her ammunition clip dropped from her submachine gun and clattered to the floor. Some of the bullets scattered. She knelt down to retrieve the banana-shaped clip, and Cinque, charging in, leaped over her, waving his own submachine gun at the startled people in the bank. As they came through the door, I got my own carbine out into the open and pointed it at the assistant bank manager at the rear desk as well as at two women at nearby desks.

At the same time, in a loud, strong voice that just about froze everyone in the bank, Cin shouted: "This is a holdup! The first motherfucker who don't lay down on the floor gets shot in the head."

Fahizah ran around waving her submachine gun and kicking and hurting customers and screaming: "SLA! . . . SLA! . . . Get down on the floor over there and you won't get hurt." I glanced over my shoulder in time to see Zoya vault beautifully over the partition which separated the tellers and their cash drawers from the customers. She too was screaming and kicking at the tellers who had flopped to the floor too close to the cash drawers.

I don't remember saying or doing anything other than point my carbine at the people on the floor in front of me. The assistant manager said later that he had asked me where he should lie down and that I did not respond. On his own, he joined the others who were bunched together in a group on the floor, belly down, glancing up at me. I happened to notice at this point that the bolt of my carbine was off to one side rather than closed and flat. It struck me that the carbine was not operable. I remembered vividly, however, not to point it toward the front of the bank where the other SLA people were. Cin had positioned us in such a way that we would not accidentally shoot each other. I knew that if my weapon were pointed in his direction, he would shoot me. I glanced up and down the bank, anxious for it all to be over and to get out of there. Everything seemed to be happening so fast with the sounds of bedlam all around me, and yet it also seemed to be taking too much time. I was confused. Then I remembered suddenly that I was supposed to be making a speech. In the loudest voice I could muster, I managed to get out: "This is Tania . . . Patricia Hearst . . ." And I could recall no more of what I was supposed to say.

I heard Cin shouting out numbers and it was time to go. In the same instant, or so it seemed, I heard the rapid shots of a submachine gun and I caught sight of an elderly man stumbling out of the doorway, his back to me. I actually saw his jacket rip open as the bullets struck him. Fahizah was in a crouch, firing away. I don't really know what happened after that. My mind shut down, went blank. But I must have left the bank when my number, Nine, was called. And I must have jumped over the man who had been shot, because he was lying there on the sidewalk, just beyond the front door. But I don't recall seeing him or anything else.

I remember stumbling into the station wagon and Cin climbing over my lap, as he was the last one into the station wagon. We sped away and within one or two minutes we made our switch to another car, a green Ford LTD, which was parked near a school no more than a half mile away from the bank. I sat in the middle seat in the rear, feeling numb and slightly sick to my stomach, flanked by Cin and Fahizah, as we proceeded at moderate speed back to the safehouse. Cin kept us on the alert for police cars, traffic signals, and pedestrians. At each intersection, someone would call out, "This street is clear," or "Watch out for that car." Cin put a stop to all extraneous talk, but Fahizah did lean over and tell me, "It's a good thing you remembered to say your name."

When we arrived at the safehouse on Golden Gate Avenue, Zoya passed the stuff bag full of money over to Cin and we were about to follow him into the apartment, except that he was so unfamiliar with where we lived that he attempted to enter the wrong building. Once that was corrected, we climbed the stairs to our third-floor apartment as quietly as possible, not saying a word. Zoya and Yolanda drove off in the two cars to "dump" them in a public parking garage under the Japanese Center on Geary Street in a distant part of the city.

Once back in the safehouse, they broke out in laughter, broad grins, and congratulations. Gelina spilled the bills out of the stuff bag onto a blanket spread on the floor. The money cascaded all over the place and she began to gather it in a heap, laughing, stuffing one twenty-dollar bill into her mouth, saying, "It looks so good, I could eat it." Cin stationed himself at the front window, looking out through a slit. He ordered everybody to cut out the comedy, to remain serious and on the alert until the two other sisters had returned safely from getting rid of the rented cars. Only then, he said, would the operation be over and would we count the money.

Someone switched on the radio to catch the first news bulletins. What we heard was the popular new rock song "Money, Money, Money."

CHAPTER

EIGHT

THE SPOILS OF WAR from the Hibernia Bank operation included much more than the money taken from the bank. It was the victory itself, the successful blow against the capitalist system. In the aftermath, the SLA soldiers were gripped by an irrepressible exhilaration as they recounted their battlefield exploits. The sense of self-satisfaction and self-importance was unmistakable. The bagful of green bills, spread out on the floor in front of us, was treated rather casually as merely a business transaction: Expropriations were a necessity of life in the course of a revolution.

Cin tried hard to subdue the joy and delight in the hearts of his combat-tested soldiers, insisting that they maintain their army discipline. But he was fighting a losing battle against the news bulletins. Even he was finally swept up in the awe and public surprise as radio and television programs were interrupted with the sensational news of the "daring daylight holdup" of the Hibernia Bank by the SLA, aided and abetted by the kidnapped heiress Patty Hearst. At first, there was only speculation and then came the confirmation from the FBI: Patty Hearst had been photographed in the bank, holding a carbine on bank personnel and customers. Then came more speculation and commentary: Had Patty Hearst been a willing participant? Or had the SLA members been pointing guns at her all the time, forcing her to take part in the startling holdup, in which two men had been shot? By the time the evening television news came on, eyewitnesses were describing the "military precision" and the "commando-type raid" of the SLA inside the bank. There was a hint of awe in the media accounts: The SLA, which had been the subject of a massive FBI search for two and a half months, had pulled off a bank robbery in San Francisco, shot two men, and escaped unscathed. The Ford station wagon and the small red Hornet were found on Lawton Street near Thirty-first Avenue, and the FBI and San Francisco police were making a house-to-house search for the SLA *in that area.*

My comrades loved every minute of it. Both our radio and our television set were kept on all day and late into the night. They flipped dials and adjusted the sound to take in every possible description of their exploit. Cin proclaimed that the expropriation proved once and for all that the SLA was a true, determined revolutionary army, fighting in the streets, raiding capitalist institutions to finance the revolution which would bring down the government. It would prove once more to all other radical groups that the SLA really meant business: that the SLA preferred action to words. It would rally *the people* to our side. The oppressed masses would be heartened to join in the fight with the SLA. It would throw fear into the hearts of all the authorities. The revolution, led by the SLA, was on its way now. Thus spake the SLA General Field Marshal.

I felt sick to my stomach. It seemed unreal and degrading, seeing myself on television, being identified so publicly with the SLA and with that bank robbery. I sensed that I had, in fact, crossed over some sharp line of demarcation. Was I truly on the other side now, allied with the SLA? Even though I had joined the SLA before the bank robbery and recited that "stay and fight" tape, somehow seeing and hearing it proclaimed on television and radio, for all the world to know, made it official. For me, suddenly it became plain: there was no turning back.

We had been in the apartment for about an hour when Zoya and Yolanda returned from ditching the last two cars. They were greeted warmly with bear hugs and kisses by all the others. Being naturally undemonstrative under the best of circumstances, I had to force myself into joining this little SLA ceremony. It was one of the SLA prescribed practices to demonstrate our comradely love by hugging and kissing everyone who returned from any mission, even if it were only shopping at the corner market. A peck on the cheek in greeting was one thing but SLA etiquette called for kissing full on the lips.

There was no disguising the elation in the room, even though Cin tried to maintain seriousness and discipline in his little army. "Okay," he declared, "now we will count the money." But he kept a guard posted at each of the windows and at the front door, saying he did not want "the pigs" to catch us unawares. We sat in a circle around the heap of money and each of us counted and stacked the bills and then we reported our amounts to Cinque. He diligently added up the totals and, with a broad smile, announced the take: $10,660.

Cin divided the money into stacks of $1,000 and handed each of us one stack. We were to keep the money on our persons at all times, he told us. He did not want all of the money to be kept in one place in case we had to abandon the safehouse suddenly. Also, if one person had all of the money it could present a problem should that individual be captured or killed. It had to be kept on our persons because a backpack might get lost or abandoned, but we were not likely to lose our pockets. Cin would often walk up to us and demand that we produce the money so that he could be sure that we were carrying it. If ever anyone were separated from the group, he or she would not be marooned without money. Whenever the SLA had to make purchases, we all would pool our resources, the expenditures would be extracted, and then the remainder would be divided equally again. Each soldier in this army had to be equipped to operate alone at any time, if necessary. It also was an axiom of the SLA that if any of us got into trouble on the outside, under no circumstances were we to return to the safehouse and endanger the lives of the others. Hence, it was important that everyone be armed and equipped for survival at all times.

Cinque did not express any particular satisfaction or dissatisfaction over the amount of money taken from the bank. Fahizah commented that it was too bad that the bank vault had not been open. "We could have gotten away with millions," she said. But evidently money was not all that important to our leader. In the SLA lexicon, money was an evil of the capitalist state. When the SLA revolution was won and the new utopia installed, money would be outlawed; free and open barter of all goods and services would prevail. Cin seemed much more pleased with the seizure of the bank guard's revolver than with the money. "It's a good thing that bank had an armed guard 'cause it gave us the opportunity to seize an enemy's weapon," said Cin. "Wasn't no trouble at all taking that gun away from that old man." He laughed. "I let him be for a while and waited for him to go for his gun. If he had, I would have shot him dead. But the old guy just stood there, so I spun him around, threw him up against the wall, and took this revolver from him." Cin's sense of morality sometimes seemed to be straight out of the stories of the wild West.

He turned the gun over to Teko, our weapons expert, and Teko, after examining it, roared with laughter, saying the bank guard had left the first (firing) chamber empty and would hardly have been able to shoot it out with anyone, even if he had had the urge. It was a .38-caliber Smith & Wesson revolver in excellent condition, with five bullets in the six chambers.

Rather formally, Cin presented the revolver to me, saying, "This is for you, Tania, your personal sidearm. Keep it on your person at all times and learn how to use it." Teko added that he would be happy to give me instructions and Cujo said that he would make me a leather holster. Accepting the gun, I tried to judge Cin's demeanor and attitude toward me, but he was acting cool and businesslike. I knew that I had been the only one who failed to carry out her assignment. I had not made that speech in the bank. Yet I had gotten my name out and my presence there was unmistakable and being prominently reported by the media. I could not figure out what was in Cin's mind: I watched for some sign. Was I in danger? Would he punish me to set an example or would he just let it go as unimportant?

Their own review of the operation was constantly interrupted by news bulletins, reports of eyewitnesses, and commentaries. Several aspects of these reports were inaccurate and Cin declared that we would have to prepare another communiqué in order to "tell the people the truth." As the news media reported that the SLA had not hesitated to shoot down two innocent bystanders in the street, Fahizah explained over and over again that she had shot the man in the bank only because he had refused to obey her orders. She had told him to come into the bank and join the other captives. Instead, he had panicked and tried to run out and she had fired in order to protect the operation. Cin reassured her that her actions had been absolutely correct. "The people got to learn to respect the SLA and do what we tell them," he said. "We don't want to hurt innocent people, but if they get in our way, there is nothing else we can do. You did just right, sister!"

The victim was identified on the news as Peter Markoff, the owner of a nearby liquor store, who was coming in to deposit his receipts in the bank. He was fifty-nine, but with his silver-gray hair he appeared to be older. He was hit by a single bullet, which went through his right buttock and right leg. I had thought that any man in the line of fire of a submachine gun, firing .30-caliber bullets, would be dead, but somehow he survived. A second man entering the bank at the same time, Eugene Brennan, who was seventy years old, also was wounded—in the hip—by Fahizah's shots. Cin thought he had wounded another man when he fired on the street during our getaway. As this was described by eyewitnesses on the news, I wondered why I had no recollection of Cin firing outside the bank, when I must have been at his side.

Cujo bemoaned his disappointment that the police had *not* arrived in time. Then they would have been ambushed by the backup team. That, Cujo declared, would really have proved to the world the determination and strength of the SLA. Gelina gleefully recounted the story of how a middle-aged woman had stood at the window of their backup car at the height of the robbery, exclaiming, "Oh, how exciting!" and refusing Gelina's advice to duck down behind the car, lest she get shot. "You should have seen the look on her face when we roared out of there, after you!" Gelina said.

The euphoria lasted all through that day. While the comrades would never be so bourgeois as to brag too openly, they reveled in all the publicity. Several of them even credited me with forcing the fascist media to pay attention to the SLA actions. "If it weren't for Tania being there," exclaimed Gelina, "those pigs would not be giving us all this air time and newspaper space." Zoya was dispatched on a quick mission to the neighborhood grocery store and that night we celebrated with a dinner of chicken and spaghetti. At the criticism/self-criticism meeting that night, I managed to mumble an apology for my failure in the bank.

"I'm sorry I did not get that whole speech out," I said, with considerable trepidation. "It all happened so fast, I didn't have time."

"Yeah," said Cin. "I noticed that." He gave me a hard, cold stare.

"I'm really sorry," I said. "I started to say it all, but then it was time to go. But it is my fault. I should have started earlier."

"Well, you did remember at the last minute, so I guess it's all right," said Cin, and I sighed with relief.

With the hundreds of photographs taken by the bank cameras, all of us who had gone into the bank were correctly identified and federal warrants for our arrest were issued. Donald DeFreeze, Nancy Ling Perry, Camilla Christine Hall, and Patricia Michelle Soltysik were wanted on charges of bank robbery; Patricia Campbell Hearst was wanted as a "material witness" on the same charges. But bail was set for each of us in the same amount: $500,000 each. The state of California issued felony warrants for the arrest of the backup team: Bill and Emily Harris, William Wolfe, and Angela Atwood. The charge was obtaining driver's licenses by fraudulent means.

Zoya was furious that the authorities had cited me only as a material witness, saying that this clearly showed the state's favoritism toward the rich and privileged. Yolanda agreed with her. But Cin had his own ideas on the subject, and he prevailed. Those charges were just legalisms, he said, and did not mean a thing in a practical sense. I could be picked up and arrested as a material witness and then charged with bank robbery or anything else. "You don't think all of you in the backup car are going to be charged with just having phony driver's licenses, do you? Hell, no, we're all going to be charged with the bank robbery the same, in or out of the bank. They're just trying divide-and-conquer tactics now by bringing different charges, so maybe someone will crack. And it won't make any difference with Tania here. If the feds get her alive, they gonna put her away in jail for a long, long time. Make no mistake about it. She's a revolutionary now and there ain't no way out for her or for any of us, at all.

"We are all revolutionaries and the penalty for revolutionaries is death," he declared. "The pigs don't want us alive. They know what we are and they want us dead. We're all under the death penalty. You all better remember that!"

Cin expounded on the subject for some time and no one disputed his analysis. His words had a somber effect upon all of us. When his own mood changed, he would lecture us on how the authorities now realized how powerful the SLA had become, how appealing it could be for the poor people, and, finally, how the revolution was now beginning to pick up momentum. So we all had to be more than ever on the alert for a surprise raid and we had to train now even harder for future actions.

In the confines of that gray, dingy room, with the sun and daylight kept out by the heavy draperies, Cin's words seemed more and more prophetic as the authorities promised the public that the SLA would be hunted round the clock until we were found. The press reported that the FBI was conducting house-to-house searches. San Francisco's mayor, Joseph Alioto, ordered the police chief "to activate a special investigative team to devote full-time to tracking down the kidnappers of

Miss Hearst." Asserting that the SLA members were "killers, extortionists, and third-rate intellectuals," the mayor declared: "We have indulged them long enough."

Evelle Younger, the state's attorney general, echoing the same sentiments, asserted that he thought the police and FBI had been too "timid" because of their concern for my safety. "I think the moment of truth has long since passed for Patricia Hearst," he declared. Then the highest law enforcement official in the land, the Attorney General of the United States, William Saxbe, delivered his own opinion bluntly. In a press conference in Washington, he said he had come to the conclusion that Patricia Hearst "was not a reluctant participant" in the holdup. He condemned the SLA as "common criminals" and said, yes, that included Patricia Hearst, adding that, of course, he expected the FBI to pursue its duty and arrest all of us as soon as possible. Thus, according to the Attorney General of the United States, I was a "common criminal."

My father responded in the press the next day, accusing Saxbe of making "irresponsible statements" and talking "off the top of his head." My mother joined in, saying, "It's always been my understanding of American justice that a person is always presumed innocent until proven guilty. I just hope the Attorney General won't make any more prejudicial statements." It was obvious to me that my parents were shocked and hurt. My mother insisted that she was not convinced by the bank photographs that "the gaunt-faced girl in the wig is my daughter." Steven Weed held a press conference to declare that *he* was convinced by the evidence of the photographs that I had been coerced at gunpoint into participating in the bank holdup. The FBI, through its Director, Clarence Kelley, and its San Francisco agent-in-charge, Charles Bates, appeared to play it neutrally: I was wanted in connection with the bank robbery and it would be up to a grand jury to decide whether or not I had been a willing participant.

Overall, however, the Attorney General's view that I was a "common criminal" seemed to prevail in public opinion generally. It was reflected in the news media day by day, as the stories about me became more and more hostile. Appearances were taken at face value: I had proclaimed my choice "to stay and fight" and I had taken part in the bank robbery. At first, I resented being publicly labeled a "common criminal" and despaired that so few could empathize with my real plight. But then, thinking it all over before falling asleep one night, I realized that Saxbe's condemnation was a blessing in disguise. His views helped persuade Cin and the others that the authorities were convinced that I was acting voluntarily. It occurred to me that if Saxbe, the FBI, the police, and others all had believed that I had been coerced or brainwashed, then Cin would have devised still another "action" to place me center stage with the SLA. And it would have been worse, more violent, than the bank robbery. He would have continued such operations until the world was persuaded that the child of the oppressor had joined in the struggle to help free the children of the oppressed. He believed it and he wanted the world to believe it. My being on the FBI wanted list made me one of them. They accepted me now, more than before. They became more friendly and open and, on my part, I tried to heed their criticisms and advice and to become more friendly myself.

The one threat to my being accepted within the SLA was interjected by, of all people, Steve Weed. He meant well and ironically he was right, and yet he could not have caused me more potential harm than by refusing to believe that I had willingly chosen to stay and fight, as I had declared in my last tape-recorded message. Steve had managed in some way to contact Régis Debray, the French Marxist philosopher who had been close to Che Guevara and the original Tania Burke. Further, Steve had persuaded Debray to write a letter, which was published in the *Examiner* a few days before the bank robbery. Debray called the SLA to task, saying the real Tania had lived among the workers and had studied socialism for many years in order to become a dedicated revolutionary and that it was dishonest and cynical of the SLA to force a kidnap victim to take her name and represent her. Accompanying Debray's letter in the *Examiner* was a message from Steve, asking me to contact him or a mutual friend and let him know "the real situation"—had I really joined the SLA willingly or was I being coerced?

On top of that, after the bank robbery, he called a press conference and insisted that the bank photographs proved to him that I obviously was thin and gaunt, under duress, and had had a gun pointed at me all the time I had been in the bank, and that I was not a free, willing participant in the holdup. Of course, he was right. But he also was ridiculous. I was exasperated by his old intellectual myopia. Did he think I had the freedom to pick up a telephone and tell him, and not everyone else, that I was a hostage? Did he think the SLA would allow me to stroll down the street and mail a letter to him? He asked me "to relieve the anguish of your friends who fear for your safety and your life." But how could I do that without endangering my life? If I could contact anyone, I would have much preferred to contact my mother and father, or Trish—without running the risk that my words would be published and get back to my "comrades" in the SLA.

No, I thought, there is absolutely no way I can reach back to my family or friends. They could not rescue me, and I certainly did not want the FBI coming around. No, I had cut myself off from them completely. I had crossed over. And I would have to make the best of it. The locks and bolts were still on the door at Golden Gate Avenue. My "comrades" were as violent and dedicated to their revolution as ever. My own course was still to live from day to day, to do whatever they said, to play my part, and to pray that I would survive.

Once I came to accept in my own mind the stark reality of my new life—that I was now a part of the SLA—that what would happen to them would happen to me—the racking turmoil within me subsided. My everyday life became somewhat easier. All I had to do was to go along with them, and that in itself became easier day by day. It was not difficult to agree with "my sisters" that Steve Weed's attitude toward me, as revealed in his open letter, was chauvinistic, sexist, and bourgeois. Zoya fumed, saying that Steve acted as though he had owned me and that he wanted me back, as though I were a piece of property. All of the SLA women insisted that the trouble with Steve and with all bourgeois men was that, in the final analysis, they could not abide the thought that women could think and choose for themselves. It was easy to agree with Cin as he condemned the whole bourgeois world for accusing me of being brainwashed because I no longer agreed with their middle-class values. It was they who had been brainwashed over the years, Cin insisted, and it was we who made ourselves free to see the truth. The more I agreed with them, the more accepting of me they became and the more they left me alone to rest and to find some peace in this revolutionary maelstrom.

My good-comrade policy even extended to having sex with General Teko. He had helped me in my weapons instruction, the combat drills, calisthenics, and he also offered all sorts of helpful hints on how to become an efficient urban guerrilla. Then one day he came to me and said that he had been very patient; he had waited for me to be more comradely toward him and he thought that now was the time for us to spend the night together. I tried to tell him that I did not feel quite up to it yet, but perhaps later. However, he insisted. It was all on the basis of my being a good SLA comrade. He had a need. I should want to satisfy that need out of the goodness of my heart and my willingness to serve the cause. So, I served the cause, and I noted that all the others approved. Nevertheless, sex did not endear General Teko to me at all. He was a vain, brash, volatile little man and he would wait a good long while, I thought, before I ever felt comradely enough to approach him. It was ironic that all of the SLA sisters believed in the liberation of women, and yet the men in this cell acted as though the women were there to serve them sexually. It was even more peculiar that none of the other women appeared able to see what I could see.

Even though I was still treated as the rawest, dumbest recruit, when it came time to write our communiqué on the bank robbery, I felt that I could write my own script as well as they could. All the points had been discussed over and over again and I was as familiar with the SLA lingo as any of them. But Cin decided that Gelina was the SLA expert on writing the Tania script and she would write it, so that the media would discern no difference in it from the previous tapes. Everyone agreed that while Cin would do the official communiqué, the important points should be repeated in my script because the media always favored the Tania script in choosing the excerpts which were most often broadcast.

The euphoria over the bank robbery gradually turned into paranoia as Cin became convinced that the FBI and the San Francisco police had hundreds of men scouring the streets for clues to the whereabouts of the SLA. Cin told us that the bridges and roads leading out of the city were under constant surveillance and that the FBI and police were making a systematic house-to-house search of the entire city. They had to be doing this, Cin reasoned, because they realized that the SLA revolution, following the bank robbery, was gaining momentum and had to be nipped in the bud if it was going to be stopped at all. To compound matters, the police had released a composite drawing of a black suspect in the rampaging Zebra killings, asking the public's cooperation in capturing that man. The composite remarkably resembled Cinque!

Cin believed that the entire Operation Zebra was a police plot designed to capture him and to put an end to the SLA.*

Cin feared that a massive, vengeful police hunt was closing in on the SLA. We had thumbed our noses at the pigs and now they were seeking us with a vengeance. Our photographs had appeared in the newspapers and on television and so, said Cin, it was far too dangerous for any of us to venture out in the street. As our food supply dwindled, Cin paced the floor, drinking his plum wine, pondering the dilemma: How could we get food and still not venture out of the safehouse?

His answer was astounding. He decided that he would go out ringing doorbells in the neighborhood; he would identify himself and enlist new recruits into the SLA to help us get food and get on with the revolution. Fahizah thought the solution was brilliant. I thought he was drunk. "They're all poor people in this neighborhood," Cin explained, "and now that they know who we are, they'll all be willing to help." Teko thought it was a good idea, but dangerous. The others agreed. Teko suggested that if Cin went out ringing doorbells, he should take a backup team with him, just in case there was any trouble. To that, Cin agreed, although he insisted the backup team was hardly necessary. *The people* would welcome him with open arms, our leader promised.

It was on the second or perhaps the third night following the bank robbery that Cin went out to ring doorbells, accompanied by Teko and Gelina as his backup team, standing off to one side, out of sight, but ready to take action. That meant they would shoot to kill if their leader was threatened. The first door he tried was in our very own building. He returned, eager to report that the woman did not want to jeopardize her husband's job as a city (MUNI) bus driver. Everyone thought that was very encouraging, but Zoya and then the others suggested that ringing doorbells in our own building was just too close for comfort.

---

* The wanton street killings of whites, which had begun five months earlier, had claimed the lives of at least fourteen persons in San Francisco, and had led to the police Operation Zebra, in which all young black men were being stopped on the streets for an identification check. I was told long afterward that the SLA was never suspected at all of the Zebra killings. The composite drawing was made to look like any medium-sized black man because the police had absolutely no clue as to the identity of the Zebra killers. In fact, the composite looked so much like one man involved with the killers that he turned himself in and led the police to the four Black Muslims who were later convicted.

Cin went out again, promising "to cruise the neighborhood 'til I find the right doors to knock on."

The three of them were gone for quite a while and I sensed that the mother hens back at the roost had begun to worry about their rooster's safety. But Cin, Teko, and Gelina returned full of smiles. Four or five people had slammed their doors in Cin's face, not believing he could be who he said he was, or not caring. But then he had been welcomed with open arms by a young woman who was a Black Muslim. "She said she was so happy to see me," Cin explained. "I told her I was Cinque, the leader of the SLA, and I showed her my talisman, and she said she was so thrilled to meet me in person. She knew all about the SLA. She said she'd do anything she could to help the SLA. But she said it was her sister who was really political, her sister was the one I really wanted to see, and they would both help if I'd come back later when her sister was home. So I said I'd send someone for them . . ."

Cin played out the scene for us, line by line, acting as though it were the most natural thing in the world for poor people, picked at random, to want to join in the SLA revolution. This was merely the start of the recruitment drive to enlarge the ranks of the SLA. He had absolutely no doubt at all that he had found some true believers. No one voiced a single suspicion that one of the people approached might turn us in to the police. "We're really rolling now," declared Cin. Perhaps Cin was right, after all. This revolution which I had doubted so much might really be more widespread than I had believed. How else could he simply go out, ring doorbells at random, and return with new recruits? I was truly impressed.

The next evening, Cin dispatched Gelina to the apartment two or three blocks away, instructing her to lead the Black Muslims there back to our safehouse. He gave her the talisman he wore around his neck, which would identify her to the woman he had met there. Her name was Jamellea. Before Gelina left, however, Cin delivered a long lecture on how we were to act in the presence of these new comrades. We were to conduct ourselves in a military fashion, maintaining discipline at all times, standing guard at the door and windows, and, above all, we were to speak only when spoken to. "I'll do all the talking because this is a business meeting and I'm the leader here, so I don't want any of you being disrespectful to your leader," said Cin, and we all nodded. Then we waited.

When they arrived, there were seven of them, four adults and three little girls. They crowded the bare, little room which was our safehouse, the first outsiders I had seen here since my captivity. I hung back as Jamellea, who was a tall, massive woman of about twenty-one, introduced her sister, Retimah X, who was about half her size and about five years older, her sister's husband, Rasheem, and her "man," Brother Ali, who was in his mid-forties and huge, at least six feet six. Cin welcomed them all as his "sisters and brothers," but before he could start his introductions, Brother Ali, looking around, asked to see Tania.

"There she is," said Cin, pointing to me.

"She doesn't look like her," said Ali.

"Smile for the man, Tania," said Cin. "People don't recognize you unless you smile, like in your pictures."

So I smiled for the man, introduced myself, and explained how happy I was to join in the people's struggle for freedom, and generally went into the speech I was supposed to give in the bank. That satisfied Ali as well as the others.

Retimah positively gushed. She and her sister had followed the activities of the SLA from the very start, clipping the newspapers, taperecording all the communiqués heard on the radio. They listened to the tapes over and over. In fact, she said, she and her sister had taught the children the meaning of the seven heads of the SLA cobra. Would we like to hear the girls recite? Whereupon the three little girls, standing in a row, singsonged in Swahili the names and the meanings of the seven heads of the cobra. When we had all applauded and oohed and aahed over the performance, the girls began to jump up and down in a clenched-fist salute to "The African People . . . The African Nation . . ."

Cin expounded on the plans of the SLA to lead a revolution of the blacks and the oppressed, starting in California and rolling on across the land. In glowing terms he spoke of all the ethnic groups who would join in the fight, so that when the revolution was won, the country would be divided into regions run independently by separate races and ethnic groups, with equality for all. The blacks would have their own nation within the United States, the Latinos would have theirs . . . On and on he went in his dream of glories to come, addressing most of his charms and words to the two women. They absorbed it all, star-struck. However, I thought the two men might be resenting Cin's attention to their women, although I could not be certain.

"But where are all the blacks?" Rasheem interrupted. "I don't see any blacks here except you."

"Oh, this is a white unit," explained Cin. "I'm here just to help them get organized and trained 'cause these brothers and sisters are going to lead the other white units who have joined in the struggle. We do need blacks in this particular unit right now, and that's why I want you to join this here unit for a while. Then, later, you can be transferred to a black unit, and you can become leaders, because we're growing all the time."

I made myself as inconspicuous as possible, sitting in a corner farthest away from the discussion, playing with the little girls and keeping them occupied, as Cin went through his recruiting pitch. The smallest of them was no more than three years old and the other two looked to be about seven and nine years of age. I could overhear the four Black Muslims hemming and hawing and being less than eager to join up with the SLA. Retimah X, who was feisty and the most articulate of the group, explained that they all wanted to fight with the SLA, but the men had their jobs and needed to earn a living and she and her sister had to take care of the children. "Could we be SLA soldiers and do it part-time?" she asked. To this, Cin countered that they give the little girls away to someone—only temporarily, of course—so they could devote their own lives to the important struggle. Both women were aghast at this suggestion.

Cin backed off, suggesting that they could help the SLA by remaining aboveground and buying supplies for us. That was our immediate need, said Cin. Now that the FBI and the police knew the SLA was in San Francisco, it was too dangerous for any of us to go out on the street until the heat eased up. They all agreed that they would be happy to be of that service and Cin handed them some money with instructions as to the food they should buy and deliver to us the next day. Of course, they all agreed to keep this association absolutely secret. Retimah assured Cin that they had always been very careful in following the SLA activities. They had even taught the children to refer to Cin only by the code name they used for him. At home, she explained, they referred to him as Jesus. Cin liked that.

"Greetings to the people, this is Tania. On April 15 my comrades and I expropriated $10,660.02 from the Sunset Branch of Hibernia Bank. Casualties could have been avoided had the persons involved kept out of the way and cooperated with the people's forces until after our departure."

Cin and I sat in the small hall closet one more time, facing each other, our knees drawn up to our chests, our scripts propped in front of us. Tape recording was old familiar territory by now; I did not need any prompting. A seasoned performer, I thought I knew what they wanted. I put into my voice a strength which I really did not feel. I was getting better at my calisthenics, combat drills, weapons instructions, and I was still eating peanut-butter sandwiches every day, and yet my old physical strength and good health seemed never to return to me. I was tired all the time, nervous and weepy. But for tape-recording communiqués, I could perform. It was my major contribution to the SLA. We all knew that the media drooled over messages from Tania. No one else in the SLA could get the coverage and publicity that I could. Being an asset to the SLA was like life insurance to me. I could have written the script myself, I thought, better than Gelina. I now was familiar with their turns of phrase and favorite buzz words like "expropriate" and "struggle" and "consciousness." However, the script was Gelina's; I was only the performer. Cin did put in his two cents literally. Just before our recording session, he decided to add two cents to the amount we had taken from the bank. It would drive the bank auditors up the wall, he said. In any event, the thrust of my message was for me to persuade the world that I had joined the SLA and participated in the bank holdup voluntarily, and further, to taunt my parents by referring to them as "pig Hearsts" and calling my father "Adolf."

Complimenting me on my performance, Cin indicated that he wanted me to remain in the closet with him while he read his part of the communiqué. He smiled at me as though we were co-conspirators. Then he turned serious, even stern, as he focused his attention on a final study of his script. When he spoke, his voice sounded official, without emotion, as if coming down from on high:

"Greetings to the people and all sisters and brothers behind the walls and in the streets, elements of the Black Liberation Army, the Weather Underground, and the Black Guerrilla Family, and all combat forces of the community.

"I am General Field Marshal Cin speaking.

"Combat operations: April 15, the year of the soldier.

"Action: Appropriation. Supplies liberated: One .38 Smith and Wesson revolver, condition good; Five rounds of 158-grain .30-caliber ammo. Cash: $10,660.02.

"Number of rounds fired by combat forces: Seven rounds.

"Number of rounds lost: Five.

"Casualties: People's forces, none. Enemy forces, none; Civilians, two.

"Reason: Subject one, Male. Subject was ordered to lay on the floor face down. Subject refused order and jumped out the front door of the bank. Therefore the subject was shot. Subject two, Male. Subject failed or did not hear warning to clear the street. Subject was running down the street toward the bank, and combat forces accordingly assumed subject was an armed enemy-force element. Therefore the subject was shot.

"We again warn the public. Any citizen attempting to aid, inform, or assist the enemy of the people in any manner will be shot without hesitation. There is no middle ground in war. Either you are the people or the enemy. You must make the choice . . ."

Cin went on to expound on his interpretation of Operation Zebra, in which the police were stopping and interrogating black males throughout San Francisco. At great length, he accused the police of launching Operation Zebra in an "attempt to entrap the SLA Forces and more precisely to assassinate myself." The enemy, according to Cin, wanted to stop him and the SLA from rallying the people to the SLA cause. "In short, he [the enemy] knows that the SLA is building an army of the people, that is the army which by its very composition can truly destroy the enemy and free the people . . .

"And if we look closely we begin to see the truth that Operation Zebra is a planned enemy offensive against the people to commit a race war. This could possibly be the only way the enemy can stop the SLA from bringing all the oppressed people together against the common enemy."

As I listened to Cin's exhortations in that little closet it finally got through to me with a new clarity that what he was saying was more than mere rhetoric or propaganda. He really believed. He honestly thought that the SLA was a big, growing, fearsome army and not just three men and six women. He was convinced that the poor people were supporting his crusade in ever-increasing numbers. He really believed that the government (whether it would be the city, state, or federal government was never entirely clear) would soon declare martial law in order to confine or curtail revolutionary violence, and as a result the blacks and poor people would rise up in armed protest. He really believed that increased oppression would spark the people's revolution. And he really believed that finally the United Symbionese Nation would be born and he, Cinque, would be the father and founder of the new nation.

My comrade sisters and brothers in the SLA simply loved Cin's communiqué. They termed it beautiful. They said Cin was awakening the people to the truth. They said the people were unaware that with the re-election of Richard Nixon in 1972, a military-corporate coalition had taken over the United States in a silent coup. Moreover, that coup was now being threatened by the SLA, because once the mass of people realized what was happening in their land, they would rally to the SLA's leadership. Cin assured all of us that the conflict was coming to a head. He was sure that the government would declare martial law by the summer, and when it did, the SLA would take action in the streets and fight back and then the people would come to our side in droves. When the pigs began to put blacks in jail, when they imposed curfews which forbade people from being out in the street after dark, when the National Guard marched through the cities, then the people would rise up and rebel because then they would be able to see oppression in the raw. The revolution would start in earnest. As government oppression spread into the blue-collar neighborhoods, Cin told us, the factory workers would start joining the SLA crusade. Finally, when the poor whites and poor blacks saw the light and joined ranks with one another and with the SLA, then the revolution would be won. On top of all that, Cin envisioned a time when our revolution would be joined by all the poor blacks and poor whites who were in the military services. They would rebel against their leaders and offer their military skills to the SLA forces. It was a gigantic scenario of things to come. Was it all fantasy? I began to wonder. I began even at times to believe. What everyone around me was saying with such sincerity began to make sense. There did seem to be panic in the streets of San Francisco. The police were demanding that all black males carry identification with them. They were being stopped and checked and given police Z cards for identification. I did not want to believe that such things were happening, but I could not *not* believe them, for they were all so insistent.

Teko suggested that he add a message to our latest taped communiqué, appealing to the whites to join in the revolution. Cin thought that was an excellent idea. So Teko tape-recorded his version of the meaning of Operation Zebra, which did not differ from that of Cin, but added this:

"The enemy has kept us [blacks and whites] divided for hundreds of years and for at least that long the pig has made uncountable attempts at eliminating the rising tide of black revolution. But black people, by their strength and determination, have survived this fascist onslaught. Black people, more revolutionary than ever before, are armed and angry and now the SLA is proving that black people ain't alone, that the thing the pigs hate and fear the most is happening, is growing: the people's army of irate niggers of all races, including whites, not talkers but fighters. The enemy recognizes that the people are on the brink of revolution and the enemy will do anything at any cost to prevent this."

The SLA was particularly pleased with its work on this communiqué. Cin declared it would fire the opening salvo in the coming revolution. Devising a media event for the delivery of the tape, Cin wanted the tape delivered to the Western Addition Project Area Committee (WAPAC), one of the few San Francisco organizations participating in the PIN food program of which the SLA approved, and he wanted it delivered by Retimah X's nine-year-old daughter. She was to hand a wrapped package, containing the tape, and a homemade SLA poster to the woman at the desk, and say, "This is from my father," and then walk out. The media would play up the point that children were now a part of the SLA, said Cin, and that would be a message to the people that whole families were in the SLA. But Retimah thought it over when she got home and then rejected the idea. Instead, one of the Muslims dropped the package on the steps of a high school and the news media reported the tape had been sent to the police. Nevertheless, the reaction was immediate: Another message from Tania, this time proclaiming that not only was she a member of the SLA but she also was a bank robber.

Meanwhile, we prepared for Cin's revolution, talked about it all the time, increased our combat and weapons drills, simulated battles and target practice, stripped our weapons and reloaded them, renewed our criticism/self-criticism meetings, and fantasized our own brave new world. None of us ever left the safehouse. Our Black Muslim comrades visited every other day or so, bringing us food and supplies and the newspapers. They came with the children all the time because, Retimah said, they were always asking, "When can we go see Jesus again?" Cin talked to the girls gently, telling them revolutionary stories in the simple language of fairy tales. Once, the oldest girl disclosed that she had had a dream in which she saw herself killing "a whole lot of pigs." That touched Zoya's heart, for she commented what a sweet, sensitive child that girl was.

One evening, Cin asked the two men, Brother Ali and Rasheem, to go out and buy the SLA some transportation, a van or a station wagon. He also asked Jamellea to look for a larger, safer place for our next safehouse. "This pad is getting hot, with all the pigs out there looking for us, and so we better move on." It also was getting near the end of the month, when another rent installment would be due. During the week that followed, Brother Ali and Rasheem bought a ten-year-old wreck of a station wagon for six hundred dollars.

Our training became more and more arduous. Cin never let up, exhorting us to become good soldiers in preparation for our becoming future leaders in the revolution. He spent a good deal of his time planning and plotting privately with Teko in one corner of the room. Then he announced a new plan: Our combat unit would be divided into three separate teams, each capable of operating independently, each to be the nucleus of a future combat unit, and in time, as the revolution spread, each of us would lead another team and then another full combat unit. Thus, there would soon be nine separate SLA combat units operating throughout California. From time to time, he took each of us aside for private consultation on our future roles in the SLA and the glories to come.

With me, Cin explained that the bank robbery was an important turning point. Now every one of us in the SLA was a wanted criminal: there was no longer any possibility of anyone turning back. Aside from himself, he said, no one in the SLA had had a true criminal record and the possibility had existed that one or more might decide to give up the struggle and return to their old bourgeois lives. But now that was impossible, especially for me. My own task ahead was to bear down on my combat drills, increase my proficiency as a soldier, and at the same time think of the people, love the people, and become a leader in the new Symbionese Nation. His talk with Cujo apparently had a profound effect upon that young man. Cujo changed his ways that very same day. He did more push-ups, he no longer dozed off, he threw himself into his combat drills with a fierceness that was awesome. Soon everyone there was complimenting Cujo on his newfound self-discipline and dedication to the struggle. Long into the night, Cujo told me of his dreams of leading combat teams through the streets of San Francisco, killing pigs, and freeing the oppressed people.

None of the others shared their new orders with me, but I could not help but note a new determination in their activities. But, at the same time, a new sense of fatalism seemed to creep into all of their thinking. Everyone began talking of the "long struggle," of the difficulties they would encounter in fighting the pigs and in winning the people over to their cause. Cin talked constantly of the probability that he would not live to see the installation of the Symbionese Nation.

Then the others took it up. Yolanda expounded during one lengthy discussion on her belief that the revolution definitely would not be won in any of our lifetimes; nevertheless, it was a worthy goal to which to devote our own unimportant personal lives. I once asked Cujo privately why he was doing all of this if he did not expect to live to see the results. He replied that he would go down in history as one of the leaders of the revolution and, although he preferred to live to see the glorious day, it was enough for him to have faith that it would come even after his death.

Being ever practical, I could not understand why they were fighting for something which they did not believe they would live to see accomplished. But I kept my mouth shut and my thoughts secret, knowing full well that I was already being criticized and distrusted for not wholeheartedly committing myself to the cause. They attributed that to my "bourgeois, ruling-class hang-ups." Cin promised us that in the Symbionese Nation of the future the cities would be adorned with statues and monuments and parks dedicated to our memories. We would have everlasting glory. In my pragmatic mind, no matter how confused I might be about some things, I definitely preferred the present to Cinque's vision of our martyrdom. But, while I wanted no part of any heroic death, I had made my pact with the devil.

CHAPTER

NINE

MOVING OUT OF THAT one-room apartment was a full-scale military operation, planned and plotted down to the last tactical detail. There were only nine of us, but Cinque acted as though he were planning the logistics of transporting an entire army through enemy territory. The basic decision to move had been made a few days after the bank robbery. With Jamellea looking for another safehouse, Cin managed to convince every one of us that the police or FBI could be expected to bust in upon us *at any second*. He was certain that the pigs were methodically closing in on the apartment at Golden Gate Avenue. He reasoned that if he were in command of the enemy forces, *he* certainly would be conducting house-to-house searches, patrolling the streets and blocking off the bridges and main roads that led out of the city.

As a counter-strategy, the SLA would have to become more mobile, Cin decreed. We could not remain encumbered with so much excess equipment and all the books and papers we had accumulated. We would have to strip down to essentials for the coming guerrilla war in the streets. We had to be capable of striking at the enemy and disappearing into the urban jungle of San Francisco. We had to travel light. "Take only what you absolutely need," Cin ordered, "only what you can carry on your back."

Every item in every file in every carton was inspected, discussed, debated, and decided upon. Books were weighed for the importance of their content as well as their poundage. Very few survived. The closetful of clothing had to be left behind. We would take only one change of clothes and one disguise each. There was a flurry of objections to that dictum. Several sisters argued that we needed disguises to get about on the streets. This drove Cin into one of his furies.

"The trouble with you people is you're always thinking too small," Cin said. "You're too shortsighted too. Trouble with disguises is they make people think 'sneaky.' You're all thinking sneaky. You got to be bold. This war is escalating. It's going to be all around us, pretty soon. Then it won't be safe for anybody to walk the streets, with or without disguises. We're in the middle of a war. All these disguises will be useless. When we go out on the street, we'll be going out to fight, not to sneak around . . ."

Weapons, ammunition, bombs, and dynamite, of course, were essential: we would leave none of them behind.

As the heap of newspaper clippings, notebooks, papers, books, and miscellaneous items to be discarded grew into a small mountain in one corner of the room, the problem of disposal perplexed all of us. The security of garbage cans in the streets of this downtrodden neighborhood was not to be trusted. Cin thought the police probably were checking garbage cans too in their search for clues to our whereabouts. Fahizah had tried to burn SLA documents in the safehouse at Concord when Remiro and Little had been captured the previous January, but the police had discovered the SLA list of potential kidnap victims at that time, including my own name. Strangely, the police had neglected to warn anyone. If they had, I would never have been kidnapped at all. Cin was determined this time to leave the FBI and police no clues of any value.

For two weeks, we had been disposing of the paper work involved in the planning of the bank robbery. It was astonishing how much of it had accumulated—planning notes, diagrams, photographs, drawings, street maps with notations. All of this material was being systematically shredded by Yolanda and put into a large shopping bag, labeled HOT STUFF, by the side of the toilet. Each of us was depositing a handful or two every time we used and flushed the toilet. Still, we had a good deal of that incriminating evidence to get rid of.

As the day of our departure drew nearer, the anxiety within the small apartment increased, guard duty became more intense, the pros and cons of every tactical step were discussed ad infinitum. Jamellea had found us a new safehouse, as directed: a four-room flat with a back door where our security could be maintained without the prying eyes of neighbors. But it was in the Hunters Point District, which was a predominantly black neighborhood of San Francisco. There was much concern in the cell that white people in the area would stand out so conspicuously as to warrant police investigation. However, Cin did not seem to think that the point was germane. If we were to free the poor people, we should be able to live happily among them. We needed only to don our disguises to get there, Cin declared. After that, we would be among friends.

As we cleared out the closets and cupboards, swarms of cockroaches scurried about the kitchen over the counters and across the floor, and Cujo cried out that no one was to kill them. He liked cockroaches, he said. He sympathized with their plight. They were poor, oppressed, living creatures and did not deserve to be killed because of bourgeois distaste. So the cockroaches were spared by the SLA, which was bent only on executing the true enemies of the people.

The disposal problem was resolved on the day we were to depart the Golden Gate Avenue safehouse. It was decided to "drown" all of the written evidence. The bathtub was filled with hot water and we dumped books, papers, and whatnot into the water, noting with glee how long it took each item to sink to the bottom. Cin defied the famous FBI laboratories to resurrect clues obliterated by the hot water. Gelina thought of adding all of the cooking condiments, spices, and colorings to the hot bath water. Later, she poured in various hair dyes. The mixture turned to a bilious, opaque brown. Teko thought of adding some SLA "Ajax" to the mixture and, with Cin's approval, poured a bagful of cyanide crystals into the water. Cin gleefully announced he would leave something personal for the FBI and, in front of us all, he began to urinate into the bathtub. Teko and Cujo quickly joined him. Not to be outdone, Gabi mounted the tub, with a foot on opposite edges, and let loose a yellow stream, as the comrades roared with laughter. The other sisters, however, declined her invitation to join in this escapade. Nevertheless, everyone seemed to enjoy the prospect of the FBI, with its usual painstaking search for evidence, having to sift through that mess.

The strain of packing and moving gave way to a mood of manic silliness. Rather than try to erase all the evidence and wipe clean all of our fingerprints, Cin decided that we should leave so many clues that the FBI would become hopelessly confused and bogged down with "evidence." Teko, with a cry of joy, began to leave his fingerprints all over one wall, dabbing out messages, so that when the FBI dusted for fingerprints, they would discover his message: "Fuck you, pigs." Cujo took up the game by scrawling on another wall in large letters: "DA DA O MI," which was some kind of secret greeting of the Black Guerrilla Family, a prison group, with which he had been associated. At his urging, I wrote: "Patria o Muerte—Venceremos," and signed it "Tania." My writing was very small and tentative, for I could not fathom how all this writing would help the revolution. But the others seemed to be enjoying themselves, scribbling messages with pens, pencils, markers, lipstick, and even spray paint. By the time we had finished, the four walls were covered with graffiti. The left-over food and garbage was strewn about. The place was a shambles. Only Zoya, in her fastidiousness, voiced an objection. Looking around the place at the end, she softly commented, "I don't think it looks nice to leave the place like this." But for the others, it was the only blow they could strike at the time against the FBI, who we presumed were only hours behind us.

As a final touch, Teko composed a merry word of caution which he inscribed on the wall of the bathroom for those who would come after us: "Warning to the FBI, CIA, NSA, NSC, and CBS— There are a few clues in this bathroom. However, you will have to wait until they are dry. An additional word of caution: ½ (one half) lb. (pound) of cyanide (potassium cyanide) crystals have been added to this 'home brew' —so, pig, drink at your own risk. There are also many additional juicy SLA clues throughout this safehouse. However, remember that you are not bulletproof either. Happy hunting, Charles." Teko was very proud of this composition, especially his taunting of Charles Bates, of the San Francisco FBI office.

Late at night, with our bags packed, we dressed to go. Cin, clean-shaven and with heavy makeup and rouge on his cheeks, was disguised as a woman, complete with bra stuffed with tissues and a new wiggle to his walk. Teko, in dark blackface and a medium-sized Afro wig, strutted about the room as happy as a minstrel singer, lowering the pitch of his voice as he spoke endlessly, mimicking the voice of a Negro of the Deep South. To me, he looked like a cheap imitation of Al Jolson in *The Jazz Singer*. But he was as joyful and as self-satisfied as I had ever seen him. He could not tear himself away from the bathroom mirror. In fact, he kept suggesting that he was so sure he could pass as a black that he wanted to go out and mingle with the local people.

At the last minute, we had learned that the house Jamellea had rented for us would not be ready for occupancy for a few days. But it was impossible to remain with the mess we had made and Cin was determined not to spend another night at Golden Gate Avenue. He instructed Jamellea to find an out-of-the-way motel for us, with three adjoining rooms, so that we would not be separated in case of attack. She was to tell the management that we were a traveling rock group.

Gelina, with her expertise as a former actress, helped everyone with applying the blackface. With her large theatrical makeup kit at hand, she explained that it was not good enough simply to apply one color out of a tube. She mixed colors on a palette and stroked on multi-toned complexions for each of us. She was meticulous in covering every inch of exposed skin—face, hands, wrists, inside the ears, over the eyelids, on the inner edges of the nose. Once all of my exposed skin area was covered with a yellowish-brown greasepaint, it was overlaid with a white talcum-type powder and then patted down with water so that the mixture of greasepaint, powder, and water coagulated into a remarkable semblance of cosmetic makeup. A huge Afro wig of black hair with a tint of red completed my disguise. Looking at myself in the mirror, I thought that on a dark street corner I could easily be mistaken for a hooker. Gelina was delighted with my transformation. She, however, had the best disguise of all. Dressed in a conservative pants suit and a modest, short Afro wig, her face made up perfectly, she looked like an attractive, young, black businesswoman.

Cin had divided us into three separate teams for this operation, according to the rooms we would occupy at the motel. He kept his bedmates, Gelina and Fahizah, with him and assigned me to stay with Teko and Zoya in another room. The middle room would be occupied by Cujo, Yolanda, and Gabi. The five locks were removed from the apartment door, the makeshift drapes taken off the windows, the large weapons, backpacks, ammunition, and equipment were packed into boxes, our small arms were hidden on our persons. We sat there, all dressed up in blackface, the room in shambles, ready to go.

Our Black Muslim friends, when they arrived, were astonished at our appearance. I have no idea what they really thought, seeing all the whites of the SLA in blackface and our stalwart leader disguised as a swishing, big-bosomed woman. But, aside from their surprised expressions, they said nothing. The effectiveness of our disguises, however, was proven when none of them could recognize me or Zoya or

Yolanda or Gelina. The four of them were, in fact, so stunned that they hardly noticed the condition of the apartment.

The trip to the motel in Hunters Point was made in two shifts, and as far as I could tell in the second contingent, we did not pass a single police car nor did we see a solitary person as we pulled into the large parking lot and made our way into our motel rooms. My room was small and simple with two single beds, a side chair, and cheap, worn carpeting. Off came the greasepaint and traveling clothes. Out came the combat clothes and boots, the weapons, sidearms, ammunition pouches, and belts. We were an army again, combat ready, and secure. Three-hour night watches were established for each team in each room. It was long past midnight before we were ready to go to bed and then, not unexpectedly, as the raw recruit, I was given the 5 to 8 A.M. watch.

With no more than three hours' sleep, I felt overtired and nervously wide awake, sitting on the floor beneath the drape-covered window, listening for unusual sounds, occasionally peeking out upon the empty, pitch-black parking lot. This eerie room in a strange location with its paper-thin walls seemed far less secure from police bullets than had our safehouse on Golden Gate Avenue. But then I thought that perhaps Cin did know more about police methodology than I did. He certainly had the experience. Nevertheless, I felt nervous and frightened. Not trusting my senses to protect me from a surprise police attack, I was alert to every little sound in the night, even the creaking of a bed every time Teko or Zoya turned over. I would never have thought it possible, as frightened as I was, but Teko and Zoya caught me asleep on watch when they woke up the next morning. My punishment was fifty extra push-ups that day, and a thorough dressing down.

Two nights and two long days we spent at that motel doing next to nothing. Teko discovered that our room shared a common wall with the next room and that by removing the medicine chests in both bathrooms, we could climb from one room to another without venturing outside and showing our white faces. Cin, in the third room, was the only one who ever sneaked outside for a short trip to the middle room, where our "team leaders" held their meetings.

I preferred to lie in bed, pretending to read a book or an SLA document. I slept much of the time. We were all under instructions to keep everything quiet, not to raise our voices, to do nothing which might conceivably attract attention. Actually, except for one cleaning woman who was turned away, we gave no one any reason to give us a second thought and aroused no suspicions. Food was delivered to us each night by our Black Muslim cohorts, who handed in bags of Kentucky Fried Chicken and accouterments through the back window, so as not to arouse suspicion by appearing each night loaded down with provisions.

However, I did have to put up with Zoya at close quarters and her criticisms of me were unrelenting. Aside from my lack of determination as an SLA soldier, she continued to challenge me on my use of the English language. Her campaign on this subject had begun soon after I had joined the SLA and intensified my anxiety as it went on, day after day. She complained that I still talked like a "rich, bourgeois bitch" rather than an SLA soldier fighting for the poor people. I had picked up the use of the SLA street vulgarities, peppering my speech with such words as "asshole" and "fucking" this or that, but I still used words that were unfamiliar to the common people. They slipped unconsciously into my speech, words such as "panacea" or "recalcitrant." Each time, Zoya would stop me and ask, "What does that word mean?" Earlier on, I would define the word and she would insist that she did not have my background and did not understand such words. I came to realize that, of course, she knew such words as well as I did. But she did not think the poor people would understand. It all seemed rather condescending, I thought, but I had to make a conscious effort to watch my speech, especially in her presence.

We moved out of the motel late on the third night, wearing disguises and blackface, and once again we reached our destination without incident. I was so petrified with fear of the police stopping us that I seemed to breathe normally only when we walked into our new safehouse on Oakdale Avenue without a shoot-out. Our new headquarters was a duplex, one part of a freestanding, ramshackle old house in the middle of a black ghetto. It looked as though it had not been occupied for months, and consisted of a front bedroom, a living room, a kitchen, and a small utility room. Thick cobwebs filled just about every corner of the high ceilings; mounds of dust had accumulated where the greenish-yellow walls met the floor. It was larger than the apartment at Golden Gate Avenue, but by an other measure it was clearly a step down from our former abode.

The new safehouse was secured by attaching our old bolt locks to the doors, hanging our old drapery rags with their surveillance slits over the windows; the weapons were taken out and made ready for combat, and, finally, new night watches were established, one person covering the front of the house, another the rear. The only furnishings were three double mattresses and a single cot the Muslims had bought for us from Goodwill. These were placed near the front and back doors for added security and we all flopped down anywhere to sleep. In case of a police assault on our safehouse, the mattresses would be thrown up against the wall to give added protection to those inside the house. Somehow, Fahizah took possession of the single cot in the front room and never gave it up.

As we settled in at Oakdale, resuming our day-to-day routine of combat drills, exercises, and marathon discussions, a new intensity crept into our lives, a combination of revolutionary zeal and sheer paranoia: We were running out of time. We were mesmerized by Cinque's certainty that here we were in May and the revolution was going to begin in earnest sometime this summer, in only a matter of months. He insisted that we had to train harder to prepare ourselves for the leadership roles that each of us would have to assume when the fighting took to the streets. Every day, Cin talked of the revolution. It was spreading across America, starting in California and inundating the country, like a giant wave. Nothing could stop it, except our being discovered and killed by the pigs. They knew it as well as we did, Cin insisted, and that was why the police were out in helicopters searching for the SLA all over the city. He raved madly about helicopters, which, indeed, flew over Hunters Point every night, their searchlight beams lighting up the streets, their engines roaring. I would tremble with fear as the windows shook each time one passed low overhead. Those helicopters were invading the privacy of all the black people who lived in this section of the city, he declared. Fuming over this injustice, Cin promised us that one night he would shoot down a low-flying police helicopter. He knew exactly where to aim. He knew all about helicopters, he told us, claiming that he had once worked for a helicopter factory. With a high-powered rifle and his expertise, it would take but one shot. A police helicopter had been brought down by a rifle bullet in Oakland some time ago and Cin swore it was time again to bring down another one. On more than one night, Cin went out into the backyard and shook his clenched fist at a helicopter roaring overhead. No one doubted anything he said. They praised his superior knowledge. Of course, the police craft were really backing up patrol cars in pursuit of criminals in this high crime area, a not unexpected nightly occurrence. I should have been able to reason this out well enough and yet I too believed Cin's explanation. How could I know why those helicopters were up there almost every night? Maybe they were searching for us.

Changes had come over me subtly since I had been brought into this strange world of the SLA. In time, although I was hardly aware of it, they turned me around completely, or almost completely. As a prisoner of war, kept blindfolded in that closet for two long months, I had been bombarded incessantly with the SLA's interpretation of life, politics, economics, social conditions, and current events. Upon my release from the closet, I had thought I was humoring them by parroting their clichés and buzz words without personally believing in them. Then, following the nightmare of the bank robbery and being branded along with them as a "common criminal," a sort of numbed shock set in. To maintain my own sanity and equilibrium while living and functioning day by day in this new environment, I had learned to act by rote, like a good soldier, doing as I was told and suspending disbelief. Cin had instructed me on more than one occasion that I must be careful to gain control over my own mind and not allow negative thoughts to intrude. Those negative thoughts were products of my past life, my bourgeois upbringing, and now, as a true revolutionary, I took care to cast such thoughts and doubts aside. I told myself not to think them, not to allow them entry into my consciousness. Struggling against my thoughts was easier than struggling constantly against my new environment. As though I were in the Army, drafted into service against my wishes, I came to accept that there was no way out and I had better make the best of it. This was an entirely new world for me, so different from my protected, affluent former life. Perhaps what Cin told me *was* true. Perhaps I had been completely out of touch with the world while studying, as he said. Revolutionary movements were erupting all over the world and I had not known of them. Cin pointed out press reports of guerrilla uprisings in Asia and Africa and the Middle East. Perhaps Cin was right in his certainty that an incipient revolution was starting in the United States. How else could he ring doorbells at random and bring back supporters to run errands for the SLA? How else could he be so sure that the black people in this neighborhood would protect us from the police, if he called upon them for help? My only source of information or news analysis all this time was Cinque and the others in the

SLA. We lived in a world of our own, never going outside our safehouse in Hunters Point. Reality for them was different from all that I had known before, and their reality by this time had become my reality.

Although I was fully accepted as one of them, I was still the "weak sister" in their army, criticized constantly for being too bourgeois, unable to shed the vestiges of my privileged upbringing, unable to change my upper-class speech patterns, unable to learn the military discipline and combat skills of the others, and, finally, not being sufficiently determined to catch up with their superior dedication to the cause. Though I tried to mend my ways, they were right. I moped around a good deal. I was distracted, disturbed, frightened out of my wits, depressed, and generally miserable. I broke down and wept many times. For me, life was far worse at Oakdale than it had been at Golden Gate Avenue. I simply could not keep up with the intensified training, which was much more strenuous than it had been before. I could not run around this house with heavy equipment on my back for the hours that were required of all of us. I would collapse in exhaustion. I became genuinely ill and too weak to learn how to tumble and do shoulder rolls, with a pack on my back, a carbine in my hand, and holstered revolver on my hip—and come up in a firing position. I had to plead with Cin to excuse me from that exercise and convince him that I was not malingering.

I was much better at the less strenuous weapons drills. They had tacked to the walls life-size pictures of policemen, with pig's faces, drawn on paper shopping bags, and I learned how to slink along the floor in a semi-crouch and quick-draw and fire "at the pigs." I could load and unload and strip and put together all of the weapons in our arsenal. We were armed with loaded weapons throughout the day, alert for any police attack, but for practice and drills we unloaded our weapons and practiced dry-firing in all sorts of simulated predicaments. Teko, for instance, would stand in front of me and we would quick-draw against one another, as I practiced aiming at his chest or his head. He would report whether my hand had been steady or whether I had wavered and missed him. If I "missed" him, he would announce that I was "dead," killed by a "pig bullet." We practiced our point and slack maneuvers for a team of three, one person forward in action, backed up by two soldiers behind him, or two forward and one backup.

Because this safehouse was on the ground floor, with no one beneath us to hear our stomping, our training was intensified. We now did indoor jogging, shoulder rolls, and shooting practice with BB guns. Calisthenics became much more vigorous and our weapons practice increased. Now there was no worry about anyone hearing the metallic clicks of the bolt actions of our guns. We were on the move all day long, from morning to night.

In preparation for the outbreak of the revolution, Cinque announced at a meeting one night that he had decided upon a new second-in-command. Fahizah, who had held that position since the formation of the SLA, did not have the necessary military skills to provide the leadership we would need in the guerrilla warfare which would soon be upon us, he said. "Our sister was fine for the position—dedicated, hardworking and capable—when our intelligence operations were so important, writing our Codes of War, and getting the message across to the people," Cin said. "But now, everybody knows us. Now we are entering a new phase, a military phase. So we need a second-in-command whose strengths are in knowing military action.

"Therefore," declared Cin, "I have decided to promote Teko to the position of General and second-in-command."

In a moment of stunned silence, everyone looked to Fahizah for her reaction. Her face seemed to crumble in pain. She was surprised and hurt. After some hesitation, she said falteringly, "I think brother Cin is right. He is doing this for the welfare of the SLA, to make us stronger. It's nothing personal, I know. Cin is our leader and he knows what's best. So . . . I think he has made the right decision."

But then the floodgates opened. "I think it's shitty and sexist," exclaimed Yolanda. In measured, mean words, which scarcely hid her anger, she launched into a long harangue on her revolutionary principles: Women were every bit as capable as men in every phase of revolutionary action. Teko was no better than anyone else, man or woman, as a soldier or a leader in the SLA. Two men at the head of the SLA would be an insult, she declared, to every woman who wanted to fight in the revolution. If the SLA was to be true to its principles, if the sexes were to be truly equal, then there should be a man and a woman in the top two positions of command.

"But that's sexist in itself," Teko shot back. "To think that a woman should be second-in-command just to have a woman there in that position—that's sexist. With my military training, I do have more military experience and I know more about weapons and maneuvers than Fahizah. That's just true. And it's got nothing to do with being a man or a woman."

Reason, of course, did little to persuade Yolanda; she was jealous of the man she had married. They had a fierce love-hate relationship; they were inseparable, dependent upon each other, and yet not a day went by without their bickering and fighting with one another. Zoya, too, bluntly opposed Teko's promotion. Not only was it inherently sexist to have two men at the head of the SLA, Zoya declared, but beyond that she did not believe Teko had the personal qualities needed in a leader. The discussion went on for well over an hour. Cin proclaimed that Teko had come a long way in recent weeks and had displayed new qualities of leadership and in planning operations. But Zoya still found him wanting. "Teko is just too emotional," she declared. "He flies off the handle all the time. He acts first and thinks later. We need a leader who can make the right decisions when something has to be decided on the spot. Teko is not good at that. In fact, he's very weak in that area. Too often, his decisions are wrong. He does not think things through."

But the others sided with Cin, and I kept my mouth shut. I liked Fahizah much better than I did Teko. But she was not much of a leader, I had to admit to myself. She was far too mystical and otherworldly, vague at times. More than anything else, she worshipped Cin and echoed everything he said. Yet one could reason with her. Teko as second-in-command frightened me. He had a terrible, unpredictable temper and would lash out at the slightest provocation, besides being arrogant, nervous, and close-minded. Disagreeing with the General Field Marshal was useless in the long run. He rarely changed his mind and dissent disturbed him. As the controversy over Teko raged on well into the night, Cin finally put a stop to it, saying, "The real problem with this group is that there are too many chiefs and not enough Indians."

"That's a very racist remark!" shot back Zoya, who automatically reacted to any word or phrase which contained the slightest derogatory implication.

"Don't you tell *me* what's racist!" shouted Cin, outraged. "You got some nerve lecturing me, a black man, about racism. Don't you ever do that again. Nobody here has got the right to tell any black man about racism. Besides, you should all keep in mind that I'm your leader, so you just stop contradicting me. 'Cause I know what I'm talkin' about, and you don't."

A silence fell over the group. Their guilt over being white and not black was unanswerable. So Teko was installed as second-in-command. Fahizah took it very well. She went about her own training and her chores with the same dedication to the cause as before and never once challenged Teko's orders. I could not say the same for Teko. From the night of his promotion, he became increasingly arrogant. He strutted about, lording it over the rest of us, criticizing everyone, with the exception of the General Field Marshal. Teko's fights with Yolanda became so violent that the two of them came to blows on occasion and stopped only when Cin interceded.

And yet, only a few days later, when Cin announced that he had drawn up a reorganization of the SLA into three permanent teams, Teko and Yolanda banded solidly together in fighting Cin and everyone else, because Cin's plan would have separated them. His plan was the culmination of discussions on the future role of the SLA which had begun back at the Golden Gate Avenue safehouse. For the revolution, Cin announced, the SLA would divide itself into three teams, each with three members, based upon each person's strengths and weaknesses. The teams would operate as completely independent, self-sufficient units, training together, taking actions together. Once we took to the streets, we would go our separate ways, never meeting again except for occasional War Council meetings of all the SLA units. Each fire team would recruit followers and build itself into another full combat unit. Then each unit would split again into three-member teams and build more combat units. In time, each of the original nine of us would lead a fully complemented combat team in the ever-growing Symbionese Liberation Army.

First, Cin picked the leaders of the three teams: himself, General Teko, and General Fahizah. No one objected to that. Then he announced that on his team would be Gelina and Zoya. On Fahizah's team would be Cujo and Yolanda. On Teko's team would be Gabi and Tania.

Teko screamed in protest. "That's not fair! You've stuck me with the two weakest ones here. Our team would be crippled from the start. With Tania and Gabi, it couldn't work out. We're not strong enough to survive. They don't have the skills yet and I couldn't protect both of them. . . ."

He wanted Yolanda on his team. "Yolanda and I should be on the same team. We complement each other. We always work well together. We know each other so well, our strengths and our weaknesses, we would make a very strong team together, and I don't care which of the others you give me, Tania or Gabi, but I need Yolanda."

Several of the sisters pointed out that it was agreed that couples should not be on the same team because personalities and personal conflicts would intrude upon the team's efficiency. They argued that Teko and Yolanda, being married, had been together too long already and that they were always fighting with one another. They wanted single-minded dedication to the cause. "We don't think couples should be together on future actions," declared Zoya, who, of course, was the most ardent feminist in the group.

"But we're not a couple," protested Yolanda with passion. "We've stuggled very hard for a long time to get rid of that bourgeois mentality. We're not monogamous. Our marriage has nothing whatever to do with anything. We've struggled so hard to be free and independent of each other. It's very unfair for people to assume we cannot operate on any other level, other than being married. It's not fair."

Yolanda continued, saying, "Let's examine the situation logically," gave example after example to show how well she and Teko operated together as a team. She talked and talked, reasoned and argued, cajoled and pleaded. Pretty soon, tears were streaming down her cheeks. No one could ever get the last word when "struggling" with Yolanda. For hours, late into the night, the debate raged, with shouts and curses as well as tears, and finally Yolanda wore them all down. The teams were juggled and reorganized. Yolanda went on Teko's team, with me. Gabi was switched to Cinque's team, joining Gelina there. And Zoya moved to add strength to Fahizah's team, which Cujo did not like very much. The two of them never got along except when Zoya wanted to have sex with him. She treated him as an overgrown, stupid adolescent. He thought that she was envious of his natural male strength and that she was a terribly bossy shrew. I myself did not like Teko at all and I felt even more uncomfortable in dealing with Yolanda. I could not quite figure her out, but I could sense the bad chemistry between us. Perhaps it was that I knew she disliked and distrusted me more than did anyone else. Nevertheless, those were the new SLA teams, wrought out of an all-night marathon of radical minds, designed to conquer the world.

From that moment on, we did everything by teams. Teko, as leader, devised imaginary combat situations and Yolanda and I would try to figure out the best solution to the problem offered. Most of our point and slack maneuvers involved one person going into "an operation," being backed up by the other two, or two involved in an action, backed up by the other one. Thus, if two comrades were positioned to ambush a police car, the third might be farther down the block, guarding the street against a surprise attack from a second police car. Or if one of us went inside a building, the second might follow at a distance and the third would stand guard inside or outside the door. The backup person or team was there for protection, obligated to open fire upon any enemy interruption. To fail to protect a comrade in the course of a combat operation was the very worst offense listed in the SLA Codes of War. The penalty for such a failure was death. Instant death. Being shot on the spot, without trial, without recourse. As we played the game, even if five carloads of police arrived on the scene of an action, the backup team, whether one person or two, had to open fire on the police in order to warn and to protect the others. In all the drills, there was no provision for surrender or for fleeing. A team operated together, succeeded or failed together, lived or died together.

From my very beginning with the SLA, I had heard Cin protest over and over again that he would never be taken prisoner by the police. Better to die, he said, than to endure the tortures inflicted upon revolutionaries in prison. Atrocity stories were a standard topic of conversation. They seemed to know of prisons all over the world: in Chile, the Philippines, South Africa, Rhodesia, Iran, and Vietnam . . . especially Vietnam. They spoke of brutal beatings, electrified cattle prods, electric shocks to the genitals, chains, whips, ceaseless interrogations, solitary confinements in bare cells . . . Everyone proclaimed it was better to die under fire than to rot in a fascist prison, helping no one while you died anyway, an insignificant death. As strange as it seems to me now, at the time, although my will to survive was as strong as ever, I accepted that part of the SLA philosophy too.

Each time a group discussion centered on the future of the revolution, a new, deeper dimension of fatalism crept into the conversations. My comrades waxed poetic on "how beautiful it will be to die for the revolution." We were fighting for the future, certain to be victorious, even though we would not live to see the glorious day of victory. Still, our willingness to die for the cause would prove to the poor and oppressed people of this country that the SLA was truly dedicated, that the SLA meant what it said, that we were willing to struggle to the death to achieve our goals. We would be martyrs. We would go down in history. . . . It was especially important for us, as white people, to prove to black and other oppressed people that we were willing to die for their freedom. Only in this way could the others come to trust us as whites. . . . Death filled the center room where we held our meetings every night.

The fatalism of fighting and dying for the cause, rather than depressing anyone, seemed to increase just about everyone's determination. Gelina threw herself into the combat drills with a new, noticeable verve, determined to be more determined than anyone else. Her usual laughter and good cheer faded away as she concentrated soberly on running, tumbling, crouching, firing her weapons longer than anyone else. She even took Gabi under her wing, helping her with the drills.

Cujo changed more than anyone else, going deeper and deeper into his own self, disciplining his body to achieve his self-imposed daily two hundred push-ups. He was a big young man, very strong and well coordinated, and, as he trained, he seemed to grow stronger and more self-sufficient day by day. He needed to prove himself worthy of becoming a general in the revolution, he confided to me. When not physically training, he spent hours studying maps and then drawing them from memory. He planned imaginary "actions" and conferred with Cin about them. Days would go by when he would not say a word to me or to anyone else. He slept alone. There were no more complaints about stomachaches. He took no more naps during the day. He was determined, changing before our eyes. In return, he was receiving constant praise from everyone for his change in attitude.

As the days went on, there was less and less socializing between members of different teams. We were preparing ourselves for the day when the three teams would separate, each going its own way, spreading the SLA war against the ruling classes. In order to facilitate a planned recruiting drive, Cin took out our Polaroid camera and ordered that a series of group photographs be taken. Except for Cin and myself, the others took turns in snapping the group pictures, so that each photo pictured eight of us looking happy and determined. The photos were to be used by each team to prove its SLA identity to new recruits in building up the army.

Our next combat operation was going to be our biggest one, Cin announced, for we were to advance the revolution by going out on "search and destroy" missions to shoot down and kill policemen. During the night, we would roam the streets, ambushing policemen wherever we found them, on foot or in their patrol cars. This would be outright guerrilla warfare. We would strike fast with heavy gunfire and then disappear into the night. In the early-morning hours, each team would invade a civilian home, take control of it throughout the next day, sleeping and standing guard in shifts, and then depart on another "search and destroy" action under the cloak of darkness on the following night.

At first, of course, people would resent the invasion of their homes, but they would learn that the SLA would never harm them. In the homes, Cin said, we would explain the revolution to the people, even try to recruit them. The SLA would attack only the police and other enemies of the people and before long "the people" would come to understand our mission and would welcome SLA combat teams into their homes.

The effect of this unrelenting guerrilla warfare would be to force the police and even the National Guard to take countermeasures against us, which would entail increasing police oppression in the black and poor neighborhoods. That naked use of force would enrage the people, who would rise up and join the SLA in battling the ruling class. Cin loved the scenario so much that he convinced himself that it could not fail. The only two questions he spoke of were when it would all begin and how long it would take. But we already knew the answers: It would begin in the summer and we would not be alive to see the victory. We all lived under his spell, preparing for the day it would all begin. Without fully realizing it, I still lived under the impression, as I had in the closet, that the SLA was much bigger and much more powerful than I could see with my own eyes. Others would join in once it all began. Confined to that dank, dark safehouse, we lived in a world of our own.

The only live contact we had with the outside world during all this time was with the four Black Muslims and their three children. Every second or third night they would come to Oakdale, loaded down with bags of food and supplies, and they would remain to have dinner with us. They told us the news and the street gossip concerning the SLA and the police hunt for us. Our photos were up on "Wanted" posters in every post office. The FBI search was always "red hot." The SLA photo of me, with beret and carbine against the SLA flag, had become a popular WE LOVE YOU, TANIA poster in Berkeley and the East Bay Area. While the conversations always focused on SLA activities and radical causes, with the Black Muslims there those evenings were always more social than they would have been otherwise. Cin told stories to children and adults, trying all the time to entice Retimah into joining the SLA. Fahizah managed to lure Brother Ali away from the group and they would disappear into a back bedroom for a while and then return with silly, telltale grins on their faces. They were an incongruous pair, Fahizah being less than five feet tall and Brother Ali being well over six feet. Fahizah gave him up, though, after she contracted a terribly annoying case of the crabs.

Brother Ali, who said he taught at a Black Muslim school, always came to Oakdale carrying a worn leather briefcase, which he kept close to him, saying it contained important school papers. But Cin came to suspect that Ali might have a secret tape recorder in his briefcase, recording our conversations. One night, as planned, Teko and Gelina managed to go through the briefcase while Ali was otherwise occupied. Afterward, Teko reported what they had found: Muslim literature, bottles of cheap perfume, sticks of incense, and a stack of pornographic photographs.

After that, Cin trusted Brother Ali with a considerable amount of cash, with which he was to go out and purchase three vans for the SLA. "'The whole Bay Area is getting too hot for us now," Cin told Ali, "so I think we might be movin' on to some place else pretty soon." Cin did not trust the Muslims well enough to tell them where we were going. They didn't need to know.

Cin had become totally paranoiac about the police closing in on us in San Francisco. We were having false alarms constantly. In the high crime area of Hunters Point and with a social center of some sort across the street from our safehouse, police cars were always zooming by and sometimes stopping at the building across the street. Each time a police car stopped, the SLA went on combat alert with automatic weapons, gas masks, and ragged nerves. One never becomes accustomed to peering out a window at uniformed armed policemen and worrying whether or not this time they have come for you.

Cin believed that our search-and-destroy missions would be much more effective in sprawling Los Angeles, where we could strike fast and escape in that urban jungle which had no natural boundaries. San Francisco was a small, contained city (population approximately

750,000) on a peninsula, which Cin said had been cut off by road-
blocks at its two bridges and the narrow neck of its peninsula, but he
thought we still could get through. His decision to move to Los Angeles caused considerable consternation among the others. They argued
for days that the first rule for guerrilla warfare was to know your territory and none of them were familiar with Los Angeles. Cinque
dismissed those arguments out of hand: He knew Los Angeles because
he had been brought up there, he said. The rest of us would learn the
terrain by studying street maps.

I too had spent part of my childhood in Los Angeles, but not in the
areas Cin had in mind. We studied maps of Watts and Compton, two
black ghetto areas, and also Griffith Park, where Cin thought we could
hide when necessary in the heavily wooded areas. We also memorized
the fastest escape routes out of the city.

Apart from the combat drills and exercises, Teko and Yolanda spent
most of the day together, planning future actions for our team, while I
tried to stay out of their way. I sat most of the time slumped in a
corner, reading weapons manuals or road maps, feeling miserable and
sorry for myself. As our team commander, Teko was impossibly arrogant and domineering, ordering us about and criticizing our work. I always did as I was told, like a whipped dog, but Yolanda almost always
fought back. In her own mind, she never ceased to believe that she
could do everything better than Teko could. When it came to planning,
conferring, or just talking, however, she was truly in her best element.
She could wear down and outtalk anyone. The two of them went on for
hours talking with one another, ignoring me even when I tried to join
in as a member of the team.

Finally, Cin himself noticed that I was being ostracized and he
brought it up at a meeting one night. "You're not being very comradely
toward sister Tania here," he told Teko and Yolanda. "She's always sitting alone in a corner and you two are off by yourselves doing whatever the hell it is you're doing."

Teko tried to explain it away, saying that I was welcome to join
them any time I wanted, but that I did not seem very interested in their
planning or discussions. Others joined in the criticism, saying they were
too much of a couple to allow a third person in.

"What's your opinion, Tania?" asked Cin. "Come on, say what you
think."

"Well, we're not much of a team," I admitted, with great trepidation, feeling my heart pump heavily in my chest at the idea of criticizing Teko. "They seem to have an exclusive relationship and don't seem to need me. They never speak to me."

Yolanda, quickly sizing up the situation and the inherent danger to the continuance of her team, began to apologize profusely. Soon she was in tears, explaining that Teko and she had become too intent upon their work and had been neglecting me. She promised that they would mend their ways. Teko then self-criticized himself as a team leader for being negligent and unaware of my feelings, promising to make amends.

After that meeting, both of them were revoltingly ingratiating, going out of their way to invite me to join them every time they were holding a meeting. But their saccharine sweetness hardly masked their disdain. "Tania, Teko and I are going to work on escape routes and methods," Yolanda would say. "Would you like to join us?"

"No," I would reply with my own feigned politeness. "I still have to do my push-ups." I had decided in my own mind that, of all the SLA, these two were the most evil as a matter of innate personality. I hated them.

Late one afternoon as I moped about, Cin sidled up to me and tried to cheer me up in his own way. "Hey, sister, what's the matter? You feelin' down?"

"Yeah," I said.

"You want to fuck?" He said it most casually, as though he was ready to do me a favor.

"No, no, thanks," I replied. "I just feel sort of sick, but I'll be all right . . ."

"Any time, you know."

"Yeah, thanks." It was the last time he would ask.

Brother Ali found and bought three used vans for us, two Volkswagens and one ancient Chevrolet, which we parked several blocks away from our safehouse. For their services, Cin told them they could keep the ten-year-old station wagon they had been using for running SLA errands. Not long after that, however, we learned that the police had discovered our old safehouse on Golden Gate Avenue. It was the infestation of cockroaches in the building, compounded by the filth we had left behind, which brought the landlord to the apartment, I think. As a result, Cin told the Muslims to get rid of the station wagon he had given them because it had been observed near the apartment and associated with us.

A few days later, Rasheem burst into the safehouse unexpectedly, excited and out of breath, exclaiming, "The pigs found the station wagon!" He told Cin that he had abandoned the car on a street as directed, but returned to it a day later for an important errand. When he could not get the car started, someone on the street had walked up and told him that the car was hot and under police observation. The man himself had seen the police take the battery out of the car. Rasheem said he had rushed to our safehouse to tell Cin right away.

Cin was furious. "You dumb son of a bitch, you jeopardized our security . . . you probably led the police right here . . ."

"No, no, I didn't do that," Rasheem cried in fear. "I went roundabout, took three buses, and made sure I wasn't followed. I thought you wanted to know right away."

Cin sent Rasheem away, instructing him to inform the others to keep clear of our house for the next two or three days, and then, when Rasheem had left, Cin announced, "We're leaving tonight. . . . This place is hot."

A meeting of team leaders was held and Teko reported back to Yolanda and me that we were to plan to make our own way down to Los Angeles that night. We would meet the others again at eleven o'clock the following morning at a location that, for security reasons, only the leaders would know.

In a flurry of excitement and fear of an imminent police raid, we packed up. But before we left, Cin told us that we had to clean up so that not a speck of dirt showed anywhere in this safehouse. When the police had discovered our Golden Gate apartment, Cin said, they had "twisted" the story, so that the press had not reported our little "joke" but instead had announced to the world that the SLA had been living in filth and squalor, like pigs in a pigsty. He wouldn't give them that opportunity again.

It was somewhat after 11 P.M. when we departed the city by the bay. The SLA had a rendezvous with death and did not wish to waste a moment in getting there.

CHAPTER

TEN

WE DROVE THROUGH the night down Route 99, the least-traveled north-south highway, passing through California's farm country, Fresno, Bakersfield, and dozens of small towns, encountering only light, local traffic. Despite the highly publicized manhunt for us, we thought it unlikely that the state highway patrol would be checking this road or that the local police would be awake at this time of night. Nevertheless, on the floor in the back of the rattling, bouncing Chevy van, I felt like a trapped, caged animal—terrified.

Security was uppermost in my mind and I could not rest comfortably with the thought that if we were stopped by the police, I would be trapped. Teko and Yolanda might fling open the doors and escape into the night, but there would be no chance for me. With no windows in the back of the van, I would not dare open the rear doors for fear of being shot instantly. Yolanda was doing most of the driving, with Teko riding shotgun in the passenger seat and occasionally changing places with her. I could see the backs of their heads and shoulders and could hear the murmur of their voices. But once again they were ignoring me, as if I were a piece of baggage. Our automatic weapons were hidden beneath a blanket on the floor of the van, ready to be used. I alternately sat or stretched out on the bare metal floor, but there was no way, no position, in which I could make myself comfortable, much less sleep.

When I stretched out, the bouncing of the moving van got me in the small of the back. If I curled up on one side, the jarring struck my hip, and sitting up, with my back against one wall, the movement over the uneven roadway jostled my entire body. There was an eerie strangeness to it all, passing through these unfamiliar towns in the deep of night, leaving San Francisco behind me, presumably forever. How long would it be before I would be tested in the revolution that Cin had prophesied? I could not face the terror of shooting at people—and of being shot at. I told myself that it simply could not happen . . . or would not happen . . . Cin had been just talking. . . . But the bank robbery had happened. . . . Why was all this happening to me . . . ? Why not to someone else? Anyone else? Why me? I would leap in fright at the slightest unexpected noise, a knock on the door, the rat-a-tat of a jackhammer, or an accidental jab in the ribs. Yet, another part of me insisted that it could not happen; I would not be killed; I would somehow survive. Cin's revolution might indeed come to pass, the SLA might succeed or it might fail, but I would somehow live through it. I could not go on with the contemplation of my own death. I taught myself to live without thinking beyond the present moment. One can function that way day by day. I did not think of my parents, my sisters, my friends. I did not think of escaping. It never occurred to me to pick up a submachine gun and blast the two people I hated so much, who sat there with their backs to me, unprotected. They were my comrades, and Teko was my General.

Toward morning, they allowed me to drive for about forty-five minutes, while Yolanda stretched out in the back of the van. We reached Los Angeles at about eight o'clock, found our meeting place, and then drove around the streets of Los Angeles for the three hours we had to wait for the others to arrive. We were numb, all of us, from that all-night drive and, I think, Teko and Yolanda were talked out.

At 11 A.M., the forces of the Symbionese Liberation Army rendezvoused in peace and quiet at a little, block-square park, whose name I no longer remember, to make final preparations, as Cin had put it, "to start the revolution." Our three vans were parked, not together, but within sight of one another. Yolanda and I waited nervously, keeping watch, while Teko attended a "leaders" meeting in Cin's command vehicle, the red and white VW van with matching curtains. Actually, I thought it was rather nice being outdoors in the daylight and sunshine, watching men and women stroll by so nonchalantly, unaware of the SLA presence.

After more than an hour, Teko returned to report that we were to scout the area, studying the terrain, while Fahizah's team would find us a new safehouse, and Cin would set up security precautions in the area—all of us meeting here again at 5 P.M. The entire operation proceeded smoothly. Teko was certain that we were much safer in Los Angeles than in San Francisco because the police in southern California had no idea whatever that we were in their area. When we launched our first action, Teko said, we would take them completely by surprise.

Teko returned from the five o'clock meeting in Cin's van glowing with news: Fahizah had located a marvelous, cheap safehouse for us. It was in an all-black neighborhood and it had no electricity, but it was only seventy dollars a month. Best of all, the landlord was a "cool dude" who had photos of Malcolm X and Martin Luther King on his walls, and he had said he "loved freedom fighters." In fact, Fahizah thought the landlord, who called himself Prophet Jones, had recognized her, because he had kept asking if they had ever met before at political demonstrations. Fahizah, of course, had denied it, but she thought Prophet Jones to be so trustworthy that she had asked Cin's permission to reveal to Prophet Jones that we were the SLA. We would be among friends in our new safehouse and we could begin recruiting. Cin okayed the action, but told Fahizah to take Zoya in with her as a backup, just in case of any trouble.

Fahizah's team drove off to rent the safehouse, and we waited for her return. When Teko had come back from that meeting he told us laughingly that Prophet Jones "must be some kind of a brother, because when Fahizah told him that she was from the SLA, he didn't believe her." Our new landlord was tremendously suspicious of all white people, Teko said, with admiration in his voice. Finally, to prove her identity, Fahizah had whipped her submachine gun out of her shopping bag and had shown him her holstered revolver beneath her jacket, and he had said, "Okay, but you better be from the SLA, 'cause we love freedom fighters here . . . but if you're pigs, you're goin' find yourselves in a lot of trouble."

Our plan was to arrive at the safehouse late that night, when the neighbors would not notice us, Teko said, and then we would play it very cool once we were inside. Prophet Jones had warned Fahizah that if the neighbors found a bunch of whites living in that house, they would be very suspicious, no matter who we were.

We drove about the city, passing the time until our next rendezvous. We stopped at a takeout place to buy a pizza for dinner and ate it in the van. We made two other stops, trying to make contact with people who might help the SLA. One was a woman whom Teko and Yolanda had known at Indiana University. Teko went to see her and came back to tell us a strange story which even he found hard to believe: The woman had greeted Teko as an old friend and asked him what he was doing these days. When he told her he was with the SLA, she replied, "What is the SLA?" She had never heard of it. Teko did not know where to begin to explain. Then he spotted a copy of *Time* magazine on her coffee table and in it he found an article on the SLA. She read the article and became terrified of her old friend. Teko had all he could do to calm her down. Help from her was out of the question.

The other stop was at the home of a black woman whom Yolanda called Utommu. She was the mother of Lumumba, a black prisoner with whom Yolanda had become wildly infatuated while visiting him before she and Teko had gone underground with the SLA. The woman was either not home or not answering her doorbell. However, her name was on her mailbox and Yolanda professed certainty that Utommu would be eager to help the SLA whenever Yolanda could reach her. We tried again just after dusk and this time Utommu was home. Yolanda went in alone, and when she returned to the van, she was positively glowing. I'd never seen her so excited and happy. She was bubbling over with news about Lumumba: He was due to be released from prison soon. She could hardly wait for their reunion. She gushed on and on, not at all hiding her emotions over the man. Teko barely managed to suppress his jealousy. After all, they both believed in open marriages.

Our new, "great" Los Angeles safehouse was located on West Eighty-fourth Street in Compton, a black ghetto which borders on Watts. We drove through the area sometime after eleven o'clock that night, the three vans in a row, and pulled up in front of an old, dilapidated, unpainted wooden shack. It was a cottage and not an apartment, as Fahizah had said, consisting of only two rooms and a long, narrow kitchen. It was unfurnished. It had running water, but no gas or electricity and therefore no hot water, no cooking facilities, and no lights.

No one complained about Fahizah's choice. We all went to work making the house secure with locks on the front and back doors, covering the windows with our old surveillance drapes, and checking out our escape routes. A way to safety was the prime essential of any guerrilla operation, Cin lectured us. As we went through this operation, I could not shake off a lingering despair and depression. It seemed to me that the SLA was sinking lower and lower, despite all of Cin's talk about the imminence of our revolution. Since its inception, the SLA had gone from a rather nice safehouse in suburban Concord to the house where I had been kept in Daly City and then to the smaller apartment on Golden Gate Avenue and on to the dirty, empty house in Hunters Point and now to this shack which was barely fit for human habitation.

Well after midnight, our landlord, Prophet Jones, suddenly appeared at the front door. I was astounded at the sight of the man. He was the biggest, blackest, strongest man I had ever seen. At least six feet five, broad-shouldered and muscular, he looked like a well-proportioned giant. His hands were enormous. Alongside of him, Cinque looked like a slight adolescent boy, half his size. Prophet Jones could have throttled him with one hand. And yet, Cin held his own with this huge man, acting every bit as tough and fearless as the giant. Prophet Jones, if not downright suspicious, seemed to be very wary of our strange group of three men and six women. In the shadows of the living room, where we were all gathered, lighted with only two or three small votive candles, Cin launched into an exaggerated history of the SLA and its exploits, explaining that we had come to Los Angeles to start the revolution which would free all the black oppressed people of the United States. Of course, he pointed me out as the SLA's prized convert, a soldier who had given up all her wealth and privileges to join in the fight for freedom.

Prophet Jones peered closely at me through the gloom and after a moment's hesitation he shook his head in wonderment and asked: "Why is all her hair cut off like that?" I don't think Cin expected that question. But he came up with an immediate answer: " 'Cause I like it that way."

"How come if you are freedom fighters, you went and killed a black person like Marcus Foster?" Prophet Jones asked.

At great length Cin explained his theory that the Oakland Superintendent of Schools had been an undercover CIA agent who had been trying to identify and segregate the children of black radicals so he could send the children off to prison. But Prophet Jones looked skeptical, questioning why there weren't more blacks in the SLA. Cin gave his usual discourse on the subject. He told Cin that we were in an all-black neighborhood where whites were not tolerated and even the police came into the area at their own peril. He told a gruesome story of how an undercover narcotics agent had been discovered several weeks before and how he had been taken out into an empty lot and shot with his own gun. He told Cin in one breath that he believed we were the SLA, but in the next breath he warned us that if we were undercover police, we would not survive long around here. Prophet Jones wished us "Good luck!" as he left, but he was still shaking his head as if he did not fully believe us.

Cin laid down strict rules that we were not to venture outside the house, day or night, and we were to keep our voices low so that we would not be heard by passersby. He instructed us to cup our hands over our cigarettes when we smoked at night so that no one could see the telltale red glow. It would be best if the neighbors did not know we were in the house, but even if they found out that the house was occupied, he did not want them to suspect that nine people were living here. That would certainly arouse suspicions and breach our security.

Security was our watchword twenty-four hours a day, every day. If Hunters Point in San Francisco had been heavy with the presence of police, this black ghetto on the edge of Watts, burned in the blaze of black violence in 1965, was saturated with police surveillance. Police helicopters hovered overhead here too every night; patrol cars vroomed down our street just about every hour, traveling in pairs for their own security. Looking out from the slits in our surveillance drapes, I could see drug deals being made on the street. I could see black men stop and stare at our house. It was plain that the neighbors had learned that white people were living here. A feeling of claustrophobia came over me. We were trapped inside this house, or so it seemed. No one went outside after the first day when Zoya and Yolanda ventured to a grocery for some spot shopping. We did have our survival supplies, canned food and army field rations. Dinner, our main meal of the day, was reduced to a slimy, cold mixture of canned spinach and okra, flavored with bits of canned mackerel. That far I could not go with my comrades. I resorted to eating the survival rations in my backpack, bits of hard processed beef, crackers, and sometimes Kipper Snacks.

While the feature-story writers in the news media were portraying the SLA as a band of idealistic radicals, however misguided, who were involved in sex orgies and daring exploits against the establishment, conjuring up romantic tales of adventure, we were sinking into the depths of psychosis. We were cut off from the outside world and lived in an isolated realm of our own. We had only our battery-operated radio for news. The radio played all day long and most of the night too and Cin would often hear song lyrics which contained for him special allusions to the revolution. Over and over, Cin would stop us all and yell, "Hey, listen to this," and we would all focus on a song's lyrics for a hint of our revolution. I never doubted that the hidden meaning was there, only that I was not sufficiently knowledgeable to understand what our leader heard. We worked all day at our revolution with as much if not greater intensity than ever before—combat drills, physical calisthenics, weapons practice. Added to all this were new classes of instructions on knife throwing and how to slit someone's throat.

Cin had detached a closet door, set it up against a wall, drawn the outline of a man on it, and then practiced throwing a large bayonet knife at it. He was remarkably good. He hit the target from varying distances, the point sticking into a vital area of the body, the handle quivering upon impact. But despite all his efforts at teaching, with the exception of Fahizah none of us could come close to his adeptness with a knife as a weapon. We all wore sheathed survival knives, with six-inch blades, on our webbed belts, purchased for us in an army surplus store in San Francisco by Retimah. Although I practiced for hours, I could never even strike the target with the point of the knife, much less stick it in. Most of the others were not much better. Fahizah gave instructions on how to sneak up on someone from behind and slit his throat. But that did not meet with much success either. The SLA was not going to win this revolution by the point of a knife.

We practiced our drills by teams and Teko was frenetic in pushing Yolanda and me to ever greater feats in trying to outdo the other teams. He wanted us to be the best. And, from what I could see, we were the worst. Fahizah's team seemed almost naturally gifted in their point and slack maneuvers, their fast draws, their rapid firing. Zoya was a natural athlete and Cujo was manic in his determination to become the perfect urban guerrilla. By this time, he had withdrawn almost entirely into himself. Not only did he not speak to me, he spoke to no one, except when absolutely necessary. He was off somewhere in a nether world of his own. Gabi held back Cin's own team, for she was as unnatural and ungainly as ever in anything physical.

In one bitter, exhausting combat drill, when we all were racing through the house with full equipment and vaulting over a door laid horizontally across a doorframe, Cin stood off to one side, urging us on and kicking stragglers as they began their jump over the three-foot-high obstacle. "Jump!" he cried, and kicked me in the behind. It was humiliating and frightening. Each time I rounded the course and came to the door, I would be haunted with the fear: Would he kick me or not this time? The intensity built up, as Cin shouted, "Keep going, keep going; in combat you're gonna get tired, but there's no stopping. Keep going!"

At one point, he gave Gabi, who was just ahead of me, a ferocious kick in the rear end, which clearly was much more than an ordinary boost. I don't know how many times she had been booted at this point, but she stopped suddenly in her tracks. She turned on him, glaring, her fist raised as though to strike him. "Who the hell do you think you are, kicking me like that?" She trembled with rage. "Don't you ever do that again!"

Instead of stepping back, Cin advanced bellicosely to within inches of her face and taunted her: "Well, what the fuck you going to do about it?" Gabi just stood there, trembling with rage. "Get your ass over that obstacle and keep running. . . . I'll kick you whenever I damn please. Now, move."

Gabi simply caved in. She stepped over the door and then began running across the living room, into the bedroom, through the hall, and back again. This time at the door, Cin stopped her.

"Why didn't you hit me then, like you wanted to?"

Gabi stood there, quivering, all the fight taken out of her.

"Why don't you hit me now?" Cin stuck out his chin. "The trouble with you, sister, is that you're still just a product of your white, middle-class upbringing. You don't have the guts to act on your emotions. Poor people, black people hit back when they're mad. They strike out at people who hurt them. That's what our revolution is all about. But you . . . you ain't learned that yet."

Poor Gabi was so upset that she simply broke down and wept. She stood there, big and ungainly in her ugly, disheveled combat clothes, with her arms dangling at her sides, embarrassing tears rolling down her flushed cheeks. At the moment, she was a most miserable, pathetic human being. No one came to her aid. We just stood there and watched. Gabi had no real friends or supporters in the SLA. Cin taunted and belittled her for quite some time, proving his dominance over her, and there was nothing she could do about it. For the rest of that day and well into the next, Gabi kept to herself, trying to hide her humiliation, as if she were a sick animal licking her wounds. The rest of us left her alone in a sort of silent understanding. Why didn't she up and quit the SLA? Why didn't she sneak away and escape all of this torment? Because she couldn't, any more than I could.

In retrospect, I suppose all of us were suffering from a combination of group hypnosis and battle fatigue, our anxieties and fears stretched to the breaking point. I had made my adjustment mentally to this fugitive life: I accepted orders and did as instructed, without questioning. But physically, I ached with a dull pain all the time. I was tired before the day was half over. My stomach cramped up in spasms at unexpected moments. My menstrual periods were so irregular I lost all track of them. I wept more and more each day. The tears would just come, welling up in my eyes and flowing down my cheeks. I am not sure that I even felt miserable anymore. This was my normal way of life and crying had become a part of it.

At a meeting one day, I noticed for the first time just how gaunt and sickly all of my comrades had become. Bereft of sunlight and fresh air, their skins had turned to the pasty color of flour. Cin appeared more yellow than black. Fahizah's cheekbones protruded in clear outline from her face. I thought I was seeing her death mask when I looked at her.

Death stalked the foul air in that safehouse. More than ever before, all of them talked of death. Hardly a day or night went by but that someone mentioned death and others quickly took up the subject. They went beyond the concept of death being beautiful. It became a necessity. The subject came up at meetings and in casual conversations again and again. The only way the SLA would ultimately prove to the people that it meant what it said was by dying for the cause. It would be "too demoralizing" for the oppressed people to see freedom fighters sent to prisons, where they would be kept helpless by their oppressors. There were already too many freedom fighters in prison. Besides, the SLA Codes of War prohibited surrender. We were obligated to fight to the death, without surrender. Either we would win the revolution or we would die fighting for it. Only then would the people understand that even though we were whites, we truly meant what we had said in all our communiqués. We would be heroes or we would be martyrs. . . .

And it all made sense to me. Cin assured us that civil war had already
begun in the United States. The police were working overtime to suppress small uprisings here and there, which were not reported in the
press. They were trying to smother the embers of revolt. But they
would fail. The revolution would burst out, beyond police control,
fairly soon, and the SLA would be in the forefront of the battle.

One night, when we had gathered for a meeting in the back room,
Cin solemnly announced that he had an important message for all of
us. That brought instant silence and full attention. He lifted his head,
contemplating the ceiling, as though his thoughts were far away, and
then he gazed at each of us in turn. "Sit up straight!" he hissed at
Yolanda, who was sprawled out sideways. She quickly assumed the
correct position, legs crossed in front of her, back straight, looking
directly at him. He nodded in assent. Then he paused once again, as if
deciding a weighty problem. We sat on the floor in a circle, around a
small candle glowing in the darkened room. "I really am a prophet. I
am here on earth to lead the people. I know Fahizah always believed
that, but I didn't really know until today. . . ."

He went on in a subdued, mystical tone of voice. He did not quite
say he was descended from God or instructed by Him, and yet that was
what he implied. I thought it strange beyond his usual strangeness.
Maybe he's having some kind of breakdown, I thought, looking
around at the others for their reactions. But they all sat there in rapt
attention, in awe of the man, who had a glass of plum wine in his hand.
Fahizah was murmuring, "Oh, yes, yes, yes . . ." and the others were
nodding their heads. With the equanimity of absolute certainty, Cin
declared that he would write a book which would impart to *the people*
all of the wisdom and knowledge and experience that he had garnered
during his lifetime. The people needed to know *the truth*. Most
revolutionary books were out of date or out of touch with current life
in the United States. They had been written too long ago about
revolutions in other countries. The only one who had come close to
presenting America with the truth was George Jackson. His book,
Blood in My Eye, was "pretty good," Cin said, but "George" had
spent so much time in prison that he had lost touch with the people on the street. "I've been touching the people like George never did,
and I can tell them from the heart what is really happening in the
street," Cin solemnly told us. "The people need to know and I need to
tell them." His tone of voice was very strange, as though he were im-

parting to us secrets from some mystical world beyond our under-standing. It was an eerie meeting, as if Christ were talking to his Disci-ples. I went to bed that night with the shivers.

The next morning, I warily approached Gelina for her opinion of Cin's behavior. I admitted bewilderment at the thought of him being a prophet. "What did you think of what Cin said?" I asked.

"Oh, he went overboard a bit," Gelina said lightly. "He may have sounded a little weird, but it doesn't really mean he got a message from God or anything. Being a prophet is just an expression. No big deal." Then she added, "Remember, Cin's our leader and he really is some-thing special. So his being a prophet or not really doesn't make much of a difference. . . . Don't worry your little head about it. . . ."

Gelina was probably right, I thought, for that day Cinque did not act any differently than he had before. He still kicked ass, drank plum wine almost all the time, and continued to demand and receive blind obedience from his troops. Looking back, I can see that not only Cin but every one of us had been stretched by fear and nervous tension be-yond normal endurance. With our daily combat drills, strenuous physi-cal exercises, and a poverty level intake of food, we were all suffering from combat fatigue before even going into battle. We had turned in upon ourselves in our own private worlds, and beyond ourselves we only had each other. Fahizah had become utterly mystical, as if floating through time and space. Cujo had turned into a lonely fanatic, talking now with no one at all. Gabi sulked most of the time by herself. Teko and Yolanda reverted to their old selves, treating me with undisguised disdain, as they planned and plotted their future glories in the revolu-tion and battled their own internal furies. The atmosphere in that dirty little safehouse was overwhelmingly oppressive. As a soldier in the Symbionese Liberation Army, I was in dire need of rest and rehabil-itation. The only relief I could find was in crying.

It seemed to me that everything was going steadily from bad to worse. But Cinque explained that this primitive living under hardship conditions was deliberate. It was our preparation for our combat and house-to-house take-overs once the revolution began in earnest. It would not be long now, Cin promised, before the three teams went out independently on their search-and-destroy missions. I heard him say every day that the revolution was coming, that "things are moving fast now," and "it won't be long now . . . the signal will come . . . the sign . . . and we'll go out and kill lots of pigs . . . and that'll get things really moving . . ." In my own misery, I could not truly believe that all he said would actually happen and at the same time I could not bring myself really to doubt him.

Luckily, after about a week in Los Angeles, I got my very first chance to get out of the safehouse when Yolanda made contact with Lumumba's mother and set up a secret meeting for that night in Griffith Park. We went out as a team, Teko, Yolanda, and I, in Cin's red and white VW van, for it was the newest and best-looking of our vehicles. We were on a recruiting drive. Teko and Yolanda were to try to make contact with black revolutionaries in the area who might want to join the SLA or to help us. They would do all the talking, of course, and I was to limit myself strictly to my usual smiling role of Tania, explaining that I had voluntarily joined the SLA. Otherwise, my team role was that of backup.

Lumumba's mother climbed into our van at Griffith Park along with her young boyfriend, James, who had been a cellmate of her son's. She was introduced to me by her Muslim name, Utommu. Yolanda had said on the way to the park that she and her boyfriend as well as Lumumba were true revolutionaries. When I saw her, the woman had fear written all over her face. Her eyes darted here and there. She refused to take off the gloves she was wearing, admitting openly that she did not want to leave any fingerprints or any other sign that she had been with the SLA. She warned her boyfriend, James, to wipe his fingerprints from anything he touched in the van. I went through my spiel as Tania, wearing an Afro wig, and smiling broadly so that I would be recognized. After exchanging pleasantries, Teko began throwing questions at them about the radical and revolutionary movements in Los Angeles. He gave them a long lecture on the SLA plans to start the revolution here in Los Angeles. James allowed that he knew of at least one cell of black activists who were training for armed combat. But despite all of Teko's rhetoric, James insisted that his group of revolutionaries would not want to ally themselves in the struggle with any whites, not even the SLA. Yolanda, recounting all that she and the others had done to help black revolutionaries in prison, cajoled James into assenting at least to meeting with our leader and allowing Cinque to explain the wonderful aims and goals of the SLA. James said he would discuss the proposal with his friends and let us know. But it did not seem to me that he was very eager to align himself or his friends with our cause. Nevertheless, upon our return Yolanda gave Cin an enthusiastic report on the possibilities of expanding our little army.

The very next day, Cin gave our team another assignment out on the street: to buy certain items of heavy clothing—wool socks, long johns, blue jeans—which we would need when we went into combat. Cin favored Teko and Yolanda for such outings because they were considered the least recognizable. Teko had grown a dark beard and mustache and looked nothing like his "Wanted" poster photographs, and Yolanda's regular features were so nondescript that the simplest of disguises made her unrecognizable. But as we were making final preparations for the outing—for this was considered a military operation, as were all ventures beyond our safehouse—Zoya commented, "I don't think Tania should go out on this operation . . . she's too upset to function properly . . . she could just break down and start crying when she's needed as backup."

I could see the doubt in Cin's eyes but I never wanted anything as much as a chance to get out of that oppressive safehouse. "I'm perfectly all right," I told Cin, "and I want to go out on an action."

"Gelina would be much better on this action and safer too," argued Zoya.

"That's not fair," I shot back. "I'm capable enough now to be backup on this operation and I'm on their team and it's only right that I fulfill my responsibility as a member of Teko's team. . . . We're supposed to stay together on all actions and I want to do my part."

That appealed to Cin's sense of order and, thank God, after some more discussion he decided that it was right that I should go out with my team. But he warned me to confine myself to backup and to stay in the van at all times and not to risk being recognized. His word was law and so I put on my Afro wig and my blue horn-rimmed glasses with clear lenses and prepared to go. It was a strange day altogether. Everyone was feeling low. The mood around the whole place was uncommonly somber. When we kissed our comrades goodbye as usual when parting, several of them looked to be on the verge of tears. There were none of the usual, lighthearted cries of "adios."

In the red and white VW van, Yolanda drove, Teko rode shotgun, and I sat on the bare metal floor in the back of the van with the weapons. It was a warm, sunny day—mid-afternoon of May 16, three and a half months after I had been kidnapped—and my spirits lifted soon

after we left and headed toward the shopping area of the Inglewood
neighborhood of Los Angeles. I could feel the fresh, sweet air flowing
from the two front windows into the back of the van and, looking
out on the street, I could see people of all sizes and ages, people
going about their everyday lives in perfectly ordinary safe ways.
Even Teko and Yolanda were in a good mood, making small talk and
enjoying the outing. It all seemed so safe, so normal. We made one or
two brief stops while Teko went out to buy some of the items on his
shopping list. At the second stop, Teko and Yolanda returned smiling
happily and told me that while in the store they heard the "SLA National Anthem" playing on the Musak. It demonstrated for them that
the SLA was alive and well and flourishing among *the people*.

For the major items we needed, however, Teko spotted another
store, which he pointed out to Yolanda on Crenshaw Boulevard, a
wide, busy thoroughfare with two lanes in each direction, separated by
a high concrete divider running down the middle. Yolanda circled
around and parked inside a large shopping-center parking lot, directly
across the street from the store Teko wanted.

"Stay in the van," Teko told me. "We won't be gone long."

I watched them stroll across the boulevard, climb over the center
divider, which was about two feet high and adorned with some green
shrubbery, and walk into the store. It was a two-story building, nothing
fancy, with a glass front topped by a painted sign:

SPORTING GOODS
MEL'S

I kept a watch on the front door of the store for a while and then, a
bit fearful that passersby might notice me, I slunk back into the rear of
the van and began thumbing through the pages of an afternoon newspaper which Teko had bought on one of his earlier stops. It all seemed
rather dull. There was nothing in the newspaper that seemed of the
slightest importance. I idly turned the pages, looking at the headlines
and the advertisements. It occurred to me that they had been gone for
a long time, longer than I had expected. But I was not sure. I did not
have a watch. So I continued with the newspaper, not consciously
worried or even concerned.

Perhaps about twenty minutes had elapsed after Teko and Yolanda
had left the van when I glanced up from the paper to witness an
astounding scene.

In a flash of recognition, I took it all in instantly. Teko was on the ground in front of the store, struggling fiercely. Several men were atop him, trying to pin him down. Yolanda was being held firmly in the grip of another man and she was trying to kick him and to free herself. Another man was jumping about, also trying to subdue Teko. In that same instant, I could see both Teko and Yolanda looking over in my direction. They were staring right at me, waiting for me to take action. I immediately knew what to do. I had been trained and drilled in this very combat maneuver over and over again. I scrambled to pick up the proper weapon, the one with the heaviest firepower, Teko's submachine gun. Moving toward the front and leaning over the driver's seat, I shoved the sawed-off weapon out the window, resting one hand on the window frame. Holding it with the other, I aimed it over their heads and, despite my awkward position, pulled the trigger.

The drill was to fire over their heads to allow my teammates to escape. But the gun jumped out of my hands and sent the first bullets into the center road divider. I could see chips of concrete flying in the air. I grasped the gun tighter and aimed higher, at nothing in particular. Again it jumped in my hands, almost out of control. They had told me there would be no recoil. But there was. Nevertheless, I kept my finger pressed on the trigger until the entire clip of thirty shots had been fired. It was over in a matter of seconds, the first time I had ever fired that weapon with live rounds in it. I then reached for my own weapon, the semi-automatic carbine. I got off three more shots, this time higher in the air, before I realized that Teko and Yolanda were free, running toward the van, while the others were scrambling for safety.

My comrades dashed aboard the van and in an instant Teko had the engine roaring. We screeched out of that parking lot, the tires squealing, and sped down the boulevard. I was rolling all around the back of the van and could feel the adrenaline flowing through my body.

"Did I do right?" I called out to Teko. He turned to me and snarled, "What the fuck took you so long?"

I had no answer for that. Had I not acted quickly enough to satisfy him? It all seemed to happen so fast. Teko swung the wheel so that the van veered around a corner. I was slammed violently against a side wall, weapons flying everywhere. Then he straightened the wheel and I slid across the bare metal floor to the opposite side, with nothing to grab or to hold on to.

Suddenly I was struck for the first time with what I had done. I could not believe that I had actually fired that submachine gun . . . that I had actually helped in the escape of these two people whom I hated . . . that I had had my first real chance to escape from their clutches and I had not taken advantage of it. . . . Why did I do it? If I did reach for a weapon, why Teko's submachine gun first, before my own weapon, with which I was familiar? It was against my own self-interest. So, why? The only answer I could find that satisfied *me,* which later was bolstered and reaffirmed by expert opinion on the subject, was that I acted instinctively, because I had been trained and drilled to do just that, to react to a situation without thinking, just as soldiers are trained and drilled to obey an order under fire instinctively, without questioning it. By the time they had finished with me I was, in fact, a soldier in the Symbionese Liberation Army. In training me, Cinque had succeeded well. As backup, I had been obligated to protect my comrades, to shoot over the heads of any enemy engaged in close-quarter combat with my comrades. The penalty for failure, in combat, according to our Codes of War, was death. That had been drilled into me. Cin had also instilled in my mind that one employed the weapon of heaviest firepower first in such situations. That was why I had reached instinctively for the submachine gun, which I had held only once before for that famous "Tania" photo, rather than my own personal weapon. I know and believe that now. But at the time I was astounded that I had actually fired that submachine gun. All during the training I had never quite believed that it was for real. I had thought it was all a game of some sort, a make-believe designed by these people whom I had to humor in order to win their approval and stay alive. But I had gone along with their combat drills for so long and for so intensive a period that I had, in fact, learned, as a soldier learns, to act and to react instinctively—like Pavlov's salivating dog. That flash of insight into what I had done and the significance of it was at the time but a brief glimpse of reality, like a sudden streak of sunlight through a hole in dark, rolling cumulus clouds, there one instant and gone the next.

CHAPTER

ELEVEN

We WERE RACING down the streets of Los Angeles, weaving in and out of traffic, braking hard at intersections, turning corners, speeding up, slowing down. Yolanda, as lookout, could see no police cars following us. But Teko, very excited, was sure someone was following us; then he thought he had lost him. He drove like a madman, cursing his misfortune at the sporting-goods store, his bad luck to run across a "junior G-man" in the store clerk, furious that anyone had been "slick" enough to clamp handcuffs on one of his wrists and mad at himself for allowing it to happen. He shook that wrist with the dangling handcuffs in the air, insisting that he had been tricked, taken by surprise. In his frustration he spewed out a stream of invectives.

Yolanda was very angry with him. "What did you take?"

"Nothing."

"You must have taken something."

"Nothing. Just a little bandolier I thought we could use. Shit, it only cost a couple of bucks."

"Jesus Christ, that was stupid," Yolanda commented.

"How was I to know the store had a fuckin' junior pig there?" Like an irascible little schoolboy, Teko fumed and fussed, refusing to admit his mistake, blaming it all on the unexpected presence of the "junior G-man," who even had handcuffs at the ready for mere shoplifters. As we learned later, Teko was not far off the mark. The store clerk was a young man named Anthony Shepard, a college student majoring in police science and working part-time at Mel's.

In bits and pieces, it all came out. They had shopped together in the store, picking out heavy sweat socks and long underwear, all without incident. But when Yolanda went ahead by herself to pay for the purchased items, Teko spotted the bandolier, a belt which would hold shotgun shells, and, on the spur of the moment, without thinking too much, he decided to steal it. He stuffed it up his sleeve. And he thought he had gotten away with it until the store clerk accosted him on the sidewalk outside the store. Of course, he could not allow himself, a General in the SLA, to be detained and possibly arrested for shoplifting.

All the while, I was being bounced about in the back of the van. At one point I thought I had cracked a rib against a sharp edge of something. But it was no time to complain. For several days afterward I would ache with pain. Bruises and huge black-and-blue welts would discolor a good portion of my body.

It was remarkable that Teko could control that speeding, rocking van and do so much talking at the same time. It was Yolanda who thought to ditch the van before the police started their search for it. She was sure it had been identified. Teko agreed. We would commandeer another car.

"Is Cin going to be mad!" Teko cursed. "I lost my gun in that fight in the street, and it's goin' to blow our cover. The pigs'll know we're in L.A. . . . They're sure'n hell goin' to trace it. Then the heat's goin' be on, real good. Shit . . ." They talked on and on about the Colt revolver, which Yolanda had purchased in an Oakland gun shop shortly before they had gone underground and had registered in her real name, Emily Harris. Teko explained that he had not had time to draw his gun before he realized the seriousness of the attack upon him. By that time he had been thrown to the ground, and when he tried to draw his weapon then, the two men on top of him wrestled the gun away. He was furious about it all, until Yolanda managed to change the subject to our need for finding another van or car or some way to ditch the van. Then they argued about how to go about that.

"There's a car, right there!" Yolanda exclaimed, pointing. "They're just parking, there."

Teko came to a screeching halt and they both leaped out of the van.

He threw open the sliding side door, reached for his weapon, and rammed a fresh clip into his submachine gun. He slammed the door shut but not before ordering me to collect all our gear and be ready to leave when he returned. Yolanda followed on his heels to help him commandeer the vehicle. Once they had left and after that wild ride, the momentary stillness in the van was unnerving.

In a matter of moments, Teko was back, commanding me to follow him. I stumbled out of the van, carrying two bags full of weapons and ammunition, and followed Teko to the Pontiac idling at the curb. Later, Teko would tell me that when he and Yolanda emerged from the van, he spotted a car stopped in the middle of the road and in it was that same young "store pig" who had accosted him before. Teko advanced on foot toward the car, his submachine gun at the ready, and finally "the store pig retreated," backing his car down the hill until he was out of sight. In recounting that action, Teko sounded very proud of himself, but Yolanda wondered if he could have even hit the car, much less the man in it, without his eyeglasses, which he had lost in the scuffle at Mel's.

We roared away in the Pontiac. I had just about settled into the cramped back seat when that old car just sputtered and died not more than two or three blocks from where we had started. We were stopped in the middle of a T-intersection. Across the street we all spied another available vehicle, a small blue station wagon, at which a Mexican family was gathered, trying to unload a lawn mower.

"Let's go!" said Teko, and they were out of the dead Pontiac in an instant. I had to wiggle my way with the bags of guns past the front seat and out the door. By the time I reached them, standing off a way, Teko was explaining: "We're the SLA and we need your car. . . . We're not stealing it. . . . You'll get it back. . . . But we need it right now."

"Sure, sure," said the man, gaping at the submachine gun in Teko's hands, the handcuffs dangling from one wrist. "Take it and use it long as you like."

The man gingerly handed Teko the keys and then he and his son moved fast to roll the lawn mower off the back of the station wagon, a Chevy Nova. Meanwhile, two or three cars had screeched to a stop around the stalled Pontiac. I looked around at the strange tableau. Teko waved me forward and into our new transportation and away we went, unobstructed and unmolested. After all, we were an army; they were civilians.

As we moved away, this time with no one in pursuit, Teko's mood lightened and he now seemed delighted with our adventures. Things were going our way now. There was something positive about being in a combat operation after the weeks and weeks of safehouse confinement. "Weren't those Chicanos just great?" Teko exclaimed. "You see, minority people really do believe in the SLA and what we are trying to do. . . . That fellow just gave us his car. He knew we really needed it. He understood we weren't stealing it. . . . Black people and Chicanos are like that. They'll share with you, if they think you really need something." He went on and on, oblivious to the fact that the submachine gun in his hands had obviously frightened that poor man out of his wits.

All of this was turning out very well, according to Teko. It all went to show how well we operated as a team, how good our training and our combat drills had been, how wise Cinque had been in his planning. We had nothing to worry about, Teko declared with great bravado. We could not go back to our safehouse. Cin had forbidden it as too risky and potentially dangerous for the entire cell. But Cin had anticipated something like this. It was arranged that in case of trouble, we would join up with the others at midnight in a drive-in movie. If that meeting didn't work out, we had a fail-safe plan. On our first day in Los Angeles, at the leaders' meeting, Cin had given the group leaders a list of dead drops. Teko knew where we could leave messages for the others and meet up with them a few days later, when the furor over Mel's had died down. Meanwhile, he said we had enough money and could always expropriate more. As a team we could take evasive action, avoid the police, and operate on our own, as Cin had originally planned. Right now, said Teko, we had to find ourselves a safe car, one which would not be reported to the police as stolen. Either we had to commandeer a car or a van and keep the driver with us or we had to find a car we could buy. Then we would be totally safe.

It never occurred to us that the worst blunder had been abandoning Cin's VW van. Under orders from General Teko, I had removed only "essentials." Inside the pocket of one of the gun carrying cases left in the van was a parking ticket, which noted that the van had been parked overtime just one or two blocks from our West Eighty-fourth Street safehouse. It would lead the police there, but at the time we were unaware of this. The parking summons, which should have been paid or destroyed immediately, was negligently tucked into the pocket by Yolanda and forgotten. So much for meticulous planning.

We cruised down the streets of Inglewood in search of a safe vehicle, stopping once in the parking lot of a junior college and then going on to a small neighborhood shopping center at about dinnertime. We left the station wagon to walk around. Teko had his submachine gun concealed under his red woolen camping shirt, clasping it to his side by keeping his left elbow tucked in. People were milling about, completely unaware of our presence, as we walked through the parking lot, searching for another vehicle to commandeer. Teko sighted a camper pulling in and coming to a stop. It would be perfect: a mobile hideout. Prospects looked good when the driver alighted from the camper—a hippie in his late twenties with hair down to his shoulders and a scrabble of a beard on his face. He had a small boy, apparently his son, with him.

"Hi, brother! How're you doing?" Teko greeted him with a broad smile.

"Hi, brother," he answered. "Just fine. How're you doin'?"

They clasped hands in brotherly greeting, as Yolanda and I stood a few feet away.

"Well, it's like this," said Teko. "We're the SLA and we need to use your camper . . ."

Teko had gotten no further in explanation when the young hippie threw up his hands in fright and took off, crying, "No, no, no . . ." Teko chased right after him. It was a short race. The fellow had no wind at all. He came to a stop and slumped against a parked car, his arms thrown over his head as protection, like an ostrich with his head in the sand. Teko was enraged. He grappled with his machine gun, trying to get it out from under his shirt, muttering that he would blast him to kingdom come. The hippie just kept crying, "No, no, no," his chest heaving with great sobs.

With Yolanda right behind me, I caught up with Teko and grabbed his arm before he could dislodge his machine gun, shouting into his ear, "Teko, no. . . . Just forget it. . . . It's not worth it. . . . You'll just bring the pigs down on us. . . . Please, leave him alone. . . . He's not worth it. . . . Let's get out of here." Teko finally let up, came to his senses, but still shaking with rage, he gave that young fellow a dire

warning of what would happen to him if he dared to report this encounter to the police. Teko stalked off, with Yolanda and me trailing
him, and we left that shopping center still trying to calm down our
emotional and volatile team leader. As we cruised about in a quiet residential area in search of the right vehicle to beg, borrow, or steal, Teko
lectured us on the rectitude of the SLA cause, the cowardly perfidy of
the white man, even those of the counterculture, and the hope of the
future residing in only the black man, the Chicano, the Orientals, the
non-whites . . .

Our next means of transportation was spotted by Yolanda—a Ford
Econoline van about five or six years old and apparently in good condition, parked on a side street in a section called Lynwood. A "For
Sale" sign gleamed out of its back window, with address and telephone
number. It was so easy. We circled the block a couple of times, eyeing
the residence, and making our plans, and then we parked about a block
away and around a corner. Yolanda walked back to the address.

Sure enough, after a short wait, we saw the van come around the
corner, with Yolanda at the wheel, and pull up across the street from
us. She waved us over. It had been so simple. Yolanda had gone to the
door, met the young owner of the van, asked to test-drive it before deciding whether or not to buy it, and when she came to where we were
parked, she asked if she could take her two friends along for the ride.

The young man opened one of the side doors for us and found himself looking at a scowling, bearded urban guerrilla with a submachine
gun cradled in his arms. "Get in the back," Teko snarled. We climbed
aboard as Teko, now adept at this recital, informed the young man that
we were the SLA, that we intended only to use his van for a short time,
not to steal it, and if he cooperated, if he did nothing stupid or flaky,
he would not get hurt. The young man replied that that was perfectly
all right with him, so long as he did not get shot. As Yolanda drove the
van away, we made ourselves comfortable on the carpeting which covered most of the floor in the empty rear compartment. Teko rested
against the back of the front seats, the submachine gun in his lap, and I
sat in the middle of the van, propped against one of the sides, with the
young man directly across from me.

It was now past seven o'clock and beginning to get dark. Teko told
Yolanda to try to find a hardware store; he wanted a hacksaw to get
the handcuffs off his wrist. In response to Teko's questions, the boy in-

troduced himself as Tom Matthews, a high school senior, seventeen years old. Teko asked, "Do you know who this is?" The boy gaped at me, and Teko announced, "This is Tania!" His eyes widened in recognition. Teko and I grinned. We had here an appreciative audience and Teko lost no time in trying to impress the lad with the SLA exploits and our struggle to free the poor people from the oppression of the ruling classes. Tom was interested, asking why, if we were revolutionaries, did we rob the Hibernia Bank, and Teko explained at great length how difficult was our cause. We needed money to finance our struggle; we were at war, official war because the SLA had declared war on the United States government; therefore the bank robbery was not an ordinary bank robbery, it was an expropriation of funds from the enemy. Tom Matthews nodded his head in agreement; he understood our reasoning. At a nod from Teko, I launched into my set speech about changing sides after I had been kidnapped, taking part in the bank holdup voluntarily, and now fighting on the side of the poor and the oppressed.

He seemed genuinely interested and displayed absolutely no fear at all, as if this were all a merry adventure. His only concern was whether or not he would be set free by the following afternoon, because he was scheduled to pitch in an important baseball game for his high school. Teko reassured him he would be home in time for his game.

"We're all going to a drive-in movie tonight where we're going to meet some of our friends. Then we'll take off with them and you can have your van back," Teko told him. Having heard the shrill news reports on the car radio of our misadventure at Mel's Sporting Goods, we were certain that the others had fled the safehouse and would meet up with us at the drive-in movie. I for one could hardly wait to rejoin our comrades. Teko's leadership had brought us nothing but trouble. Once we were back, I thought, Cin would revise the makeup of our teams and I would get away from these two.

In the midst of explaining to the young man how the SLA intended to lead the revolution, Teko told me to remove any live cartridges that might be in the chambers of our weapons: he did not want any of them going off accidentally and killing someone. The boy's eyes widened in awe as he watched how deftly I could remove the ammo clips, eject the live cartridge from the chamber, shove the shell back into the clip, and then ram the clip home again in the weapon. It was as though I were giving a performance. Before long, Teko was trying to recruit the lad. "It would be great, Tom, if you decided to join us," Teko declared with great sincerity. "You could lead a Youth Unit of the SLA."

Tom Matthews commented that while he could see our point of view, he was not into politics and he did not want to join the SLA. No offense intended, of course. Of course.

Finding a hacksaw in the suburbs of Los Angeles at that hour of the night, somewhat after 7 P.M., when most stores were closed, was more difficult than we had imagined. At the first two stops, Yolanda returned to the van to report they had no hacksaws. Each try was considered a risky combat operation. We would pull up close to a hardware store, with our escape planned, Teko at the wheel with the engine running, me stationed at the side door, ready to open it in the event that Yolanda was recognized and had to make a run for it. At the third store, our hostage offered to cut down the risk by going in for the purchase, but Teko thought better of it. Yolanda, on that try, returned happily, waving the bag with the hacksaw in it.

With our hostage concealed under a blanket, we pulled into the Century Drive-In Theater, without incident, in time to see the whole double feature. Yolanda went out to get us all hamburgers and soda, while Teko tried to saw the handcuffs from his left wrist. He swore in frustration as the steel cuffs slipped away under the grinding of the hacksaw. His hand had begun turning blue, his circulation cut off. Finally, Tom took over, and while Teko held the cuffs steady, our high school baseball player conscientiously and carefully sawed his way through the steel ring around Teko's wrist.

Holding up a small section of the cuffs, Tom asked, "Gee, can I keep this, as a sort of souvenir?"

"Sure, kid," replied a grateful Teko, rubbing his freed wrist.

After we had eaten, Yolanda placed one of the large soda cups upside down on top of the speaker stanchion outside the van. It was our identification so that the others could find us among the anonymous vehicles parked in the drive-in. Our meeting was set for midnight, but we thought that one of them might come by earlier. It had all been carefully planned beforehand. A confident Teko instructed us all to relax and enjoy the movie. The main feature was *The New Centurions,* which was about the exploits of the Los Angeles Police Department, and, of course, Teko rooted for the bad guys. Thoroughly engrossed in the film, Teko would urge them on: "Kill the pigs . . . shoot, shoot, kill the pigs . . ." For safety's sake, we kept Tom Matthews hidden under a thin blanket in the back of the van and, as I watched the movie, from time to time I noticed his body trembling and I would pat his head in reassurance. I thought I knew how he must be feeling. But then, perhaps I did not. For he seemed to be enjoying his kidnapping far more than I had when I was kept under a blanket on the floor of a car taking me away from Berkeley.

Yolanda left the van several times to scout around in hopes of finding one of our comrades. She was very anxious to link up with them again, concerned that they might not be able to spot our identifying paper cup in the dark. Teko was far less concerned. Not unhappy over having command of our team foray, he insisted that Cin had anticipated not being able to meet on the same night of an action. We would just have to leave our messages at some dead drops, lie low for a few days, and then we would link up again. Even in whispers, lest Tom Matthews overhear them, their argument was fierce. When our comrades had not shown up by midnight, Teko wanted to leave, but Yolanda insisted upon waiting until the end of the movie. They discussed all the possibilities ad infinitum. But finally, at 1 A.M., we followed the long line of cars out of the drive-in. No one contacted us outside the drive-in theater either. I missed the security I had felt with the others in the safehouse.

Teko instructed Yolanda to drive out to the Hollywood Hills, where we could park and get some sleep, but Yolanda pleaded with him to allow her to drive past our safehouse, just to check it out, not to stop. Teko argued that was contrary to all the rules of urban guerrilla warfare. Besides, he said, he was positive the others had left the safehouse once they heard the radio reports of our escapade at Mel's. But Yolanda pleaded and pleaded and, though I could not see her face, I was sure she had her tears flowing to bolster her argument. At last Teko relented and we drove down West Eighty-fourth Street, surprised at the amount of traffic out that late at night. Undoubtedly, from what we learned later, the police already had traced that traffic summons, located our safehouse, and had it staked out as we drove by. But just as we could not recognize their unmarked cars, they did not suspect Tom Matthews' Ford van. The safehouse, as we went by it just once, was empty. Our friends had flown. We could tell because the windows were bare. The surveillance drapes had been taken down.

With a road map on his lap, Teko directed Yolanda up Mulholland

Drive, a long, winding road up a mountain, and near the top, on a deserted side street, we parked and agreed to get some sleep. Teko set the guard watches, and the only one who got a full night of sleep was Tom Matthews. He slept straight through, unperturbed.

Bright and early the next morning, we started the new day with a fierce argument over stealing another car. While Tom Matthews lay asleep at about six in the morning, Yolanda insisted we should waste no time in finding another vehicle. She simply did not believe Tom's protestations that his family would not worry about his being away for the whole night. Nor did she think he would be so amenable if kept hostage for another day. He seemed to have enjoyed his adventure less and less as the hours wore on the previous night. When he woke up, Teko told him we were going to expropriate another car and let him return home. Teko also reassured him that we did not want the small sum of money he was carrying with him. "We only take money, kid, from people who can afford to finance the revolution," Teko said. "In fact, if you think you need some bread for gas, we can give you some, though we really don't have much." Tom declined the offer.

Teko and Yolanda, of course, argued over strategy for getting another car. Teko's idea was hardly subtle. He proposed that we wait at a stop sign or traffic light and commandeer a car simply by jumping aboard and overpowering the driver. Yolanda suggested that she and I pose as hitchhikers, and once we were picked up, we would point our guns at the driver and take over his car. That was far more practical, she insisted, than Teko's plan. They argued over that. Teko, as our leader, did not particularly like any sign that he was not in command. Neither of them consulted me. I was their foot soldier; they were generals. But once they decided upon the hitchhiker ploy, I protested. I could not do it, I told them. Just could not do it!

"That's too fuckin' bad," Yolanda said. "We're not asking you to do this, we're telling you. We made a decision and you have to do it." In spite of everything, my mind automatically rejected the idea that I could shoot someone.

Upset and flustered at even the possibility, I hemmed and hawed and made excuses. I did not know where to hide my revolver, I said. Yolanda, though she had abandoned her wig when we left the Pontiac in a rush, still had her purse. But I did not have a purse or anything else into which I could put my revolver. I stuck it in the front of my slacks, but the butt protruded beyond anything my blue raincoat could hide. Finally, I tucked the .38 in my slacks at the small of my back and hiked down the road with Yolanda until we reached another intersection. The shooting at Mel's had been bad enough, but I really had not had time to think about what I was doing when I acted, and at the Hibernia Bank, I did not have a choice, but this action, taking over a car at the point of a gun, seemed to demand a deliberate, conscious action on my part. And I doubted whether I could do it. As we walked down the road, Yolanda outlined the plan of action. There was a cold asperity in her voice. She did not think much of me as a comrade- or soldier-in-arms or as a reliable revolutionary. She did not doubt my conversion to the cause. But she was convinced that what she considered to be my pampered, spoiled former way of life had made it impossible for me to be a good urban guerrilla. And she did not hesitate to warn me of the consequences of my failing her. I was frightened and I worried over my ability to perform.

But, just as Cin had said during my training, the SLA was stronger than the enemy. A fairly new and shiny LTD stopped for us and a smiling middle-aged businessman, a building contractor, as he later told us, beckoned us into his car. Yolanda took the front passenger seat and I climbed into the back. I don't think he got much further than "Where are you pretty girls heading for?" when Yolanda pointed her pistol at his belly and announced who we were. The man virtually crumpled in fright at the name Symbionese Liberation Army. It was soon obvious that he would do anything we demanded in order to stay alive. Yolanda made him climb over the seat and into the rear of the car, while she took the wheel and headed us back up the road.

Our leader was delighted with our prize of war. The car was less than a year old and luxurious by our revolutionary standards. Teko wasted no time in relieving our new prisoner of his wallet and informing him of the conditions of his arrest by the people's army. We moved our belongings out of the van, appropriated a blanket with which to keep our new prisoner hidden, and Teko wished Tom Matthews well. Of course, he also told Tom to be careful about what he told the pigs because we had his address and we could always find him again. Upon taking our departure, Teko shook Tom by the hand and told him to count to a million and to take plenty of time doing it before he started home in his van. As an afterthought he again offered the boy money to buy gas, but Tom declined with a polite "Thank you," and, if I remember correctly, he wished us well, with a good deal of sincerity.

In contrast to Tom Matthews, our new prisoner did not enjoy any part of his adventure with the SLA. He was kept down on the floor in the back of the car and covered with the blanket for all of the eight hours we held him prisoner. Teko went through his wallet and identified him as Frank Sutter and announced that the SLA was expropriating the two hundred and fifty dollars in cash Teko found there. Teko told the prisoner we were keeping his wallet too, just in case we needed to find him again. Then he went happily through his usual explanation of the struggle and goals of the SLA, informing Mr. Sutter that as a civilian, even though he was a member of the bourgeois, capitalist ruling class, the SLA would not harm him in any way —so long as he did not impede our actions. This time I did not have to do much talking because Teko was very happy lecturing the prisoner on the evils of capitalist oppression and the glories of the poor and oppressed minorities. Mr. Sutter was so frightened and upset that our leader at one point became surprisingly solicitous of his health. "You don't have a heart condition or anything like that, do you?" Teko asked. "Because we really don't want you to take sick or die on us." Mr. Sutter, gasping for breath under the blanket, reassured our leader about his health. "Well, I'm glad to hear that because if you did have a bad heart, there'd be nothin' we could do about it," Teko commented.

Our leader was verbose, alternating dire threats of violence against society with rosy platitudes of the revolution which would change everything. He became exasperating. If he would only shut up, I thought. Each time we heard a radio news report on the SLA, Teko would launch into his own interpretation of the events. He was furious over news reports that the SLA was believed to be in Los Angeles because he, William Harris, had been identified as a shoplifter, trying to steal a pair of sweat socks. "It wasn't sweat socks, it was a bandolier," he would screech, adding, "And I didn't steal it."

Our first mission that day was checking for and leaving messages for Cin and the others at all of the prearranged dead drops. Teko, whispering into Yolanda's ear so that our prisoner could not overhear him, directed her to five different locations in the areas, I believe, of Compton and Inglewood. One message was taped beneath the sink in the ladies' room of a small coffee shop, another was stuck to the underside of a mailbox outside of a post office. Yolanda was most anxious about our separation from our comrades, but Teko, who enjoyed being in command, spent a considerable amount of time reassuring her. A few days or even weeks on our own would not hurt the cell, he told her. I barely managed to stifle a groan at this thought.

Our second mission was the purchase of a car through the classified ads in the morning paper, checking out the inexpensive ones we could afford. Each time we stopped so that Yolanda could make inquiries from a public phone booth, Teko would explain to Frank Sutter that we had to keep up our contacts with other units of the SLA. He wove a great mystery of the action we were involved in for our frightened prisoner. We spent eight long hours in that LTD with Mr. Sutter before Yolanda found another car to buy. She made the purchase herself, an old Corvair that looked ready for the junk heap. But it only cost three hundred dollars and the seller was a Latino woman who hardly spoke English and, according to Yolanda, was completely unsuspicious of her. The only thing unusual that Yolanda noticed was the number of what she called "piggy-looking people and cars" in the area. Little did we suspect that in buying this car we were no more than four or five blocks from where Cin and the others were hiding out in a small stucco house on East Fifty-fourth Street.

Now with two automobiles, we moved away from this area, traveling in tandem, toward Griffith Park. Teko intended to leave our prisoner and his car there, while we departed in the Corvair, which Frank Sutter, being kept under that blanket, had never seen and therefore could not possibly describe to the police. Yolanda drove the Corvair, following right behind us, as I drove the big LTD at a moderate, law-abiding speed. Teko, now next to me in the front seat, directed me onto a freeway, where we stayed in the right-hand slow lane all the way. I could see the Corvair behind us in my rearview mirror. When I took the exit ramp for Griffith Park, however, she was gone.

I could not understand or explain how Yolanda had missed the turnoff. Teko fumed. Neither of us knew what to do. Volatile as ever, Teko cursed her, me, the Los Angeles highway system, the bourgeois establishment, and his own rotten luck. We could not get back on the freeway at that point, nor hope to catch up to Yolanda by way of a side road. So Teko decided that we should proceed to Griffith Park and wait for Yolanda there.

We parked slightly off the main road leading into the park and we waited. We expected that Yolanda would leave the freeway at the next

exit and make her way back to the park. How could she miss us? She
had to find us; we could not find her. So we waited. It was early afternoon on a bright sunny day and the traffic on that road was fairly
heavy. Cars whizzed by us. If the police came by and stopped to
inquire, we would be hard-pressed to explain what Mr. Sutter was
doing under a blanket. After a while, Teko told me to start the engine
and keep it running, just in case we needed a fast takeoff. He began
muttering that we would have to leave the area fairly soon. We could
not just sit there waiting. What if Yolanda's car broke down? What if
she had been taken into custody by the police?

"Look, if Yolanda doesn't show up, we're going to have to waste
this guy and just take off by ourselves," Teko whispered to me.
"Yolanda will have to fend for herself."

"She'll show up," I replied. "She's got to show up pretty soon now."

We waited. It was excruciating. Teko constantly reassured the prisoner, telling him, "We're waiting to make contact with some of our
comrades and then we'll let you go. . . . Just take it easy." But to me,
every so often, he would whisper, "We've *got* to get rid of this guy, so
we can get a good head start in this car. We can leave his body in the
bushes. Nobody will find it for days. . . . Yolanda ain't coming."

"She'll be here . . . she'll show up . . . she's just lost . . . but she'll
be by pretty soon now . . ." I sat there, frantic, watching all those
other cars going by, praying and willing with all my strength for her
car to show up. I had no doubt at all that Teko was quite capable of
executing our prisoner.

This uncertainty went on for the better part of an hour, and when it
seemed hopeless to wait any longer, as a last resort I pleaded with
Teko to try the parking lot of the park, where we had met with
Lumumba's mother and James. Perhaps Yolanda could not find this
road, I said; if she entered the park by another road, then in all likelihood she would head for the parking lot which we had used before. So
we drove further up into the park until we found the parking lot, where
we waited. Finally a distraught Yolanda showed up. She had hopelessly
lost her way after missing the freeway exit, could not find her way back
to the park, and had to stop at a service station for directions.

We drove on up the road, toward the Observatory, and when we
stopped and Teko removed the blanket, Frank Sutter was clearly
terrified. Teko told him that the SLA had decided mercifully to spare

his life because he was a civilian. We would leave him off by the side of the road. He was to wait there for a half hour and then start walking down the road. He was not to hitchhike. He would find his car parked about a mile away, with the keys under the front seat. He was not to report any of this to the police. If we saw his face down the road within that half hour, we would shoot him on sight. If he went to the police, we would find out about it, and since we still had his wallet and knew his home address, we would come back and seek our revenge. This was war, Teko told him, and he was being spared only because he was neutral; if he cooperated with the government, the SLA would kill him as an enemy.

A mile down the road, Yolanda was waiting for us. We left the LTD as promised and drove off, confident that Frank Sutter would not go to the police, not immediately at any rate. Teko expounded on how well we had operated as a team; we had been tested by events and emergencies since Mel's, and we had come through with flying colors. The police would have no idea where we were at this time. We could have been hundreds of miles away. We were safe. Teko roared with glee each time we heard a radio news report concerning a police raid on the SLA hideout on West Eighty-fourth Street. Hordes of police had gathered and crept up on the house and thrown tear-gas grenades and then stormed inside—only to find it empty. The SLA, one step ahead of them, was gone.

In deciding where we could best lie low for the next few days, Yolanda suggested Disneyland, in Anaheim, where we could easily get lost among the tourists. She had worked in Disneyland one summer during her college days and knew of many small motels near the world-famous attraction. Teko thought her idea brilliant. We could do no wrong. We headed south from Los Angeles for some thirty miles to Anaheim, and while my two SLA generals reviewed our situation and planned future strategies, I lay curled up on the back seat, thoroughly drained of energy and yet too exhausted to fall asleep. I feared that Teko could not help but get us into some more trouble. He seemed to be made that way. As we reached Anaheim we heard on the radio the news report that the police were surrounding another suspected SLA safehouse and were preparing to assault it. But their mood was by then one of near-euphoria. Teko scoffed at the stupidity of the pigs trying to trap the SLA. "Even if they had ever been there, by the time the stupid pigs raid that house, our comrades would be long gone. The pigs won't find nobody home, just like at Eighty-fourth Street." He laughed.

Disneyland, even from the outside, looked enormous and inviting. It had been years since I last visited it as a child, so young and innocent and carefree. But now I knew I could never see it again, as much as I may have wished, for there was too much risk that I would be recognized. It was well after five o'clock, perhaps nearer to five-thirty, when we pulled into the motel parking lot. Teko told me to get under the blanket on the floor of the car in order to stay out of sight while Yolanda went in and registered for a room for two. They would sneak me into the room to save money and for security in case the police had been alerted to look for two women and a man registering at any motel. Teko himself said he would walk about for a while, though he would keep an eye on the car. After Yolanda had registered, we drove around to our motel room and moved in. We now had only our weapons with us, having lost the clothes and the groceries we had bought when we abandoned Cin's VW. The room seemed marvelously big to me and clean, with two large double beds and a color television set. Teko headed for the TV as soon as we got into the room.

"It's live. . . . Look, it's live," Teko exclaimed, shaking all over, pointing. We gathered around the set and watched. There in living color we could see what seemed like a regular cops-and-robbers show: an army of policemen, wearing gas masks and battle fatigues, surrounding a little white stucco house. At first we had thought it might be a tape recording of the raid on the Eighty-fourth Street safehouse, but we soon realized that this was another house and the announcer kept repeating that the SLA was trapped inside and had refused the police's demand that they come out and surrender. Within minutes of our turning on the TV set, the shoot-out started.

The emotional shock was devastating. Shots rang out and my body reverberated as though struck. Tear-gas canisters were fired into the house. Clouds of smoke and gas poured out of the front windows, followed by a fusillade of submachine-gun fire from the house in response.

"That's our people in there," screamed Teko. Yolanda began sobbing. Teko changed channels and it was all the same, perhaps a different angle, a slightly different scene, but it was all the same, like a war news film out of Vietnam. Hand-held cameras jerked every which way while the news reporters described in simplistic detail what we could see on the screen. As Teko impatiently switched channels, we saw the same scene over and over again but we did get a variety of synopses of what had happened earlier, before we had reached the motel. Apparently Cin and the others had taken over that house on East Fifty-fourth Street in the Compton area during the previous night or in the early hours of this morning. They were holding the black occupants of the house hostage, the newsmen said. But they were all trapped inside, surrounded by an overwhelming force of Los Angeles police, more than one hundred of them. And they had refused to surrender. The police had called on them again and again—perhaps twelve different times—to come out with their hands up and they would not be hurt. But no one had come out. Furthermore, there were contradictory reports on how many SLA members were inside the house. Neighbors who had visited the house before the police arrived reported that Patricia Hearst was inside. Others said she was not. Over and over again, the news reporters speculated, but no one knew for sure. Finally the police had fired tear gas into the house and the shoot-out had begun.

I watched all this, trembling, on the floor, leaning against the foot of one of the beds. Yolanda was propped up on the other bed and Teko sat on the edge of the foot of that bed, rocking back and forth, changing channels on the television set, and screaming out in defiance his own interpretation of the shoot-out: The SLA would not be holding black people hostage—the black people would have welcomed the SLA and they were now fighting alongside the SLA against the oppressors. The SLA would never surrender. Cin had already told the world that. This was a shoot-out to the death, as Cin had prophesied. If our comrades had to die, this was the best way. They would take a lot of "pigs" with them. They would kill ten for every one of the SLA slain. The "pig reporters" were only interested in Patty Hearst, not in what happened with all the others in the SLA. . . .

The truth was, as we learned from reports later, that Cin and the others had come to that house, at four o'clock in the morning, because it was the only one around showing a light at that hour, and he had bought his way in—for one hundred dollars. Cin, drinking his usual plum wine all day, had stayed in the house with all the others, sending some neighborhood children out for groceries. He also apparently was talking to all the neighbors, telling them the SLA had arrived on their doorstep.

At one point during the shoot-out, a black woman stumbled out of the front door, screaming hysterically. She was thrown to the ground by the police and dragged away. She had been inside the house all this time, sleeping, and had come to in the middle of the gun battle, barely managing to escape with her life. As she struggled, she was kicked, sat upon, and finally handcuffed and subdued. Teko screamed out for revenge.

As the shooting continued, Teko swore he saw the silhouette of Cin running past a window, bobbing and weaving in his own characteristic manner. At another point, the camera caught the fiery blast of a shotgun coming out one of the front windows and Teko identified the shotgun and the man behind it as Cujo. Cheering them on, Teko predicted that if they could just hold out until dark, at least some of them would be able to escape.

"We should go up there and help our comrades!" Teko cried out. "We could blast the pigs from the rear and fight our way in, so our comrades can escape."

"It's no use, Teko. We'd be so outnumbered we'd just be killed and it would serve no purpose," Yolanda said sadly.

"We should go anyway. . . . We should die with our comrades. . . ."

"No," said Yolanda. "Cin would want us to live and to fight on. . . . That's what we've got to do."

"Oh, I wish I was there with them," Teko moaned, punching his fist on the bed.

It went on for a whole hour, a mini-war in the black ghetto of the city where movies are made, all of it in living color on television. It was barbaric, overwhelming, unbelievable. And then the house caught fire. It went up in flames in an instant. Teko screamed in agony, cursing the police for using what he called incendiary grenades to burn out the SLA, whom they could not conquer with bullets. The whole house was soon engulfed in angry flames. Teko swore that only incendiary grenades could ignite a house in that fashion. (The police later insisted that no incendiary devices were employed, attributing the fire to two one-gallon cans of gasoline, said to have been brought into the house by the SLA, which were ignited either by a bullet or by the tear gas.)

With flames shooting up through the roof and the television reporters saying that no one could live much longer inside the house, the police again and for the last time called upon the SLA to surrender: "Come out. The house is on fire. It's all over. Throw your guns out of the window. You will not be harmed."

The reply was a burst of gunfire from the house. Teko cheered through his tears.

A few minutes later, the gunfire from within the house ceased and the police stopped shooting. Only the fire continued. Then one of the walls and finally the whole house collapsed in flames. It was all over. The only sound of shots came from exploding ammunition within the burning house.

Teko and Yolanda fell into each other's arms, clutching one another in grief and misery. Teko was hysterical, sobbing, "It's all my fault. . . . If it weren't for Mel's . . . I killed them. . . . I didn't mean to, but I did it. . . . Oh, I should have been there with them, shooting it out to the end. . . . Oh, I wish I were there. . . . I wish I were dead too."

"Don't say that, Teko, don't say that," Yolanda sobbed. "It's not your fault. . . . Cin would want you to live and to carry on the struggle. If it had to happen, it's better that we were not there, or we'd all be dead. This way, our team can live to fight again."

Slumped on the floor at below eye level with the television screen, I was mesmerized. Everything was happening around me and I was feeling nothing. Teko and Yolanda's wailing became louder and louder, blending with the incessant bleating of the TV news reporters, and I heard it all over a dull buzzing ring inside my head. Numbed but perhaps on the brink of hysteria myself, I crawled away on all fours to the bathroom and locked myself in. I did not want to be with them any longer; I could not take any more of this.

I sat in there alone for I do not know how long, with only the mumble of the sounds from the other room reaching me. I don't know for sure what I thought. I tried to collect my thoughts, but they ran through my head as through a sieve. I could not stand the two people in the other room. I could not believe what I had just seen on television. I could not resist projecting myself into that shoot-out witnessing my own death. Some of the TV reporters had been saying I was in there. I knew that if I had been in there, the police would have behaved precisely the same way. Why would they do anything else?

Cin had told me it would be that way. If I had been there, I would be
dead now. I could not believe Cin really was dead. I just could not believe it. Yet it flashed through my mind that I was glad he was dead.
Glad that all of them were dead. They deserved to die for what they
had done to me. They had expected to die in this cause, but they had
no right to expect me to die with them. But then I corrected myself:
That was a bad thought to harbor. The shoot-out had been barbaric.
I really did not wish them to die in that way. In fact, I really did
not want them to be killed because now I was left with the Harrises, for whom I felt no comradeship whatever. My fear of them intensified. My life in the SLA would be even more miserable from now
on.

I sat there on the floor in a stupor. I was a soldier, an urban
guerrilla, in the people's army. It was a role I had accepted in exchange for my very life. There was no turning back. The police or
the FBI would shoot me on sight, just as they had killed my comrades. . . . I sat there sobbing—not for my comrades but for myself.

Teko banged on the door with his fist. "What the hell you doing in
there? . . . Come on out here, now!"

Yolanda was displeased with my conduct. "You really are not showing the proper respect for our fallen comrades, Tania. You must stay
here with us and watch the news. Perhaps one of our comrades got
away."

Shocked and subdued, the three of us sat on one of the beds
watching ghastly scenes from the "mopping-up" operations. After the
fire department had doused the flames, a police team, garbed in fatigues and gas masks, searched the remains of the building for bodies.
Nothing was left of the house but charred rubble. The newsmen announced that no one could possibly have survived that fire. The only
question was how many members of the SLA had been inside the
building. And, of course, whether Patty Hearst had been inside. Only
the identification of the bodies would provide the answers. It was gruesome. But we talked of the possibility of someone having escaped. It
was possible, said Teko. Perhaps the others had broken up into teams
and only Cin's team had been inside the house.

Teko continued his running commentary on the news. As we
witnessed on television the removal of some of the bodies, Teko described how difficult identification would be. The intense heat of the fire
would have melted the gas masks our comrades were wearing. Further-

My parents in front of their Hillsborough home. (Photo credit: San Francisco *Examiner*)

Lines for the People in Need food giveaway. (Photo credit: UPI)

Some of the graffiti at the Golden Gate Avenue apartment. At right are some of the locks used for security. (Photo credit: UPI)

The Los Angeles Police Department found this picture, taken by Zoya, of the SLA. First row (left to right): Me, Gelina, Fahizah. Second row (left to right): Yolanda, Cujo, Cin, Teko, Gabi.

One of over 400 photographs of the Hibernia Bank robbery, showing three guns pointed at me.

The destruction of the Los Angeles safehouse in which six SLA members were killed. (Photo credit: UPI)

UNITED STATES DEPARTMENT OF JUSTICE

FEDERAL BUREAU OF INVESTIGATION

WASHINGTON, D.C. 20535

April 19, 1974

RE: DONALD DAVID DE FREEZE   PATRICIA MICHELLE SOLTYSIK   PATRICIA CAMPBELL HEARST
     NANCY LING PERRY   CAMILLA CHRISTINE HALL   MATERIAL WITNESS

TO WHOM IT MAY CONCERN:

The FBI is conducting an investigation to determine the whereabouts of these individuals whose descriptions and photographs appear below. Federal warrants charging robbery of a San Francisco bank on April 15, 1974, have been issued at San Francisco, California, for Camilla Hall, Donald DeFreeze, Nancy Perry, and Patricia Soltysik. A material witness warrant in this robbery has been issued for Patricia Hearst, who was abducted from her Berkeley, California, residence on February 4, 1974, by a group which has identified itself as the Symbionese Liberation Army (SLA). The participants in the bank robbery also claim to be members of the SLA.

DONALD DAVID DE FREEZE
N/M, DOB 11/16/43, 5'9" to 5'11",
150-160, blk hair, br eyes

PATRICIA MICHELLE SOLTYSIK
W/F, DOB 5/17/50, 5'3" to 5'4",
116, dk br hair, br eyes

PATRICIA CAMPBELL HEARST
W/F, DOB 2/20/54, 5'3", 110,
lt br hair, br eyes

MATERIAL WITNESS

NANCY LING PERRY
W/F, DOB 9/19/47, 5', 95-105, red
br hair, haz eyes

CAMILLA CHRISTINE HALL
W/F, DOB 3/24/45, 5'6", 125,
blonde hair, blue eyes

If you have any information concerning these individuals, please notify your local FBI office, a telephone listing for which can be found on the first page of your directory. In view of the crimes for which these individuals are being sought, they should be considered armed and extremely dangerous, and no action should be taken which would endanger anyone's safety.

Very truly yours,

C. M. Kelley

The first "Wanted" poster after the Hibernia robbery. (Photo courtesy FBI)

Jack Scott. (Photo credit: UPI)

The house where Wendy Yoshimura and I were arrested. (Photo credit: Wide World Photos)

Wendy Yoshimura. (Photo credit: San Francisco *Examiner*)

more, the ammunition worn on their belts probably exploded, destroying whole sections of their bodies. He talked as though he knew it all, comparing this shoot-out with the devastation he said he saw in Vietnam. My empty stomach turned at the grisly horror of it all. My eyes wanted to see no more, my ears to hear no more about the fate I had so narrowly escaped.

Shortly after 10 P.M., the television cameras picked up the scene of my parents, accompanied by my sister Anne, disembarking from an airliner at Los Angeles International Airport. They had come from San Francisco to be on the scene, to find out if I was dead or alive. Teko vented his fury at the attention given by the capitalist press to my family. It was as if no one cared at all about any of the others in the SLA, he said. To me, it all looked surreal. I felt no emotion whatever upon seeing them after so long a time. In fact, it occurred to me that they looked dead, as if they were in another world far apart from mine. The connection between us had been severed forever, I thought. In a close-up of the three of them, as my father spoke briefly into a microphone, I noticed that Anne, the typical younger sister, was wearing a favorite jacket of mine. I could not believe that I would be thinking of such a silly, irrational thing at a time like this. It made me feel foolish and selfish and, at the same time, I felt a sharp pang of longing for my mother and father and for my sisters. But I dismissed such thoughts as "badthink," unworthy of an SLA soldier.

As we watched the eleven o'clock news summary, Yolanda talked of the future: we had to send our condolences to the families of our slain warriors, we had to return to the San Francisco Bay Area to recruit and rebuild the SLA, we had to fight on in memory of the lives given in the cause. She turned solemnly to Teko and said, "Do you realize that now you are the head of the Symbionese Liberation Army? You are now the General Field Marshall of the SLA."

"Yes," he replied softly, "I will do my very best to carry on the struggle as Cin would have wanted. . . ."

"Tania," she said, turning to me, "we both have to give Teko all the respect that we gave Cin because he is our leader now. We've got to try harder than ever before to cooperate with each other. . . . We've got to work as a team all the time . . . and we've got to support Teko because now he is our leader."

"Yes, of course," I said, "I'll really try. . . ."

When the eleven o'clock news ended, Teko announced that it was time for us to turn in and get a good night's sleep. We were all exhausted, red-eyed from weeping, spent. Yolanda turned to me and solicitously asked, "Tania, do you want to make love with us tonight?"

"No, thanks," I said, and climbed into the other bed, alone.

CHAPTER

TWELVE

AT UNEXPECTED MOMENTS I would visualize what must have gone on inside that bleak, little house on Fifty-fourth Street. Whole scenes would streak through my mind and then be gone. Reliving past moments with Gelina, Gabi, Fahizah, and the others, I knew that all of them had to have been living with the anticipation and terror of that ultimate shoot-out. It had been an all-pervasive fear, a knowledge of what would certainly come to pass. Whether it was clear and close up or at other times buried deep inside, it was always present, an integral part of their consciousness. When the shoot-out finally came, it might well have been anticlimactic. Each of them had lived through it mentally so many times before. They did what they knew they would have to do: die for their cause. The revolution had given them a reason for living, as well as for dying. I had been conscripted, but they were fanatics—true believers. Street-wise and paranoid about the police hunt for the SLA, Cin must have known "the pigs" would find him there. People were going in and out of the house all day long. Word spread through the neighborhood; it had to reach the police. Cin had chosen to stay and fight in that little stucco house.

All he had to do was take off and flee when the children went to school. But perhaps he had grown weary of flight and fear and claustrophobic loneliness. Maybe he was simply drunk that day. But I had seen him drink the cheap wine all day long, as he reportedly had on that last day, and never totally lose control of his senses and

awareness. More likely, though, he had chosen this day for his martyrdom, deciding that they would all go out in a blaze of glory. Cin's
mood that day might have been one of mystic euphoria as he com-
muned with his people. And the others? Did they all trust him so
implicitly at the end that no one raised the question of the danger of
remaining in that house? Perhaps Zoya might venture a conflicting opinion. But once Cin made up his mind, his word was incontestable.

In the days that followed I went over and over in my mind the
events and possibilities of that shoot-out. But only later could I put the
confused pieces in place. One possibility came to mind in various
forms: If I had been in that house at the time, Cin would have walked
me outside as a hostage and in the glare of the police floodlights he
would have demanded an airplane and safe passage for all of them to
Algeria or Cuba or Libya in exchange for my life. What would the Los
Angeles Police Department have done then? There was no getting away
from it. I was a "common criminal," a soldier in the SLA, in the eyes of
the Attorney General of the United States and down through the FBI
and all the police forces in the country. They would shoot me on sight.
I firmly believed that. I had no reason to doubt it. Not only had Cin
told me that, but I had witnessed it live on television. The police had
not asked me, Patty Hearst, to step aside or to step outside when they
opened fire. For all they knew or cared, I was in that house with my
comrades. Once I had been a kidnap victim, but now I was a hunted
criminal. The sheer horror of seeing that shoot-out, that mini-war, with
thousands of shots being fired back and forth, and that final conflagra-
tion, completely devastated me, for while I was not there physically,
every nerve in my body told me that I was part of it.

More than nine thousand bullets were fired during that hour-long
siege, according to the police reports, and, incredibly, not until the final
moments was *anybody* killed or wounded. The six people inside the
house fired an estimated four thousand rounds and fortunately, despite
all of Cin's dire predictions and Teko's expectations, not a single policeman was wounded or killed. According to the official police report,
which came out later, when the fire became too intense to bear, Cin
and the others retreated to the rear of the house, pulled up some floorboards, and snuggled together in the earth beneath the house. When
the fire and heat advanced upon them, Fahizah tried to sneak out of
the crawl space into the backyard in an attempt to reach the next

house. Gabi came out behind her. But Gabi panicked and opened fire upon the police stationed behind the house. They returned the fire. A single shot hit her in the forehead between the eyes and she died instantly, the first to go. Then Fahizah whirled about and opened fire with her hand weapon. She caught two bullets in the back, severing her spine. She fell to the ground, dead. At the same time, Gelina, who was next in the crawl-space tunnel, reached out and pulled Gabi back under the house. There was to be no escape.

The heat was so intense that neither the police nor the firemen on the scene could approach the blazing building. They all heard the rapid explosions of bullets in the crawl space under the building. Apparently the ammunition in the SLA gun belts and bandoliers exploded from the intense heat. Finally, the entire building collapsed.

After long hours, when the police were able to dig through the rubble, they found Gelina in the crawl space leading out of the house. Further back, beneath the floorboards, they discovered Cin, lying on his side, his face pressed up against a ventilation screen; Zoya was crumpled over his body; Cujo was lying alongside of Cin, to his left. Several had died of smoke inhalation and burns. Fahizah's body was outside where she had fallen, only a few feet from the back corner of the building. Gabi's body was buried deep beneath the rubble and was not found until two days later.

But on the night of the shoot-out, we in the motel room in Anaheim knew only that two male and three female bodies had been removed. We held to the hope that one of the sisters had escaped. Yolanda forlornly wished that Fahizah had survived; she was small and smart and perhaps had managed to sneak away from the house. I agreed with her. I am certain that Yolanda and I wanted Fahizah to have survived for the same reason. We both preferred for her to take over the command of the SLA. We did not trust Teko's judgment. Of course, neither of us dared voice this.

It was not until the next day, Saturday, that the authorities gave names to the charred remains and we knew that Fahizah had not survived. Positive identification was announced for Donald DeFreeze (Cinque), age 30; Angela Atwood (Gelina), age 24; Patricia Soltysik (Zoya), 24; William Wolfe (Cujo), 23; and Nancy Ling Perry (Fahizah), 26. Teko, Yolanda, and I could not believe that Gabi, of all people, had survived that holocaust. So we had given up hope before

Gabi's body was discovered the next day as the police dug more deeply into the ruins of that house.

All during the weekend, the press speculated upon my whereabouts. Teko and Yolanda were livid because as each body was examined by the coroner and identified, the press announced that that body was *not* mine and my parents were the first to be notified. The sixth and final body was thought to be mine until dental records could be consulted. The press attention given to me and to my family was excessive and I spent a good deal of time apologizing to Teko for the unfairness of the coverage. The anguish my own family felt through those days of uncertainty—not knowing if I was dead or alive—must have been the most terrible part of their long ordeal. Yet none of it touched me at the time. I thought of myself as long lost to them, cut off from all of my past, friends and relatives. In my own mind, I could see no way of crossing over to them. I believed my parents had given me up as lost forever and that they no longer even wanted to see me again. I was convinced that there was no way I could come out in the open now, without the police or the FBI gunning me down as they had the others. I spent that Saturday and Sunday crying, deep in a bottomless quagmire of depression. I wept so much that I ached with pain.

At a press conference, the Los Angeles coroner, Thomas Noguchi, openly expressed his own astonishment at the manner of the deaths of the six SLA members. "They died compulsively," he said. "They chose to stay under the floor as the fire burned out. In all my years as a coroner, I've never seen this kind of conduct in the face of flames." But then he astounded us when he announced that, in his opinion, Cinque had committed suicide by shooting himself in the head in those final moments when the others had died all around him. He said there had been powder burns in the head wound that had killed Cinque, the bullet entering the right temple and exiting slightly higher up on the left temple.

"That's a chickenshit, motherfucking lie!" Teko screamed, jumping up and down all over the motel room, ranting that the "fascist pigs" were trying to falsify and distort the heroic deaths of the SLA and its leader.

"Oh, we've got to send out a communiqué and tell *the people* the real truth, so they'll know," wailed Yolanda. "It's so important that the people know that we were all willing to die for what we believed. . . .

Cin told them, but we've got to remind them. . . . We can't let them discredit our leader with a lie like that. . . . And we've got to send condolences to the families of our fallen comrades."

Teko and Yolanda went on making plans. They were forever making plans, talking of carrying on the struggle, the need to regroup, to rebuild the SLA, to continue the revolution, to free the oppressed people. As far as I remember, I lay curled up in a fetal position in bed, sleeping, dozing, staring out into space, feeling weak and sick. By the end of the weekend, both Teko and Yolanda had changed their appearances, disguising themselves beyond recognition. We had to move on. This motel was too expensive for our remaining resources. While driving about with Frank Sutter on Friday, Yolanda had bought new wigs and new clothes. Her new hairdo of soft curls of gray and dark brown hair added ten years to her age and changed her appearance dramatically. Because she had been identified at Mel's, she bought herself green slacks and a new blouse. She got a new shirt for Teko since his red lumberjack shirt also had been identified in the news reports. Teko dyed his hair and beard blond, which gave him a startling new appearance. My new wig turned me into a pale blonde with a shag cut and that was deemed sufficient as a disguise.

We moved out of there early that Monday morning, heading south, and after some looking we found a modest, transient motel in Costa Mesa, where we rented a room by the week which had a hot plate and small refrigerator—all for forty dollars. They signed in as a married couple and sneaked me in, which obliged me to hide in a closet every time someone came to the door to clean up or to ask a question.

The plan was to lie low for a week and then move north, back to San Francisco, where we knew the terrain and had a much better chance of finding friends and supporters. On Tuesday, the district attorney of Los Angeles announced that the three of us were wanted on charges of kidnapping, armed robbery, assault to commit murder, and at least another dozen charges. This hardly surprised us. In fact, it made Teko feel much better and more important. As a general in the SLA, it had disturbed him that he and Yolanda were wanted only on some minor charges while I was wanted for bank robbery. Now he was getting his due in publicity and notoriety and he reveled in it. In our little motel room with its one double bed and small card table, Teko never let an opportunity pass to remind me of his grave responsibility as the new

General Field Marshal of the SLA. The corollary, of course, was that I owed him my complete allegiance and obedience, as we all owed a responsibility to the memory of Cin and our fallen comrades.

On a small black-and-white TV in the room, we followed every scrap of news and rumor concerning us and the SLA. A gigantic police hunt for us was under way. We were sighted in all sorts of places in Los Angeles and in San Francisco. He rejected the idea of surrendering. That was out of the question. We were still an army, even if we were reduced to the size of a small guerrilla band. But, he said, we could still strike at the fascist beast, like the flea that torments the dog, and in the end be victorious. Teko decided we would leave for San Francisco on one of the heaviest-trafficked days of the year, Memorial Day, and we would travel on the busiest highway in broad daylight, hidden in the midst of the holiday travelers.

In a series of criticism/self-criticism meetings, we studied the mistakes of our comrades in order that we might learn from them. The SLA should never have come to Los Angeles, we reminded ourselves, because urban guerrillas should operate only on terrain that they know intimately. San Francisco and the Bay Area was our true territory. The SLA should have had two safehouses, not one, so that when forced to leave one, Cin and the others would have had a backup hideaway. When leaving the Eighty-fourth Street house, they should have split up into teams and arranged to meet at a later date. They had remained together only for their own feelings of security. They felt safe with each other. Under the circumstances that had been a grave mistake. Upon taking over that house on Fifty-fourth Street, either they should have kept everyone there hostage or they should have moved out at daybreak. Teko pledged that under his command we would not make those same errors. We all agreed that as a team we did very well when "jammed" at Mel's and afterward. Teko's own gross mistake there was touched upon only lightly. It was a very sensitive subject. But he did try to explain to us that he had shoplifted the bandolier only because he thought it might arouse suspicions if he went up to the counter and tried to pay for it. That might have tipped off the store clerk to his true identity. Yolanda never failed at these meetings to emphasize our need for better, more trusting relationships among us as the sole remaining members of the SLA. It was her well-meaning attempt, I think, to assuage their cold treatment of me and to calm Teko's temper. Our most dire needs, of course, were a safe place in which to hide and money with which to buy food. Teko had gathered together all the cash we had and it came to something less than two hundred dollars.

We departed on Memorial Day morning. "The pigs can't stop everyone on the road on a holiday weekend," Teko declared. We traveled up Interstate 5 in heavy traffic from Los Angeles to San Francisco and not only were we not stopped, we witnessed no other cars being investigated by the highway patrol. Yolanda had her Mauser automatic in the front seat and Teko, who had lost his gun in the scuffle at Mel's, was armed with my .38, which he had taken from me. I lay curled up on the back seat, resting my head on the armrest, with a blanket covering most of me, playing the part of a sleeping child. The idea was to avoid the appearance of two women and one man in a car heading for San Francisco. On the floor in the back was the vinyl duffel bag Yolanda had bought to hold our other weapons, a submachine gun, a shotgun, a carbine, our ammunition belts, our sheathed survival knives, and bags of ammunition. We ate snacks in the car and did not stop at all, except for refueling. They never did say in so many words what we would do if stopped; but surrender was unthinkable and against our Codes of War. We could hardly escape in any race with the police in the dilapidated compact car Yolanda had bought for some three hundred dollars. What if it simply broke down on the road? Then what would we do?

But the car did not break down. It chugged along the highway for more than nine hours and then through the busy, familiar streets of San Francisco. It sputtered and died on Oak Street in the Panhandle section of Golden Gate Park. We pushed it to the curb and Teko tried to get it started, as people gathered to watch and to give advice. By then it was early evening and the tree-lined street was alive with all sorts of people doing all sorts of things—Kung-fu exercises, bicycling, strolling, staggering about in drunken or spaced-out stupors. We were on the edge of the Haight-Ashbury District, former home of the flower children, which had now been taken over by the hippies and drug addicts of the 1970's. Finally, we pushed the car a few blocks to a service station. Yolanda and I hung back while Teko went into the station alone and left the car there to be repaired.

The three of us, the most wanted trio in the United States, returned to sit on a park bench in the Panhandle, discussing in full view of all passersby what we should do next. Yolanda, in her trusty little encoded address book, found the name of a woman she had known in Berkeley who lived within walking distance. So, while Teko and I remained on the park bench, with the red bag containing our submachine guns at our feet, Yolanda went off to beg for a place to stay for the night. She was turned away, although they did give her fifty dollars.

"Why didn't you tell me your sister Gina lived in that building?" Yolanda asked me, having been told that by her friend.

"Gina and her husband used to live there. I forgot all about it. But they moved out over a year ago or more."

"What a weird coincidence," she said.

Yolanda then came up with the name of a college friend or acquaintance whom they had not seen since leaving Bloomington, Indiana. The question was: Could this friend, named Mark, be trusted? After some discussion, Teko and Yolanda worked out a plan. They sent him a bouquet of flowers with a card that said: "From Honeysuckle ⚹1." It was a joking code name that referred to the apartment they lived in while at Indiana University, Teko explained. Then Teko telephoned Mark to test the reception he would receive. We were invited, Teko exclaimed, proud of himself. Mark was living with a friend, also named Mark, in a flat in one of the remodeled Victorian homes that are so distinctive in San Francisco. It was directly across the street from the Panhandle.

We were greeted rather warily. Mark was obviously frightened. He fed us quickly and took us to our accommodations: his storage space, which once had been a coal bin, in the basement of the house. He locked us in there for the night—for our own safekeeping, of course, he explained with profuse apologies. I slept fitfully that night on a bare concrete floor in utter darkness.

Teko touched Mark for fifty dollars the next morning. It was apparent that Mark never expected to see that fifty dollars again but thought it well worth the price to be rid of us. By telephone, Yolanda located a motel where we could have two bedrooms, one large, one small, for the price of one, on Lombard Street near Van Ness, in the heart of one of the city's busiest business districts. We traveled there, halfway across the city, by bus, carrying with us our flaming red duffel bag filled with guns. It felt claustrophobic to be crammed in with so many people, wondering whether anyone would recognize us.

That motel too was only a stopgap, Teko announced. We would stay there only for as long as it took Yolanda to find us a suitable safehouse. She was looking in Oakland, across the bay, where it was cheaper. Since the police were looking for us as a threesome, Teko decreed that we should not go outside together. In fact, he decided it was safe outside only for Yolanda. He and I were too well known to take too many chances. So Teko and I stayed in the motel room, eating snacks and watching television and chain-smoking.

After a two-day search, Yolanda found and rented for us an apartment in a working-class, racially mixed neighborhood a few blocks from Mills College in Oakland. In glowing terms, she described the place—one large room with a double bed plus a kitchen and a small dining nook—and the security aspects of the neighborhood, particularly the predominance there of older blue-collar working people, where the "pigs" would least expect to find us. She and Teko spent so much time planning our move across the bay, with detailed street maps, alternate meeting places, and dead drops, that I finally tuned out and stopped listening. Since our car had not yet been repaired, we had to travel again by bus.

For security reasons, we split up. Yolanda and I set out first, going by city bus to the downtown bus terminal and then transferring to an inter-city bus which would take us across the bay to Oakland. We were loaded down with bags stuffed with all our belongings. Yolanda had a shopping bag and I carried the duffel bag containing our guns. Teko was to follow later. So, with the police and FBI presumably in hot pursuit of us, there we were, traveling through the streets of San Francisco at a snail's pace by public transportation.

When we got out at Mills College, with three or four blocks to walk to the apartment on Walnut Street, I was exhausted, struggling to carry those heavy weapons. As I stumbled along, dragging the bag beside me, Yolanda, who had been treating me as if I were a moronic army recruit, became furious. "You're being too conspicuous," she hissed. "Try to carry that bag higher; make it look light."

"I can't. I can hardly carry it at all."

No amount of her exhortations could get me to lift the heavy bag any higher. In fact, I worried about the sounds of the guns rattling. We certainly were conspicuous, struggling down that city street. In disgust General Yolanda took up one handle of the heavier bag and together we made our way to the apartment. It was plain but clean, several rungs above our previous safehouses in Los Angeles and at Hunters Point. In fact, I thought it had the feeling of a safehouse, an aura of permanence and safety after our hustling from coal bin to motel. The important point, for me, was that Yolanda had rented it by the month. We could stay here and rest.

Teko arrived about an hour later and lost no time at all in complaining about the security aspects of the apartment. He was simply pulling rank, giving Yolanda a violent dressing down for choosing such an apartment. It was in the back of the house and had no view of the street in front or of the steps leading up to our door. We could be taken by surprise at any time. There was no back escape route open to us. The walls were so thin; the neighbors could hear our every word. "How could you be so stupid as to take a place like this? Didn't you think of security at all?" Teko demanded. He proceeded to give Yolanda a stern lecture on security. Of course, she fought back and they were into one of their old bickering, raging arguments. They played one-upmanship, always trying to catch one another at fault so he or she could justly be criticized.

As time went on in that small apartment, they fought more and more each day over petty, ridiculous issues. Teko liked to command, to order us about arbitrarily, and Yolanda's natural inclination was to defy him. He had the stereotypical small man's pugnacity, always needing to be right and to prove his strength and superiority. They would stand toe to toe and scream violent curses and abuse at one another. More often than not it was Yolanda who would strike the first blow, although sometimes he did. Yolanda would haul off and, with all her strength, punch him in the stomach, not once but as many times as she could before he socked her across the room. The barnyard vulgarities and genital metaphors were hardly unusual, but both of them, being long married, knew each other's weak points and sensitivities. It did not take much to goad Teko, a violent, nervous little man by nature, into one of his rages, but Yolanda was an expert at it.

"You just couldn't resist shoplifting, could you?" Yolanda screamed at him on more than one occasion. "You don't think, you just do things that are stupid and dangerous, and you'll probably do something to get us killed too."

That was usually her final verbal thrust before Teko hauled off and punched her.

Sometimes I interceded when their fighting went on longer than usual. "What are you two doing?" I once screamed over their screaming. "Everyone else has just been killed and you two are fighting like enemies, instead of being comrades. Do you want the neighbors to call the police in to stop a family dispute . . . ?"

When I quieted them they would usually sulk at opposite ends of the room. But just as often, they would both turn on me. My objection to their battles was strictly bourgeois. I did not understand them and they were true revolutionaries. It was good to fight. I objected to their physical fighting because of my rich, bourgeois background. Poor people fought all the time, expressing their anger as well as their love physically. It was more honest that way. I was just too uptight. And on and on . . .

Their criticisms of me became a litany. I was a spoiled rich brat, a symbol of what was wrong with the capitalistic society. I was too weak ever to become a good soldier, a good revolutionary. I didn't really love the poor, oppressed people as I should. I was too cold. I did not care enough. I was a millstone around their necks, a liability to them. I was too recognizable to be trusted on any outside actions by myself. I was holding them back because they had to drag me everywhere they went. I was hindering their freedom of action. They were stuck with me.

I cringed because, as with all good attacks, there was a degree of truth in all they said, and I knew it. I was depressed and weepy all the time; I was not a good soldier, not as good as they were in combat skills, and I was not pulling my full weight.

I worried constantly about being too much of a liability to the SLA. If Teko ever reached that decision I knew he could easily rationalize the need to kill me. He would never announce it, of course. He would take me out somewhere, execute me, and hide my body where it would never be found. At the same time, I also knew I was their greatest asset. As Tania, I was a symbol of the greatest success of the SLA.

By this time, I entertained no doubts whatever about my future. I thought of myself as a soldier in the SLA. I had joined and agreed to their recruitment and thereby had given up all of my past life. Thoughts of my family, friends, and acquaintances of my past life almost never entered my mind, and when they did I criticized myself for such bourgeois thoughts as mercilessly as Teko or Yolanda would have. I did not ever want to think of them anymore. The SLA was my whole life. Everything Teko, Yolanda, and I did day by day revolved around "the struggle," the revolution, the war to overthrow our capitalist government and to free the oppressed people. There was no other reality for me.

In our interpersonal relationships, Yolanda could be cold and cruel and calculating. But Teko did not carry a grudge; he lived almost entirely in the present. He never seemed to remember the past, not even the immediate past. Thus, he could fight violently with Yolanda one evening and an hour or so later ask her to make love with him, and she would refuse.

"That's not comradely," Teko would say. "Come on, let's fuck."

"I don't want to," she'd retort.

"Come on, I have a need."

"I don't."

"Well, you're supposed to satisfy my need."

"Shit, that's sexist. What about my needs?"

"What are your needs?"

"My need is to be left alone, not to fuck you when I don't want to."

She rejected him every night that we were at that Walnut Street apartment and so Teko turned to me with his inimitable "Let's fuck!" and I never refused him. I did not know how. I was a soldier in the Symbionese Liberation Army and I did as I was told. Teko would make his demands upon me only occasionally and always when Yolanda was out of the apartment. There was nothing loving, romantic, or even affectionate in this. He was the General Field Marshal and he had a need. I had no feelings whatever. In fact, much of the time I was half drunk, feeling no pain, on mountain red wine.

Soon after we had settled in at the apartment, Teko sent Yolanda out for a gallon jug of mountain red, which he claimed he needed for "medicinal purposes" to calm his nerves. But with that gallon jug being replaced almost daily, I think I was outdrinking him, sipping wine throughout the day and for most of the night: I was never roaring drunk but I was good and numb. At the start, Teko said only Yolanda should go outside because only she could pass easily among people. But after three or four days, Teko became so nervous and irritable being cooped up that he redyed his blond hair to a dark red and trimmed his beard to a wispy goatee. Then he too ventured outside.

For the very first time since I was kidnapped, I was being left alone for hours, sometimes for most of the day. I suppose I could have walked out of the apartment and away from it all. But I didn't. It simply never occurred to me. My fear of the police outweighed my hatred for the SLA. When Teko and Yolanda were both away, I stayed in bed, wallowing in self-pity and sipping mountain red and crying. It was easy not to think at all.

This was a time of despair and emotional upheaval for all of us. Yolanda had begun working on a communiqué which would eulogize our slain SLA comrades. They were much in our minds. With or without my imbibing of wine, I was in a constant state of deep depression. It hung upon me without specific reason, deadening my mind, my emotions, my body. When Teko's mood deepened he too would complain, but Yolanda would challenge his right to feel sorry for himself.

"Revolutionaries don't despair," she would say in her flat, Midwestern accent. "Revolutionaries fight on. . . ."

"It's all so crummy living like this . . . I wonder if it's all worth it . . . no one seems to care," Teko complained one night, pushing the beans around on his dinner plate.

Yolanda gave him that cold glare of her steel-blue eyes. "Then why don't you just turn yourself in to the pigs?"

"I didn't mean that, you know," said Teko.

"Revolution means struggle and true revolutionaries knew it would be a long, hard struggle. We knew it from the start. Our comrades did not give up. They didn't give up even when the pigs were killing them. . . . We don't have it so bad. There are no pigs at our door. There are people starving all over this country. We just have to put up with not enough food. We can at least do that, can't we?" Yolanda was off on one of her interminable revolutionary lectures, hardly pausing for an answer to her rhetorical questions. Teko and I knew the litany. But she was always one up on us, the stalwart, resolute mother hen with a need to lecture and teach her wayward children.

Our greatest prevailing concern, aside from eluding the police dragnet, was money. Yolanda had had to pay out a month's rent in advance before we could move into the apartment. Now we were just about flat broke, down to about twenty dollars, and back to eating rice and beans and celery and not much more. Teko proposed a quick robbery—to hold up someone on the street, snatch a purse, or anything fast and simple. We needed the money to carry on and we had to act, Teko said. But Yolanda would agree to a robbery only if it was thoroughly planned out in advance and provided with a backup force. They fought over this at length, of course.

"We're so fucking white, bourgeois, chickenshit scared," Teko
stormed. "Blacks go out all the time and snatch purses when they need
money. They don't plan everything down to the last detail. They act.
But we whites are so uptight we have to do surveillance and plan and
all that crap."

"But it's so dangerous, so unsafe, to just go out and pull a stupid
caper," Yolanda argued. "Suppose we got caught on a chickenshit
holdup? We'd be the laughingstock of the radical movement. Think how
it would look to the world and to the people we're struggling for! It's
much safer to try to reach our old friends. Some of them will come
through. They owe it to us and to our fallen comrades. Besides, we
have got to build up our ranks again. We've got to operate as an
army, not a bunch of stickup artists." This was an ongoing argument,
especially when Yolanda returned from one of her outings and bitterly
reported being turned down by one or another of their old radical
friends in the Berkeley area. A onetime close friend with whom she
had worked in Berkeley had given Yolanda twenty dollars but had told
her not to come back again. A doctor who had helped the Harrises go
underground after the Marcus Foster shooting had refused even to
come to the telephone. A Berkeley girl who had worked with Yolanda
in the Venceremos prison program, and who had even attended some
of Joe Remiro's gun classes and shooting practice, had been even more
cruel.

"Don't call me, ever," this girl told Yolanda. "Stay away from
me. . . . I don't want any part of you or the SLA. . . . Just go away."

"Listen, sister, we're supposed to be comrades," Yolanda had told
her.

"Get lost!" was the final reply.

Angry and embittered, Teko and Yolanda looked upon these rejec-
tions as outright betrayals of the revolution. They condemned such
people, in their own words, as "fucking liberals who call themselves
revolutionaries, but when it comes time to do more than just talk, they
turn into chickenshit pigs." Yolanda, before she went out seeking help,
always consulted her encoded address book, and a person was never
approached unless Teko and Yolanda agreed that such an attempt was
safe. For instance, they dismissed contemptuously all of the radical
group living at Peking House in Berkeley, where they and the SLA
were well known. Yolanda considered all of them "unworthy of our
trust" and Teko feared that the house was probably under pig surveil-

lance and riddled with pig informers. I could not offer much. Friends from my past were not likely to help the SLA. Teko and Yolanda had pretty much reached the bottom of their own list when Yolanda came up with the name of Kathleen Soliah.

She had been a very close friend of Gelina long before the SLA had been formed, a fellow actress and radical who had worked with Gelina as a waitress. But she had been considered too flaky to be trusted with the underground activities of the SLA. They did not know Kathy Soliah too well, but Yolanda thought it was worth a try, in the memory of poor Gelina. . . . Besides, Yolanda had her address.

For several days Teko and Yolanda discussed the wisdom of approaching Kathleen Soliah. We had read in the newspaper that she had been a prominent speaker at a memorial rally for the slain SLA members in the Ho Chi Minh Park in Berkeley. They did not know if she was under police surveillance or, even if not, whether she could be trusted to help us. So many of their former friends had turned out to be just big talkers. They preferred to approach only those whom they knew well. But we were at the end of our rope, broke. The choice was down to a holdup of some sort or try Kathy. They decided to approach Gelina's friend. In her gray wig and a nondescript dress, Yolanda went out to do it alone. She returned, ecstatic.

Kathy had not been home, so Yolanda left a message that her aunt had stopped by and was given the address of the bookstore in which Kathy worked. At the bookstore in Berkeley, a block or so from campus, Yolanda recognized Kathy working at the cash register. Customers were coming and going from the register desk, so Yolanda wrote out a short note: "Meet me at the church." There was only one church nearby, which was around the corner from the bookstore. Then she approached the cash register and ever so sweetly asked, "Excuse me, dear, but could you tell me what time it is?"

Kathy turned to reply, looked at her, took a second look, and her jaw fell open in astonishment. Yolanda smiled her sweetest smile and handed her the note, saying, "Oh, would you be good enough to throw this away for me, please?" Kathy stood there, stunned. Yolanda had to take her hand and place the note in it and close her fingers around it. "Thank you," called Yolanda, and she strolled out of the bookshop.

About twenty minutes later, Kathy arrived at the empty church excited and out of breath. "Oh, I'm so happy to see you . . . you have no idea . . . I'm so glad you came to me. . . . I recognized you after a moment and I couldn't believe it, but then I knew it was you." She said she had telephoned her boyfriend, Jim Kilgore, and he had gathered up all the cash they had on hand. This Kathy turned over to Yolanda, saying she knew we would be in need of funds. Then she had telephoned her younger sister, Josephine, and Jo had understood and would withdraw all her savings from her bank for the SLA.

"She was so right on," exclaimed Yolanda, happy in recounting the meeting for us. "She knew we needed money. I didn't even have to ask her. Her consciousness was right there." There was enough to pay for the repair of the Corvair, so that same day Teko went to pick up the car.

We were all to meet Kathy and her boyfriend the following night in a drive-in movie in Oakland. The arrangements had been made. Then we would have time to work things out, Yolanda said, for Kathy had promised that she wanted to do everything she possibly could to help us.

Under the impetus of that successful action, Teko and Yolanda worked far into the night on the communiqué they had been preparing to tell the people our side of the story about the shoot-out. Yolanda was writing the eulogies for our fallen comrades, which I would recite on the tape, while Teko was working furiously on his first message as the new head of the SLA. He intended to set the record straight on what had happened and to appeal to others to join in the continuing struggle. We could not allow the pig lies to remain unanswered in history, Teko fumed.

Just prior to meeting them at the movies we held a meeting to discuss how we would act around Kathy and Jim. We had to appear strong and determined, upset by the loss of our comrades but not defeated. Under no circumstances would we admit that Teko stole *anything*—it would make us look too "un-together." We had to appear to be united, as if we had no personal differences.

When darkness had fallen we drove to the theater and parked in the section that was showing *The Sting*. A few minutes after the film had begun, we locked the car and walked to the refreshment area, mingling with the crowd. While Teko stood back, Yolanda and I met Kathy in the ladies' room. She was a tall, lean, intense girl of about twenty-seven, with long, fine, light brown hair. We led Kathy outside to meet Teko and she explained that Jim Kilgore was with her, waiting in her car. "Yes," said Teko. "Let's use your car." It fell in with his plan not to allow them, for security reasons, to see our car.

They were parked in the movie section showing another feature, a soft-core porno film called *Teacher's Pet*. We piled into the back seat of the car, while Jim and Kathy sat in the front seat. Jim Kilgore looked like the typical intellectual, unkempt Berkeley student, with wire-rim spectacles, six feet tall with medium-long brown hair, wearing a wrinkled T-shirt. He also had, I noticed, a little paunch. Once safely in their car, with the movie speaker turned down, we went through the formal introductions. We kissed and hugged Jim and Kathy as though we had known each other all of our lives.

Within the anonymity of the darkened car, the floodgates opened and the conversation flowed with intensity. I did not need to give my set speech. They knew all about me, or thought they did, and they approved. Kathy remarked that she admired my courage and commitment in joining the SLA. She was very emotional, talking very rapidly in a sharp little voice, sometimes seeming to be on the verge of tears.

Over and over again, she told us how much she had loved Angela Atwood (Gelina) and how disappointed she had been that Angela had not trusted her enough to invite her into the SLA. She would have wanted to join, to make the real commitment to the cause that both she and Angela had believed in. But she had been away on a vacation in Mexico when Angela had gone underground, and although she had hoped and even expected that Angela would contact her, she had never heard from her again. Angela had been her very best friend, and had shared their hopes and dreams. And then Angela had gone off and made her life's commitment to the SLA without her. She had been crushed, devastated, and racked with the guilt of inadequacy, of being helpless, when she had learned of Angela's horrible death.

She wanted us to know that she and Jim were ready now to do anything they could to help us. They had been part of the radical movement in Berkeley for three years and they knew lots of people who they thought would want to help also. There was much love, she said, in Berkeley for the SLA and what it stood for. Kathy had graduated from the University of California, Santa Barbara campus, with a degree in theater arts, and Jim had given up his graduate studies in economics so they could come to Berkeley together in search of people with their own political beliefs. Her brother, Steve, who was one year younger than she, had followed them to Berkeley later that year, 1971. He had dropped out of Humboldt State College in northern California, in his junior year, where he had been a track star, to be closer to his sister. Kathy's younger sister, who was about twenty-one, had come to Berkeley two years later. They were obviously a close family and Kathy was the leader. In explaining all of this, Kathy said that Josephine would gladly follow her lead in helping the SLA. In fact, said Kathy, at her suggestion, Jo had withdrawn her savings from her bank in order to help. Kathy handed the money over the back of her seat to Yolanda— $1,500. Yolanda thanked her sincerely. Kathy thought a bit and then added that Steve was more into the hippie movement than into politics and she was not at all certain he should be told about our activities. "I don't know how he will react and I want to think about it a little more," she remarked.

Kathy talked about a number of friends in the radical movement who she thought would also like to aid the SLA, saying that most of her friends sympathized with the aims and goals of the SLA and admired their courage. Teko, of course, gave her the standard lecture on the need for action rather than words, the efficacy of urban guerrilla warfare, the concept of how a small group can inflict innumerable blows upon the body of the capitalist state and bring it all crashing down. Kathy responded that she was ready and willing to go underground with the SLA and take part in any actions that were planned.

"No!" exclaimed her boyfriend. "I don't think any of us should get into any action now. It is just too hot for that. The pigs are really out in force around the Bay Area. I think you ought to lay low for a while . . . do nothing, until the heat lets up."

Teko, although he agreed with Jim Kilgore, did not like being told what to do. He was trying to act cool and collected, but he seemed to me to be rather pompous in his role as General Field Marshal. Nevertheless, he did tell Kathy that she and her friends could do more for the SLA at this time by staying aboveground and above suspicion.

For instance, Teko remarked, we were now preparing a communiqué for the people on the shoot-out. Could she get us a tape recorder by tomorrow? Of course, replied Kathy, eager to help. Could she arrange for someone trustworthy to deliver the tape to the Pacifica radio station in Los Angeles? We did not want the pigs to know we were in the Bay Area. Of course, said Kathy.

Teko, as our leader and spokesman, gave them an abbreviated and much edited summary of our activities, mentioning the incident at Mel's but in this version denying that he had stolen a pair of socks, as reported in the press, or a bandolier or anything. As he put it, he had been pounced upon for no reason at all and we were forced to shoot our way out of that predicament. Jim Kilgore questioned him on why the SLA had chosen to kill a black man like Marcus Foster, who had seemed to be such a good superintendent of schools. Teko tried to explain the SLA reasoning, but Jim remarked that most of the people in the radical movement just did not understand it. Teko did not like the implied criticism one bit, dismissing it as a sheer lack of understanding. The impression that Teko tried to create was simply that we in the SLA, who had taken action, were the professional revolutionaries. All the others, including Kathy and Jim, were mere amateurs. Teko did control his temper admirably. Yolanda was as sweet and as sympathetic as I had ever heard her. She seemed to drink in and absorb with the keenest interest everything that Kathy had to say and she hardly blinked an eye when Jim Kilgore raised a question or two about the wisdom of some of the SLA activities. No one called on me for my opinion and I just sat there listening to them and catching glimpses of silent, silly sex scenes on the huge movie screen beyond the windshield of the car. The meeting went on for the better part of two hours and even that did not seem enough time to cover all that needed to be said.

At one point my mind must have wandered from the subject at hand, for I suddenly became aware that Teko was talking about the possibility of our leaving the Bay Area and seeking a safe haven somewhere else. Kathy was saying, "I know a man who may be able to help you get across the country or to anywhere else you may want to go. He's a radical sportswriter and he knows just about everybody and he runs a sort of underground railroad for political fugitives. I know he's helped a number of people get away from the pigs."

His name was Jack Scott and he had been a sportswriter for the magazine *Ramparts,* published in Berkeley. He was, according to Kathy, a champion of black athletes, had written a number of books on how blacks were being used and ripped off in organized sports. As sports director of Oberlin College he had hired as his assistant Tommy Smith, the black track star, who was one of the two American blacks who had raised a clenched fist upon winning a medal at the 1968 Olympics.

Teko, who was an ardent sports fan, lost his revolutionary cool and said, "Wow!" He had heard of Jack Scott and said that he certainly would like to meet him. Kathy, excited at the prospect, promised to try to contact Jack Scott, who she thought was in New York.

As the movie ended, they made plans for meeting the next day. Teko refused to tell them, however, where we were staying or how they could reach us. "We'll contact you!"

Jim Kilgore was insulted. "Don't you trust us?" he asked.

Yolanda, the appeaser, explained that even when she was a trusted comrade in the early days of the SLA, she had been blindfolded every time she was driven to the SLA safehouse in Concord. It was nothing personal. It was a fundamental tenet of security that the location of a safehouse was never to be disclosed to anyone who did not have an absolute need to know.

Jim thought that was ridiculous, carrying security too far. But Kathy calmed him down. "They know what they are doing," she told him. "It's their own safety at stake and they have a right to be ultra-cautious. I understand." So Teko worked out with them a series of coded messages by which we could telephone their apartment; once they received our call, they would go to a specific public telephone booth and at a specific time we would call them there. "Never say anything important on your home phone," Teko said. "It may be tapped." We left them there, refusing their offer to accompany us to our car, and made our own way back separately but in sight of one another. Teko was suddenly very security-conscious.

Returning to our pad on Walnut Street, Teko was positively euphoric. The SLA was back in business.

CHAPTER

THIRTEEN

IT WAS MEANT to be a show of strength, a declaration that despite our terrible defeat in the shoot-out, the Symbionese Liberation Army was alive and well and determined to continue the struggle. It was also designed as a recorded memorial service for our fallen comrades, which would rally radicals and revolutionaries to our ranks. The shoot-out and fiery death of our comrades had given rise to a new wave of sympathy for the SLA, at least among some of the leftist groups, radicals, and liberals in the country. Teko particularly was heartened by various sightings of spray-painted signs on walls in the Bay Area proclaiming, "The SLA Lives!" So it was with great diligence and concern that we worked steadily for three whole days in our one-room apartment in Oakland on our post-shoot-out communiqué, which became widely known as our Eulogy Tape.

I should say *they* worked steadily for three days. Teko and Yolanda disdained my offers of help, although I thought by this time that I could write SLA propaganda as well as they could. I knew all the buzz words and phrases. But Teko and Yolanda had such a low regard for the value of anything I said that they seldom, if ever, consulted me. Perhaps they recognized me for the zombie that I had become. They sat on the floor at opposite ends of the room, writing furiously on pads of yellow legal-sized paper. Teko had insisted on the tablets as "proper equipment" and Yolanda had reluctantly gone along with the "extravagance" of the pads. Every so often they would read me a line or a

section and ask, "How does this sound?" Invariably, I would praise
the effort.

Yolanda was masterful in composing the eulogies that I would record. For all of those who had died in the fire, she incorporated their
favorite sayings as well as their own familiar personal struggles. Thus,
she painted Cujo as "the gentlest, most beautiful man" whom I had
ever known, "the great love of my life." It was far from my true feelings for Cujo, but I thought it appropriate for his eulogy, where exag-
gerations are expected. She wrote of Gabi, whom we all knew as awkward in her physical movements, as having practiced her combat drills
so that her shotgun "was an extension of her right and left arms." Gabi
would have liked that line, I said, in complimenting Yolanda on that
eulogy. She did as well for all the others.

It had been decided beforehand that I would read the eulogies so
that they would get wide publicity. Teko, as the new General Field
Marshal of the SLA, was to give his interpretation and analysis of the
shoot-out and subsequent events, as well as a rallying call to radicals
and oppressed people everywhere. Yolanda had become in effect the
new intelligence officer of the SLA because she was the most adept in
writing, typing, making appeals, and, in my opinion, planning. She also
was the only one of us able to move freely about the area. Every day
she went out and bought the major newspapers so that we could follow
what the authorities were doing or saying about us. She had met with
Kathy and picked up the promised tape recorder. She was also very
good, when her ego was not pointedly involved, at appeasing and
manipulating Teko. She had held him back from issuing a communiqué
in the week that followed the shoot-out, insisting that the SLA should
not rush to put out a sloppy piece of work and risk being laughed at.
"We have to deal from a position of strength at all times" was her oft-
repeated dictum. In Teko's part of the communiqué, she edited his
words only for grammar and repetition, complimenting him on how
good and how effective his message was. Teko had tried to make the
tone of his address formal so that it would sound reminiscent of Cin's
communiqués. He reverted to Cin's ploy of referring to other radical
organizations and some nonexistent groups as part of the SLA. But in
his own mind Teko was certain that other organizations would be
happy to join ranks with the SLA if only they were given the chance.
Some of the media reacted afterward in astonishment at what they
called Teko's wild and bizarre message. But it was truly Teko as he

was. What he said in his communiqué was what he believed and had been telling us all the time. His strength, for what it was worth, lay in his own single-mindedness. He was certain of his beliefs, certain that the revolution was in progress, certain that he was right and the rest of the world was wrong:

> To those who would bear the hopes and future of our people, let the voice of their guns express the words of freedom. Greetings to the people, the Black Liberation Army, the United People's Liberation Army, the Black Guerrilla Family, the Weather Underground, and all freedom fighters of the United Symbionese Federation and the New World Liberation Front!
>
> This is Teko speaking. Yolanda, Tania, and I extend profound feelings of revolutionary love and solidarity to General Field Marshal Cabrilla [who had issued a communiqué a few days earlier, on behalf of the United People's Liberation Army, extolling and honoring the fallen members of the SLA] and all soldiers of the United People's Liberation Army, to all elements of the Anti-Aircraft Forces of the SLA, to Combat Unit ⚡4 of the Black Liberation Army, to comrade Martin Sostre and all other comrades, brothers and sisters in Amerikkka's concentration camps.
>
> To our beloved comrades-in-arms Osceola and Bo, we echo the words you could have often left us with: *A luta continua . . . venceremos* [The struggle continues . . . we will win].
>
> We have come together in many different cells, squads, and military-political units. We have taken many different meaningful names. But we are not hung up on names, for, as comrades-in-arms, we are one in our struggle for freedom. The determination to eliminate our common enemy by force of arms has united us. To our comrade sisters and brothers of the Black Liberation Army and all other fighters, let it be known that the Malcolm X Combat Unit of the Symbionese Liberation Army proudly takes up the banner of the New World Liberation Front.
>
> The Malcolm X Combat Unit of the Symbionese Liberation Army left the San Francisco Bay Area in a successful effort to break a massive pig encirclement. It had become clear from other SLA elements and from the people in the community that the pigs were preparing to trap us on the San Francisco peninsula. We knew that there was a great risk in setting up a base of operations

in San Francisco, which is a natural trap. The area was very small, surrounded by water, and with limited choices for breaking a major encirclement. However, we accepted this potentially danger- ous condition because we saw the importance of making solid con- tacts in the oppressed communities of this city. We considered ourselves to be an underground unit; however, the majority of our unit's members moved about freely, and in the five months we were there, we made many good contacts.

We decided to move our base of operations to southern Califor- nia, concentrating on the Greater Los Angeles area with its vast oppressed communities and more favorable terrain. In April the War Council dispatched an Intelligence and Reconnaissance Team to Los Angeles. Its mission: to make some additional contacts and survey the area. Based on the favorable results of this mission and the concentration of pig activity in the San Francisco Bay Area, our unit slipped out of San Francisco and into Los Angeles on May Day, 1974.

On Thursday, May 16, 1974, three members of the Malcolm X Combat Unit of the SLA were sent out to buy a number of items needed by the unit. At Mel's Sporting Goods store in Inglewood, a pig-agent clerk named Tony Shepard, attempting to show his alle- giance to his reactionary white bosses, falsely accused me of shoplifting. It was impossible to allow a verifying search by a store security guard because I was armed, and therefore we were forced to fight our way out of the situation.

The pigs originally said that a forty-nine-cent pair of socks were stolen and that this was what caused the shoot-out at the store. The people found this very difficult to believe when it was pointed out that we had already purchased over thirty dollars' worth of heavy wool socks and other items. This, apparently, became in- creasingly confusing to the pigs, who later charged that an ammu- nition bandolier was the item taken, supposedly to make the accu- sation more believable.

The policy of the Symbionese Liberation Army has always been to avoid shoplifting, because of the heavy risk involved to the whole unit. We cannot afford to have soldiers busted on humbug charges. However, we realize that the combat and support ele- ments run a great risk of being jammed whenever we move about aboveground. The most unfortunate aspect of this situation was that the pigs then learned that SLA elements were in the Los Angeles area. It appears that even with this knowledge, the pigs would not have located our comrades if a collaborator named Mary Carr had not snitched to the enemy.

On Friday, May 17, 1974, a CIA-directed force of FBI agents, Los Angeles City, County and California State pigs, with air support and reserve assistance from the United States Marine Corps and the National Guard, encircled elements of the Malcolm X Combat Unit of the Symbionese Liberation Army. The result of the encirclement was that the people witnessed on live television the burning to death of six of their most beautiful and courageous freedom fighters by cowardly, fascist insects. In most cases when an urban guerrilla unit is encircled by the enemy, it can expect to take great losses, especially if the enemy has time to mobilize a massive force.

Our six comrades were not on a suicide mission, as the pigs would have us believe. They were attempting to break a battalion-sized encirclement. By looking at the diagrams of where their bodies were found, it is clear that they had split into two teams, moved to opposite sides of the rear of the house, and were preparing to move out of the house by force. The heavy automatic weapons fired from the front of the house was a diversionary tactic to force the pigs to concentrate some of their forces in the front. The two dynamite-loaded pipe bombs were to be used as fragmentation grenades to clear a path through the cringing pigs who had started the blaze by firing incendiary grenades into the house.

Cin, Fahizah, Zoya, Cujo, Gelina, and Gabi died of smoke inhalation and burns before they could get outside. The pigs want us to believe that the fire was started by the SLA, that it was caused by SLA Molotov cocktails, or by accident from pig tear-gas grenades. This is pigshit. The SWAT squad, FBI, and LAPD would have had to go into the house to clear it out. They showed their true cowardice by using incendiary grenades to cause the fire that killed our comrades.

For those that don't know, incendiary grenades burn at such an incredible temperature that they melt steel and armor plate in a matter of seconds and are impossible to extinguish.

The pigs want the people to believe that the bad-ass tactics of the SLA guerrillas drove the fascists to use such barbaric force.

But we say that the SLA is a reaction to fascism. The SLA uses automatic weapons and homemade bombs because the pigs have automatic weapons, artillery, and hydrogen bombs.

The pigs want the people to believe that General Field Marshal Cinque Mtume committed suicide. To this absurdity, the SLA responds by quoting our beloved comrade brother. He often said, "We must not fear death, for to fear death is to put our fear of pig terror before our love of the children and the people's struggle for freedom." The pigs have historically focused on eliminating Black leaders. Many have been murdered and imprisoned in Amerikkka's concentration camps.

For over a year the pigs couldn't find Cin to murder him, so they attempted to isolate him from the people with pig propaganda. First they worked on the most blatantly racist Whites with their traditional "crazy-Black-nigger, escaped-convict-rapist" routine. Next we learned that Cin was a plum wine alcoholic. This obviously was the White racist, Liberal answer to the logic that a Black revolutionary leader could order and assist in the assassination of a jive-assed, pig-agent school superintendent.

It followed that the White supremacists and bourgeois Black elements of the revolutionary left so-called leadership would be pimped with ridiculous tales of links between the SLA and the CIA—that Cin was and had been a paid informant for the Los Angeles Police Department and the California attorney general's office. If this were true, we dare these fools and collaborators to explain Cin's reward for his deed—a life term in California's concentration camps.*

White, sickeningly Liberal, paranoid conspiracy freaks and spaced-out counterculture dope fiends proved their naïveté and amateurish research skills as they rambled on and on and on about the California Department of Corrections. Bizarre stories about Cin having been programmed and electrodes implanted in his brain while at Vacaville began to appear in the so-called underground press.

Cinque Mtume: the name means "Fifth Prophet." Cin was in-

---

* Actually, five years to life for armed robbery, and he was in fact a paid police informant at one time.

deed a prophet. The pigs would have the people believe that Cin was just, as they would say, another dumb nigger. They continually attempted to undermine his leadership by propagandizing that Cin was being offed by Whites, that he wasn't smart enough to be the brains behind the planning and execution of the successful SLA actions.

To this display of racism we say, go on into the Black community and ask the people if Cinque Mtume was not a prophet. Ask the people if they think he was being used by Whites. The people know that a Black man in Amerikkka does not need conscious Whites to push him into leading a revolution. Racists cannot believe that middle- and upper-middle-class Whites and a daughter of a superfascist ruling-class family would ever have reason to follow the lead of a beautiful Black genius, revolutionary warrior, and give their lives for the people. Sick-assed racists would have us believe that White women who follow the lead of Black revolutionaries are only mindless cunts enslaved by gigantic Black penises.

The cringing pigs who faced the firepower of Gelina, Gabi, Fahizah, and Zoya know much better.

Racists believe that it is impossible for white men to denounce White racism and follow revolutionary leadership of Black men, but the SLA proved this theory to be a sick delusion. Cinque Mtume, himself, was the spirit of Frederick Douglass, Gabriel Process, Denmark Vesey, Marcus Garvey, the Scottsboro boys, Medgar Evers, William E. Burghardt Du Bois, Malcolm X, Martin Luther King, Emmett Till, little Bobby Hutton, Fred Hampton, L. B. Barkley, Jonathan and George L. Jackson, Mark Essex, and every other Black freedom fighter who came before him.*

To racist slander, the SLA and all the people say: Death to the fascist insect that preys upon the life of the people.

And now, after our comrade brother fought valiantly against a battalion of pigs—a battle witnessed by millions—these same chickenshit pigs are trying to have us believe that General Field Marshal of the Symbionese Liberation Army, Cinque Mtume, killed himself. Cin was so determined to kill pigs that as long as

---

* Teko loved to show off his knowledge of black history.

his heart was beating and that there was any air in his lungs at all, he would fight, even if his only weapon was his body. We all know that revolutionaries do not kill themselves. Revolutionaries kill the enemy.

Cin was the baddest member of the SLA and therefore our leader. Our five White comrades who died with him were among his students and had learned well. They, too, showed incredible determination and courage. Cujo, Gelina, Fahizah, Zoya, and Gabi did not commit suicide, as the pigs would have us believe. Pigs tell us it is suicidal for Whites to join Blacks and other oppressed people in making revolution. To this oinking we say, it is suicidal for the ruling class and all its pig agents to believe that they can continue to oppress, exploit, murder, and imprison an undivided revolutionary army of the people. White Amerikkkans who follow the example of our beautiful comrades and join the fight for the freedom of all oppressed people will not do so because they wish to die, but because they wish to be free.

The pigs boast that they have broken the back of the Symbionese Liberation Army. But to do this, the pigs would have to break the back of the people. The military/political leader of the SLA and five top cadre have been killed by the fascists. However, the SLA is not dead and will not die as long as there is one living, fighting member of any oppressed class, race, sex, or group left on the face of this earth. The pigs have won a battle, but the war of the flea is not over. As our dear comrade Ho Chi Minh once wrote from an imperialist prison, "Today the locust fights the elephant, but tomorrow the elephant will be disemboweled."

Our new leader was very pleased with his performance on the tape. He insisted over some of Yolanda's objections that his gutter language was the language of *the people,* that it would demonstrate his sincerity and it was the kind of straightforward language everyone would understand. Both of them urged me to put determination and sincerity into my own reading. That was one thing I had learned to do well; I considered myself an adept actress by this time, an experienced communicator of communiqués. We were at war and this was the propaganda end of it. So I read Yolanda's words in which she waxed poetic in memory of our fallen comrades:

Greetings to the people. This is Tania. I want to talk about the way I knew our six murdered comrades because the fascist pig media has, of course, been painting a typical distorted picture of these beautiful sisters and brothers.

Cujo was the gentlest, most beautiful man I've ever known. He taught me the truth and he learned it from the beautiful brothers in California's concentration camps. We loved each other so much, and his love for the people was so deep that he was willing to give his life for them. The name Cujo means "unconquerable." It was the perfect name for him. Cujo conquered life as well as death by facing and fighting them. Neither Cujo or I had ever loved an individual the way we loved each other, probably because our relationship wasn't based on bourgeois, fucked-up values, attitudes, and goals. Our relationship's foundation was our commitment to the struggle and our love for the people. It's because of this that I still feel strong and determined to fight.

I was ripped off by the pigs when they murdered Cujo, ripped off in the same way that thousands of sisters and brothers in this fascist country have been ripped off of people they love. We mourn together and the sound of gunfire becomes sweeter.

Gelina was beautiful. Fire and joy. She exploded with the desire to kill the pigs. . . .

Gabi crouched low with her ass to the ground. She practiced until her shotgun was an extension of her right and left arms, an impulse, a tool of survival. . . .

Zoya wanted to give meaning to her name and on her birthday she did. Zoya, female guerrilla, perfect love and perfect hate reflected in stone-cold eyes. . . .

Fahizah was a beautiful sister who didn't talk much but who was the teacher of many by her righteous example. She, more than any other, had come to understand and conquer the putrid disease of bourgeois mentality. . . .

Cinque loved the people with tenderness and respect. They listened to him when he talked because they knew that his love reflected the truth and the future. . . .

The Malcolm X Combat Unit of the SLA was a leadership training cell, under the personal command of General Field Marshal Cinque. General Teko was his second-in-command. Everything we did was directed toward our development as leaders and advisers to other units. All of us were prepared to function on our own, if necessary, until we connected with other combat units. The idea that we are leaderless is absurd as long as any SLA elements are alive and operating under the command of our General Field Marshal [Teko].

My part of the communiqué continued along, echoing much of what Teko had already said, denouncing fascist pigs of whatever denomination, and, finally, reaffirming my love for the people and my determination to fight and die for them. Teko had insisted upon my repeating the points he had made because he was not sure how much of what he had said would be broadcast by the capitalist press.

For this taped communiqué, even Yolanda was persuaded to add her voice to this message to the people. Though she had a hand in writing almost all of the SLA communiqués, Yolanda was shy and reluctant to speak into the microphone for public consumption. This time, however, Teko insisted that *the people* needed to hear from each of the three remaining SLA soldiers, if for no other reason than to prove that all three of us were alive and carrying on the revolution. Yolanda chose the subject most disturbing to her personally:

There's been a lot of talk about wasted lives, referring to the six dead bodies of our comrades and to Tania, Teko, and myself. There are no editorials written for the wasted lives of our brothers and sisters gunned down in the streets and prisons. The present uproar of white Amerikkka over the fate of Patty Hearst was barely a murmur as hundreds of young men, mostly black and brown, went off to die in Vietnam.

Teko played the recorded tape through and rejoiced at how well it sounded. He could not wait to get it to Pacifica radio station KPFK in Los Angeles. A hurried call was put through to Kathy Soliah and a meeting was arranged for later that day at Lake Merritt in Oakland. Both Teko and Yolanda went off with the treasured tape to give it to Kathy. They returned and told me that it was already on its way to Los Angeles. Kathy's brother, Steve, was taking it to Santa Barbara. There he would hand it over to an attorney who had been a friend of Jim Kilgore at UC Santa Barbara. Kathy said the attorney, whose code name was Jerry, would deliver it to a Pacifica radio station.

Jerry drove the tape to Los Angeles and early the next morning he hid the cassette beneath a mattress on a pile of rubbish in an alley outside the radio station. Then, from a phone booth, he tipped off the radio anouncer. KPFA, delighted at its find, broadcast the tape recording immediately, before notifying the police or FBI. Then the message was rebroadcast by sister Pacifica stations across the country and further picked up by other radio and television stations. In our little apartment, we spent the entire day and night hearing the whole tape or excerpts of it played over and over. It was a major media event—the first time the public had heard from the SLA since the shoot-out, three weeks earlier. Teko or Yolanda sat by the radio, turning the dial from station to station, stopping only when they came upon snatches of our communiqué or commentaries on it. They loved every minute of it. And it would go on the next day and the next, for there is a network of small radio stations that feature news and events of the various radical movements. Teko and Yolanda were devotees of these stations, listening to the news of the world of the radicals. It reinforced their own fanatical view of the war that they were waging against the fascist state. "Just think," exclaimed Teko, "how strong this tape will make the people feel! They will know the revolution is still being fought."

As I listened to that tape over and over again along with the gloating comments of my two comrades, I was so humiliated, I became nauseated, hearing myself say things I really did not believe, hearing Teko's boasts which were not true. What was true? Trying to sort it out for myself, it was painful to face my own true feelings, and as they came through to me, I knew I could never voice them in this room. The tangled and perplexing truth for me was that I was relieved that they were all dead and now out of my life. I had never loved Cujo. It was closer to the truth to say that I loathed him. I had hated and feared Cinque. I felt sorry for Camilla Hall (Gabi). She had apparently been led into this maelstrom by her misguided love for Zoya. She should never have tried to be a revolutionary. Of all the others, I did miss the companionship and high spirits of Angela Atwood (Gelina). She had been the only one with whom I could converse at a quasi-personal level. I felt alone with Teko and Yolanda, trapped. I could not go back to my family because of my certainty that the police and FBI would not hesitate to shoot me. I was convinced that their official policy was to shoot every revolutionary on sight. I could only go forward with the SLA into the unknown.

I was so depressed that it seemed nothing could rouse me from the heavy lethargy that weighted me down. When they were not planning new strategies, Teko was lecturing Yolanda on the elements of security in the apartment and in the neighborhood. He insisted that we should have a route of escape in the event of a surprise attack. But there was no escape route from the apartment, no hidden passages, no way to see out into the street or the one stairway which led to our apartment. Nevertheless, we stood three-hour watches through the night, presumably so that one of us could hear anyone sneaking up to the door. It mattered very little that by then it would be too late. Teko admitted that our only security was that "the pigs" thought we were in southern California and no one knew the location of our safehouse. But when our old car would not start, it became necessary to tell Kathleen Soliah and Jim Kilgore where we lived. They became our only means of transportation.

It was just about a week or so after the broadcast of our communiqué that Kathy told us that she had reached Jack Scott and he had agreed to meet with us. Kathy was very excited. We were in luck, she said, because by some incredible coincidence, Jack Scott was in San Francisco and he wanted to help. The meeting was set up in an apartment in Berkeley, north of the university campus, which Jim was house-sitting for a friend who was off on a trip to New York. Jim had to check the apartment every day because the friend had a collection of rare and valuable tropical turtles and fish.

At Yolanda's insistence, we prepared our strategy for the meeting with Jack Scott as though it were a full-scale SLA operation. We certainly did not want to appear weak, foolish, or indecisive in our meeting with him, Yolanda stated. Teko agreed: The SLA would lead from strength. We would not ask Scott for anything. Instead, we would ask him what he wanted to do for us, as if we had no particular need. Teko and Yolanda were especially interested in Scott's reputed contacts in the radical underground, especially the Weather Underground, with which they discussed the possibility of merging the SLA. For all their criticisms of the Weather Underground and its "symbolic bombings," Teko and Yolanda were impressed with the group's reputation and they envisioned a situation in which they would convince them that the

SLA tactics of violence and murder were better than the symbolic actions of the Weather People. So the strategy was to impress Jack Scott with the strength of the SLA, hoping that he would pass on the word to the Weather Underground. We did not want them to think that we would be a liability to them, said Teko. As a show of strength, we would meet with Scott fully armed and wary. Yolanda and I were to be quiet and respectful of our General Field Marshal. Teko would do all the talking for the SLA so that we would present a strong, united front.

Jim Kilgore drove us to his friend's apartment on Euclid Street in Berkeley and once there, Teko took over as though he were a general at a new army post. We loaded our weapons and armed ourselves. Teko strode from room to room, closing the blinds and windows, saying, "We need to do a thorough security check of this place before anything else." Josephine and Steve Soliah stood awestruck at Teko's performance and the display of armaments. Jim Kilgore, shaking his head in disbelief, chased after Teko, raising the shades after him. "That's the dumbest thing I ever heard of," he complained. "There's nothing that will arouse suspicions more around here in this neighborhood than pulling all the shades down so early at night." Teko yelled back at him that we would not remain in the apartment if it were not secure; we could not risk the possibility of anyone looking in and seeing our weapons or recognizing us. Jim relented on all but the front windows.

The apartment was comfortable and spacious, clean and well furnished, with one wall of the living room lined with bookcases, and it had a lovely bay window looking out upon the tree-lined street. Just wandering around this apartment, after all those motels and safehouses, lifted my spirits. It was as if I had returned to civilization. Josephine Soliah was a younger version of her sister Kathy, although somewhat heavier, and she was very quiet and shy, as if in awe of us. Steve gave the impression of being a happy younger brother to his domineering sister. No more than five feet nine or ten, he had a wispy goatee and an earring in one pierced ear, and his blond hair fell to his shoulders.

"What do you do?" asked Yolanda upon being introduced.

"Nothin'," mumbled the embarrassed young man.

Yolanda immediately labeled him a jerk for not being into the revolution. Teko offered to show him how a submachine gun worked and how a revolutionary soldier would handle it. They talked guns for at least an hour, which was the beginning of an education in combat tactics for Steven Soliah. It came out that the three Soliahs had grown up in the desert town of Palmdale, northeast of Los Angeles beyond the San Fernando mountains. Steve had had some practice as a boy shooting desert rats with a carbine, but submachine guns appeared to hold a fascination for him.

I wandered around the apartment, intrigued with the large tank of tropical fish and turtles. In one room I came across a framed photograph of the man who unknowingly was providing this apartment for us: He was posed in a park somewhere in a Kung-fu combat stance.

Aside from the fact that Teko, Yolanda, and I clomped about the apartment in our hiking boots, combat clothes, and weapons, everything there seemed so normal to me until, suddenly, we heard sirens on the street below. Panic set in. We all dashed to the front window and saw fire engines stopping at the building across the street. Teko cried out that it was a trap. "Combat positions!" Jim Kilgore insisted that the appearance of fire engines meant there must be a fire somewhere in that other building. But it *might* be a police ploy, Teko exclaimed. Jim volunteered to go down and ask around. Teko thought that too dangerous. They argued, Teko revealing all the signs of paranoia that I remembered of Cinque. But Jim Kilgore was the model of reason, insisting that *he* was not wanted by the police and he had every right to go down there and ask what was going on. We maintained our tense combat positions until Jim returned and calmly reported that there was, indeed, a small fire in the building across the street.

With all the large, comfortable rooms in that flat, Teko chose for the setting of his meeting with Jack Scott the smallest room possible, a back bedroom that was unfurnished except for a mattress on the floor. With the window shut and drapes drawn, the room was stifling. But that was the way Teko wanted it. When Scott arrived late that night, he found us there in that back bedroom, seated cross-legged on the floor in combat readiness. I could not discern from his expression what he might have thought upon first seeing us. Teko had his submachine gun cradled in his lap; Yolanda had her sawed-off shotgun across her knees, a bandolier full of shells across her chest. Both of them wore their gun belts with ammunition bags and holstered sidearms. I had a .30-caliber rifle slung over my back. It was, in Teko's words, our show of strength.

As for Jack Scott, he was unarmed and in obvious high spirits, with a disarming smile and an eager stream of condolences for our fallen comrades, as well as sympathy for and understanding of our plight as hunted revolutionaries. He was tall and athletic-looking, with broad shoulders and a trim waistline, a former track star himself, but now balding and beginning to show signs of age. After the introductions, Teko got right down to business. Jim Kilgore and the three Soliahs sat quietly by, listening and hardly daring to say a word. Teko thanked Scott for his concern over the SLA and his willingness to help and then asked, "What do you think you want to do to help us?"

That was all Jack Scott needed. Here was a man who loved to talk—even more than Teko did. In an avalanche of rapid-fire words, Scott declared that he was prepared to move the three of us to the East Coast where we could walk around in the fresh air without fear of being immediately recognized. "Look at yourselves," he exclaimed, "holed up in this little room, hugging your weapons. You all look so tired and pale and worried. You need fresh air and open country, an atmosphere where you won't have to be so paranoid."

Teko and Yolanda tried to make their usual points from the guerrilla mini-manual about revolutionaries functioning best only on terrain with which they were thoroughly familiar. But Scott hardly allowed them to complete a sentence. As soon as their meaning became clear, he interrupted.

"The West Coast is the most dangerous place you can be. The FBI, the police, everybody is looking for you," he said. "The Bay Area is the hottest spot in the country for you. But on the East Coast, you're not on everybody's mind. The police there are not looking for you, not expecting you. It would be the safest place to be. . . . You could lie low for the summer at least."

As Teko tried to defend SLA recent strategy, Jack Scott put him down effectively, and I thought: There goes our position of strength. Even our latest taped communiqué, as good as it was, according to Jack Scott, was a mistake because it had stirred up the police hunt for us in California.

He compared himself to Harriet Tubman, who had run an underground railroad to smuggle black slaves out of the South to the North during the days of the Civil War. He was running a similar underground railroad now for radical and revolutionary fugitives. He mentioned the Revolutionary Army, the Weather Underground, and several other organizations, which he said he had helped in the past.

Scott explained that he was the "director" of what he called "the Institute for the Study of Sports and Society," which published books, magazine articles, and a newsletter focusing on the political aspects of the sports world. The ISSS would serve as a perfect cover for us on the East Coast. He rambled on endlessly.

As he talked, I noticed that every so often his eyes rolled up or darted involuntarily from side to side. Either the man had the worst case of coffee nerves I had ever seen or there was something wrong with him. And yet, what he was saying was making sense. He overrode all objections. He went on to say that, without mentioning any names, he had checked out his strategy with a radical attorney whom he trusted implicitly, and the lawyer had concurred that we should go East, obviously surmising our identities.

Scott clinched the discussion by telling us that his wife was in the process of renting a farmhouse in a remote spot in Pennsylvania where he had intended to spend the summer writing a book. He would turn the farmhouse over to us. "It would be a perfect cover for you—a writer's retreat. You can say you are my research assistants. I could come out there from time to time, or stay, or not stay, whatever you want. We have a car, so we can drive you. We even have a German shepherd, who'd be good protection. Besides, it's really remote. No one comes there. You'd be perfectly safe. You wouldn't have a thing to worry about. . . . I'll supply all the money you need to live there."

Despite himself, Teko was visibly impressed. He bought the idea. Scott went on to explain how he would transport us; it would be best if we went separately, driving cross-country by automobile. "Since Patty here is the most . . ."

"Tania," interrupted Yolanda, correcting him.

"Yes, sorry, Tania. Since she'd be the most difficult to smuggle cross-country, for obvious reasons, I'll take her myself. I'll contact friends who will take you two. But for Tania, I can get my parents to drive me across the country in their car. They have a real bourgeois LTD and with two retired people in the front seat and us two in the back, we would arouse no suspicions. I know it, because they've done this before. They've helped me move fugitives and we never had any trouble. In fact, they go back a long way in helping revolutionaries. In the old country, they were connected with the IRA. So, believe me, they know what they're doing."

Yolanda, who was obviously suspicious of all this sudden largess, began insinuating questions into Scott's discourse and he would reply in such repetitious detail that he would wear down her objections with what amounted to a filibuster. He said he would ask a close friend and colleague to drive her cross-country; the friend was an associate professor at a university in New Jersey who wanted to return East anyway to visit his ex-wife and child. What kind of car? A Pinto. Whose car was it? Another friend's. Yolanda went on asking questions until Teko commanded her, "Stop asking questions! I'm doing the talking here. Understand?"

Yolanda clamped her mouth shut, glared hatefully, and said no more. The meeting lasted until dawn. At times, sitting straight up, yoga style, I would doze off and then come awake again when the discussions became more heated. For the most part, however, it all seemed quite businesslike.

Scott did lay down some conditions. If we agreed to go East, we would have to do what he advised during the whole trip. For instance? asked Teko. No guns along on the trip cross-country, Scott declared.

"Then we can't go," replied Teko. "We're at war and we cannot surrender to the pigs. So we need our guns."

"But it's too risky to travel cross-country with a carload of guns," reasoned Scott. "We may be stopped for vegetable inspection at the California border or we could be stopped for a traffic violation or anything. I could not take you with guns. It's too dangerous—not only for you, but for the people who will be transporting you."

Scott solved the impasse by promising to give us weapons on the East Coast. He said he had one or two revolvers and a carbine, which should provide us with plenty of protection on a remote farm. Teko finally agreed. Scott then said he also would provide disguises for all of us. "You can't go around like that, loaded down with guns and knives. You'd be stopped in a minute. If you want to be disguised, I'll get you jogging clothes. No one would suspect a jogger of being a revolutionary."

Teko finally announced our agreement, asking, "How soon is all this going to happen?"

"As soon as possible," replied Scott.

"How soon is that?"

"Maybe tomorrow, maybe the next day," said Scott. "But it will be as soon as I can arrange everything. . . . But, you be ready at a moment's notice."

Kathy suggested that we all stay at the Berkeley apartment until the

time came for each of us to depart. Teko accepted the invitation immediately. Jim Kilgore recommended that we take new code names. "It's
dumb and it's dangerous for us to keep calling you Teko, Yolanda, and
Tania. . . . If someone overheard us, they'd know who you were right
away." Teko thought about that for a moment and then agreed. Our
revolutionary names were our real names, he declared, but for security
reasons only we would refer to one another by our new code names.
He assigned our new names: I was Pearl, Yolanda was Eva, and he
was Frank. Kathy became Helen; Jim—Roy; Steve—J.D.; Josephine—
Lola.

After Jack Scott had left and we settled down alone in the back bedroom, Yolanda's pent-up fury exploded. "How can you be so trusting?
I don't like it. It's all happening too fast. How do you know you can
trust him? We don't know him. We just met him and he comes in here
and tells us what to do. And why should we be sent East? We don't
know anybody out there. We'd be on unfamiliar terrain, without
friends, without help, without money, without weapons. Suppose he
takes off? We'd be stuck out there, alone, and with no way to get back.
What's the sense in that? I think we ought to discuss it, struggle it out,
and then decide."

Teko's eyes bulged and his jaw jutted forward as he said through
clenched teeth, "I already decided and that's it. We're goin' East."

Yolanda started in again, but Teko cut her off. "That's it. I'm the
leader and I decided." She shut up. Then he added, "He's right, you
know. It's too hot for us in California. We can't do nothing here,
nothin' important, so we might as well lay low for a time. And I believe him. He's goin' to provide everything for us. 'Cause he believes in
us and he wants to help. Besides, he has contacts with the Weather Underground and we're going to need those contacts. He knows what he's
talkin' about. . . ."

Jack Scott burst in the next day with new shorts, T-shirts, and
Adidas running shoes for Yolanda and me, but only a pair of ordinary
shorts for Teko. Our leader was visibly annoyed, but he said nothing.
Scott announced that Yolanda was leaving for the East Coast that
night. He and I would leave in a day or so, or just as soon as his parents, who managed a small motel in Las Vegas, could drive to Berkeley. He was still trying to arrange transportation for Teko, he said, but
not to worry. It *was* all happening so fast. Yolanda still did not like it,
but she was a good soldier and held her tongue until she could com-

plain to Teko privately. That did not stop her, however, from expressing her disdain for the "bourgeois jogging outfit." But Scott insisted that she wear it. Everyone in the country was jogging, he declared, and it was far better to look like an athlete than a fugitive revolutionary.

That night the professor arrived for Yolanda and he was nothing like what we had expected. Perhaps he was on vacation, but I could not imagine what classes he taught, looking as he did. Long and spidery thin in his early thirties, he looked like a dirty, disheveled hippie with long, uncombed hair and a fierce beard. He represented everything that Cinque had despised in the youth movement. Both Teko and Yolanda protested that he would be far too conspicuous to escort a fugitive across the country. He would be stopped on suspicion for his looks alone. He turned out to be a rather shy, quiet man who quickly acquiesced to our demands that he allow himself to be cleaned up and made presentable. Kathy and Jim took him into the kitchen, sat him down and cut his hair and trimmed his beard and polished him up for the trip East.

A kiss goodbye and she was gone. It seemed so sudden and unreal: Yolanda was no longer with us.

We did not go outside to see them off, but it was explained to Teko and me that they were driving an almost new Pinto, borrowed from one of their friends, called Seanna. Another of their radical comrades, Michael Bortin, had once been a leader of the Students for a Democratic Society (SDS) on the Berkeley campus and had since become a revolutionary. Mike Bortin had just been paroled from jail a few months earlier, having served one year for a bombing escapade back in 1972. Bortin, Jim Kilgore, and Steve Soliah were close friends and partners in a house-painting business which supported all of them. Kathy and Jim, in explaining all of this, promised that they would all now pool their resources in helping the SLA. They would hold our weapons in safekeeping for our return to the West Coast and in the meantime would try to save money from their house painting to finance future military actions. They would also clean out our apartment in Oakland for us, leaving no clues behind. They understood the need for secrecy, but that did not save them from the security lectures of our General Field Marshal.

Two nights later, Jack Scott returned with his parents, John and Louise, a very nervous, frightened couple. But they seemed willing to do anything their son advised. So, without further ado, we departed

late that very night. When Teko asked, "What about me?" Jack
Scott blithely apologized for not being able to find anyone to transport
the SLA leader immediately. He would keep trying, Jack said, and if
he could find no one else he would return to ferry Teko cross-country.
It would only take a few days, he said reassuringly. Teko was not very
happy at all.

CHAPTER

FOURTEEN

WE ARRIVED IN Reno, Nevada, early in the morning. Jack Scott, brimming over with nervous energy, wanted to drive on through the night, but his parents refused to travel any further. In that gambling pleasure dome, the flashing lights and neon signs lit up the streets and there was nothing at all unusual or suspicious about anyone checking into a motel at close to 4 A.M. We took two separate rooms, one for his parents and the other for Jack and me. In my brown wig and old-fashioned blue horn-rimmed glasses, I was posing as Jack's wife. Accompanied by his parents, we were plain and nondescript, above suspicion and hardly memorable. Nevertheless, the plan was for me to keep out of sight and not to risk being recognized. I remained in the car with Mrs. Scott, while the two men checked us into the motel.

Jack made his expected pass at me that first night. As long as we were posing as a married couple, he suggested, we ought to sleep in the same bed. I told him that Teko would strongly disapprove of that arrangement. Jack's role was to take me safely across the country and nothing more. We were now in an SLA combat operation, I told him, and we both had our assignments. He accepted that with good grace.

The journey was long and essentially boring and yet I was fascinated with the tremendous expanse of America, driving for whole days through wheat fields and farmlands that seemed to go on forever. This was my first automobile trip across the country. Inside the Scotts' LTD, they talked (particularly Jack) and I listened or slept or gazed out the window. The elder Scotts informed me of all the troubles they had had in their lives, trouble with alcoholism, Mrs. Scott's heart condition, their other son, Walter. They described him as a free-lance mercenary, unpredictable and unreliable, a son they loved but did not dare to trust with any secret, such as our trip. Walter must never know of this escapade, for there was no telling what he would do if he knew anything about Patty Hearst and her story. On the other hand, they were very proud of their son Jack and his accomplishments in the sports world. They were both nervous over the enormity of the risk they were taking. Mr. Scott did all of the driving, adamantly refusing to allow Jack, despite their admiration for him, to take the wheel. Jack took pills, and it was apparent that his father did not trust him to drive.

From the first minutes on the road, not a day passed that Jack did not tell us the story of how he so cleverly helped Wendy Yoshimura, of the Revolutionary Army, to escape from the clutches of the FBI. The Revolutionary Army was the most successful of all the radical organizations doing bombings all over northern California in the early 1970's. Its leader was Willie Brandt, a Berkeley campus radical who masterminded all the Revolutionary Army bombings as a protest against the escalation of the Vietnam War.

Wendy Yoshimura, Brandt's lover and bombing cohort, had stored a cache of explosives in a rented garage in Berkeley, Scott said, and somehow that garage was discovered by the police. Brandt, Michael Bortin, and another radical were trapped by the police when they came to the garage to pick up explosives for another bombing. Luckily, according to Scott, Wendy stayed at home that night listening to a police-band radio and heard of Brandt's capture. She telephoned Scott and he sent his wife, Micki, to help Wendy clean out her apartment before the police arrived. That night they drove her to Los Angeles and she and Jack flew to New York City. Scott said he had Wendy dress up in her most demure clothes, and since it was just about Easter time in 1972, he bought her a large stuffed bunny rabbit and an Easter basket to carry aboard the plane. Thus cleverly disguised, they traveled first-class from coast to coast in comfort and above suspicion. Thanks to him, Wendy was still free, two years after her flight, tending house for one of his friends in New Jersey. The point was, he kept repeating, that the police on the East Coast were not actively on the lookout for West Coast fugitives. Teko, Yolanda, and I would be able to walk around freely without fear of being recognized and arrested, thanks to him.

Jack Scott acted so cocksure and unconcerned with the obvious dangers of this trip that I became super security-conscious. Each time we stopped for gas I tried to hide my face from the attendant. Each time I spotted a highway patrol car, I tensed. I became highly suspicious of any car on the road that seemed to be following us for any distance. This was my very first trip out on my own as an SLA soldier. Perhaps Yolanda had been right in questioning the wisdom of putting our safety into the hands of this nervous, high-strung, overconfident man whom we hardly knew at all. It was only at his parents' suggestion that, for safety's sake, we did not stop to eat or to go to the bathroom the whole day long. We drove from about nine in the morning to six or seven at night, and for those nine or ten hours on the road, I did not leave the car. When we stopped at toll booths, I averted my head so that the guards there would not see my face. Jack Scott tried to laugh away my fears, but that did not help. I wanted to hide.

We stuck to Interstate 80, the northernmost through highway, in crossing the United States. Mr. Scott drove at a modest speed in the right-hand lane, seldom passing another vehicle. On our first full day on the road, we crossed Nevada, stopping at the small town of Wells, near the Utah border. In the motel room that night, Jack brought up the subject of writing a book about the SLA. I told him Teko was very much interested in such a project, which would more fully explain the SLA to the public. Apparently, Jack was primed for that subject. He was eager to help and I learned that he had come out to the West Coast with the intention of finding us so that he could sponsor a book of that sort.

Although he was already under contract to write another book, he would be happy to find a sympathetic, professional writer. He said he knew several radical writers whom he could approach on the project. But he could help most, he explained, in finding a publisher and arranging for the best publication of such a book. He had already spoken to an attorney about it, he told me. He went into great detail on how he could set up a corporation in Liechtenstein to handle the finances free from taxation and government scrutiny. The money earned by the book would be paid to an aboveboard, legal corporation or foundation and then funneled to us surreptitiously. In that way the SLA could be assured of money to finance the revolution and still be free of government encroachment. I told him that he ought to speak to Teko about the project.

It certainly gave Jack something more to talk about on our trip across the country. The routine was always the same. Mr. Scott drove and Jack talked. No one questioned me very much about the SLA. When they did, I gave them the stock SLA answers, which came easily to me now. Jack was so happy talking about himself that he seemed very little interested in my own experiences with the SLA. He and his parents accepted me fully and without doubt as an SLA soldier. That status placed me on a rather exalted pedestal in the world of radicals and protesters. After all, hadn't I robbed a bank, shot up Mel's Sporting Goods, and sent those tapes? They were obviously impressed. I was not one to be trifled with.

Our fifth day on the road, we passed through Youngstown, Ohio, into Pennsylvania and late that night we made it to the Poconos, south of Wilkes-Barre and Scranton. There we ran into trouble. We could not find two available rooms at any motel because of the crowds that had come for the Pocono 500 auto race. Tired and road-weary, the Scotts got into a bitter argument. Jack wanted to push on for another two hours and reach New York. His parents wanted to keep looking for a place to stop overnight. Finally, we did find one available room and Jack insisted that his parents take that room while he and I drove on to New York. Mr. Scott hated turning over his car to his son, as though he felt he would never see it again in one piece. But Jack prevailed, largely because the two older Scotts were clearly exhausted.

It was well past midnight, after a long day on the road, when we reached Jack's neighborhood on New York's upper West Side. He parked the car in the street and we walked a couple of blocks on dark sidewalks, flanked by tall apartment houses and ancient brownstones, to the small apartment house in which he lived.

"Oh, comrade, it's so good to see you!" Yolanda ran across the room, smiling. She hugged and kissed me with genuine emotion. She seemed truly happy to see me. Strangely enough, she imparted a sense of warmth and safety to me: I was home again and in her care. That's how dependent I had become. I felt much better, far safer being in this apartment with Yolanda than I had felt out there in the open, traveling across the country with the Scotts, who were strangers to me.

Micki Scott was strikingly tall and thin, in her early thirties, with pale white skin and short, dark, curly hair. She greeted me affectionately and within a few minutes I sensed that she was a nice, warm person. It was more than I had any reason to expect, given all the characters I had been meeting, but it came to me that here was a woman who was straightforward and open.

The introductions were barely over when Yolanda exclaimed, "Oh, you'll have to excuse us, my sister and I have to have a meeting. . . . It won't take long; we'll be right back." She led me into a back bedroom, repeating how happy she was to see me. Alone, she eagerly wanted me to tell her everything that had happened since she had left California. "How was your trip cross-country?" she asked. "Oh, all right," I replied, telling her how much Jack Scott talked all the way and about the book project. I told her all that I could remember.

"Did you make it with Jack?"

"Oh, no, nothing like that," I said.

She could hardly wait to tell me of her trip. "We had a great drive across the country," she said with a broad grin. "We were getting it on all the time. In fact, we hit it off so well we couldn't even wait to get to Reno. We just pulled off the road and started to fuck. But then we pulled ourselves together and drove straight through to Reno. We shacked up in a motel and fucked all night long . . . it was fabulous. . . . But later," Yolanda added, "we realized how stupid we'd been . . . I mean, what if a pig had driven by and seen us! What a dumb way for me to get busted!"

Emily Harris was as happy as I had ever seen her. She told me how much she liked Micki Scott. The farmhouse in Pennsylvania had been rented for us, she said, and she was eager to spend the summer there. She also told me of going to Bellevue Hospital in New York City to visit a free clinic, where she was tested for pregnancy, something she feared back on the West Coast. Jim Kilgore, who had flown in from the West Coast to pick up the Pinto, which he was to drive back, accompanied her to the hospital clinic. Emily told me of giving them a phony name. But when they asked for the names of her mother and father, she had to think fast, as she put it, and came up with the names of Mary and Joseph, which she thought was hilarious. Oh, yes, she added, the pregnancy test was negative. The only wrinkle in the whole fabric was the indecision over how to get Teko to the East Coast. No one had gone to get him. He was still there, stranded.

We ended up that night in the Scotts' bedroom with Jack and Micki, talking. Dark red and blue bulbs gave the room a subdued, exotic aura. The Scotts played their favorite record album for us, *Country Joe and the Fish,* explaining that the music was truly revolutionary, but that the best way to enjoy and to understand it was to be "stoned out of your mind." They also played an album called *Cuba Va,* which Yolanda immediately recognized. She told us that Teko had named her Yolanda after a song of that name from that album. I had never before seen Yolanda so relaxed and carefree. We shared a joint with the Scotts. I worried about the Codes of War, which forbade drugs, and it occurred to me that no one was paying any attention at all to the security of the apartment. I asked Yolanda about it and she just giggled. "Don't worry, Tania, it's perfectly safe here. . . . We're with good people," she laughed, bouncing up and down on the bed.

We had frequent mix-ups with names at this time, stumbling over our own code names. I still thought of her as Yolanda, while the Scotts and Kilgore frequently called her Emily, and when she herself thought of it, she would say, "Call me Eva, my code name is Eva now." In the same fashion, I responded to the name Tania or Patty and tried to grow accustomed to answering to my new code name, Pearl, which I did not like much. But it was all done in a rather lighthearted atmosphere, free from the rigid discipline of the SLA under Cinque's command.

Jack Scott showed me the small office in the apartment out of which he conducted his Institute for the Study of Sports and Society (ISSS). Lined with bookshelves and crowded with books, manuscripts, and loose papers, an old file cabinet, a small desk, and a telephone, this tiny room was his national headquarters. Jack explained that he was in touch with black athletes and radical writers throughout the country, in addition to his contacts with major sports figures throughout the world. He bragged that he was in a position to publicize the bad deals black athletes were getting from their white coaches. He even had taken on the University of Alabama's famous football coach, Bear Bryant, for some of his supposed misdeeds and had been publicly denounced as "an enemy of sport" by none other than the Vice-President of the United States, Spiro Agnew. Jack Scott was proud of himself. He was terribly busy with all his activities, he let me know. He sent out a periodic newsletter to sports people nationwide, pointing out the radical political implications of events in the sports world. He was currently involved in something he could not tell us about with Bill Walton, the basketball player, and he also had to write his own book, and was planning a trip to Cuba.

So . . . he and Micki could not spend the whole summer with us, as planned, at the farm in Pennsylvania, though they would be there on and off. Instead, he had invited a trusted close friend to baby-sit the farmhouse for us, running errands and buying food and supplies in town so that we would not have to expose ourselves. We were to pose as researchers for ISSS, working on his book. In any event, the farm was in a rural area and it was highly unlikely that anyone around there would drop in. We would be perfectly safe.

Our "baby-sitter" turned out to be an attractive Japanese girl in her late twenties who had been keeping house for a friend of Jack's in New Jersey. When she arrived at the apartment, she was introduced as Joan Shimada, but it was only a matter of seconds before Yolanda and I reached the obvious conclusion that this was none other than the Wendy Yoshimura whom Jack talked about so incessantly.

She had the classic small, regular features of the Japanese, with smooth, creamy skin and straight black hair cut short at the chin with bangs which reached to just above her eyebrows. She was calm and friendly and sane, with the nicest smile. It was difficult to keep in mind that this quiet, cheerful young woman was a revolutionary, and a fugitive from charges involving explosives. We all discussed arrangements for the farm and the part Wendy would play. Jack made it clear that he was paying Wendy six hundred dollars to stay with us at the farm and would buy her a car to replace her beat-up little red VW bug. I gathered that she was agreeing to the arrangement largely because she was indebted to Jack Scott, who had helped her escape.

"When is Teko going to be brought out?" Yolanda asked. The question came up again and again and each time Jack would give a noncommittal answer. Apparently, he could not find or did not really care to find anyone willing to take Teko cross-country. "We can't just leave him stranded," Yolanda argued. "We need him with us . . . or we will just have to go back to him."

"I just can't find anyone to bring him," Jack complained. "If you can't wait anymore, I'll just send him a plane ticket and he can make his own way to the farm."

"Oh, no, he can't do that . . . he's too hot for that!" Yolanda cried, furious by this time.

"Okay, okay, I'll fly back and drive him to the farm myself," said

Jack, assuring her that he fully intended to live up to everything he
promised us. The important thing, he insisted, was for us to get to the
farm, feel safe there, and get to work on our SLA book.

The Scotts were running things and they appeared to be highly organized and efficient. Micki went out shopping for clothes for me and
Yolanda and for food for the farm. Jack's parents arrived by bus from
Pennsylvania to pick up their LTD. Jack was ever busy with all the
details involved. For me, the two days in the New York apartment
seemed easy, free of harassment. For the first time in months, I had decent food and hot showers and books and magazines to read. Jack and
Micki went out for long walks at night and Yolanda went down for
briefer periods to call Teko from a telephone booth in the street. I even
grew accustomed to the frequent police and fire engine sirens of New
York which could be heard in the apartment, realizing that they were
not for me. Jack repeatedly made the point of how much safer the East
Coast was and would continue to be for the SLA. Nevertheless, I
declined his invitation to go out and see New York. I felt much more
safe and at ease remaining in the apartment.

We drove to the farm in the dead of night in two little VW beetles,
Wendy and I in her car following Micki and Yolanda in the Scotts' car.
There was not an automobile or a person or a light to be seen in the
provincial town of Honesdale, which was about thirty miles or so northeast of Scranton. The farm was located up a country road, several miles
beyond the outskirts of the town. The farmhouse did seem spacious,
even if everything in it was old and plain. There were three bedrooms
upstairs and a living room, dining room, big kitchen, and large screened
sleeping porch on the ground floor. The next morning we were able to
see our new hideout properly. It seemed ideal: not a neighbor in sight,
although there was at least one house farther up the road. The farmhouse was situated on the rise of a hill from which we could see broad
fields with high grass all around us. Farther down the hill in back of
the house were three ponds rimmed with tall white birch trees. Beyond,
there was a large lake, where we could swim and fish. The air was
clean and chilly in the morning, warm and bright the rest of the day.
We were hidden in the foothills of the Pocono Mountains among non-
working or abandoned farms, a summer retreat for city dwellers. One
incongruous note amused me: On the balustrade of the balcony off the
second floor were large wrought-iron circles containing the letters

P A I X. Someone long ago had fashioned this simple farm as a place of peace.

Actually, I did have one full week of peace in that farmhouse, and then Teko arrived. Yolanda was happy and relieved to see him safe and sound and reunited with us. The hugs and kisses were prolonged. He had shaved off his mustache and beard and his hair was cut short and back to its natural dark brown color. But he had not changed. He had no "thank you" for Jack, who had driven him to the farm. He demanded to see the weapons they had supplied us with at the farm. Then he flew into a rage. The .38-caliber revolver was loaded with blanks, and we were given no live ammunition. The carbine, which Jack admired, was a present from one of his old professors. The rifle was old, filfthy and rusted out, and also without ammunition. They were useless. As for the Scotts' guard dog, we had left twelve-year-old and feeble Sigmund behind in New York.

Jack and Micki stayed for dinner and slept over that night. But they explained to us that they had to leave because they were scheduled to take a contingent of black athletes to Cuba and thought that they might even meet Fidel Castro there. Teko was visibly impressed.

But the next day, after the Scotts had left, Teko turned his wrath upon Yolanda. "What's wrong with you? Where are your brains? I leave you in charge for a little while and what do I find? You're all sitting around here on your asses, doing nothing. What kind of security setup have you got? Nothing! What kind of cover do we have? We have a wanted fugitive to go out and get us supplies . . . an Oriental who will stick out like a sore thumb in these parts. What's your problem, Yolanda? Have you forgotten already? Our comrades have been killed, we're supposed to be carrying on the revolution, and here you are—on vacation. What have you been doing all this time? What?"

He thought Yolanda had made a terrible deal with Jack Scott in accepting Wendy Yoshimura as our helper on the farm and he said so in her presence. Then he turned his charm on Wendy. What had she been doing all this past year? She had been underground, she replied. What, no bombings? No, no bombings. "Well, what the fuck is wrong with you? Are you in this revolution or not? You're certainly not helping anybody house-sitting in New Jersey!" Wendy simply stalked off. Later, when he caught her reading a book about French separatism in Quebec, Teko lambasted her unmercifully for wasting her time on such a bourgeois irrelevant subject. "Why aren't you reading about the pressing problems that are confronting this country here and now? Why aren't you reading George Jackson and books like his?" Wendy answered him back and before long they were nose to nose in a furious argument.

Teko accused her of being lazy and wasting her potential for Third World leadership. "The Third World people are the most oppressed in this country and all over the world," Teko declared, "and they more than anyone else have the most need to overthrow their oppressors. You could become their leader in this country, if you only would work at it. As an Oriental, you're in a position to take that leadership either in the SLA or elsewhere. But you should be working at that and not anything else."

Wendy argued back that she had no wish to be fronted off as a token Third World leader. It simply was not in her nature to lead anything, she told him, and she did not have any desire to lead blacks or Indians or even Orientals. "Besides," she told him, "all that crap about Third World leadership is racist in itself and based upon white guilt."

Neither of them really persuaded the other. But Teko thrived on such encounters. Before his first full day at the farm had ended, he and Yolanda were squabbling with one another as before. He had an instant opinion on everything and expected each of us to follow his dictums. Teko intended to rule the roost.

Wendy Yoshimura's first shopping mission for Teko was to buy bags of sand and cement. He mixed these with water in five-gallon planter buckets and fashioned fifty-pound barbells for arm- and leg-strengthening exercises. He had Yolanda make ankle weights for our jogging. She sewed sand into socks to make five-pound weights which we would wrap around each ankle for our morning jog of either a half hour or a full hour. Teko measured out a one-mile course, to be run as fast as one could, and he stood there timing us by the second hand on his wristwatch. At first, we did our runs on a long flat driveway which connected the house to the barn, and when we had mastered that, he had us running up and down the hills on the farm. For me, the hills were sheer torture. I could swim, ride horseback, play tennis and basketball, and had always considered myself a fair-to-good athlete, but I never could run or jog with any ease. With Teko standing there or running alongside me, hovering over me with his relentless criticisms, I would become so upset that I would invariably begin to hyperventilate. As often as not, I would fall to the ground in exhaustion and tears before completing Teko's course. Wendy, to whom running seemed to come naturally, tried to comfort me. "I feel so sorry for you," she would say. "Just lie there a minute or two and try to catch your breath." I got no sympathy at all from our General Field Marshal. His exhortations were worse than the exercises and running.

"You're all getting too soft," he would often shout. "There's a war on and we've got to get in condition. How can you forget it all so soon? This place has not been touched by the revolution . . . so with all the peace and quiet around here, you forget what we're here for. We're supposed to be getting ready for the big struggle and how in hell can we do that if we're not in condition?"

We worked out with our makeshift barbell, did push-ups and sit-ups, hand stands and head stands, shoulder rolls and waist bends, deep knee bends and jumping jacks, and, of course, jogging with weights and running without weights, and that was all before breakfast.

Yolanda, for one, took Teko's lectures about preparing for the revolution very seriously. She got up every morning before anyone else. She exercised with a frenzy, pushing herself to near-exhaustion. To discipline her mind as well as her body, she allowed herself to eat only small portions of food. She deliberately chewed only half sticks of gum, as she said, to learn to live with deprivation. In order to stay abreast of current fashions, she studied the clothing ads in the New York *Times*. "Even though we're underground, we should know what's going on in the outside world in order to help us come up with disguises," she said. Her pleasure came from telling Wendy and me of all her efforts and acting superior to the rest of us.

I remained in a world of my own. It seemed to take all my energy just to get through the day. I was still all skin and bones, weighing not much more than ninety pounds, my cheeks sunken in, my flesh a pallid color despite all the sunbaths I took in the fields beyond the farmhouse. There were days when I did not speak with anyone, not a word. I would wander off by myself to a remote part of the farmhouse or off somewhere in the woods, and do nothing. Wendy would admit to me later that she thought I was a strange sort of creature, a dull vegetable without a mind of my own. My relationship with Wendy at the time was based upon what Teko wanted it to be; I told her what he wanted me to say. Teko re-emphasized that he, Yolanda, and I must always be the picture of unity and solidarity to all outsiders. We were the SLA.

Wendy Yoshimura, the Scotts, the Soliahs, Kilgore—they were all outsiders. We were the real revolutionaries, the cadre, the true leaders of
the coming revolution. Therefore, no matter what our own personal
differences might be, we had to present a solid, united front to the
outside world.

For the first few days Teko and Yolanda managed to conceal most
of their arguments, but before the week was out, it was all out in the
open. They were screaming and screeching at each other. Wendy was
astonished. At the Scotts' apartment in New York Yolanda had given
Teko such a tremendous buildup that Wendy had concluded that she
worshipped him.

Despairing of me and hating Bill Harris, Wendy gravitated to a sort
of personal companionship with Emily Harris. They went off on long
walks together around the lake, sharing their thoughts and struggling
out their own personal problems. Emily was very good at these lengthy,
heart-to-heart talks. It was only later that Wendy would discover that
Emily Harris was entirely two-faced in all her personal relationships.
While she may have sounded sweet and understanding, in fact she was
cold and deliberate. Teko could be domineering and mean and
irascible, but one knew what to expect from him. Yolanda was much
more difficult. She was devious and unexpectedly hurtful; she would
use your confidences against you, striking out on your weak points and
personal embarrassments. Although she fought bitterly with Bill Harris
almost every day, she always shared with him everything that she had
learned from Wendy or from anyone else. Theirs was a solid love-hate
relationship that defied ordinary comprehension. Nevertheless, for the
time we spent on that Pennsylvania farm, I became an outcast, with no
one in whom I could confide.

The best part of the day for me was when it was over. We would sit
in the living room, listening to the radio or reading or just talking. The
criticism/self-criticism sessions were forgotten for the time being. Bit by
bit, Wendy Yoshimura told us about herself and her life. Her parents
were American-born and when the Japanese attacked Pearl Harbor in
1941, her father had tried to enlist in the U. S. Army. He was rejected.
Soon all the Japanese people here, her mother and father among them,
were sent to internment camps in remote areas of the country. Wendy
had been born in one of those concentration camps. After the war her
parents decided to make their new life in Japan. She was brought up in
Hiroshima, or what remained of it after the atomic bomb had fallen

there. When she was eleven, her parents returned to the United States and settled in Fresno, California. She was put in the second grade, instead of the sixth or seventh, because she could not speak English. She was an outsider among Americans. But she caught up and went to college in Oakland at age nineteen, studying art. At college, she was entirely apolitical until her fourth year, when she became involved with a man who was a radical and who "opened" her eyes to the social injustice existing in the United States. Just before graduating she met and fell in love with another radical activist, who, in 1969, turned her focus in life from art to the Vietnam War, racism, sexism, and all that was wrong with America. That man was Willie Brandt.

Willie Brandt was Wendy's ideal. She described him as warm, humane, good, loving, caring, handsome, masculine, and dedicated to changing the American political system. She joined him in harvesting sugarcane for Castro in Cuba in 1969; she joined him in his bombing of banks, nuclear laboratories, police cars, and other political targets beginning in 1970. Willie was the head of the infamous Revolutionary Army, which was formed that year. She was the Army's only soldier. Brandt's method of operation was simply to ask any of his many radical friends if they would like to join him in a bombing. But, as Wendy explained, they were all "symbolic bombings." They were not designed to kill or to hurt anyone. They were carried out late at night and a manifesto was always announced. The idea was to draw the public's attention to what was wrong with this country. She estimated that Willie was responsible for at least forty bombings over a two-year period. It was pure luck that she had not accompanied him on the action when he had been arrested at the garage where he had gone to pick up his explosives. Michael Bortin went with him that night and on his first action was arrested with Willie in 1972.

Teko could not resist dismissing the symbolic bombings as useless and futile in changing the face of Amerikkka. Only revolutionary killings of the police and prominent business and political figures would serve to bring on the class struggle, he declared, spouting SLA philosophy. Wendy retorted, "I don't see you or the SLA doing that much . . . all you do is sit around and plan." But General Teko insisted that the great days of the SLA were still to come. The revolution was just beginning; the SLA would lead it and would, in the end, be victorious. . . . And so it went.

Teko found fault with just about everything that Wendy Yoshimura did. It drove him wild to see her out on the sleeping porch with the Sunday New York *Times* spread out all around her, as she refused to do any exercises or combat drills on a Sunday. "You're so bourgeois!" Teko screamed at her one day. "What would Willie say if he saw you laying around like that when there's work to do?"

"Willie would never put anyone down," she replied coldly. "He would say that every single person was a revolutionary at heart and if you were willing to stand up for what you believe, no matter how you did it, that was revolutionary enough. He understood that everybody was different. Anything anybody was ready to do was all right with him, and no more. He would not insist, like you do, and he would not force anything on anyone."

But Teko was so doctrinaire that he believed that no one else could possibly be right except himself on matters of radical philosophy and the revolution. He objected to the books Wendy read on feminism, foreign affairs, or philosophy. And, in addition to all that, he tried again and again to lure her to bed with him. She refused to be "comradely." Point-blank, she told him she did not want to have anything to do with him physically, now or ever. But Teko was thick-skinned and hard to put off. Finally, she told him she would take no orders from him at all: "I don't care if you're the head of the SLA. I am not under your command. I'm not in the SLA. I don't want to be in the SLA. I'm here only because I promised Jack that I would stay to help you out, to run errands and stuff, and only for this summer. After that I'm through with you—totally."

Wendy was obviously unhappy with her situation on the farm. The local people in town were hostile toward her. The storekeepers were surly and one even insulted her to her face, calling her a Jap. She was unaccustomed to this kind of blatant prejudice, not having experienced it in the San Francisco Bay Area, which has a large Asian community. But she would stick it out with us because she had given her word to Jack Scott. Wendy preserved part of each day as her own, when she wrote in her journal or penned a long letter to Willie Brandt. She exchanged letters with her lover by using an intermediary, who copied them and sent them on.

Of course, Teko and Yolanda complained that her journal and her letter writing were a breach of security, even after she explained that all names were written in code and that no outsider would understand the true import of the letters or the references made in them. That did not satisfy them. Yolanda was particularly caustic in her criticism of her writing to Willie.

"I don't understand why you're so upset about this," Wendy remarked one evening, and I blurted out, "She's jealous because she can't write to her boyfriend Lumumba in prison." Yolanda and Teko both turned on me in fury. "That's a flagrant violation of security," Yolanda cried out. "You keep SLA business to yourself, sister, or you'll find yourself in real trouble." I shut up instantly and crawled back into my shell.

The Scotts visited the farm once every week or two and that helped relieve the boredom and sense of being confined. We all talked of the SLA book we were to write, but no one got anything down on paper. It was much more difficult to write a book than to practice and train for the revolution.

The Scotts' visits became less and less frequent until finally, toward the end of July, they arrived to announce that for security reasons we had to leave the farm and move to another, more remote place on the other side of the Pennsylvania–New York border. They babbled on about their being investigated by the government because of their upcoming trip to Cuba and they were afraid the authorities might find out about this farmhouse in Pennsylvania. Unfortunately, said Jack, Micki had rented the place in her own name and they could not very well have us living in a house which could be traced to them. So, said Jack, Micki had disguised herself in a long blond wig and, posing as an artist and giving a phony name, had rented us a farmhouse in Jeffersonville, New York, a remote community of small dairy farms near what they called "the Borscht Belt" of hotels in the Catskill Mountains. We did not have much choice and Jack swore the New York farmhouse was more remote and safer than this one. He urged us to leave that night, promising that he and Micki would return to wipe away all fingerprints and traces of us from the Pennsylvania farm. We did a general but thorough cleaning up and late that night we departed for our new safehouse in the Catskills.

Tucked away off a narrow country road near nowhere in particular, our New York hideout was an old, abandoned dairy farm with a huge barn that had once been a creamery and bottling plant and a one-room wooden farmhouse with a carport alongside of it. Inside, it had an open floor plan, a kitchen area and a step-down living room about fifteen by thirty feet. There was also a small bathroom and a sleeping loft which could be reached by a ladder in the living room. Although the house was not much, the acres of untouched land all around it were beautiful. Thick woods of pines and white birches surrounded us. The August days were hot and humid, almost tropical, and I delighted in the crashing summer storms of rolling thunder and crackling lightning that flashed from the sky down to the earth. It was magnificent, awesome. Those storms made me come alive again, if only temporarily; otherwise, I was pretty well sunken into a permanent state of depression.

At the dairy farm we went on with our calisthenics and combat drills, but this time General Teko devised a new method of torturing us into condition. He instituted practice guerrilla-warfare maneuvers, staging mock search-and-destroy missions by dividing us into two teams: the pursued and the pursuers. If Wendy and I were the team to be pursued, we would be given a three-minute head start. We would have to run like mad up the hills, through the woods beyond the house, across a dirt road, through a field and up another hill, and through even more fields. Our goal was a stone wall about two miles from the farmhouse. Or we could stop and hide at some point in the woods and try to ambush our pursuers. When we were the pursuers, chasing Teko and Yolanda, we could proceed as fast or as slowly as we wished, always on the alert for an ambush, but the object was to catch up to and either capture or kill the other team.

Strategy, tactics, guile, alertness all played a part, as well as physical fitness. The game became more strenuous day by day. Teko and Yolanda played with the utmost seriousness. He insisted that we play this game as if our lives depended upon it. When Teko leaped up from behind a rock and shouted, "Bang, bang. You're dead!" he meant it.

Whenever Wendy and I were pursued, no matter how fast we ran or where we hid, we were always captured or killed by Teko and Yolanda. They could outthink and outrun us. When we pursued them, we were always ambushed. They never tired of the drill and the opportunity to prove their superiority. Wendy soon stopped taking the game seriously; she decided it was good exercise but otherwise ridiculous. In fact, she told me in so many words that she thought Teko was a complete, all-around idiot. I was shocked and defended Teko according to the precepts of the SLA that I had learned. He was our dedicated leader and the only one we had and therefore was deserving of our respect, even when we had differences with him.

Jack Scott finally appeased Teko on the matter of weapons by bringing up two BB guns, and Teko set up a target-shooting range for us inside the cavernous dairy barn on the property. I got the housecleaning job of picking up all the pellets after our target practice. Jim Kilgore sent us several books on revolutionary philosophy and economics and Teko gave me reading assignments to further my education. The favorite summer reading in our enclave was *Prairie Fire,* which was a sort of history of the United States according to the Weather Underground. Teko and Yolanda spent hours dissecting that book for my edification.

I also had classes in "people's elocution," as Teko cracked down on my bourgeois manner of speaking. "You sound more like Katharine Hepburn in one of her movies than you do a revolutionary," he told me. My prep school diction offended him. It would only alienate me from the people, according to Teko, so I had to consciously try to speak with double negatives, incorrect grammar, and, above all, I had to learn how to drop my final *g*'s. These classes were ongoing. I was corrected and criticized day and night by Teko or Yolanda. There seemed no escaping them.

Living at such close quarters in the one-room farmhouse, however, increased our tensions and conflicts. There was no getting away from one another after sundown. I got two black eyes that month on the farm. Once I said something which Teko interpreted as "disrespectful" and he hauled off and socked me. The other time he hit me for "insubordination" which I did not understand. Once, he almost struck Wendy. His clenched fist was raised. But she stopped him cold. "If you lay a hand on me, ever, you son of a bitch, I swear to you I'll stick a knife in your gut. I'll get you one night when you're sleeping. Just once, and you've had it." We all knew she meant it. Teko spluttered something or other and backed off.

Strangely enough, during this period Teko and Yolanda seemed to get along better than ever before. They were positively lovey-dovey, taking long walks together, talking with one another to the exclusion of Wendy and me, sleeping together, and, as far as I could see, actually enjoying one another's company. It was at that time Wendy discovered that Teko had knowledge of everything she had confided to Yolanda. She knew it because Teko was throwing up the personal information to denigrate everything she believed in. It was only then that Wendy reappraised the relationships among the four of us. She never told me what kind of picture Yolanda had painted of me for her, but she did remark, "I'll never trust her again." She felt that she had been demeaned and insulted and used, for Yolanda had acted so warm and caring but, in fact, had been using her, sucking all the information she could out of Wendy and then feeding it to Teko for future use. So this quiet and wise woman turned to me and we began to have longer and more intimate talks. She opened my mind to horizons somewhat broader than those of the SLA.

After a while, forced to accommodate ourselves to one another, we all slipped into a routine that was easier to live with. Teko and Yolanda made more frequent trips away from the farm. They went into Monticello together. Teko bought two pairs of eyeglasses, replacing for the first time the pair he had lost in the scuffle at Mel's, and she bought new contact lenses. Teko wandered off one day to take a look at Grossinger's, the ultimate bourgeois hotel resort, which was not far from our farm. He returned with reports of luxuries, comforts, and decadence the likes of which he could scarcely believe. He had picked up a yarmulke skullcap, which he had worn so that he could walk around the hotel grounds among the many Jewish people there without arousing any suspicion. On another occasion, he took Yolanda with him to see the sights at Grossinger's with her own eyes.

Teko was so proud of being able to pass himself off as Jewish, wearing his yarmulke, that he insisted that we all get to work improving our disguises for future actions. He sent Yolanda out to get me a new red wig, a maternity outfit, and Ace bandages to wrap stuffing around my middle. For hours I practiced painting on freckles, so that I had it down to an art and could get myself ready as a red-haired, freckled mother-to-be in a matter of minutes. Even though Yolanda looked nothing like any of her "Wanted" photos, Teko wanted her too to improve her disguises. Because she acted so well as a middle-aged or old woman, Teko tried to persuade her to remove the bridge she had in her mouth and go about partially toothless. "You'll look like a poor person," he said. "Poor people always have bad teeth." But Yolanda was self-conscious about her teeth and absolutely refused. Then Teko tried to get Wendy to make herself up as a white person and she refused. She told me she thought he was "absolutely out of his mind" if he thought she could fool anyone about her Asian origins.

One small incident among many had a profound effect upon me and my own thinking, which I managed to hide from all the others. It was a Sunday and Wendy once again was refusing to take part in any of Teko's exercises or drills. He was castigating her for her lack of discipline and determination. "What are you going to do if the pigs show up here and they surround the house? How are you going to defend yourself? You won't take any target practice with us and, when the time comes, you won't be ready to fight the pigs. So what are you going to do then? Huh? What are you going to do?"

He was standing, glaring at her as she sat on the grass, and she answered him straightforwardly: "I know what I am going to do. I'm going to walk out of the house with my hands up!"

Teko was shocked. "Those pigs aren't going to let you walk out of here," he retorted. "They're going to shoot you down like a dog."

"Well, I'm going to take that chance," she said. Then she added, "I know they're going to kill me if I stay here and shoot at them. That's for sure."

Yolanda tried to reason with her: "It's really better to die for the people, sister, than to be locked up in prison. It's too demoralizing for the people to see their freedom fighters go to prison."

"I don't think it's demoralizing at all," said Wendy. "It should give the people hope that one day that person will get out of prison to continue the struggle."

"No, they never get out," declared Yolanda. "They are murdered in prison."

"No, Willie is in prison and he's going to get out," Wendy said. "You really can't do the revolution any good at all if you're killed. And I don't intend to get killed, not if I can help it."

I sat there, saying nothing, hardly noticed, but I was so relieved to hear someone else say for the first time what I felt: I wanted to stay alive; I did not want to have to die for the revolution or anything else. I told myself what I had been afraid to think before: If the police came here, I too would surrender. No matter what they did to me, I would walk out with my hands up. This was the first thought of opposition to the SLA Codes of War that I allowed myself to harbor.

Unfortunately for Wendy and me, the idyllic relationship between Teko and Yolanda did not last very long. The professor who had driven Yolanda to New York arrived one day for a visit. It was obvious that his only reason for coming was to see Yolanda. She became so sweet, girlish, and flirtatious that Wendy and I had to suppress our own giggles. It was amusing to witness the change in her demeanor and the intonation of her voice and, at the same time, to watch her husband seethe with jealousy, which he tried so hard to conceal. After all, it would be the height of bourgeois sentiment to oppose anyone's free will in sexual matters. To make things even worse, the professor was the very opposite of Teko: he was tall, thin, and muscular. Ever so casually, they announced that they were going for a walk in the woods. They fooled no one, nor did they intend to. Wendy and I sat outside the house, waiting, and, sure enough, ten minutes later, Teko came out and announced he was going jogging.

He returned in about forty minutes and without a word went into the creamery barn. We could hear the shots of his target practice. After a bit, I went into the barn and saw him shooting at a hand-drawn silhouette of an extremely tall man. Sitting down on a table to watch, I remarked lightly, "That's a pretty tall target there." He glared at me and just went on shooting. When Yolanda returned she unabashedly told us all: "We had such a nice walk."

Later, after the professor had left, Teko turned upon her and screamed, "I went out for a jog, you know, and there you were with him, like animals, fucking on the side of the road!"

"Well, you found what you were looking for," she shot back.

"Yeah, well, you know that was a breach of security, doing that in the woods, don't you?"

"Well, fuck you, I enjoyed myself for once."

Teko was even more dictatorial and difficult to live with in the days that followed.

At long last, Jack Scott showed up one weekend with the writer he had promised for the SLA book. He was introduced to us with much fanfare as a Ph.D. from an Ivy League university who had attended school in London. An old radical friend of Jack's from his Berkeley days, he was now teaching at a small college I had never heard of in Canada. His claim to fame was having been arrested in Britain during a school demonstration for, as he put it, "shitting on a picture of the Queen." He was a most unattractive, overweight man in his mid-thirties, with long, stringy hair. The idea was for him to write the book for us and Jack to get it published.

The writer decided to tell the story of the SLA in question-and-answer form, followed by a general summary of the reasons and philosophy behind all of our actions. The writer would ask the questions and Teko, Yolanda, and I would answer them. Before he began, however, we would all go over the questions and prepare our answers prior to reciting them into the tape recorder. Of course, we would have the opportunity to edit and change anything we wished so that the final result would be satisfactory to us. He pulled two tape recorders out of his suitcase and announced that for safety's sake he would record our answers on both recorders and he would keep one set of tapes, just in case anything happened to us.

He began tape-recording Teko. Jack Scott stayed at the farm only to see us get started that first day and then he left. Even going over the questions before recording, we ran into trouble trying to get the SLA version of our story onto the tapes. Teko answered his questions with bravado on the formation and early days of the SLA, but when he listened to the playback, it just did not come out the way he had intended it. Yolanda was fiercely dissatisfied with her first try at describing her early life and her conversion to the cause. She decided that in order for her story to come out right she would take the tape recorder alone into the bathroom. Finally, she suggested that we transcribe all that we had recorded and go over every line with great care.

We all had trouble in explaining my conversion to the SLA. The three of us went over the questions and our proposed replies, but the writer had difficulty accepting our answers. He was shocked when I told him of being kept locked up in a closet for two months. He had never suspected such a thing from his preconceived notions of why and how I had joined the SLA. Teko tried to explain that my being kept prisoner was not so bad. "It was a big closet," he explained. The writer asked, "How big?" Teko could try to twist facts and stretch the truth to fit his own version of what had happened, but he could not bring himself to lie outright. We struggled to find the right words prior to being recorded. For instance, I said that the SLA had not "kidnapped me" but rather that they had "rescued me" from my blighted, bourgeois life, and had led me to true freedom. The whole thing was an exercise to me, a sort of propaganda action. The purpose was to glorify the SLA to the outside world and my kidnapping and conversion were just difficult spots in the story to explain in terms of the freedom-fighter image of the SLA. I was not to worry for a minute about truth or accuracy, but rather how my tale would fit in with the propaganda we had been feeding ourselves and now wanted to serve to others.

The writer obviously had trouble believing us or believing that he could put together a book that would be believed. Aside from the content, Teko was also dismayed at the tone of my voice. He complained that I sounded drugged or under duress when I spoke into the tape recorders, much as I had sounded on the very first tape I had made in the closet with Cinque. I found the whole project upsetting. I did not want to be exploited publicly with such pronouncements as this book would contain. It would be forever embarrassing to me and to my family. It was just one more ugly thing I had to do in my present circumstance.

The writer stayed out there with us for a full week, going over questions and answers and taping each of us, and he came out two more times for additional taping during that month of August. Each time, Wendy would pick him up at the railroad station and then drive him back, and each time Teko would worry about what Wendy might be telling him privately, knowing full well her low opinion of him. However, Teko never allowed the writer to take any of the tapes with him away from the farm. He was determined that no one else should ever hear the sound of my voice on these tapes because it would be a clear admission of my diminished capacity.

Our friends on the West Coast were not forgotten. They were supposed to be earning money to finance the revolution by painting houses, while we were waiting for the Coast to cool off so that we would be able to return.

From the start of the summer, Wendy drove Yolanda into town every third night for her telephone calls to Kathy Soliah or Jim Kilgore to check up on the West Coast activities of our new comrades. Wendy almost always made her own personal calls at the same time, either to Mike Bortin and Seanna in San Francisco or to her friend in New Jersey. There was no way Teko or Yolanda could stop her or control her because she frequently went into town shopping by herself. But they both agonized over what Wendy might be telling her friends. Wendy denied ever revealing anything of our activities, but to me privately she freely admitted that she told her friends everything that was going on. She did that because she trusted them and if she couldn't let off steam that way, she would go out of her mind. Nor did she hide her true opinions from the writer on his trips to and from the railroad station in Monticello.

As time went on, Teko became more and more suspicious of Jack Scott's loyalty to our cause. They had had their political arguments every now and again, usually about the extent of violence needed to bring about change in America. But with the taping of the SLA book and the difficulties in getting it to come out right, Teko came to believe that Jack was more interested in the book than in us. It occurred to him that if Jack Scott ever got his hands on these tapes, he could anonymously turn us in to the police and then, after our deaths, he would have the SLA book all to himself.

Once that idea had entered his thinking, there was no end to the scenarios our leader could construct whereby the Scotts could profit financially by betraying us to the authorities. Sheer suspicion led Teko to the conclusion that the only reason the Scotts were laying out so much money to support us was to reap the rewards that an SLA book would provide for them. The various scams and rip-offs the Scotts bragged about led us, Wendy included, to distrust them. That led Teko to the decision to kill Jack and Micki Scott. He told us that the only way he could do it safely was to wait for an occasion when they came up to the farm together but without the writer. Then he could take them for a walk in the woods, murder them, and bury their bodies out there.

The Scotts did come up the following weekend late in August, arriving late on Friday night, but the writer showed up early the next morning. The Scotts had brought roast beef and other food for a celebration meal because we had by then accumulated a fairly large batch of tapes which constituted a rough draft of perhaps half of the intended book. They tried to make a festive affair of it, but there were many underlying stresses. Yolanda, for instance, thought it was terribly bourgeois of them to spend money on a roast beef dinner when they knew that we were in desperate need of cash. It showed, she said, their lack of feeling; it demonstrated that they were not true revolutionaries.

Teko nagged Jack for a means for us to return to the West Coast. Our comrades out there had not earned enough money, he said, to finance our trip back. Jack replied that he had put out so much money renting these two farmhouses for us that he did not have enough to pay for our way back. We were, in effect, stuck in the hinterlands of New York and the rent would come due on this farm at the end of the month. Yolanda suggested that we could return to the Pennsylvania farmhouse, for we knew that it had been rented until October. But Jack insisted that would be too dangerous. Micki interrupted to say that returning to that farmhouse was impossible because the farm had been sold.

On Sunday, when all of us were outside playing volleyball, Teko returned to the house and took all the tapes out of a cabinet in the living room and hid them away in the barn. At dinner that night, he announced that contrary to prior plans he had decided that he could not allow any of the tapes to be taken out of his personal control. They were not in final form and they contained too much incriminating evidence against the three of us in the event that we were arrested. Jack, Micki, and the writer were shocked and visibly shaken. They tried to convince him that the tapes would be safer with them than with us, but Teko would not relent. In the midst of the argument, the writer got up to walk around and casually glanced into the drawer which had contained the tapes. They were, of course, gone. And that was that. "We will transcribe them for you," Teko said, "and we'll let you have them when we think it is safe."

When they had left, Yolanda promptly said, "I just don't believe the farm in Pennsylvania has been sold. I think they lied, and I just don't trust them anymore."

"Yeah," said Teko. "I wish we'd killed all of them when we had the chance."

The next day Yolanda set out to find a new place for us to stay. With Wendy as her chauffeur, she found a small place to rent near Poughkeepsie, a small city further up north, which she thought might be suitable. However, the landlord demanded rent in advance and Con Edison insisted on a ninety-dollar deposit to cover gas and electricity bills, and we did not have that much money in our coffer. On the way back, she and Wendy were surprised to be stopped at a police roadblock. But they were passed through without incident: those police were looking for two men who had held up a bank that day. The Harrises found it hard to believe that there could be any crime in so rural a town. Teko went out the following day to inspect the possible new safehouse, but vetoed the place as not nearly secure enough for our purposes. He spent the rest of the day criticizing Yolanda and Wendy for their stupidity in even suggesting the Poughkeepsie apartment.

We were expecting the Scotts that afternoon and I could not help but worry that Teko really would carry out his plan to silence them and bury them in the woods. But Micki arrived alone. They must have had their own suspicions about us, for never again did they come to the New York farm together and that saved their lives.

Micki strolled up to us smiling. "Hi, guys."

We were all seated on the lawn in front of the house when Yolanda confronted her. "Why did you lie to us about the farmhouse in Pennsylvania?"

Micki paled. Her face suddenly turned ashen.

"What do you mean, lie to you? The farmhouse was sold a few weeks ago," she responded.

"No, it wasn't," Yolanda said coldly. "You lied. I called and found out. It's empty and still rented to you."

"How dare you think I would lie to you!" Micki declared angrily. "After all we've done for you, it's outrageous of you to check up on us. We just can't get through to you and get you to trust us."

"Well, you were lying," said Yolanda.

While the argument was going on, Wendy moved behind Micki, filched her pocketbook, and looked through its contents in search of a gun. Teko had set up the maneuver beforehand in the hope that Micki might be carrying a gun that we could use better than she could. But Wendy found no weapon and replaced the bag.

"Jack and I think it's too dangerous for you to be out at that farmhouse," Micki admitted. "It's rented in my name and if the police ever, ever, trace you being there, we'd be in deep trouble. It's not fair for us to take that risk."

"Well, we just have to go back there," announced Teko. "We have no place else to go until we can get back to the West Coast. How about it? Can you get us back to the West Coast?"

"Jack and I have been trying to figure it out and I think we can help you a bit." Micki explained that she and Jack were going to close up their New York apartment and move themselves and the ISSS operation to Portland, Oregon. They had been invited to live with Bill Walton out there. So they figured that they could take me cross-country with them in a moving van they intended to rent for their move. But Yolanda and Teko would have to make their own way across the country. Wendy would decide for herself whether to return to New Jersey or come back to the West Coast.

So a workable truce was declared between the Scotts and the Harrises. With our money running low and the worry about buying food, I was happy enough to be returning to the San Francisco Bay Area. All we had with us were the jogging clothes that Jack had given us and these were now less than adequate. The weather was changing and the leaves were beginning to turn color.

CHAPTER

FIFTEEN

OUR STRATEGIC DECISION, made after intense planning via long-distance telephoning, was not to return to San Francisco after all. Instead, we decided to begin anew in Sacramento. The capital of California was only ninety or so minutes by car from the Bay Area and its great advantage to us was that neither we nor our new recruits were known there. The Soliahs, Jim Kilgore, Mike Bortin, Seanna—all were very well known in the Bay Area. They could hardly join in SLA operations without the risk of their friends, if not the police, becoming highly suspicious. Sacramento also would be less dangerous for us; we could carry out our combat operations in the Bay Area and hide out in Sacramento. The plan therefore was for the Soliahs to rent a safehouse in Sacramento and then divide their time between it and their usual haunts in the Berkeley-Oakland area and gradually, without arousing any suspicions, disappear from view. Sacramento also had another distinct advantage: Joe Remiro and Russ Little had obtained a change of venue from Oakland for their trial for the Marcus Foster murder. They would be tried in Sacramento. We wanted to be on hand for that event.

Bill and Emily Harris could hardly wait to get back. Kathy Soliah had informed us that she had made contact with someone who was allowed to visit Remiro regularly and who was willing to work with us to plan their escape. If Bo and Osi could be sprung from jail, the SLA would once again have an experienced cadre of revolutionary leadership, according to Teko. Besides, our California comrades would have to be "whipped into shape" if they were to become SLA soldiers fit for action. Teko and Yolanda considered them too intellectual and too flaky to be trusted. They had none of the discipline required of true revolutionaries. They had spent years in the radical movement, studying the literature, attending the usual lectures, rallies, and demonstrations, rapping with one another, but they had never *done* anything. Teko meant to correct that.

The first two weeks in September that we spent at the Pennsylvania farm was a busy, upbeat time. These were the weeks, according to Teko, for our final preparations for re-entering the war zone of California. Aside from our calisthenics and combat drills, almost all of our time was spent in transcribing and editing the tapes for our SLA book. Yolanda, who had once worked as a secretary, did most of the transcribing, although Teko took over when she got tired. As a typist, I was hopeless: slow and inaccurate. Both of them would be screaming over me before I finished a page. In all, I transcribed only about twenty pages of typescript from the tapes. Teko worked primarily on his own material, rewriting what he had said on the tapes as he typed and then correcting what he had typed and then retyping that. It took him forever and Yolanda hovered over him, complaining all the while. When Yolanda did the typing, Teko paced the floor in frenetic anxiety, eager to burn the tapes as soon as they were transcribed. Again and again, he declared that no one must ever hear my voice on those tapes, because it would undo everything we were working for in the book. "Tania's voice sounds just like it did on that first [SLA] tape," Teko said. As soon as Yolanda finished a tape, Teko would take both copies out behind the barn and burn them.

He and Yolanda went off together each evening for long walks, during which they planned our future strategies. That left time for Wendy and me to talk and become better friends. As she described her days with Willie Brandt, I came to realize that she would never have become a terrorist if she had not become romantically involved with that particular man. She was deeply immersed in the feminist movement during this period and explained to me that she would never have taken to violence if it had not been for Willie. She was convinced that the capitalistic system was basically and fundamentally unfair to minorities, but she believed that the system would have to be changed in the hearts of the people. She hated violence. Even though terribly frightened, she had gone along with Willie on his "symbolic bombings," but she had tried to stop him from some of his wilder schemes. In telling me all of this, Wendy was using me as a sounding board, I believe, as she was facing the truth of her relationship with her old boyfriend. He had controlled her. Now she had come to wonder seriously about their future relationship. She still loved him but had begun to doubt to some extent whether she would be willing to join him again when he emerged from Soledad Prison. She had changed too much during the past few years, and had become too much of a feminist, to return to their old relationship.

The amount of work we had to do in the time remaining kept Teko's rages somewhat under control and so the tension eased a bit. I found that I now could run up and down the hills fairly easily, so long as I ran alone. When Teko or Yolanda insisted upon running with me, I ended up hyperventilating. In the drills, I found to my surprise that I was surpassing Yolanda, who, despite all her determination, could not learn to throw a ball (in lieu of a hand grenade) any distance at all. Although my two seniors still insisted that I had a lot to learn in combat skills, it was evident to me that I was a vastly better soldier than I had been at the start of the summer.

The Scotts arrived suddenly one afternoon with a rented van and their little Volkswagen bug and announced that we were leaving that night. Teko still refused to turn over any of the tapes or transcripts of the book, telling Jack only that we would be in touch with him on the West Coast when we had our book in suitable form for him to sell. We spent hours cleaning the house, wiping our fingerprints from the walls, counters, and furniture. The Scotts then announced their plan to get rid of their Volkswagen by abandoning it somewhere away from the farm. They then could say it had been stolen from a New York City street and claim the insurance on it. They had their rented van packed with their clothing and ISSS file cabinets. With Teko's help they smashed all the windows, slashed the upholstery, and thoroughly vandalized the car. Then the Scotts drove off to leave the VW in a field some seven miles away from the farmhouse.

We took off that night in the van, Micki, Jack, and I, heading for Interstate 80 and the West Coast. Jack talked incessantly. Bill Harris was a hard man to deal with, he said, because he was so distrustful, despite all that the Scotts had done for us. So, Jack asked, would I trust him? Would I tell him the SLA plans? Where were we headed for? How could he get in touch with us? What was my destination?

But I was under instructions not, under any circumstance, to trust him or to tell him anything of our plans. I told him simply that I did not know. I was to be picked up in Las Vegas and brought to the West Coast. I did not know where, I told him. Perhaps it had not yet been decided. I did not know. He had to accept it. But he talked on. And on. And on.

When we reached Cleveland the next day, Micki announced that she was getting off there. She had decided to visit some friends in Ohio and said that she would fly the rest of the way.

Somewhere in Indiana that night we were stopped by a state trooper. As the officer approached our car, Jack warned me to act natural, to look straight ahead and not at the policeman, but also not to flinch or try to hide. A flashlight was beamed into our van from Jack's window and I was mostly in the shadows. Of course, I had freckles painted on my face, a wig of red hair, and a bath towel wrapped around my middle under my slacks to give me the appearance of pregnancy. Nevertheless, I had to do everything in my power to stop myself from shaking with fright. I was still a beginner at this sort of thing. Jack Scott, however, was as cool as could be. He leaned out the window so that the trooper could see him without shining his flashlight into the van. Jack engaged him in conversation and before I knew it they were talking about football, sounding like the best of friends. We drove off with a polite warning and no speeding ticket. Jack was not humble about his own performance, replaying it for me with an explanation of the subtleties involved, all the way to Las Vegas.

We headed down from Salt Lake City on Interstate 15 directly into Las Vegas, arriving at Jack's parents' apartment shortly after noon. As we walked in, I was surprised to see Micki lounging on an inflatable mat in the swimming pool. She greeted me warmly but with no explanation. She had said she would be going on to San Diego. In the apartment, Jack appeared nervous for the first time and it soon became obvious to me that he did not want anyone to come upon me so close to his parents' home. I spent the night there because he was unable to reach Jim Kilgore on the West Coast. The whole family was disturbed, in fact, because they had just received a cablegram and a phone call that brother Walter was on his way in from Libya. They feared what he might do, which was anything as long as it was the least expected, if he stumbled onto the fact that the family was involved with Patty Hearst. The very next morning, Micki went out and rented a motel room on a side street off the Strip and told me to stay there until Jim Kilgore arrived. They would be in touch with news and with whatever food and necessities I required. So I stayed in the room by myself, curtains drawn, television set droning on, and I waited. Jack had paid for two days.

Jim Kilgore arrived on the morning of the second day, looking red-eyed and haggard, saying he had sat up on a bus all night. It had been a miserable trip of twelve hours or so and it would be, he told me, just as miserable going back. The delay was not his fault. Josephine Soliah had not been able to rent a safehouse in Sacramento until the previous day. Jim had our return tickets on him and not much money left over. So we had to vacate the motel at noon and kill time until the bus left.

Getting through six hours in Las Vegas as fugitives without much money presented a real problem. Jim showed me the .38-caliber revolver he had stuck in his waistband: Teko had insisted over the telephone that he come armed. Jim was my guardian, my protection, and he was not too happy about it at all. We could not go into any of the casinos. Security patrolmen were all over the place. We were afraid to go into a hotel for the same reason. We did not have enough money for another motel room. We did not come upon any movie houses. We searched out greasy spoon restaurants and small, poorly lit coffee shops and they were not easy to find in this brightly lighted city. Jim tried to reach Jack Scott for help, but Jack would not come to the phone and we were told not to come to the Scotts' place. So, for the most part, we wandered the streets.

I had never seen or been seen by so many people in the eight months since my kidnapping. It was the first time that I had been out in the open for so long. I was close to absolute panic. A virtual agoraphobic, I feared everyone who cast an eye upon me. I wanted to run and hide, to crawl down a hole, to do anything to get away. But all we did was walk. Each time I came to the verge of panic, I concentrated upon controlled breathing. By the end of the day my feet were so sore that I could hardly stand. I was leaning helplessly on Jim Kilgore's arm, listening to his reassuring words which did not reassure me at all. At any moment I expected recognition and the alarm being sounded. I envisioned an FBI agent emerging from a hiding place and shooting me down. I did not feel at all like a revolutionary freedom fighter. Boarding that overnight bus to Sacramento came as a blessed relief.

When we arrived, Kathy Soliah greeted us with open arms and a broad smile on her face. Alongside was her brother Steven, who was quiet and withdrawn, and now clean-shaven. Kathy and Jim talked and exchanged stories on our drive to the safehouse on W Street in the center of Sacramento, a low-income neighborhood of small, run-down houses. Our place was little more than a wooden shack, a house that had been divided into two units. The front room facing the street was a small bedroom and behind it was a modest-sized living room and behind that the kitchen and bath. Josephine, the "baby" of the Soliah family, greeted me with warmth and concern. I was put off at first by the ridiculous wig she was wearing. She looked like a young girl trying to look older, but at least she had made an attempt at a disguise.

They were all very kind to me and solicitous of my health and well-being and it took me a little while to adjust to this treatment. Slowly, I began to relax. No one was shouting orders at me; no one was shouting at all. Since it was agreed that I was to stay out of sight, we sat around most of every day and talked and got acquainted. We talked of our schools, the books we had read, our upbringings, and the state of the world. Jim Kilgore, and Kathy too, suggested the names of books they thought I should read. After a week or so, Jim brought up a stack of books for me. They thought the SLA had been too much into action and too little into fundamentals of the communist and socialist viewpoint of history. They told me the SLA had failed to rally others to its cause because much of the SLA propaganda did not make sense. We ate and slept well and rested. Jim and Kathy did not go out shopping as much as they went out shoplifting. They were masters at it. They came back with steaks and chops and fancy desserts and, according to them, such a diet was all part of the counterculture. It was perfectly appropriate for them to rip off the establishment supermarkets: everyone knew the chain supermarkets were ripping off the people with their bloated prices.

Two weeks slipped by for me most pleasantly as I came to know Kathy and Jim and Steve and Josephine. Oh, we all had code names, Helen, Roy, Lola, and myself as Pearl, but we hardly used them. After all, there was no one watching and we were becoming friends in communal living. Since that awful shoot-out, I had been, in effect, the Harrises slave, doing what I was told, never questioning, operating by rote, living day by day on a mere survival course. But here in Sacramento, I was being treated as a person, and the people around me were not, as Teko had declared, flaky at all. They were nice, normal revolutionaries, and far more reasonable than anyone I had ever met in the SLA.

All this came to an abrupt end after two weeks. The Harrises arrived, looking like tourists from the East, clean-cut, combed hair, a devoted couple. They came in with happy smiles, saying that they had had a great trip, traveling by train, stopping in Chicago, where Yolanda had grown up, spending a day there visiting the zoo and favorite places of her childhood. They looked around the house, peered out the windows, and then Teko, the General Field Marshal, threw a screaming fit. Not more than fifteen minutes had passed since their arrival and everything in the house changed.

"You're all a bunch of assholes," he suddenly shouted. "Where's the security around here? What are the arrangements? I don't see how you people intend to defend yourselves. What have you been doing all this time? What?"

He thrust his chin out at me and let me have it. "What's wrong with you, Pearl? Eh? You know better than this. You should have asserted some leadership. You should have told these people what to do. Haven't you learned anything yet?

"Where are the guns? For Christ's sake, you've been here two weeks and you haven't even unpacked them. Don't you have any weapons at all in this joint?"

By this time he had me cowering in the corner of a couch. Then he turned upon Kilgore. "You're supposed to be protecting her? What kind of defense plans have you drawn up? Do you really think this is a safehouse? As a safehouse, it's a joke! It's just the kind of place the pigs would expect us to be in—the worst-looking house on the block. It's a giveaway, not a hideaway. What were you all thinking? And what would you do if the pigs come in on you? You can't escape, 'cause you got no escape routes laid out. Jesus, you don't even have the doors locked!"

They were all terribly embarrassed, feeling guilty and unworthy, and Teko made the most of it. The weapons were stashed in a footlocker with the television set on top of it in the living room. Teko practically hurled the TV set aside to get at his beloved weapons, and of course they were there, unloaded and not cleaned or oiled since we had left them. The cars were parked just behind the house, and that, of course, was a gross breach of security. Teko called for an immediate meeting on security. He insisted upon reports from each of them on what they had done all summer to help the cause of the revolution. He criticized each of them in turn. He delivered a long lecture on the precepts laid down by Cinque. He told them that if they wanted to join in the revolution with the SLA they had better get serious about the business of revolutionary, guerrilla warfare. They needed to be physically fit, combat-ready, security-conscious; they had to adopt the attributes practiced by successful revolutionaries from China to Cuba. They were unworthy of the great tradition. And the Soliahs and Kilgore took it from him because he had been through so much and they, as yet, had not.

In the next few days Teko and Yolanda set about getting everyone in the SLA combat unit organized. The windows were covered with heavy drapes, locks and dead bolts were purchased for front and back doors, combat positions and escape routes were worked out and explained to everyone. Teko instructed, shouted orders, cursed, grew exasperated, and barked new commands. Yolanda backed him up. Both of them reminded all of us of Cinque and the others who had given their lives for the cause. Calisthenics, combat drills, and jogging were reinstituted. The Soliahs and Kilgore escaped the full measure of SLA training, for they took turns staying with us in Sacramento and returning to their usual haunts in the Bay Area. Kathy and Jim were known radicals and both of them had been questioned several times by the FBI about the whereabouts of the SLA. Kathy said she had told the pigs, "Get lost . . . see my lawyer . . . I've been instructed to say nothing to you at all." It was agreed that for the time being they would make sure they were seen in the Bay Area, and then would just fade away from the radical scene. An abrupt disappearance would bring the police after them.

Toward the end of October, with the weather beginning to change, the Harrises called for an "organizational meeting" of all the new recruits. It was the first of many that went on long and violently through the night, starting after dinner and fading into exhaustion around five or six in the morning. By this time, only two weeks after the Harrises' return, I had once again been reduced to a state of exhaustion, thoroughly dependent upon them as before. This was partially accomplished, I think, by forcing me to run four miles a day. Each day, accompanied by the Harrises, I would run through the streets of Sacramento and around the football-field track of a nearby high school. But at that first full meeting, both Teko and I learned to our surprise that these troops did not automatically follow the commands of their leader.

For this weekend meeting, along with the Soliahs and Jim Kilgore, came their good friends Michael Bortin and Seanna. Mike Bortin was perhaps only five feet nine but he seemed like a big man. He was muscular and tough-looking with wild red hair, two chipped front teeth, a tattoo of a large dragon on his arm, and a prison tattoo of a clenched fist on his broad chest. Seanna, a pretty student nurse with a pear-shaped figure and long, dark brown hair and blue eyes, was far more sane and down-to-earth. Her role seemed to be to try to curb Bortin's exuberance and keep him out of trouble. By way of introduction, one of the first stories Mike told us was of having tried to slit the throat of John McCone, the former Director of the CIA, who lived south of Los Angeles. He and Seanna had discovered McCone's unlisted telephone number and, posing as college newspaper reporters, had succeeded in setting up an interview in McCone's home. But at the last minute, she had refused to go through with the plan and they had never kept the appointment.

Mike had brought with him another prospect for the SLA, a girl introduced to us under the pseudonym of Bridget. Her parents were lifelong socialists and she herself a member of the Socialist Workers' Party, which, as I understood it, was to the left of the U. S. Communist Party.

Bridget sat quietly through that entire first organizational meeting, listening and hardly saying anything. Yet she was the only one of the Bay Area group who came up with a robbery plan. Bill Harris had bitterly castigated the Soliahs and Kilgore for not doing anything all summer long. They were supposed to have been financing the SLA while we hid but they had barely earned enough money on their painting jobs to support themselves. Nor did they have any other fund-raising plans. According to General Teko, they were "hopeless intellectuals" who would "spend all their time reading and studying, while doing nothing to help the people." The SLA, if it were to function smoothly, needed funds to buy supplies and weapons. Money was once again our most

pressing problem. Bridget said that the manager of the Berkeley bookstore in which she worked always walked the day's receipts across the
street to the bank and that he could easily be held up on his way to the
bank. After much discussion, the idea was turned down as being too
risky and too close to home: eventually the police would focus on her
as a radical and that might lead to us.

Kilgore pressed the need for the SLA to "legitimize" itself in the eyes
of the left-wing movement by steeping its actions more in the ideas of
acceptable left-wing philosophy. He insisted that all of us needed to
read more of the classical Marxist literature so that we could build
upon a solid base. Only in that way could we hope to attract a large
following. Kathy supported him in suggesting that we had to revitalize
our propaganda unit if we hoped to win the hearts of the people. Both
the Harrises ridiculed the idea of more study. They insisted we needed
more actions, which would advance the all-out war between the state
and the people.

Basic differences in revolutionary philosophy surfaced at that very
first meeting, but they came to a violent boil only after a month or so,
when the Soliahs, Kilgore, Seanna, and to an extent Mike Bortin discovered that they could not dissuade Teko and Yolanda one iota from
the SLA codes and declaration of war against the United States. Bill
Harris insisted that he as General Field Marshal was the political-mili-
tary leader of the group, that his word was law and must be obeyed:
only with a single leader could an army function.

A week or so later, Bridget sent word through Mike Bortin that she
wanted nothing more to do with the SLA. She considered us an
anarchistic group which had no viable plans for a real revolution nor
any idea of what kind of society would supplant the capitalist state if
and when it was overthrown. Bill Harris was furious. He insisted that
she come to the safehouse and say what she had to say herself. Bridget
refused to waste her time by attending another meeting and sent word
to Bill Harris that he was living in a dream world, that there was no
Symbionese Federation, no Symbionese War Council, no Symbionese
Nation. She condemned the SLA for having no discipline, no structure,
no organization, and suggested that we all ought to wake up and join
some other organization, like the Socialist Workers' Party, and try to
be of some use to an organized radical movement in the United States.
That was the last of Bridget in the SLA.

As our all-night meetings went on, there was a struggle to reach a meeting of the minds between the Harrises and the others on all sorts of important points. The others did not want to follow blindly a single leader, especially Bill Harris. They thought actions should be undertaken by majority vote. They wanted a more democratic structure for our group. Nor did they want our actions necessarily to be done under the emblem of the SLA. That would bring the most heat down upon us, they said, and besides, they did not feel beholden to the SLA or to its Codes of War.

Bill Harris threw temper tantrums. He shouted and screamed at the stupidity of the others, while Emily tried to reason with them, talking ad infinitum, weeping, cajoling, and pulling out all the stops. She succeeded in making them all feel guilty, saying over and over that Cinque and the others had given their *lives* for this cause and now they were trying to obliterate the proud name of the SLA. It seemed to win Kathy Soliah's allegiance each time, and whither Kathy went, so went her sister Josephine and her brother Steve. Seanna announced that she could not commit any violence, but she would be part of the propaganda unit and would, with Josephine Soliah's help, make posters and print communiqués for the group. But she stopped coming up to Sacramento for meetings. Mike Bortin remained gung ho, eager to turn the world around by any means of violence.

About a month after the Harrises arrived, Wendy Yoshimura returned to San Francisco from the East Coast with two friends. When Wendy came up to the safehouse in Sacramento her own verbal battle with Bill Harris lasted half the night. Their fights were partly personal and partly philosophical, but they did not see eye to eye on anything. No matter what our leader said, Wendy absolutely refused to live with us in Sacramento or, finally, to have anything more to do with us. She denied that she was a security risk. She would not admit to Teko that she had revealed anything about the SLA to her New Jersey friends. By the end of the night, however, she allowed that she might join in a combat operation of the SLA, but only if she approved of that particular action.

As all of these fights went on, Bill Harris became impossible to deal with. He would not listen to reason; he talked condescendingly to everyone; he criticized and found fault, and when anyone disagreed with him, he would fly into a screaming rage. While we sat on mattresses on the living-room floor, he would stomp about, snapping his fingers, and spew curses upon the recalcitrants. At times he became so violent he had to be physically restrained and warned to keep his voice down. He worried everyone. The walls were thin and we could not imagine what our neighbors in the next duplex would think, hearing the goings-on through the night. We did keep a radio blaring next to the common wall in the duplex to muffle our voices.

Our military-political leader also committed some very stupid blunders because of his inherently impulsive nature. On one shopping trip to a grocery store, he shoplifted a small paring knife worth sixty-nine cents, and then, back at the safehouse, he had the gall to take it out of his pocket and brag about it. Yolanda and I exchanged knowing glances of astonishment; our reactions were immediate and identical. But it was Yolanda who lashed out, saying, "What are you trying to do? Get us all burned, like you did to the rest of our people?"

Wham. She got a black eye for her outburst.

I got a black eye from him for having the audacity to argue over a single word in the SLA manuscript that we were editing. That too was insubordination and disrespect in the eyes of our leader.

About this time, Yolanda persuaded Teko to tell the others the truth about his shoplifting the bandolier at Mel's Sporting Goods. The lie he had told Kathy and Jim upon first meeting them became an embarrassment when Kathy mentioned explaining the events at Mel's to her friends in the Bay Area. So, at a criticism/self-criticism meeting one night, Teko admitted to them that while he had not stolen sweat socks from Mel's, he had indeed shoplifted a bandolier. They were all surprised, but Kathy was furious.

"Why did you lie to us?" she asked.

"I was too embarrassed to tell you the truth," said Teko. "I was afraid you wouldn't help us if I told you the truth."

"You're always saying we all are comrades and our relationship is based upon truth and then you go and tell us such a crummy lie," Kathy retorted. "We told our friends that you were railroaded and now you tell us the pigs told the truth."

Emily commented that that was why Teko was now telling them the truth, because he did not want to live a lie with his new comrades.

"But how do we know you won't lie to us again, if you would lie about that?" Kathy went on. "There's nothing so terrible about stealing a bandolier that you could not share with us. It's as if you didn't trust us . . . as if you did not respect us enough to share that with us.

"Did you steal anything else that we should know about?" she asked.

"No, never!" Teko swore. Yolanda and I again exchanged knowing glances.

It was a very emotional encounter on all sides. Teko wept while trying to explain shoplifting that bandolier and the memory of the horrible shoot-out and fire hung in the air as Emily began to cry and to plead for understanding. "We did what we thought was best at the time," she said. "What more can we tell you?"

Bill and Emily Harris got their way most of the time. They simply wore out their opposition. Beyond that, they did command a certain respect from the others because of the reputation of the SLA as the most celebrated revolutionaries of the seventies. Bill Harris *was* the most knowledgeable when it came to guns, shooting, robberies, and violence. It was he who came up with the first plan for an expropriation action acceptable to all the others.

Teko, who once worked in an Oakland post office, remembered that certain stores in Berkeley used the postal system for sending cash receipts to banks and that those cash receipts were picked up by regular mail trucks every day. With meticulous planning, surveillance, maps, and charts, he worked out an action for Jim Kilgore and Kathy and Steve Soliah. It was brilliant in its audacity. Jim followed a particular mail jeep as it picked up a package of money from a Berkeley pharmacy and continued on its regular route. Then one day, Kathy posed as a housewife trying to address and stamp a letter as she stood by a roadside mailbox. The jeep stopped and as the driver waited for her letter, she engaged him in conversation, distracting him. Then Steve rode by silently on a bicycle, dipped his hand into the open jeep, and pedaled away with the money parcel. The mailman went on about his duties, completely unaware of the theft. That action netted a little more than one thousand dollars.

The planning for breaking Bo and Osi out of the Alameda County Jail in downtown Oakland was much more intricate and involved. At the start, word was sent to them that we were back in the area by having Kathy visit them wearing a necklace dangling a clenched fist, fashioned from a fork. Bo and Osi would recognize it immediately as coming from Teko. Given to him by a prison inmate whom he used to visit, Teko wore it around his neck all the time as his personal symbol. It also was a signal between him and all SLA members that Teko was communicating with them through whoever wore that clenched fist. But

Bo was especially cautious and he double-checked: If we were who we said we were, then we would know the answers to these questions:

"At the New Year's Eve party, who was the girl with the sticks?

"Who was the blonde who came late?"

Only the original members of the SLA had been at that 1973 New Year's Eve party in the safehouse at Concord, which was after the Marcus Foster killing and before my kidnapping. Of course, the Harrises immediately knew the answers. The girl with the sticks was Fahizah, Nancy Ling Perry, who had been telling fortunes with her I Ching sticks. And the blonde who had arrived late was none other than Yolanda.

Once the line of communications was open, we sent word to each other indirectly through a chain of messengers. We would tell Kathy what to say to Sally, a friend of Joe Remiro's, who visited him frequently; she would either talk to Bo or Osi directly or ask that one of their lawyers pass on seemingly innocuous messages to them. Their answers would travel along the same chain.

To help us with our planning we received a sealed letter in longhand from Joe Remiro containing various diagrams of the interior of the jailhouse, which was on the tenth floor of the county court building, along with details on the number of guards, their shifts, their duties, and the jailhouse procedures and routine. Yolanda transcribed the notes in her own handwriting so that we could all study copies. The original letter was destroyed so that it could never be traced to Bo or Osi. In early December, Bill Harris set up surveillance on the exterior of the courthouse and particularly the alleyway and tunnel which led to an elevator connecting directly to the jail. Just about all of our aboveground comrades—Kathy, Josephine, Steve, Jim, Mike, and even Seanna—took turns logging the activity at the entrance to the jail. Messages were passed back and forth. The subject came up at every meeting. Emily waxed poetic in describing the benefits of having Osi and Bo back in the cell, praising their individual leadership abilities. She was obviously attracted to Russ Little and hardly tried to conceal her hope that we would all vote Joe Remiro, who had had battle experience in Vietnam, to be our new leader. Teko in turn did little to hide his jealousy of both men. After all, he was being threatened on the two most important aspects of his personality—his masculinity and his leadership.

Toward the end of January, a more pressing matter became a top priority: money. Finding that we were running short of funds once again, Bill Harris announced that we had better start looking for a suitable target for another expropriation. As our leader he pointed out all the tactical problems involved for a successful action. It was Emily who came back from one search with the target, a small savings and loan association bank located in a shopping center on the northern outskirts of the city. What recommended it above all other targets was the escape route it provided. Emily rubbed her hands with glee as she explained that right next to the bank was a narrow alleyway which led out of the shopping center into a purely residential neighborhood with quiet open streets. Once we got through that alleyway we would be scot-free. The getaway car would take off from there. Bill Harris objected but said he would check it out.

The Guild Savings and Loan Association, in Arden Plaza, earned another plus when it was discovered to be outside the city limits of Sacramento. That meant it was not covered by the city police, but fell within the jurisdiction of the county sheriff's office. There were no more than five deputy sheriffs on duty at any one time, trying to cover an immense area on the periphery of the city.

It was on February 4, the anniversary of my kidnapping, that Bill asked me to accompany him in checking out the Guild Bank. Though I was reluctant to leave the safehouse, I had never learned how to say no to General Teko.

On the way back, walking along a street, Teko noticed a car traveling slowly alongside of us with a woman driver peering out curiously. Then she drove on, but a few minutes later, Bill noticed the same car again. This time it pulled up to the curb and the woman asked us directions. Teko rattled off some phony directions to get rid of her. But she continued to look at me and then suddenly asked:

"You know, you look so much like Patty Hearst!"

I was stunned. Though I was in my SLA-approved disguise— freckles, red wig, and horrible blue spectacles—I had never believed it to be an effective camouflage.

"Oh, people tell her that all the time," replied Bill Harris with casual cheer in his voice. "This is my wife and she does look like that there Patty Hearst."

"Oh," said the woman before driving off.

"Shit!" said General Teko as we ran to the bus stop. I did not go out of the house, aside from our daily jogging, for a long, long time after that encounter.

We had no idea whether that woman would report her suspicions to the police but we did know that thousands of people had called their local police and the FBI with stories of having seen me. Young women driving vans were being stopped and asked for identification almost every day all over the country by zealous policemen. I carried identification with me at all times in the name of Sue Louise Gold. Kathy had sent me a birth certificate in that name while I had been in Pennsylvania. False identifications were easy to come by in the United States. All one needed to do was to look up death certificates for persons of the same age and sex and then request by mail a birth certificate for that person. While in Sacramento, Emily and I enrolled in the local city college so that we would be issued student identification. I told them at the college that I was married, and I received an identification card in the name of Sue Louise Hendricks, with a color photograph of myself as a smiling, freckled, red-haired, married student. Now I had two identifications. Teko had suggested that I use Anderson as my married name so that my initials would read S.L.A., but Yolanda nixed that idea. "Too smart-assed," she declared.

Even so, I tried to stay safely inside the house, curled up on the beat-up old couch, reading one of Jim Kilgore's books. Most of them were textbooks in economics or politics or sociology and of an extreme left-wing persuasion. But they were educational and I preferred burying myself in a book to coping with Bill Harris' outrageous orders for my self-improvement. I had paid my dues in the SLA. I knew my combat drills. I could do shoulder rolls and crouches. I could fire any of the weapons (in practice) from any of the accepted positions. In fact, I was the only one of the three who had fired the weapons at all. I could field-strip, put together, and load every gun in our arsenal. So General Teko turned most of his attention to his new recruits.

In our private meetings, while the others were away in Berkeley or Oakland, Teko and Yolanda would tell me that we had to humor our new comrades with their book reading, political discussions, and all their theorizing. It was a complete waste of time, Teko said, but soon they would come around to our way of thinking. "We're the revolutionary cadre of the group and we've got to show them the way," Teko said confidently. "All the others right now are just a bunch of intellectual amateurs." I was sure that Jim Kilgore and the others thought that they were influencing the thinking of the Harrises. What they did not realize was that neither Teko nor Yolanda was ever really listening to them. The Harrises were fanatics: only they knew what was right. In the evenings, when our day's work was done, Teko and Yolanda would huddle together in a corner hatching their secret plots. Sometimes they would bounce an idea off me: What did I think about getting a dog so that our safehouse would appear less suspicious? What about bombing the federal probation office in Sacramento? Did I think we could pull off the execution of California's attorney general, Evelle Younger? What about kidnapping his wife, Mildred?

When they were not scheming, they usually watched one of the countless television cop shows that were shown on all of the networks at the time. Teko's favorite was *S.W.A.T.* "You can learn a lot about the pig's tactics by watching these programs," our leader declared. As for me, I tried to stay out of the cross fire. During our meetings, I remained silent most of the time. When called upon for an opinion, I always agreed with my SLA comrades. That is all the newcomers ever heard from me.

My twenty-first birthday passed with little notice. Emily made up a greeting card of sorts which said, "Happy Birthday, Comrade. You really should try harder to struggle with me. After all, we are sisters." Bill handed it to me unceremoniously, as though such bourgeois sentiment was beneath his contempt. "This is from Yolanda," he remarked with a sneer, "so read it, 'cause it's the way she feels." As for himself, he made no other mention of the occasion, nor did he even sign the card.

On the condescending premise that the others were hopelessly unable to take any action themselves, Teko and Yolanda alone laid out the detailed plans for holding up the Guild Savings and Loan. They drew the diagrams, listed the cars and weapons needed, and outlined the actions to be taken by each of the participants. Teko sent word to Wendy Yoshimura of the planned robbery and she replied through Mike Bortin that she wanted nothing to do with it; she would not even attend any meetings. All of the others were sent out to inspect the bank and its environs. Then the fights began. Teko unmercifully berated Wendy in her absence for her lack of commitment. But Seanna stuck up for her, saying Wendy had every right to decide for herself what she would do and would not do, and all the others agreed. Seanna wanted no part in the robbery either.

For the Guild heist, Teko told me that he intended to use only the others. "They need to get their feet wet, get some real action behind them," he said. "It'll build up their confidence and get them absolutely committed to the cause." The original plan was for Bortin and Kilgore to go into the bank and commit the actual robbery. Steve would drive the getaway car. Bill Harris would stand outside the bank with his submachine gun for backup. Kathy would drive the switch car. But Mike and Jim objected to the excess of people involved who would be likely to draw attention to the robbery. They did not want Bill standing outside the bank with a submachine gun. They did not want anyone manning a switch car. They wanted as few people involved as possible. But Kathy wanted a piece of the action. So it was agreed that she would be posted somewhere nearby as an observer, timing the arrival of the police in order to give her something to do. Teko would play no part in the robbery. Steve would park the switch car himself. The four participants practiced every part of the action over and over again, under the critical eye of Bill Harris.

Our two captured comrades were not forgotten during the preparations for the Guild action. The plan to free Bo and Osi from what Teko called "the pigsty" was worked out in conjunction with their own wishes. The break would be timed for late one afternoon on a weekend when only four guards were on duty at the jail. It would occur in the guards' room, next to the conference room, when Bo and Osi were led out of their cells to meet their trial attorney. At a prearranged time, they would attack the one or two guards in the room with sharpened pencils, overpower the guards, and use their keys to open the weapons locker. At the same time, we would drive a rented car into the courthouse tunnel beneath the building and one of us, probably Bill Harris, would make his way up the special elevator which led to the jail. He would be carrying a submachine gun and would aid the two prisoners in their escape. They would leave the courthouse in the car waiting for them in the tunnel and then switch to another car two blocks away. Sally would drive the switch car and the two of them would go deep underground somewhere in the Bay Area, until we felt it safe for them to join us in Sacramento.

Sally was invited up to Sacramento to discuss the arrangements. Mike Bortin, who did not want to be recognized by her, wore a ski mask throughout the entire meeting. Sally thought the escape plan was crazy. It would never work, she said, because the courthouse and the jail facilities were built like a fortress, with locked doors which could be opened only by some special buzzers in a control center. She wanted to free the two men as much as we did, for it was obvious that she had become romantically involved with Russ Little during her jailhouse visits. Emily tried hard to convince Sally that the plan would work because it was so bold and unexpected.

The jailbreak planning went on for more than a month, and Kathy met with Sally regularly at least once a week in San Francisco in order to coordinate the plans. Jim Kilgore, however, hated the idea and led the opposition to it. The whole plan was "crazy," he insisted. "If anyone goes up in that elevator, it's tantamount to committing suicide," he argued. "At best, you'd be only saving the sheriff's department the gasoline it takes to get us to jail." Mike Bortin became very emotional in his argument that we *had* to go ahead, no matter what the risk, because we had been leading Bo and Osi on for so long to expect our help. "It's wrong to play these mind games with people in prison. . . . It's really cruel letting them think that you are going to help them, when, in fact, all you are willing to do is to talk."

As time went on, however, the others wavered as they came to see the high risk involved. Mike Bortin too finally decided that it was hopeless. "I know that jail and they'll never get out. . . . Maybe they got one chance in a million." The others were not very happy about the prospect of all the shooting that would be involved. Each in turn said no. Bill and Emily ended up pleading with the others. "It is our duty to try to free our comrades in prison," Emily cried. "They are two of the founding members of the SLA and we need them. We owe it to them to blast our way in, to help them . . ."

But Jim Kilgore spoke for all the others when he flatly corrected her: "No, it's not *our* duty to sacrifice ourselves to free them."

It was another of those all-night, emotion-packed meetings. Nothing Teko could say nor all of Emily's tearful pleading could sway the others. They argued the logistics of the escape plan down to the finest detail and it became evident that if even one element in the plan went wrong—if Bo and Osi failed to overpower the guards or if they could not open the gun locker or if they could not open the doors or if we failed to get up the elevator to help them—then the whole plan would fail, jeopardizing us all.

General Teko made the final decision: We did not have enough firepower for the plan to succeed; it would be foolhardy to go through with a plan that we thought would fail; we would not go through with it and we would so inform our two comrades.

Bo and Osi were not pleased. The message we got back from them was: "Fuck you."

CHAPTER

SIXTEEN

FROM THE SIDELINES, I watched our four top recruits go through their paces in preparation for the Guild Savings and Loan Association operation. Kathy and Jim and then Steve and Mike Bortin had moved in with us on W Street for the final week of planning and rehearsals. Like a tough, veteran drill sergeant, Teko instructed them on every detail and made them do everything repeatedly. He held a stopwatch to their movements and he quizzed them on what they were supposed to know. Each one had to memorize the approach and escape routes so that if one of them got shot, another could take over the driving. Teko would call out a street name on the escape route and they would have to recite from memory the remainder of the route from that point.

Treating them like raw recruits, Teko barked out so many orders that the scene conjured up for me the vision of Cinque instructing us on the Hibernia Bank robbery. Teko was in his element. And they took it, accepting the discipline he imposed for the promise of success, though they never left off arguing with the Harrises about political theory and the organization of our revolutionary cell. At the same time they recognized what they believed was his superior experience in revolutionary action.

In the practice sessions, Steven Soliah was letter perfect. He had memorized the route to and from the bank, the name of every street on the route and the intersection where he would park the rented switch car prior to the robbery. In an ancient Chevy Impala he had bought under a fictitious name in San Francisco, he would drive Mike and Jim to the front of the bank and then drive out of Arden Plaza, around the block, and park at the outside end of the alley alongside the bank, waiting. Kathy would drive to Arden Plaza in another car and observe the action from some inconspicuous spot outside the bank.

Mike and Jim would enter the bank together. Mike, wearing a white safari jacket and a white cap to cover his bushy red hair and hide the upper portion of his face, would walk to the rear of the bank. There he would lift up a half-mask, hanging from his neck, to cover the lower portion of his face. At that point, Jim, standing at the door, would lift a green scarf over his face and from beneath a shiny, almost iridescent blue-gray raincoat he would take out his sawed-off shotgun and announce the robbery. While Jim covered the customers and the bank manager, Mike would point his fearsome .45-caliber revolver at the two tellers and empty the tellers' drawers of all the cash and money orders he could find. Jim would time the action on his wristwatch and announce when it was time to leave. At that point, no matter what Mike was doing, he would break off the action and the two men would leave the bank, run down the alley, get into Steve's car, and they would be off.

Kathy was eager to get on with her first real action and she bristled as Bill and Emily Harris repeatedly tried to refine the perfection of every detail. "We're not stupid, you know, we do have minds of our own," she told Teko. But he demanded that all of them be certain of their positions and roles in the drama. Mike Bortin performed like an old pro, calm and cool, and sure of himself. He kept reassuring our leader that he need have no worry about them at all. Jim Kilgore, however, could not hide his nervousness. As he practiced thrusting his shotgun at people and ordering them to the floor, his voice went up two octaves and squeaked. It was all he could do to keep his voice under control. But he knew what he had to do and his actions were clear and certain.

Teko had wanted Jim to be the leader of this operation, but Jim had declined, saying he was perfectly happy to have Mike Bortin in command. Kathy and Steve agreed, outvoting Teko. I sensed that Bill Harris feared the competition of Mike Bortin for the leadership of our cell. Mike Bortin would have been every bit as capable in action as Bill Harris. And, according to SLA standards, Mike, as an ex-convict, had been a more oppressed white man than Bill Harris and therefore was a more appropriate SLA leader. But Mike did not care about that, nor did he ever seem to aspire to that leadership, although he did sometimes taunt Teko with this idea. Teko continually reassured all of them. This assault was their first and was designed, as much as for anything else, to build up their confidence in taking action.

The four of them had become my "friends." They were the ones who had come up to our safehouse every week, while the others had fallen by the wayside. Seanna had stayed away of her own accord, while Josephine had slipped into the background. She had a steady job, working in a bank in San Francisco, and had shown little interest or aptitude in the revolutionary discussions and plans going on in our safehouse. But Mike and Jim and sometimes Kathy and Steve had come to my aid when Teko or Yolanda was mistreating me. I was ordered about, told to clean up after them, and generally treated like dirt. While I no longer believed everything they told me, I did not have the strength to fight back. It was useless to argue, so I tried to avoid confrontations.

More than once Jim or Mike had stopped Teko from hitting me for some alleged disrespect to his leadership. Mike Bortin had won my gratitude when he took me out one day for my required four-mile run and decided, as an experienced runner himself, that the four miles were doing me more harm than good. I had a near-asthma attack at the end of the run. He told Teko that there was too much stress associated with my running. When Teko announced that anyone could run any number of miles with sufficient practice, Mike challenged him to run ten miles with him. Teko backed down and I never went jogging with the Harrises again.

For security reasons, the four participants left the safehouse the day before the robbery. They spent the night of February 24 in a motel near McKinley Park, so our neighbors would notice no unusual activity on the morning of the action. The operation went smoothly, but not quite as precisely as Teko had rehearsed it.

When they reached the bank that morning, Jim stopped Mike from going in, saying there were too many people around. He became nervous over one man who, he thought, had looked at them oddly. When they entered the bank a minute or so later, there was one teller, not the expected two, and only one customer. Jim fumbled about, having trouble getting the shotgun out from under his raincoat. Mike decided on the spot that the teller might become upset upon seeing the shotgun, so he walked up to her and said, "Good morning." Then, when Jim got the shotgun out in the open and announced the robbery, Mike grabbed the teller by the arm and led her from one cash drawer to another. But only one had any money in it. The others were empty. Mike forced her to open the safe and he grabbed two canvas sacks of coins and a stack of money orders. He dropped all of this into a stuff bag. Meanwhile, Jim told the sole woman customer to get down on the floor and not to look up. In his fumbling with the shotgun he dropped a shell on the floor and forgot to cover his face with his scarf. It took no more than a minute and a half to do all they could and beat a hasty retreat down the alleyway.

In the getaway car, they shed their outer clothes and stuffed them into a large straw shopping bag, along with their guns and the two bags of coins. The paper money and money orders they put into a small plastic shopping bag. Within two minutes they were at the switch car, a green and white compact. Steve dropped them at McKinley Park and drove away to dump the switch car. At the park, Emily and I greeted Jim and Mike. We talked for a minute or so and then parted. They left the two bags with us. I got the heavy straw bag with the weapons, coins, and clothes. Emily held fast to the paper money. We took a bus back home, two young women who could not be connected with the bank robbery on the outskirts of the city.

While the robbery was going on, Kathy watched from a nearby store, pretending to look at greeting cards. She checked her watch and waited for the sheriff's deputies to arrive. Five full minutes elapsed before the first sheriff's car, with siren screeching, pulled up in front of the bank. Kathy walked over to become part of the crowd gathered around the bank, then went into a nearby coffee shop. From there she phoned a service station and asked sweetly that her 1956 Chevy be towed in for repairs. She gave the location and description of the car, saying that the car's registration was in the glove compartment. Lingering over a cup of coffee, she saw the bank manager enter. "They cleaned us out. . . . They took everything." Kathy smiled in anticipation. She drove back to the safehouse via the escape route in time to see the tow truck taking the Chevy safely away.

There was joy in the old W Street safehouse that day. Emily counted the bills while the others added up the rolled coins. The total came to something over $3,700, most of it in fresh twenty-dollar bills. The blank money orders were put aside and we held on to them for a while. We tried to work out the logistics of stealing an imprinting machine from a store in our neighborhood, but decided that the serial numbers on the blank money orders made them a liability rather than an asset and Teko destroyed them.

Mike Bortin could not control his high spirits over how easy the whole caper had been. All four of them sparkled with excitement. Mike and Jim said it had been unnecessary to take a shotgun into that small bank. But Teko insisted that he had been right. The firepower of a shotgun was necessary to instill fear in the enemy, even if the gun were not used. He then turned his wrath upon Kathy for insubordination and taking unnecessary risks by going into the coffee shop. However, the four of them were so happy that they did not seem too concerned over our leader's displeasure. His attempts at instilling military discipline in the group were far from successful. They left later that day so that they could be seen going about their usual business in the San Francisco area.

The next day, the Sacramento *Bee* reported the robbery in a brief, straight story. The SLA involvement was not suspected. Bill and Emily, following the classified ads, wasted no time in going out shopping for a used car, which we badly needed for our own use when the others were away. They returned with a 1966 Chevrolet station wagon, bought from a private party for four hundred dollars. Bill then took it out to get a forty-dollar paint job and we had a car of our own, still registered to the previous owner, of course.

One week after the Guild Bank robbery, on March 1, the SLA exploded in the news media across the country: Bo and Osi had made an attempted jailbreak . . . and failed. What amazed me was not that they failed but how close they had come to succeeding. Every bit as fanatical as the Harrises, they had gone through with the original plan, but without our help. At 5 P.M. on March 1, when his attorney came to see Russ Little, Little asked for a joint conference with Joe Remiro and the lawyer unwittingly passed on the request. With the two prisoners, the two guards, and the attorney in the room and the door open to the guards' room, Little suddenly leaped up and stabbed one of the deputies in the throat with a sharpened lead pencil. At the same moment, Remiro tried to knock out the other guard with one punch. To the lawyer's horror, they all landed in a tangle on the floor, Bo struggling to snatch the ring of keys away from the guard. He actually got the keys, and by trial and error found the right one with which to open the cabinet containing loaded carbines and shotguns. But by this time, the other two guards on duty had rushed to the room. Remiro was tackled at the gun locker and subdued just as he was opening it. He was only seconds away from the weapons and probable success.

In the ensuing investigation, the police found the supposed getaway car, with the keys under the driver's seat, parked just outside the tunnel leading to the jail elevator. We could not figure out who had left that car there for Bo and Osi. Kathy tried to make contact with Sally, but she refused to see her or any of us. Our attempts to communicate with Bo and Osi came to naught. Word came back from them that we had failed them and that they never wanted to talk to us again. Teko and Yolanda went over the possibilities of freeing Bo and Osi when they were transferred from the Alameda County Jail to Sacramento for trial. That turned out to be impossible. Our two comrades were transported in a bulletproof armored van within a convoy of police cars, escorted by a police helicopter overhead.

As time wore on, Teko and Yolanda became exasperated and despairing of me as a worthy comrade and revolutionary. They denigrated me in just about every conceivable way, saying that all my faults stemmed from my inability to shuck off my wealthy, bourgeois background. I sank lower and lower into my own personal misery. My hair was growing longer, but it was also falling out in great clumps. My nails were chewed down beyond my fingertips. I chain-smoked all day long and fidgeted in nervous anxiety. I spent most of each day reading books, ostensibly to further my educational base as a revolutionary but really just to stay out of trouble with the Harrises. The more Teko berated me as worthless, the more I feared him and his impetuous temper.

If Teko ever reached the conclusion that I had become more of a burden than an asset to the SLA, he would kill me and dispose of my body where it would never be found or identified. He would rationalize his need to do away with me as a necessity for the success of the revolution. I feared him acutely, as I had Cinque. I began to have recurring nightmares. In each of them I saw myself killing Teko and Yolanda, their blood flowing all around me. In some of the dreams, I would shoot them; in others I would stab them. But there was always a great deal of violence involved. I'd wake up trembling with fright, afraid to sleep. At one group meeting which went on far into the night, I hallucinated while wide awake. I saw Mike Bortin light up a cigarette and then, so casually, touch the lighted match to one leg of his trousers. He went up in flames ever so gracefully, sitting there with a smile on his face as the bright orange flames melded with the red of his hair. But then I snapped back to reality; Mike was there unharmed, quietly smoking a cigarette.

Mike Bortin's conflicts with Teko increased in intensity after the Guild robbery. While Mike did not care very much about who won the incessant arguments over radical political theory, he was not about to allow anyone to run his personal life. Teko ordered Mike, for instance, to stop seeing Seanna on the grounds that if she was not with us, she was against us and could not be trusted. Mike refused. "I trust her and I'll see her any damn time I choose. It's my life and it's got nothing to do with you or the group."

Teko called a special meeting one night to bring the group's pressure down upon Mike for his continuing use of LSD. Drugs were forbidden in the SLA, Teko insisted. Mike replied, "Bullshit." It went on for hours, this "struggling it out," but Mike Bortin said that none of them knew what they were talking about when it came to LSD. One of his greatest pleasures in life, he said, was dropping acid and running ten or fifteen miles on the beach under its influence. That was a trip he would not give up for anyone or anything. Before the night was over they were screaming at each other and Teko pulled rank to forbid the taking of any drugs by anyone while in the SLA safehouse. Mike compromised. He would not "trip" while with us, but while away from us, he was his own man and would do whatever he damn well pleased. Months later, in reminiscing about that battle, Mike confided to me that that very night, while the argument was going on, he was under the influence of LSD.

The most violent and repeated struggle within the group was over the role of the leader. The others all protested the dictatorial orders of the SLA General Field Marshal; Teko insisted it was the only way the group could accomplish anything. Yolanda slyly insinuated herself into the melee, saying that our group *did* need one leader in command and that Teko was now our leader and should be obeyed, but the group could, if it so desired, choose another leader, at least temporarily, until we found a black or some other Third World person to lead us.

This would send Teko into an orbit of vituperative fury. He recognized his wife's not so secret wish to be chosen as the leader. So did all the others, for Yolanda was not as subtle as she thought.

"Why should we be led by someone just because he's black?" Jim Kilgore demanded.

"Because only they know what direction the struggle should take. As whites, we might misinterpret things. Only a black or a Third World person can understand the plight of the oppressed masses and the SLA Codes of War say that a black person shall lead us," Emily explained.

"You're both crazy," Mike Bortin would tell the Harrises. "I know those dudes from prison and what makes you think any of them would want to be fronted off as the leader of this group?"

Kathy tried to point out that the Harrises' position was reverse racism and there was nothing inherently wrong in the revolution being led by dedicated whites. "We're all white and there's nothing we can do to deny it." But the Harrises ignored this reasoning. "You'll see," Emily would say. "When we find the right black comrade to join us, you'll all see that it's right that he be our leader."

At the end of one long struggle between Teko and Jim Kilgore, Teko conceded for the first time that perhaps it had been a mistake for the SLA to assassinate Marcus Foster. I was amazed. But he would admit only that it was a political mistake to kill a black man. He refused to budge in his argument that the Oakland Superintendent of Schools had been an undercover CIA agent, which all the others branded as ridiculous. Jim Kilgore always threw up the Marcus Foster killing as a prime example of the SLA's lack of political sophistication and revolutionary know-how.

Two weeks after Bo and Osi's attempted jailbreak, Wendy Yoshimura's photograph was blazoned on the front page of the San Francisco newspapers. We learned that the FBI was hot on our trail once again. They had discovered the Pennsylvania farmhouse and apparently had found fingerprints linking Wendy with us and with the farmhouse. In a near-hysterical panic, Wendy fled to us, asking to be taken in. Teko welcomed her with open arms.

The FBI could claim no great powers of investigation in this discovery. From the news reports, we gleaned that we had been given away by, of all people, Walter Scott. Apparently Jack's parents had bragged to Walter of their involvement with us and then Walter had wandered into the Scranton, Pennsylvania, police station to tell all. Walter, furious that his brother had involved their parents, told the police and FBI everything he knew, which was pretty much all of the story of our summer. In the farmhouse, the FBI had found a fingerprint of Wendy's and one of Bill Harris'. Jack and Micki Scott denied everything, refused to cooperate with the FBI, eluded them, and disappeared. What saved us was that none of the Scotts knew where we were now.

Late one night at about this time, however, we did have a terrible scare. I was awakened in the front bedroom by the sound of police radios outside the house. Powerful searchlights and the lights from the cars illuminated the scene. There seemed to be police all around us. I cried out, "They've surrounded the house." Everyone went into full combat readiness, crouching in the front bedroom and watching the police outside. Then we heard one of them say, "Let's get another picture and get the hell out of here."

We realized that the police had responded to a mugging not more than twenty feet from our front door. We had slept as a man was being ambushed from the vacant lot alongside our house and beaten to death.

The next morning a patrolman came to the door making inquiries. Emily, wearing her gray wig and a housedress, opened the door and said in a quavering sweet voice, "Hello, Officer. . . . No, I don't know anything about it. . . . I saw the lights and heard the commotion; I was frightened, but I saw the police were there, so I knew everything was under control, and I went back to sleep."

"Thank you very much, ma'am," said the officer, and walked away from the three most wanted fugitives in the nation.

Yolanda was concerned about the lack of security which had allowed us to sleep through this murder, but Teko thought nothing could stop us now. By this time we were looking for other places to rent in the area. Kathy, Steve, Jim, and Mike had agreed to move up to Sacramento on a permanent basis so that we could operate as a combat team and, as Teko put it, "escalate the struggle." For comfort as well as for security, we decided that we needed three separate safehouses. In this way we could not be trapped in one place. Mike Bortin, who had to report to his parole officer twice a month, decided to divide his time between the Bay Area and Sacramento, promising to be available for any and all actions we planned.

Living arrangements were worked out only after the usual struggles.

The very last thing I wanted was to be with Bill or Emily Harris; I was barely on speaking terms with them. But Emily insisted. Overriding my objections, Yolanda promised to reform, to change her ways, to try to build a sisterly relationship. She averred that she now accepted the criticisms of Bortin and Kilgore that she had been too hard on me, too critical. Emily wanted one more chance to struggle it out with me. That could best be accomplished by our living together, she said. She also wanted to live apart from Teko so that she could find herself as an individual, not bound to this man she had married when she was a young college student. I did not have a chance; I said I would try. So Emily and I moved into the one-and-a-half-room apartment she had rented on Capitol Avenue in downtown Sacramento. None of the women wanted to live with Bill Harris, so Jim Kilgore moved into an apartment on T Street with him and Mike Bortin stayed there when he came to Sacramento. This was the nicest of any of the safehouses and it was a typical Teko maneuver to claim the best house for himself. Kathy and Steve stayed on at the W Street house, and Wendy Yoshimura joined them there.

Living with Emily Harris in a studio apartment was a no-win situation. She never let up. Putting on her crying act, weeping those crocodile tears, she would plead with me, "I really want to be comradely with you, to share everything, to work together and end our competition . . . please, sister, try . . . try to meet me halfway. . . . I tell you things only for your own good. . . . I really want to struggle out our differences, so we could be good comrades . . . please . . . trust me . . ."

For about a week or ten days this went on, and then, angry and frustrated, she moved out and went to live in the W Street safehouse. Teko was furious, but Kathy moved in with me.

In the evening, sometimes we would go out for walks. I began to confide my true opinion of the Harrises. But although I grew closer to Kathy and the others, there was still an important dichotomy underlying all our relationships. The Harrises and I were the *known* revolutionaries, wanted by the police, forced to remain underground. They still were above suspicion, not on any "Wanted" posters, and free to walk about without that fear of being recognized and shot on sight.

Three separate safehouses gave us personal privacy that we had not enjoyed previously and new personal relationships began to flourish. Bill Harris frequently came to call on Kathy at our Capitol Avenue apartment and before very long he was smitten with her. For her, I think, it was an opportunity to get to know and to serve our leader in the line of duty and pleasure. She rarely discussed this with me, but I did know how Bill Harris operated on a personal level. It took a while, however, for him to discover that Emily meanwhile was sleeping with Steve Soliah every night at the W Street safehouse.

Teko was insane with jealousy. It was one thing to have an open marriage in theory and under certain circumstances, but it was an entirely different matter to him when a subordinate moved in on the general's wife. He stormed over to the W Street safehouse. Steve Soliah told me later he thought Teko meant to kill him. He displayed the gun he kept in his waistband as he accused Kathy's younger brother. "How dare you take up with my wife?" Teko screamed at him. "What the hell do you think you're doing . . . ?"

Under this tirade, Steve backed off immediately. "Forget it, man. . . . I didn't think you cared. . . . It was just one of those things. . . . You know, nothing serious. . . . If you're so hot about it, all right, I'll stop, call it all off. Hell, it's not worth it to fight about. You can have her. I won't have anything more to do with her. . . . Okay?"

Now Emily was mad at both of the men for, as she put it, treating her in such a sexist way and discussing her as though she were a mere possession. But, as Steve told Kathy and me, he certainly did not want to tangle with a crazy man and risk his life over Emily. It simply did not mean that much, if anything, to him.

Steve Soliah was an easygoing young man who lived for the day's pleasures and excitements. He did not have his sister Kathy's commitment to the SLA or to the revolution. I had long thought he was merely trying to live up to her expectations. But after his run-in with Teko, Steve turned to me and I welcomed his attention. Neither of us had anyone else within our group, although he had a steady girlfriend with whom he lived when he was in Berkeley. We were comfortable being together, talking easily about things other than the SLA, the revolution, freeing the oppressed, or changing the world. He had no problem with his own ego and did not try to dominate, teach, or make demands. For me, that alone won my gratitude.

Emily, in turn, could not conceal her jealousy and displeasure as Bill Harris softened his tone whenever talking to Kathy or gave other signs of his infatuation. Jim Kilgore was better at hiding his feelings on the matter. Before long, Jim was visiting the W Street house to see Emily through the night, but their relationship did not last long. Jim turned to Wendy, who was more subdued, less demanding than Emily, and much more Jim's type of personality. Sex among these comrades was far more private than it had been in the previous SLA cell. For one thing, it was not carried on in the open nor did anyone preach Maoist philosophy as the underpinning of their sexual needs. In fact, it was not an integral part of the group's togetherness; it was something personal and apart from our other activities.

In the meantime, the revolution was keeping us very busy. We tried a few other scams, most recommended by Kathy and Jim. For instance, Kathy and Emily took free trial sessions at various health spas, as advertised in the Sacramento newspapers, so that they could filch wallets, money, and credit cards from pocketbooks left unattended in the locker rooms. Jim and Steve frequented a city tennis court, where they lifted wallets from tennis bags or jackets left lying about. The money involved was not much, but the credit cards and driver's-license identifications and checkbooks allowed us at least one major buying spree on each separate identity, without too much risk of being detected. We bought clothes, food, and even ammunition, using the stolen identifications and checks.

General Teko ordered that each member of the group be offensively armed. Using money from the Guild bank robbery, Steve treated himself to a beautiful nine-millimeter Browning automatic, made in Belgium, which he bought from a friend. Teko eyed that handgun covetously and dropped hints as to how much he would appreciate such a gift. Steve was not about to part with it. This prompted Teko to visit a Sacramento County gun show. In a regular gun shop, one would have to register the gun, prove one's identity, and then wait two weeks for state approval of the purchase. But at a gun show, booths were set up to sell all kinds of guns over the counter with few or no questions asked. Teko and Jim Kilgore returned from the outing with wild stories of "right-wingers and Nazis" selling guns, Iron Crosses, and Nazi mementos to anyone. Teko thought it was a fine way for revolutionaries to arm themselves—buying their weapons from right-wingers. Teko returned home with a batch of brand-new handguns, a Colt revolver for himself, a snub-nosed Smith & Wesson .38 for Wendy and one for me. Jim bought a Colt for himself and a .38 S&W for Kathy. Mike Bortin finally got his own preferred weapon, a .357

Magnum, "just like the highway patrol uses." Teko ordered everyone to go about armed at all times and, when they looked askance at his order, he amended it, saying they could use their own judgment on being armed or not when out on their own. But he insisted that neither Emily, I, nor himself, as members of the SLA, should be taken alive. If accosted by the pigs, we were to shoot it out. Therefore, if any of the others were out with us, they too must be armed and prepared "to shoot it out." I did carry my .38 in a purse and Steve toted his Browning in a leather camera case he dangled nonchalantly from a strap on his wrist. Even Wendy kept hers in her purse.

With all our new weapons, Teko decided to correct a situation which had long been bothering him. I was the only one who had ever fired the submachine gun and it was driving him crazy, partly with jealousy and partly because his army was so ill-trained. We found a secluded wooded area, in a place called Grass Valley, where Teko acted as our instructor in target practice with live ammunition. I could handle my .38 and a .22 rifle but I was thrown at first by a sawed-off shotgun. The idea was to fire the weapon continuously while swinging one's body in an arc so that three or possibly four separate targets, which were spaced out on trees, would be hit. I tried repeatedly but I could not hit a single target. I was unnerved by Teko standing over me like a drill sergeant. He became so angry he berated me ferociously until I fell to the ground, sobbing uncontrollably.

"You're not hitting the targets because you don't want to hit them, that's why," he shrieked at me.

"You make me too nervous," I managed.

"Too fuckin' bad if you don't like your instructor."

During our return to the safehouse, I discovered that I had become "deaf." According to Teko, revolutionaries did not wear earplugs when shooting, and the hour or more that we all spent in the woods had left me with a steady ringing in my ears. No other sounds came through. For the next day, my comrades wrote notes to me. When my hearing did return, Teko pronounced me a hopeless weakling who would never become a good revolutionary.

The others had their faults too; they were careless. One evening, hearing the click of an empty revolver, I looked up from my reading to see Jim Kilgore playing with his .38, nonchalantly pulling the trigger as he pointed the gun at various people. When he pointed the gun at me, I could see a single bullet in the cylinder advancing to the firing position.

"Stop!" I cried out. "There's a bullet in the cylinder. . . . Don't pull that trigger again!"

"It's not loaded," he said indignantly. "I checked it."

"Don't. I can see the bullet."

Teko took the weapon out of his hands, spun the cylinder, and the single bullet fell into the palm of his hand.

On another occasion, Mike Bortin snapped a bullet into the chamber of Steve's new Browning, and then took out the ammunition clip from the handle. As his finger went to the trigger, everybody in the room realized what he had done so absentmindedly and rose up shouting a chorus of "Put that gun down! You chambered a round! Don't touch the trigger!" In fact, he became so flustered that Steve had to take the gun away from him and unload it. Teko was positively gleeful at catching Mike in such a blunder and needled him about it ever afterward.

While all this was going on, the group was intensely involved in arguing over the future course of our activities, struggling over organization and structure and our revolutionary relationships, living day to day, and planning our next bank robbery. From the week following the Guild bank robbery, Teko had begun mapping out our next action for a larger and better financially endowed bank. In the two months which followed, the group must have surveyed, diagrammed, and considered as targets fifteen different banks in and around Sacramento County, but always beyond the jurisdiction of the city police.

The new target was the Crocker National Bank branch in Carmichael, a suburb about seven miles beyond the Sacramento city limits. As with the Guild Savings and Loan, the escape route was a prime consideration. The bank's rear parking lot abutted the parking area of a large shopping center, separated from it by a Cyclone wire fence, which already had a pedestrian passage hole in it. Our getaway car could take off from the shopping center while the responding sheriff's deputies would come to the scene on a completely different street. Emily, who cased the bank, worried some about two angled mirrors in the bank, fearing that there might be cameras behind the mirrors. We finally decided that there were no cameras in the bank, and no security guard.

This would be a full-scale SLA combat operation, Teko declared, involving all eight of us. It would require four vehicles, two of them stolen for assault cars and two rented for use as switch cars. Four soldiers would go into the bank, cover the employees and customers, scoop up the money, and depart within a minute and a half. Two others, heavily armed, would provide backup directly across the street from the bank entrance. Two more would drive the switch cars, instead of leaving them parked along the escape route, as we had done before.

Then the arguments started. Kilgore, Bortin, and the Soliahs, having gained more confidence after the Guild bank escapade than Teko had envisioned, now formed a united front in arguing with the Harrises. They refused to make this an SLA action and thereby alert the police to our whereabouts. Emily argued long and hard that the SLA was a name to be proud of and that this bank robbery, as opposed to the other, would be seen as a show of strength for the SLA.

"But we're not strong," Kathy retorted. "Why pretend that we are?"

The greatest internal battle, however, was fought over who would lead the action in the Crocker Bank. Mike Bortin was favored by everyone else, but Emily not only insisted that it was sexist to exclude women but demanded that she be the leader of the assault team. She had planned the action and was senior to everyone else, except Teko, and he had chosen, as the self-proclaimed best shot, to stand guard outside the bank with his automatic weapon. That argument was not resolved until the final stages of planning the robbery. By that time, Steve Soliah, who had gone to San Jose with Kathy to find an apartment to be used as a safehouse after the robbery, was involved in a car crash that sent him to the hospital with five broken ribs. When he returned to Sacramento, he was still in considerable pain, hardly able to walk. So Steve was put on backup with Teko as a driver.

Teko, shouting down all objections, made the final decision: Bortin, Kilgore, Kathy Soliah, and Emily would go into the bank to commit the actual holdup. The two women would be disguised as men and they would speak in low voices or not at all so that the people in the bank would mistake them for men. Emily won command of the team inside the bank. I would drive the switch car for the four who had been inside the bank; Wendy would drive the switch car for the backup team. Wendy and I tried to beg off, but Teko said we were needed, and that was that. We both were grateful that our part in the action would be so small.

In preparation for hiding the stolen cars, Emily went out to rent two private residential garages, which she found through the classified ads. In one of these rentals, she committed a serious error in judgment, which we did not discover until afterward. While negotiating for a garage at Twenty-eighth and D streets, the landlord had asked her many questions, and Emily told him that she was using the garage to store her brother's Thunderbird. Then she asked if there was an electrical outlet in the garage so that he could work on his car. She never thought of the possibility that other car thieves in the area had been using private garages to strip stolen autos. Her question instantly alerted the landlord.

About two weeks before the robbery, Jim Kilgore found a good car for the getaway. At a party in Oakland, given by a friend of Seanna, Jim stole the purse of a woman who had told him she owned a neat Pontiac Firebird parked outside. He extracted her car keys and drove directly to Sacramento and put the car away in the Twenty-eighth Street garage. A few days later he came upon a Mustang parked in downtown Sacramento with the keys in the ignition and the motor running. He hopped in and drove that car directly to the other garage.

Meanwhile, as the date for the robbery drew near, Teko drilled us on all aspects of our upcoming combat action. Emily, of course, drilled with the most determination and on at least two occasions, as she practiced thrusting her shotgun forward in a menacing movement, while shouting in her best basso voice, "Move . . . get down on the floor . . . move," the shotgun dry-fired with a loud click.

"You better not take that gun," Kilgore told her. "It's got a hair trigger and besides, you don't need a shotgun inside a bank."

"Mind your own damn business," she told him. "I know how to handle this weapon. . . . You just pay attention to what you're supposed to do." She went on practicing, crouching and thrusting her shotgun forward. The shotgun dry-fired again. Kilgore complained about the excess firepower we were taking inside that bank. "It's too much and we don't need it," said Jim. "We didn't need it for the Guild action and we don't need it here. Besides, most bank robbers don't even use weapons. . . . They just pass notes. All these guns and people will draw attention to us and it could even connect it with the SLA."

But Teko would not listen. "Oh, shut up . . . you don't know what you're talking about." Teko and Yolanda knew what was best for all of us. They were in command and there was no arguing with them. Bortin, Kilgore, Kathy, and Emily went through their paces. Wendy and I recited our memorized escape routes.

The night before the action, a Sunday, Jim, Kathy, and Steve drove to the University of California campus in Davis, about a half hour away from Sacramento, and lifted California license plates from cars parked in the students' parking lot. Replacing them with stolen plates, they affixed the new plates to our own stolen Firebird and Mustang and hoped that no one would notice the switch right away. We figured that by the time the stolen plates were reported to the police, our holdup would be completed. Later that night we all met at the T Street apartment and Teko gave everyone final marching orders. He was in overall command, but in the bank Yolanda would be in charge, he said, and her orders were to be obeyed instantly. When she announced that it was time to leave, they would all leave together. Everyone knew what to do. When we left that apartment, we were combat-ready.

Early the next morning, we swung into action. Kathy and I walked from our apartment to nearby Winn Park, where we were to be picked up. Kathy wore a green turtleneck sweater, trousers, and hiking boots and in a straw bag she carried a carbine and Steve's pistol. I wore slacks and a pink flowered blouse, a brown wig, and sunglasses. Right on schedule Jim Kilgore drove up in a rented white VW van, with Mike Bortin and Emily inside. We drove to the garage at Twenty-eighth and D streets. All was quiet. Our assault team transferred to the Firebird and I followed them to a brief rendezvous with our backup team at McKinley Park. Teko and Steve were there in the blue-gray Mustang, and Wendy, disguised as a white woman wearing a blond wig and enormous sunglasses, was driving a rented Pinto. Then we made our way to the Crocker National Bank. Wendy peeled off along the route and I stopped the van near a funeral parlor a few blocks away. And waited. Nervously.

Five minutes later, not more, the Firebird roared down the street past me. Surprised at their speed, I pulled out and followed. From the rearview mirror I could see no one pursuing us. We went a short way and the assault car pulled up to the curb on a deserted street and parked. I stopped alongside and Emily, Kathy, Mike, and Jim piled into the van and I took off. "Go, go, go!" Mike shouted at me. "Go!" But I ignored him and continued along at the legal speed limit. After a while, Mike said with a sort of sneer, "Well, should we count the money?"

"No, not now," replied Emily.

"Well, you're in command, so why don't you give us some orders?" Mike asked sarcastically.

"Okay, get the disguises off. Put them in the bags. And the guns too," said Emily in a subdued tone of voice. "Pearl, don't drive too fast. We don't want to be stopped for speeding." She was wearing a heavy coat, light khaki pants, a green-billed cap, sunglasses, and a mustache. The others had ski masks and wigs.

Kathy mumbled something which I could barely hear, but it sounded as if someone in the bank had been shot, a woman. I heard Emily say, "Maybe she'll live . . ."

"No," said Jim somberly. "I saw her."

"What're you all talking about?" I asked, not wanting to believe what I had heard. Kathy then said that a woman in the bank had been shot.

"Who shot her?" I asked.

"I did," snapped Emily. "Let's not talk about it. Keep your eye on the road and your mind on the driving."

Everyone seemed nervous and worried, except Emily. She was remarkably calm, reminding all of us we were to go to our own safehouses and stay there until contacted by Teko.

I carefully parallel-parked the van near Winn Park and Kathy and I got out and walked to our Capitol Avenue apartment. Emily accompanied Bortin and Kilgore to ditch the getaway car and then to T Street, where they could count the money taken from the bank. No one was bragging about the success of this venture. Once we were home Kathy explained that at the very start of the holdup Emily had shot a woman customer. Mike had stood on a teller's counter, waving his gun at everyone, and she had emptied out all of the tellers' drawers, including the two at the drive-in window. Thanks to her sister, Josephine, who worked at Wells Fargo in San Francisco, Kathy knew enough to force the tellers to open the cash drawers with their own special keys. She had not missed a drawer. But she did not know why the woman had been shot. That had happened at the front of the bank, right after they had entered. In fact, she said, Mike had held the door open for that woman and her two companions, who preceded them into the bank.

About an hour later, Kilgore arrived unexpectedly. He was very upset. He said he was shocked when Emily had fired her shotgun. He had been right behind the woman, on his way to his assigned position, and if he had been a bit out of alignment with her, he would have caught some of the buckshot. "She was nervous and incompetent, for

God's sake," Jim exclaimed. He then drew us a diagram showing the positions of everyone, demonstrating that Emily should never have pulled the trigger while he was in the line of fire. Besides, he said, he could see no reason why she had fired in the first place. He told us she had been very nervous before going into the bank and could not resist playing with her watch. Jim told us that our assault car had been found almost immediately and had been traced to the garage on Twenty-eighth and D streets. It turned out, as we discovered later, that the Sacramento police had been alerted when Emily rented the garage and aroused the suspicions of the landlord. The police had set a loose surveillance on the garage, hoping to catch some car thieves in the act of stripping a stolen car. If the police had kept a closer watch, we would have been arrested when we came to pick up the car before the bank robbery.

Kathy and I were both upset and I ventured that the Harrises were insane. We had no radio or television in the apartment and still did not know if the woman who had been shot had survived. About twenty or thirty minutes after Kilgore had left, Emily arrived to report her version of the bank robbery.

"How's the woman who was shot?" Kathy asked immediately.

"Oh, she's dead," replied Emily airily, "but it really doesn't matter. She was a bourgeois pig anyway. Her husband is a doctor. He was at the hospital where they brought her."

The woman, who was forty-two and the mother of four teenage children, was Mrs. Myrna Lee Opshal and she had gone to the bank that Monday morning to deposit the collection of the Carmichael Seventh-Day Adventist Church. When she was brought to the hospital, her husband, a surgeon, had been summoned to the emergency room, and there on the table, he had found his wife dead.

Emily told us her shotgun had gone off by accident. She had told the woman to get down on the floor but the woman had not moved fast enough to suit Emily. So Emily thrust the shotgun forward to threaten her, and the gun had gone off. "The safety must have slipped off," Emily remarked, adding that she thought the safety was on all the time. She had been as surprised as anyone at the sound of the blast. The woman did not fall, which Emily found "interesting"; she stood there for an instant and then "melted to the floor."

Emily told us what she had heard on the radio about the robbery and commented that it would get pretty hot for us around here, now that the pigs would be investigating a killing. With that, she gaily waltzed out the door.

Kathy and I were still upset and reeling from Emily's visit when Bill Harris arrived. He told us that the robbery had netted "something over $15,000," but that we were now all involved in a gas chamber offense because the woman in the bank had been killed in the commission of a felony. He was full of his old bravado, acting the part of the hard-bitten revolutionary, tougher than all the other urban guerrillas.

"This is the murder round," he bragged as he extracted from his pocket the brass base of a shotgun shell, its plastic jacket cut away. He joked about it, but no one laughed. "If it hadn't been for good ol' Myrna, one of our comrades would be dead now. Good old Myrna, she took all the buckshot."

But everything was under control, our leader proclaimed. The police did not have a single clue that the SLA had been involved. "It's a good thing Eva didn't eject this shell, because then the pigs would have it for evidence," he told us, adding that now he was going to bury the remains of the shotgun shell in McKinley Park where no one would ever find it. He returned about forty-five minutes later in high spirits.

Teko told us he wanted us to come to T Street that night for a meeting to critique the bank action. Everyone showed up and no one was happy. Bortin was beside himself with anger. The whole thing was fucked up, said Bortin while the Harrises were out of the room. He thought Bill Harris was stupid to have put Emily in charge and to let her carry a shotgun, which he and Jim Kilgore had been against. "She fucked up with that gun in practice and she fucked up during the robbery!" If he had run the action, he said, the bank robbery would have been a simple stickup and no one would have been hurt.

At the meeting, we went over everyone's role and there was plenty of criticism to go around. Bill Harris, by way of defending his mate, accused Steve Soliah of being thoroughly incompetent. According to Teko, Steve had sat in the car with his cap pulled down over his eyes and without a round in his shotgun. "What would you have done if the pigs had come? What would you have done?" he screamed. Teko, disguised with "white-out" liquid (used to correct typing errors) in his beard to make it look gray, had covered the bank's entrance with an automatic rifle, giving Steve the signal to pull out only when he saw the assault team leave the bank.

Teko diagnosed the entire action as "a sloppy job," saying that now every one of us would be wanted for murder and that would mean the gas chamber. "Revolutionaries always die eventually in one way or another," he said. He made a long speech, using a lot of revolutionary rhetoric, the implication of which was that killing the woman was only a small occurrence in the overall picture. The others were not reassured. They were appalled at the sudden turn of events, as though they never really had imagined that anyone might get hurt in one of their escapades. I loathed the Harrises more than ever before. They were violent, evil, unpredictable, incompetent people. I felt ill.

The only agreement that came out of that tempestuous meeting was that we had all better lie low, take no action for a while, and stay close to our safehouses. Most of the news reports in the days that followed described our bank holdup as an "SLA-style robbery." We knew then that we had to get out of Sacramento. The state capital was now much too hot for us and we had made it that way ourselves.

CHAPTER

SEVENTEEN

JIM KILGORE, KATHY SOLIAH, and I were the first to leave Sacramento, relieved to get away from there and from the Harrises. The death of Myrna Lee Opshal hung over us all, and our final two weeks in Sacramento was a period of intense anxiety. Fear permeated everything we said or did.

We stuck close to our safehouses, only occasionally slinking along the streets, armed, to visit one another or to hold meetings. Everyone kept up with the news reports on the police investigation. The hunt was on. The getaway car and the backup Mustang had been found. The garage in which we had kept the Firebird was in the news. Although the police did not publicly link the crime to the SLA, some reports in the media had commented upon the "SLA-style robbery" because of the heavy artillery we had brought into that bank.

The Berkeley group began to feel the strain of being hunted and they did not like it one bit. The romance of being a revolutionary lost its glitter for them—at least for the time being. It was in that atmosphere that we all came to the conclusion that we would do far better by moving our base of operations to the familiar Bay Area.

Kathy and Jim were given the assignment of finding a house for us in San Francisco, and I went with them because everyone thought I would be too "hot" in Sacramento. Unsaid but understood was that I did not want to have to move in with the Harrises again. But before we left, Teko got a brilliant idea: We should all take one day off as a sort of farewell to Sacramento. There was a Cinco de Mayo celebration in the Mexican community of the city, marking the expulsion of the French from Mexico. Teko thought it fitting that we join in the celebration of that successful revolution. I begged to be allowed to remain in the safehouse. But Teko would hear none of that and the others thought it would be good for me to get out among people for a change. That was the last thing I wanted to do. We went to this street festival disguised and armed. I stayed close to Kathy, Jim, and Steve throughout the revelry, worrying that if I were recognized, it would come to a shoot-out in the midst of a crowd. I felt like the only sober person at a raucous New Year's Eve Party.

Kathy drove me to Oakland to visit one of her many political friends, Bonnie Jean Wilder. A short, cheerful, and bouncy young woman, she greeted me like a long-lost sister. Bonnie had proved her friendship and loyalty when she had lent her car to Kathy for "something illegal"—picking me up upon my arrival at the Sacramento bus depot. Bonnie's studio apartment, above a hamburger joint and a record shop, was located on Park Boulevard across the street from Oakland High School, and though it was often noisy there, the apartment was cozy and comfortable. We told Bonnie stories of our exploits and plans, but avoided mentioning the Crocker Bank robbery.

After a few days closed up in the apartment, Jim, Kathy, and Bonnie urged me to go out with them for dinner. "You need to get out and get around," Kathy said with much concern. "It's no wonder you're depressed being shut up and closed off from the world for so long." Against my better judgment, I joined them for dinner one night in a small Mexican restaurant nearby, where the food was good and inexpensive. Naturally, the restaurant was crowded. Despite Kathy and Bonnie's assurances in the apartment that my red wig and freckles made me unrecognizable, I was so nervous I couldn't eat. Another fear came to mind. "What if one of your friends walks in, Kathy?" I asked. "How do you explain me?" After some discussion on this point, we all agreed: eating out was not such a good idea for me, after all. I did not leave Bonnie's apartment after that night.

Under assumed names, Kathy and Jim easily rented an apartment on Geneva Avenue at the southern border of San Francisco. The others then came from Sacramento, hauling all our weapons, files, clothing, and paraphernalia in two U-Haul trailers. We spread out in the city in what we envisioned as a network of different safehouses. The plan was to slip unobtrusively into the city, spread out, and size up the security situation in San Francisco. Future guerrilla actions would be planned and then, once secure, our presence would be felt. Only the Harrises and I needed to stay under cover; the others could still go about their everyday lives. In fact, one of our first decisions was that everyone who could would get a steady job—not so much for the money but as a cover for our contemplated combat actions. Mike, Jim, and Steve went back into their house-painting business and lived with friends away from our safehouse. Kathy and Bonnie moved from Oakland to an apartment on Lyon Street in San Francisco's Haight-Ashbury District and were joined there shortly afterward by Josephine. Under an assumed name, Kathy found a job as a waitress at the Sir Francis Drake Hotel. Josephine went back to work at Wells Fargo. Wendy moved in with friends living in a Victorian flat in the Mission District. With no place else to go because the others were all out working during the day, I had to move in with my old SLA comrades on Geneva Avenue. One flight up from a dry-cleaning establishment, the apartment was large, with a living room, dining room, kitchen, and two bedrooms. It was ample enough to serve as the group's headquarters. When our criticism/self-criticism meetings went late into the night, comrades could choose to sleep over or make their way home, as they pleased.

Teko and I declared a truce of sorts in our personal animosity—we simply did not talk to one another. He branded my behavior as childish and insubordinate and declared that he would have nothing more to do with me. I had no such luck with Yolanda. I stopped talking to her, but that did not prevent her from expressing her sisterly concern for me. Her absolute faith that she *knew* what was right for me drove me wild. She also thought she knew what was right for Teko. They shouted and screamed at each other over trifles.

Teko loved to give orders. It came to him as naturally as breathing. He simply could not understand or abide people not obeying, particularly his own wife. It was only a matter of time before Yolanda announced that she no longer wanted to live with him: one of them would have to move out. So Teko moved to another safehouse we had rented on Irvington Street just over the border in Daly City, about a mile south of the Geneva Avenue apartment. Steve Soliah, who had been living with his girlfriend across the bay, moved in with him in order to be closer to the group and to the action. Jim then moved in with Yolanda and me so that no wanted members of the group would be living alone. That arrangement lasted little more than a week. Steve moved out, telling the rest of us that he could not stand living with Teko. For a while our leader lived in exile in Daly City. Finally, Jim Kilgore, who had a soft heart, said it just was not right for Bill Harris to be living alone, because he was wanted, so he volunteered to move into the Irvington Street apartment, and Steve moved in with Emily and me in his stead. Actually, that arrangement worked fairly well for the Harrises. Yolanda began to visit Teko and spend the night with him and then he began calling upon her at Geneva Avenue. It was in line with their theory of independent living arrangements, with no marital strings attached, and it became obvious to the rest of us that the Harrises got along much better when they were not on each other's nerves all day long.

Hours were spent in meetings struggling out the proper attitudes on sex in a revolutionary cell. Yolanda took the lead. She demanded the right for the women to form our own study group, even our own combat unit, so that we could work out the "true role of women in the revolution." We needed to spend time among ourselves, without men, she said, so that we could learn from one another. When Teko protested that such an arrangement would inevitably lead to a loss of the women's military skills, Yolanda shocked me. She argued that *I* had studied all of Teko's weapons manuals and could teach the others as well as he could. Teko was furious at the idea that I, or anyone, could supplant him as the group's weapons expert. But he did not object to a women's study group on the issue of the feminist's role in the revolution. However, I did conduct gun classes for the women and Teko continued to resent it. But he had force-fed me instructions for so long that I had come to know all about every single weapon in the SLA arsenal. For once, I was not the know-nothing idiot in the group; for once, I was contributing something; for once, I was receiving praise from my sisters. They, in turn, declared that it was a real victory for the revolution to receive instruction from another woman.

In our women's study sessions, held at the Lyon Street house, we all agreed that we had concentrated so much on military skills that we had neglected our personal relationships, specifically, the issue of feminism. The men had assumed the leadership roles in the cell, acting as our instructors, because they possessed the military expertise we didn't. But we had developed our own combat skills, were equal to the men in that respect, and therefore we no longer needed them to lead the revolution.

Our feminist discussions led to a consensus that we ought to work out our own policy statement on women's place in the revolution. We read and reread Shulamith Firestone's *The Dialectic of Sex* and other radical literature, such as the Weather Underground's *Prairie Fire,* and extracted for our own purposes what these books reported on feminism in the revolutionary movement. What we tried to analyze was the reason why in all of the revolutionary movements, including our own, the men were the leaders and instructors and the women were the followers and students. A further "honor" was bestowed upon me by my sisters when they elected me to assimilate the voluminous notes taken during our meetings and to write our position paper on the SLA version of radical feminism.

Our position on equality in sexual relationships held that sex should be the end result of natural friendships. A woman should not feel inhibited about sleeping with a woman she liked any more than she would sleeping with a man for whom she cared. Such inhibitions were a result of our cultural conditioning. Natural feelings of homosexuality had been suppressed by our bourgeois upbringing. But now we enlightened women should work toward developing these natural feelings.

Teko read our position paper and agreed wholeheartedly with these feminist conclusions. The bourgeois environment had made sexists and racists of us all, he declared. No matter how hard he struggled against it, he said, he recognized himself as still a sexist and a racist because of his middle-class, white upbringing. In the natural course of events it stood to reason that partners of the same sex would know how to satisfy one another better than would two of the opposite sex. But, he added, it was sad but true that he had always been uptight about having sex with a man. In theory he approved of it, but he could never bring himself to do it. Cinque had been his closest comrade. "I could sleep in the same bed with him or in the same sleeping bag, with my arms around him, but I just could not bring myself to make love with him." His voice had a wistful, faraway quality to it. As he confided his feelings of guilt Yolanda began to weep. "Oh, I miss Cin so much."

It was during this period that Emily and Kathy, who were the leaders in our feminist study group, discussed their relationship as lovers. It was only natural, I suppose, that they should test out their own theories. Kathy and Emily's relationship did not stop Bill Harris from sleeping with each of them from time to time and upon occasion with both of them at the same time. However, that did not last for very long and they sent him packing, back to the Irvington Street apartment.

Just about everyone was busy with his or her own activities, including regular jobs during the day and attending our long planning meetings at night. Bonnie Wilder was working toward becoming our own undercover agent in the Oakland Police Department. To Teko's delight, Bonnie had passed the civil service examination to become a police cadet. In time, however, she failed to pass the strenuous physical requirements for a policewoman. But she did join our propaganda unit, which included Seanna and Josephine Soliah, to make posters and write leaflets.

Seanna was in and out of our cell, depending upon whether she would quit in disgust or Teko would expel her. The final break came during a meeting on future actions.

Teko declared that our first full action in San Francisco should be the killing of policemen. That was what Cinque had envisioned as the spark to set the revolution aflame. Policemen were our enemy and they should be our prime target. When we killed enough, the police would retaliate by cracking down on the oppressed and the masses would rise up to fight them.

"That's a terrible, disgusting idea," Seanna shouted back at him. "One of the women I work with at the hospital is married to a police officer and he's a very nice person. You can't shoot policemen at random. You wouldn't know who you were killing. He might be a nice person, even if he is a pig."

"You don't know what you're talking about," retorted Teko. "A pig is a pig."

"We're revolutionaries and we should be killing pigs and pigs' families," Emily added.

"You people are sick," said Seanna in disgust. "I want no part of this. Fuck you all."

She got up to leave and Teko screamed out, "You're through; we want no part of you; you're expelled. Just keep your damn mouth shut and you won't get hurt."

But she had left.

The discussions and arguments continued that night and for the next few nights over whether or not to launch an attack upon the San Francisco police and, if so, just how to go about doing it. Mike Bortin finally blew up in exasperation: "I think all this talk is stupid and a fucking waste of time. All you people do is talk. I think you're all a bunch of sissies. If you want to kill some pigs, then you ought to go out and do it. Just walk up to a pig in uniform, put a gun to his head, and pull the trigger. Hell, it's no big deal."

"We've got to plan it," Teko argued. "If you're such a hotshot, you come up with a plan and we'll do it."

"Okay," said Mike. "I'll come up with a plan for you."

A few nights later, he took Jim Kilgore and me for a drive and told us he had found a small coffee shop called Miz Brown's, in the Richmond District of the city, where policemen on patrol often stopped for a cup of coffee. "I'll case the joint and you draw the fucking maps that our leader likes so much and we'll show them how to do it." We circled the block a few times, noticed the parked patrol cars, and I diagrammed the location of the coffee shop and the surrounding streets. Mike parked and walked into the restaurant.

A few minutes later, he returned, exultant. "I could have done it right then. There were four pigs in there and I could have blown them away. . . . We could have gone back and reported to the group that we already did it, while they were sitting on their asses." I calmed him down, saying I would draw up the escape routes and the location of the restaurant and then leave it to the whole group to decide. In return, Mike made me promise to conceal my maps and say nothing until he proposed the plan at a meeting.

At the next meeting, Mike laid it all out for them, saying it would take no more than one or two men with submachine guns to "off" everyone in the restaurant.

The plan was turned down. The Harrises thought it far too risky and dangerous. The others were against a shoot-out with trained professionals. They favored surreptitious bombings where we could hit and run.

Bortin complained that the real trouble with our cell was that we could never bring ourselves to do anything spontaneously. "Why do you have to have meetings about *everything?*" he demanded. "We haven't done anything in more than a month [since leaving Sacramento]. You people analyze everything to death. That's your trouble. If you want to kill pigs, go out and kill them. If you want to bomb a target, bomb it. But for Christ's sake, stop analyzing every little thing."

Mike stalked out and we wondered if he would ever return. Three nights later he showed up at Geneva Street and plunked down a package of Flo-Gel plastic explosives, a type used in construction work. "Here's your explosives. All you need now is some blasting caps and you're ready to go."

But Teko, angry that Bortin had acted on his own, chastised him for committing a breach of security, because the explosives, purchased through a friend in Oregon, might be traced back to us.

Mike threw his arms in the air and declared that he had had it with Teko and with all of us.

"Good riddance," said our leader, after Mike had left.

Mike's point was not lost, however, upon Jim Kilgore and Kathy Soliah. In his absence, they began to press for some action—bombings.

As tension and dissatisfaction mounted in the group, the only relief I felt was on my outings with Steve Soliah. We usually headed north to Sonoma County, the wine country of California. We went hiking in the woods, practiced target shooting, and found a secluded pond where we could go swimming. It was on one of these outings at the end of June that Steve and I ran into trouble.

We were driving on Route 1, the highway that runs along the Pacific coast, when we stopped at Gray Whale Cove in San Mateo County, about twenty miles south of San Francisco. A cliff there led down to a secluded beach, and we decided to climb down and go for a stroll. The descent was challenging, though not particularly difficult. But on our way back up, about two hundred feet from the top, we found ourselves on sliding sand and rocks. We heard shouts and looked up into the faces of three deputy sheriffs calling down to us. We tried to tell them to go away, leave us alone, that we would do just fine without them. But they passed down a rescue line and ordered me to tie it around my waist and climb back up. We did not have much choice. Steve was hauled up first. All during the rescue, one deputy was taking photographs of us for their in-house magazine. When I reached the top of the cliff, Steve threw his arms around me and hugged me, as if in relief, and whispered into my ear, "Ann Silva," the alias I should use for the police report.

The deputies, who we both noticed were not armed, gave us a mild bawling out, saying that the area was dangerous and posted, and that we had committed a misdemeanor of some sort, but they would let us go with a warning. We had to identify ourselves, so we gave them the names Victor and Ann Silva, said we were married, and recited a phony address. Steve kept fingering his camera case. Inside it he carried his fourteen-shot Browning. But the deputies were friendly and unsuspicious. Back in the car, Steve was confident and boastful. If they had tried to arrest us, he told me, he would have had no choice but to off them. I shuddered at the thought.

From the constant media reports, I assumed that everybody was looking for me. With all the photographs appearing in the press, I was certain that anyone taking a close look would be able to recognize me. Teko and Yolanda suffered no such pangs. They went jogging every morning and went out for frequent excursions. Emily could alter her appearance simply with a change of wig and attire. Bill had trimmed his beard to a goatee, cut his hair very short, wore a windbreaker, and posed, according to his whim and his gait, as either a homosexual or a tough undercover cop. Several times I went with them to drive-in movies, feeling relatively secure in the dark anonymity of our car. Only once—and I swore never again—did I accompany them to a regular movie theater.

There was an anti-Vietnam War documentary film that the Harrises particularly wanted me to see. It was a highly emotional depiction of the bloody war and of the suffering of the Vietnamese people. Bill Harris, unable to control his emotions in the packed movie house, became thoroughly involved and, naturally, he rooted for the Vietcong. All during the film, he made comments on the action in a loud, clear voice:

"Eat lead, pigs!"

"Fuckin' pigs!"

"Kiss my ass! Don't tell 'em nothing!"

Each time, Emily or I would grasp his arm or poke him in order to bring him back to the reality of the movie theater.

I sank lower and lower in my seat, expecting something to happen. How long could one go on shouting obscenities in a movie theater before attracting the attention of the management? Would Teko shoot his way out of the theater? People turned in their seats to glare at him, but no one came to stop him. When the lights came up and we walked out, people stared at us.

Later they wanted me to go with them to see *Citizen Kane,* the Orson Welles movie based upon the life of my grandfather. I absolutely refused.

"Ask me to do anything, ask me to rob a bank with you," I pleaded. "But don't ask me to go to a movie theater and get arrested watching *Citizen Kane.*"

They returned safely from that movie too and chided me. "You should've gone," said Teko. "It was real cool, a good movie, and we had no trouble at all."

After all the plotting and disputes, the target chosen for the first action in San Francisco showed little imagination. It was the police station in the Mission District. That station was one of the most popular targets of all radical groups going back to the 1960's. The police there had come under attack so often it had been reinforced with bulletproof windows, heavily locked doors, and a wall around it for protection. On the other hand, as a target well recognized by radical groups, each time it was hit, the strike was immediately listed as a blow for our side.

With no hope of penetrating that fortress, the plan as proposed by Jim Kilgore was to bomb a police car right in front of the station. When the car blew up right in front of their eyes, the police and the community would know that the revolutionary struggle was still going on. For good measure, our group decided to blow up a squad car outside of the Taraval police station at precisely the same time as the other explosion.

Wendy Yoshimura was our explosives expert, owing to her experiences with Willie Brandt and his Revolutionary Army. She recommended the simplest and safest type of bomb: gunpowder inside a two-inch pipe, attached by wires to a battery for the spark and an alarm clock as a timing device. The components were easily purchased in separate stores. We all got busy devising and testing them in the Geneva Avenue safehouse. A new esprit de corps set in among us. At last we had something "revolutionary" to do. A common purpose served to bind us together and to let us forget, at least for a while, our personal conflicts.

One afternoon, Teko and Emily tested the detonation devices, setting fire to small amounts of the gunpowder. They worked together for the better part of an afternoon on a discarded mattress in the little courtyard behind our apartment where the garbage pails were kept. Just before sunset, when the others were involved with the bomb in the living room and Wendy and I were chatting in the kitchen, I looked out of

the window and saw billows of smoke drifting by. At first I thought it
was just heavy summer fog, but then I knew.

I called to them from the kitchen. "There's a fire in the backyard!"
Just at that moment there was a pounding on the door. "Fire Department, let us in."

Because the dry-cleaning shop downstairs was closed and locked for
the night, the firemen dragged their hoses up the front stairs, through
our apartment, and down the back stairs to the little backyard. I heard
the commotion of their shouts and stamping feet through the door of
the bathroom, where I was hiding. Sparks from the Harris' pyrotech-
nical experiments in the backyard had started the mattress smoldering
and it had finally burst into flames. When it was extinguished, I could
hear Emily telling the firemen: "There were some boys out there this
afternoon, smoking cigarettes. . . . I'll be a lot more careful next
time." When they left, everyone thought it was hilarious—firemen in
our safehouse, while the whole FBI was out searching the streets of
America for us.

Two nights later, I was frantic that we were liable to be blown up.
All of them were gathered around the kitchen table, arguing about
the best way to put the bomb together, leaning over the apparatus
and being quite careless. I refused to stay in the kitchen with them, and
after I had left, most of the others joined me in the living room. Teko
insisted upon assembling the bomb anyway, while Wendy watched.

He poured gunpowder into the center of the pipe and then packed in
toilet paper, connecting the explosives by toaster wire to a battery. An
alarm clock and an on/off safety switch completed the circuit. He then
taped the bomb securely into a cardboard box and put the whole thing
into a plastic carrying bag. He made two of them, one for the Mission
police station and one for the Taraval station. Wendy questioned the
use of the toilet paper, saying that Willie had never packed his bombs
that way. But Teko would not listen.

Josephine and I were chosen to place the Mission District bomb and
Wendy and Kathy to plant the one on Taraval Street. The alarm clocks
were synchronized for late on the night of August 7. Jo and I drove to
the Mission District in our white Ford Galaxie, stopping at a service
station phone booth for a call from Kathy, saying she and Wendy were
near the Taraval District station and ready to go. We drove past the
station house, turned, and parked on a side street, the car facing away

from the target for a quick getaway. As planned, Josephine set the bomb's timer for twenty minutes and then she and I walked around the corner and back to the station house. While I strolled slowly on the opposite sidewalk, Jo crossed the street and, faster than I imagined possible, she bent down and slid the bomb bag under a police car. It was our only moment of danger, and it went by so fast that if I had blinked I would have missed seeing the placing of the bomb. We returned to the car and drove back to our safehouse.

Steve walked into the Geneva Avenue apartment about an hour and a half later. He had positioned himself in a nearby restaurant and had gone through several beers and a pizza before he finally decided that something had gone wrong. He even drove by the station, just in case he had somehow missed the explosion, and saw the bomb still under the police car.

Teko threw one of his worst temper tantrums, demanding to know why the bomb failed. We all pointed the finger at him: he had made the bomb. He denied the fault was his. He screamed at all of us, his chin jutting out, his face turning crimson, accusing us of incompetency and insubordination.

Wendy, Kathy, and Jim Kilgore (who had been their backup) returned and reported woefully that Taraval Street had been so busy that it had been impossible to plant their bomb. Teko turned his wrath upon them, saying they had no guts. Jim retorted that even if they had planted it, the bomb would not have gone off anyway.

The next day there were brief reports in the media of a dud bomb found under a police car in the Mission District. It was humiliating, especially for Teko. If we had left a communiqué, it would have been even worse. Bortin came over that day and razzed Teko over the failure. "Great job . . . great action. . . . How'd you manage to get it done?" Kilgore joined in the heckling. "It was Teko's bomb, all his," said Kilgore, " 'cause he wouldn't let anybody else touch it." Teko maintained a stony silence, but I could see he was ready to explode. I pleaded with Mike not to start any more arguments. Teko and Jim had argued late the previous night over the design of our bombs, Teko insisting that it had to be packed tightly with explosives so that the compression would cause a big bang. Jim had argued that Teko's bombs were packed so tightly that there was not enough oxygen left within the loaded pipe for the spark to ignite the gunpowder.

Jim, Wendy, and I set to work the next day on devising the proper proportions of gunpowder, length of pipe and toaster wire, minus Teko's precious toilet paper. Then the three of us, accompanied by Steve, drove up to Sonoma County, where we had previously gone for shooting practice, and there we tested two smaller versions of our newly made bombs. The test bombs were only three inches long. We hooked them to long wires and hid behind some rocks about thirty feet away. We exploded two bombs and they went off with a mighty roar. The pile of small rocks we placed over the bombs was hurtled high in the sky. Success! Smiles all around. There was no doubt that the Kilgore bomb would destroy any police car. We went home feeling very superior to the Harrises.

The next target was the Emeryville police station. We wanted to call attention to the controversial police slaying in November 1973 of a fourteen-year-old black youth named Tyrone Guyton. It had become a cause célèbre in black and radical communities. Jim Kilgore, Kathy, Josephine, and Steve scouted the Emeryville police station, trying to pinpoint the private vehicles used by the two officers who had shot Tyrone Guyton. But their efforts were unsuccessful. We had to settle for a patrol car.

Emily Harris and Steve were chosen to place the bomb at Emeryville on August 13, one week after our try at the Mission District police station. Emily and Steve left Geneva Avenue in one car, with the bomb, and Kathy and Jim, in their best clothes, departed in another car for an observation post in a motel restaurant.

The Emeryville station was on the edge of San Francisco Bay, a pleasant area near several hotels and restaurants. Having scouted the area before, Steve and Emily strolled down a walkway at the water's edge, which was a sort of popular promenade in the complex, below the street on which the Emeryville police station was located. When they came abreast of the target car, Steve scrambled up an ivy-covered slope, emerging on the side of the police car away from the station house. Within seconds, he had slipped the bomb under the car and retreated down the slope. He and Emily walked away arm in arm.

Before they got back to Geneva Avenue, we heard the news on television. "We interrupt this program to bring you a special bulletin . . ." the announcer said, and Teko jumped with joy. Jim and Kathy heard the explosion from the restaurant where they sat, joined the crowd that gathered to see the wreckage, and then returned to the safehouse in a glow of excitement. Kathy's eyes sparkled as she described the destruction caused by the pipe bomb. The police car had been completely demolished; the policemen there were running about in confusion.

"We did that action in memory of Cinque," Emily intoned. "We really did it for him."

The writing of the communiqué on this bombing gave us far more trouble than the action itself. The radical rhetoric, written by committee, with Bill Harris in the forefront:

> The explosion at the Emeryville Station of Fascist Pig Representation is a warning to the rabid dogs who murder our children in cold blood. Remember, pigs: every time you strap on your gun, the next bullet may be speeding towards your head, the next bomb may be under the seat of your car. The people and the people's armed forces will no longer quietly submit to the occupation of our communities and we will never forget the execution of Tyrone Guyton . . .
> THERE ARE TO BE FUNERALS? LET THERE BE FUNERALS ON BOTH SIDES.
> LONG LIVE THE GUERRILLA.
> DEATH TO THE FASCIST INSECT THAT PREYS UPON THE LIFE OF THE PEOPLE.

The Harrises had agreed not to sign the communiqué with the name of the SLA. There was no sense in telling the FBI we were in the Bay Area. But Emily had insisted on the SLA motto: "Death to the fascist insect that preys upon the life of the people." It would remind the people of the SLA, she said, and the police would never know whether the message came from the SLA or from a sympathetic group. We agreed to sign the communiqué with the name of the "New World Liberation Front." The NWLF was a radical group that had been specializing in bombing capitalist establishments, such as banks and corporate headquarters, in the Bay Area over the past six months. We did not know who was in the group but they had declared open season on "the establishment," inviting like-minded people to use the NWLF name in any of their own actions.*

---

* The central core of the NWLF, as in many such groups, consisted of only two individuals. From 1974 to 1978 they were responsible for almost one hundred bombings in the San Francisco Bay Area. Their revolutionary activities came to an abrupt end in September 1979, when the NWLF's accused leader was arrested and charged with the ax murder of his comrade/lover.

Our own cell thought this had been a very clever move, for the police then could never be sure just which group was responsible for which bombings. For the Emeryville action, Teko wanted to sign our communiqué as the Jonathan Jackson Unit of the NWLF, in honor of the seventeen-year-old brother of George Jackson, who was killed after he and others had stormed a Marin County courtroom and taken the judge and others hostage.

But Jim Kilgore and the others resisted. While they respected the memory of Jonathan Jackson, his name would indicate that our unit was made up of black revolutionaries and, Jim argued, that would be misleading: we were not a black unit, we were white. Bill and Emily Harris were furious. They were back at the old argument over black or white leadership of the revolution. In the end, they compromised. Our communiqué was signed by the "Jonathan Jackson/Sam Melville Unit of the New World Liberation Front." Sam Melville was a white radical and a bomber who had been killed in the Attica prison rebellion of 1971. The split name given to our unit indicated the deep split among us.

We began planning our third and much larger bombing action. This one grew out of a mishmash of old ideas and discarded suggestions. The target this time was the Marin County Civic Center, an unusual Frank Lloyd Wright futuristic building, all pink with a bright blue roof, which housed the county courthouse, sheriff's department, county offices, a law library, and a public library. Marin County was the land of the rich and bourgeois, a worthy target for revolutionaries; besides, we were familiar with it. Jim Kilgore and his parents had lived in Marin County and some of the others had gone to the Civic Center to get birth certificates which we used for our false identities.

After scouting the building, Josephine returned to tell us that she had wandered into the sheriff's office without being stopped, and if she had had a bomb with her, she could easily have planted it. She and Emily went back to the sheriff's office for another visit, but this time they were stopped and challenged. "We're looking for the law library," Emily told a deputy and he directed the SLA general and her foot soldier to the proper doorway.

As a result of that encounter, Emily came up with a plan to set off two bombs rather than one at the Civic Center—one beneath a car in the lower parking lot and the other beneath a police vehicle parked in front of the sheriff's office. Her idea was to time the explosions very carefully so that the bomb in the parking lot would explode first and then, when the deputies rushed out of the sheriff's office in response to that explosion, the second bomb would explode in their faces. Teko was delighted.

Wendy hated the idea. She pointed out that the sheriff's office and the law library were adjacent and that the explosion would draw law students as well as sheriff's deputies out to the scene. They could be killed as well as the deputies. Yolanda tried to convince Wendy that innocent bystanders sometimes become victims in the revolution. When that did not work, she told Wendy, "Those law students are studying to be lawyers and they'll go to work for some big, piggy corporation, and so they are pigs too."

Wendy tried to reason with her, saying, "But they could be radicals who are trying to change the system too, or they might want to be public defenders and to help people. You don't know who you might kill." But the Harrises were unmoved. We would go ahead with the action according to their dictates, but Wendy refused to have anything to do with us during this operation.

In the excitement, the scheme was augmented with the idea of a simultaneous bombing action in Los Angeles. In that way, we would persuade the world that the Jonathan Jackson/Sam Melville Unit of the New World Liberation Front was no ordinary group, but that we were strong enough to carry out actions in northern and southern California simultaneously.

Teko divided us into two teams, giving Yolanda command of the Marin County action, while he, Jim, and Kathy would drive down to Los Angeles to search out a suitable target there. Our actions would be coordinated by telephone. Not satisfied with the simple pipe bomb we had used before, Teko built a more powerful one, made of hard-to-find three-inch-diameter pipe. It was twelve inches long, loaded with concrete nails as well as gunpowder, for a bigger and more lethal bang. He told us the concrete nails made it an "anti-personnel bomb." He also devised a complex triggering device with a magnet and clothespins so that if the bomb were attached to a police car, it would explode when the car was driven off with one or two "pigs" in it. He was very pleased with himself and his custom-made bomb.

On August 20, leaving ourselves plenty of time, Steve and I set off from Geneva Avenue, driving across the Golden Gate Bridge into Marin County, and headed for the Civic Center complex. Our target was a "pigmobile" in the lower parking lot. Josephine and Bonnie Wilder left from our Lyon Street safehouse to place a similar bomb under a police car in front of the sheriff's office in the county courthouse. Steve was calm and nonchalant about the whole thing, reassuring me on the drive that I had nothing to worry about. It would be even easier than Emeryville. In fact, he seemed to enjoy it all, as though it were nothing more than a playful adventure, a revolutionary action out of a storybook.

We parked near a theater by a small lake within the Center. It was near dark and deserted. From the trunk of our car, Steve took out a ten-speed bicycle and reattached the front wheel. The bomb was concealed in a khaki-green canvas knapsack, which Steve strapped to his back. With the bike assembled and ready to go, Steve threw the safety switch, which would allow him twenty minutes before the explosion.

"See you in a bit," he said to me with a little smile, and pedaled off to the parking lot.

I waited nervously. It was taking him more than the two or three minutes we had allowed for placing the bomb. But then, probably five minutes after he had left, he reappeared silently at the car. "It took me a little while to place the damn thing," he said, "but everything is just fine." Deftly he disassembled the front wheel and put the bike back into the trunk and we were off and away. As we were leaving the complex, we caught sight of our blue Buick, which Jo and Bonnie were using. We drove out of the complex and up a little hill, looking for a place from which we could watch the fireworks, but when we could not find one, we drove back to the safehouse. Back at Lyon Street, Yolanda joyfully reported to us that the television program she was watching had been interrupted to report the double explosions. However, the bombs had gone off in the wrong order: first the one near the sheriff's office and then the one in the parking lot. I sighed with relief but made no comment.

Bonnie and Jo returned about twenty minutes after we did. Reporting on their mission, they told us they had parked their car nearby and walked right up to the building. Wearing wigs and dressed as students, they carried their bomb in a greenish canvas school bag with flowers all over it. Jo spotted a policewoman with whom she had talked when she had been at the courthouse a few days earlier, but they walked on anyway to the front of the building and past the entrance. At the police vehicle, they stooped down, and slipped the bag containing the bomb underneath the car, but Bonnie's wig almost fell off. So with one hand she shoved the bomb further under the car and with the other hand she grasped her wig. Then they both walked off.

The next day, Bonnie and Jo dropped off our communiqué in a phone booth outside radio station KSAN. Later, listening to the radio, we heard a disc jockey report that someone had informed the police that he or she had seen a blue Buick at the phone booth. Yolanda cursed our bad luck. She yelled at Josephine and Bonnie for driving the car right up to the telephone booth, instead of parking it out of sight and walking to the booth. "You were both lazy and now we have to ditch our best car." For Yolanda, this had turned our team's operation into a complete failure. She dreaded having to tell Teko about the Buick and her inability to handle her command. Everyone else thought the operation had been a complete success.

The other team returned the next day in defeat. Teko and Jim, both sullen, were not speaking to one another and Kathy had a black eye. Teko ranted over Yolanda and her team losing a car, and no one dared question him about the failure of his bombs or about Kathy's black eye. But bit by bit during the next few days we all learned the details of their miserable trip.

They had spent most of their time in Los Angeles arguing over what would make a meaningful and significant target for their super three-inch bomb. Teko and Jim found a convention meeting of the Veterans of Foreign Wars in a midtown hotel. They walked into the meeting carrying the bomb in an attaché case. But their appearance aroused the suspicions of the guard at the door, who had kept them in sight and then, or so they thought, had sent another veteran to keep an eye on them. They argued bitterly over whether or not to plant the bomb, and decided to leave and to try it again later.

While stopped for a traffic light, still arguing, with the bomb still in the car, Kathy in her fury had made some kind of disparaging remark about Jim's sexual prowess. He in turn hauled off and socked her in the eye. Teko, at the wheel, tried to avenge the attack, and with Kathy between them, the two men came to blows in the front seat of the car. Meanwhile, the cars behind them began to honk their horns, jolting them back to reality.

Determined to set off their bombs that evening, they cruised the streets of a high crime neighborhood in East Los Angeles until they came upon a parked police car. They attached their bomb, hidden in a garbage bag and set to go off when the patrol car was moved. Then they raced off to plant their second bomb under another police vehicle parked on the street. Feeling marvelous, they drove back to their motel to await news of their daring attack against the pigs who had killed our comrades in that blazing shoot-out. Teko talked of revenge as they waited for the news of the bombings to be reported. But the news was not what Teko had expected.

When the first car drove off, according to the news reports, the garbage bag containing the bomb was left lying in the street. A couple of young boys came upon it and began to kick it around. Still the bomb did not go off. However, some of the bomb components fell out of the bag. An adult recognized what was going on and summoned the police. All units were immediately alerted to search for explosive devices on their cars. Within minutes, the second device was found and defused. Apparently the concrete nails that Teko had added to his bomb had short-circuited the device. He cursed his bad luck and the lucky pigs who got away.

Without telephoning ahead, they drove back to San Francisco, arguing all the way. In all his megalomania and brilliant planning, Teko had not taken into account the personal jealousies of the team which he had handpicked to accompany him. Jim obviously harbored a deep resentment over losing Kathy's affections, and Kathy apparently had absorbed all of Teko's insane single-mindedness in fighting the revolution. She had become a carbon copy of Yolanda in her virulent dedication, denouncing everyone in sight for not being sufficiently dedicated and determined. Yolanda, being on the outs with Teko at that time, was more bitter than usual, harping on his shortcomings as a leader, nagging him constantly, and never missing an opportunity to allude to the significance of her combat team being better than his on our latest bombing action.

Everything pretty much spiraled out of control after that. We were splintered every which way now. Beyond the usual philosophical and political differences, we were torn apart by very real personal hatreds and piques. Teko was bristling at Jim Kilgore, not talking to me, and he was treating Steve Soliah with contempt for supposedly alienating my affections from him. The bad feelings were naturally reciprocated. Mike Bortin was half in and half out of the cell, ridiculing Teko and all of us for being all talk and no action. Blowing up empty police cars was not his idea of how to carry on a revolution. Seanna had been read out of the cell. Wendy was finally getting up enough courage to express her deep hatred of both the Harrises.

Kathy eventually recovered from her case of "Emily-itis" and became disgusted with the dictatorial ravings of both Teko and Yolanda, and of course, her attitude influenced Josephine and Bonnie. Emily in her own way was trying to glue the group back together again with her sanctimonious appeals and her carefully timed cascade of tears. But she was going about it in precisely that righteous, mother-hen manner which we had all come to loathe.

It was shortly after the Marin and Los Angeles bombings that we had another of our horrendous, all-night struggles at the Geneva Avenue safehouse and it was at this meeting that the thread holding us all together finally snapped. The immediate issue was, once again, black leadership. Teko announced that he had learned that Doc Holiday, who had been the head of the Black Guerrilla Family at San Quentin and an old friend of the SLA, had been paroled recently and was somewhere in San Francisco. He and Emily proposed that Doc Holiday (who had served fourteen years of a life sentence for murder and robbery) be approached and asked to join and to lead our group.

Everyone protested, resisted, and rejected the idea. The arguments ranged over a wide spectrum of subjects and all the old animosities rose to the surface. The living room was filled with acrid cigarette smoke and strewn with pizza crusts and empty beer and wine bottles. Jim Kilgore, the most violent of all of us in his objections, almost came to blows with Bill Harris. Emily, still trying to patch things up, lamented over the old days of the SLA when, she said, the SLA was a true army, well disciplined, determined, and leading the revolution. She went on singing the praises of Cinque and the SLA in contrast to the present state of affairs in our group. Teko joined in the accolades. Then Jim Kilgore screamed at them: "That's all a bunch of crap. What did the SLA ever accomplish? You killed a black man, kidnapped a little teenage girl, and robbed a bank. What the hell did that amount to?"

Screaming accusations flew back and forth. Teko stomped around the room flailing his arms, spittle dribbling from his lips as he tried to outshout Kilgore. Emily Harris was in tears.

"We're going out to find Doc Holiday," Teko exclaimed. "He's our black leader, the leader we need for a new start."

"We don't need a black leader," argued Kilgore. "We don't want a black leader. We're white and there's nothing wrong with that."

It came to a sudden end when Teko, in exasperation, exclaimed: "That's it. . . . It's all over. . . . We have to split up and go our own separate ways! We're going to find a black leader to lead us and you can join us or do whatever you want. You're all a bunch of chickenshit reactionaries anyway."

Teko did not change his mind the next morning. He sent Yolanda out to find a safehouse for their own new beginning. The atmosphere in the place was thick with murderous hatred. I was given the cold shoulder, absolute dead silence from my former General Field Marshal. Nor did Yolanda forgive me for having sided with the others the night before. The conflict between the Harrises and everyone else was basic and fundamental. While everyone in the group agreed that "revolution implies violence," most felt that it was not the *only,* or even the most important, aspect of the revolution. The Harrises held that violence was primary to the struggle, as it seemed to be in their personal relationships. Over and beyond that, the most serious disagreement concerned the issue of black leadership. To them, black leadership was the backbone of the SLA. But not only did I agree with the others that skin color should not be the basis for leadership; I also was reluctant to have a black ex-convict comrade of the Harrises join our cell and assume its leadership. I feared that all the others would fall under his (and the Harrises') absolute control, as the original members of the SLA had with Cinque.

Yolanda returned that afternoon with the announcement that she had rented an apartment on Precita Avenue near the San Francisco General Hospital. It was in the Bernal Heights section, in the middle of the city, a racially mixed neighborhood where she thought they could blend in unnoticed. With a vengeance, Teko went downstairs to give notice to our landlord, saying he would be leaving at the end of the month, which was about a week away. Wendy and I left with Jim and Steve to take up residence in the cramped Irvington Street safehouse in Daly City. Kathy chose to stay for a while with the Harrises to give them moral support, taking Jo and Bonnie with her. I could not fully believe that this was the end. There had been no goodbyes.

Steve and Jim went off every day to a large apartment complex painting job, where they worked with Mike Bortin. A few days after we had moved, Steve returned later than usual one evening in a state of high excitement. His father had shown up unexpectedly in the city and Steve and his sisters had had dinner with him. To their dismay, their father, Martin Soliah, told them that the FBI was looking for them in connection with radicals. The government agents had asked him to come from Palmdale to San Francisco in order to locate his children and to persuade them to meet with the FBI. Their father, deeply worried at even the hint that they were in any way connected with the SLA, had pleaded with them to return home to Palmdale. Kathy had vehemently denied the accusations, refusing to go back home, and had chastised her father for cooperating with the FBI. Josephine had broken down and cried. Steve had been deeply disturbed, certain that the FBI was close behind and on their trail—probably even watching them at that very moment.

Fearing that they were being followed, Kathy had insisted that Josephine turn her car over to Steve to ditch at the other end of the city, in the Richmond District, and Jo had obeyed her older sister. They had all made their way back separately by bus. Word came from Teko that we had to give up the Irvington Street safehouse and find other accommodations. Once again Teko did not leave it entirely to us. He showed up unexpectedly and informed the Irvington Street landlord that we were vacating the apartment. This left us with no place to live.

Looking for another apartment, the four of us were driving in the Outer Mission District one evening when we came upon Morse Street and spotted a FOR RENT sign in a window at No. 625. We stopped and Jim copied the phone number given. The next day he phoned for an appointment and insisted that I go with him, posing as his wife. "I can't, I can't do it," I pleaded. "I'm afraid to . . ." Irrational fear gripped me at the thought of actually speaking with a stranger, someone not of my own underground world. I had barely done that on my own in all the nineteen months since I had been torn from my apartment in Berkeley. But Kilgore insisted. By talking with the landlord just one time, he said, I would establish myself in that residence and be able to move freely in and out of the house. Otherwise, I would have to sneak about.

I managed to get through the interview with the landlord and on September 9 we moved in with all our possessions. The apartment, on the second floor, had two entrances, one from a stairway leading up from the front door and the other from a steep wooden staircase leading up from the backyard to the kitchen. It was a good safehouse and soon became the meeting place for the whole group, excepting, of course, the Harrises. They never came to Morse Street and the four of us never went to Precita Avenue.

Kathy told us of some wild goings-on there in which Bill Harris cursed one or another of us, fought with Emily, and continually risked bringing on a visit from the police for disturbing the peace. Their new neighbors had even knocked on their door to demand that they keep down their noise.

One evening, when our group was discussing the possibility of taking up a new life in Oregon or in Boston, I suddenly got sick of the whole thing, of all their talking and arguing and, in the end, getting nowhere fast. Almost without thinking, I blurted out, "Oh, what's the use. I'm so sick of all this, I feel like turning myself in. I'm tired of running away all the time. I just don't care anymore if I'm arrested. It's all such a worthless existence."

They were all shocked, and I heard a chorus of protestations. "You can't do that. . . . You must stay. You're a symbol of the revolution. . . . Posters of you are up all over Berkeley. . . . You give the people hope. They believe in you. . . . You must stay and fight on. . . ." Their reaction was much stronger than I had expected, and I worried that they might become suspicious of my loyalty.

"Oh, I didn't really mean it," I replied. "I'm just feeling down now and will be better in the morning." Nothing more was said about that.

But the thought was there. And yet, I felt I owed them something, something like loyalty. Still, for the first time I considered trying to reach someone in the outside world. Telephoning my parents or my sisters was out of the question. I thought they had given up on me because of what I had been forced to say on the tapes, and I thought, too, their phones would certainly be tapped. I believed that the FBI was camping in my parents' home and I was certain they had tapped the phones of all my friends. Most of all I thought of trying to telephone Trish Tobin, my best friend. I trusted her completely, but she was away at college and I had no idea how to reach her. I could not call her home. After all, it had been her father's Hibernia Bank that we had robbed. It seemed to me that I was trapped in this nether land of radicals and revolutionaries. Theirs was the only world I had. I did not really know what I believed anymore. It did not seem to make much difference. There were telephones all over the city but calling someone was beyond me. I was troubled and anxiety-ridden, for it seemed that even without the Harrises, I could find no mental peace.

In the middle of September, Kathy reported to us that the Harrises had finally made contact with Doc Holiday and had sent her to look for him at a rally in Golden Gate Park for the "San Quentin Six."* Kathy said she had found Doc lying in some bushes near the rally, stoned out of his mind and smoking marijuana. The thirty-three-year-old black ex-convict required a lot of convincing, Kathy said, before he would agree to follow her to the Harrises. They met in a motel room north of Berkeley and spent a couple of days there. Kathy had not been invited to the meeting. But she assumed, she said, that Doc had declined the Harrises' offer. He certainly had not turned up at the Precita safehouse and the Harrises were not saying another word about him.

Wendy and I spent most of the days at Morse Street talking with one another after the men went out on their painting jobs. We agreed that the essential trouble with Bill Harris was that he was a short, belligerent, guilt-ridden man who had a severe Napoleon complex, always having to prove himself in a world of taller black men. We discussed the more complex manipulative personality of Emily Harris at great length. Wendy and I got along very well together, conversation coming easily for both of us. We were alike, I think, in being rather low-key in contrast to the others. Also, we both felt lost and uncertain, not knowing what the future could possibly hold for us.

On one balmy afternoon, much like any other, we were sitting at the kitchen table, with the top half of the rear door, a Dutch door, open to allow some air into the apartment. Wendy was sharing with me a long letter she was in the midst of writing to Willie Brandt, trying to explain how and why our group had broken up. As I read the letter, Wendy got up to get a glass of water at the sink. Her letter was good, introspective more than factual, but it was very, very long. I laid it down on the table, half read, and got up to go to the bathroom. As I entered the hallway I heard a tremendous commotion on the back stairs which led to the kitchen. I turned and saw two heavyset men diving through the top half of the open Dutch door, each with one arm fully extended, waving revolvers at Wendy and me.

"FREEZE!" one of them commanded. "F B I . . . FREEZE!"

This was it. This was the moment I had dreaded for so long.

---

* The six were the prison inmates then on trial for murder in connection with the foiled prison break in 1971 in which George Jackson, two other inmates, and three guards had been killed.

CHAPTER

EIGHTEEN

THE SHOTS I EXPECTED did not come. The voice seemed to reach me from somewhere far away.

"Freeze!"

"Stop or I'll shoot!"

In fractions of seconds, as I heard the voice, I slid into Wendy's bedroom, terrified, instinctively moving away from the hail of bullets I expected. I was through the door and away, out of the line of fire, when the voice came through to me, loud and clear:

"Come out, or I'll blow her head off!"

I stopped and looked back. There was Wendy up against the wall in the hallway, just outside the kitchen. She looked over her shoulder at me. Pure panic was in her eyes. In the flash of that moment I thought of two things at once: the shotgun hidden in the wall behind me and Wendy's statement back on the farm that she did not want to shoot it out and die; she wanted to come out with her hands up. I was so scared, I literally could not move. He's going to shoot her, I thought, pushing myself forward. Then I walked into the hall toward him and raised my hands.

"Are you Patty Hearst?" he asked.

"Yes."

The other man, who turned out to be a San Francisco police inspector in plain clothes, pointed his gun at me. We were both frisked and then handcuffed. The FBI agent, Tom Padden, told me I was under arrest for the Hibernia Bank robbery on April 15, 1974. "Any weapons in the house?" he asked. We pointed to our pocketbooks and they confiscated our revolvers and then we led them to the shotgun and the two carbines we had hidden in the bedroom closets. I thought the two men were as nervous and unsure of themselves as we were. In my terror at that moment, I had wet my pants. I explained what had happened and asked if I might change before we left. Wendy and I certainly were not putting up any fight. The FBI agent gave his consent and unlocked my handcuffs so that I could do what I had to do.

They tried to open the front door in order to let two other agents into the apartment but the lock stymied them. That lock always got stuck, and I had to open the door for them. There was very little conversation as the agents took Wendy and me into custody. The long flight was over, and I was still alive.

They led us down the front stairs and past our landlord, who stood there staring, his mouth hanging open. He was probably the most surprised of us all. Nothing much was said in the automobile as we drove downtown to the Federal Building, which housed the FBI headquarters in San Francisco.

At the Federal Building, the car slowed up, coming almost to a stop before it nudged its way through a huge crowd of reporters and photographers. Obviously the word of our capture had been sent ahead and released to the media. The search for the missing Patty Hearst had come to an end. The FBI, after having been the laughingstock of the radical left, and much of the press and public, had won out in the end. As the flashbulbs went off in my face, I remembered the press pictures of Susan Saxe, a revolutionary who had recently been arrested, and, like her, I smiled broadly and raised a clenched fist in salute. This is how I'm supposed to act now, I thought. Those pictures would show me being taken off to a fascist concentration camp, like a true revolutionary. I had a role to play and I knew my part well. I did notice that Wendy looked grim.

The car was surrounded by a mass of news photographers and reporters. Some jumped on the hood for better pictures, others banged on the windows and shouted questions at me. More than anything else, I now felt giddy and euphoric, as though I were outside of everything, floating through a surrealistic Jean Cocteau film. Wendy looked as if she might throw up at any moment. We drove through a long tunnel

and into the garage and then Wendy and I were escorted into an elevator and brought up to the FBI floor. The corridors were lined with employees, standing there staring at the famous fugitive. I was literally pa-
raded before them. I must have been a sight, all ninety pounds of me,
dressed in corduroy pants, a striped lavender T-shirt, and rubber-soled
thongs on my feet. My hair was chopped short and dyed a hideous red.

I was led alone into a small room and there a female agent gave me a
strip search. Fingerprinted and photographed, I was led out of the
room, and in the hallway I caught a glimpse of Emily Harris and wondered if Bill also had been arrested. I was then shuffled into a large
conference room with a table in the center. One of the five or six
agents in the room told me proudly, "This is the room where we did all
the work on your kidnapping case. The whole room was devoted to
you." I glanced around the room and noticed that all the walls were
adorned with "Wanted" posters of me.

Several agents and men from the U. S. Attorney's office came in to
talk to me in shifts, never identifying themselves, and I became confused with the constant changing of my interrogators. One of them read
me my "Miranda" rights to remain silent, etc., and then asked me to
sign a long sheet of paper. At the top of the page I saw the words
"Waiver of Rights," and I refused to sign. He insisted that my signature
only meant that I had been read my rights as a prisoner in custody. But
I could not help but think of Cinque's advice: "Never sign anything,
never say anything, when the pigs've got you." I refused to sign and the
man, whoever he was, stormed out of the room.

Then a nervous young man brought in someone he identified as a
psychiatrist. "We want you to talk to this doctor," he said. Only later
did I discover that this nervous man was Michael Nerney, an Assistant
U. S. Attorney, already preparing the case against me. But the appearance of a doctor frightened me more than anything else. I thought
they intended to send me to a mental institution, where, according to
what I had learned in the SLA, I would be subjected to hideous tortures.
Frightened, I refused to say a word to the doctor.

After a while, they halted the questioning and led me out of the
room. In the hallway, I came upon Wendy and she managed to whisper
that both Teko and Yolanda had been arrested. We were shuffled off to
an elevator and taken up to the U.S. marshal's office on the nineteenth
floor, where I was again fingerprinted and photographed. I was put into
a wire-mesh cell so designed that I could see out but others could not

see into it. It was called a conference cage. For five or six hours I was held there alone, wondering what would come next. Wendy was in a standard, barred holding cell on my right, Emily was in the next corner cell to my left at a right angle, and Teko was led into the cell next to hers. I could see Teko and Yolanda, and Wendy was reflected in a mirrored glass which hid the marshals' desks in the center of this large room.

Talking from one cell to another, Teko and Yolanda described their arrest, which had occurred about an hour before mine. The FBI had traced the Soliahs through their painting jobs and located them working in the Pacifica area, south of San Francisco. Following them back to the city, the FBI observed Steve Soliah enter the Morse Street house and Kathy and Jim go into the Precita Avenue house. Spotting Bill Harris outside the apartment, they had staked out the place since the previous day, confirmed their identification of Bill Harris, and then sealed off the block with fire trucks and police cars. They waited until both Bill and Emily returned from their daily jogging in a nearby park and were walking up to their apartment. The two were taken into custody by a horde of heavily armed agents on the street. Teko, in shorts and T-shirt, surrendered immediately. Yolanda bolted. She got only a short way before she was grabbed. "You motherfucking sons of bitches!" she screamed, struggling in their arms. "You sons of bitches . . ." Unarmed, in jogging clothes, neither of them had a chance.

"I thought about diving through the window of a store to get away," Yolanda told me, "but I didn't think it would work."

"If only we could have got to our guns, we could have blasted our way out of there," moaned Teko, excusing himself for not putting up a fight.

Incredibly, on the day of the arrest, the FBI had not thought to cover the apartment complex in Pacifica where they had first sighted the Soliahs on their painting job. So when our arrests were announced on radio and television, Kathy, Jo, Jim, and Mike took off and went underground. Steve Soliah, hearing only that the Harrises had been arrested, rushed back to our safehouse which did not have a telephone, to warn Wendy and me. He was arrested on the front steps.

Wendy was the first to leave the holding area. She was removed from her cell and shackled in heavy chains wrapped around her waist and attached to cuffs on her wrists and ankles. She was being taken to Oakland for arraignment in the Alameda County courthouse on the old

charges outstanding against her. In all those chains, Wendy looked so
tiny and helpless, like a Roman slave girl being led to auction. She was
crying.

At last I was taken out of the cage and led off to another room. A
federal marshal told me, "We have a lawyer here to see you," and another marshal remarked, "She has to be in court in a few minutes."
The room was swarming with FBI agents and federal marshals, who
were arguing that the lawyer had no right to see me at that time, and
the lawyer was insisting loudly that he had been hired to represent me.
The attorney was Terence Hallinan, whose name I knew of only
slightly, although he was well known in the Bay Area as a defender of
liberal and left-wing causes, and was the son of Vincent Hallinan, who
was even better known for his widely publicized defenses of labor
unions and union leaders in the 1930's. He was there with my cousin
Will. Terry Hallinan got in only a few words with me, with the marshals standing right over us as we talked. Terry told me that I was to be
arraigned in court on the charges against me and that it was all routine;
he would take care of everything.

In a crowded courtroom in the same building, I was led to a table
before a judge and the charges were read out: I was charged with
armed bank robbery and the use of a firearm to commit a felony, in
connection with the robbery of the Hibernia Bank on April 15, 1974.
Feeling ragged and on display, I realized it was bad manners to chew
gum in court. I removed the gum I had been chewing since my arrest
and stuck it under the table. The courtroom itself was imposing, pan-
eled in wood with an enormous Great Seal of the United States hanging
high on the wall behind the judge's head. I remained silent as my new
lawyer pleaded not guilty for me.

Hustled out of the courtroom, I was made ready for my next trip—
to the San Mateo County Jail. It seemed that the federal government
did not have a jail of its own in San Francisco and they considered the
city jails too insecure for special prisoners. Hence, I would be held in
San Mateo on the Peninsula, not far from our old home in Hillsborough. Very much like Wendy, I was secured with chains around my
waist and handcuffed to these chains. I could hardly move, much less
escape. Nevertheless, the marshals seemed to equate fame with danger,
treating me as though I were the most dangerous criminal they had had
in their clutches in many a year.

At the San Mateo jail, I was once again fingerprinted, photographed, and booked into the jailhouse. Emily Harris was standing nearby, waiting to be booked.

"Occupation?" the woman at the desk asked.

I shook my head, unable to think of any.

"Occupation?" she repeated.

I stared at her, not knowing what to say.

"You *have* to give an occupation," she demanded.

"Urban guerrilla," I said.

She just smiled and wrote it down, and that answer was headlined in the press the next day. At the time, I glanced over at Emily and she smiled broadly, delighted.

Once in the cell area, I was stripped of my clothes, given a shower, told to wash myself and my hair with an odious disinfectant and louse-repellent mixture. Then I had to undergo still another strip search. After that they handed me a jail dress to put on. Made of coarse cotton, it was a pink hospital gown that just covered my bare buttocks. It was all I had to wear for my first week in custody.

My cell was one of three in the segregation wing of the women's quarters of the jail on the fourth floor of the San Mateo County courthouse building. It was about nine feet long and six feet wide, containing a double bunk bed and a plastic commode which combined a toilet and a sink. The walls were concrete. The cell door was made of steel bars with an opening for passing through food. Alone in the cell, I curled up on the lower bunk bed and tried to rest. Emily was brought in and put in the cell next to mine.

This was it, the cell in isolation which Cinque had described so often. I wondered when the torture and beating would begin. If the pigs were trying to humiliate and debase us with this kind of impersonal treatment, I thought, they would not succeed. If I could withstand the treatment of the SLA when I was a prisoner of war, I could stand up to whatever these people dished out. I felt remarkably calm, without emotion, as though none of this was really touching me or affecting me deeply.

A deputy came for me that night and led me out of the cell, saying that I had visitors. I did not believe him. But they led me into a small attorneys' conference room. I saw my mother and father and my sisters Vicki and Anne for the first time in almost two years. They looked unfamiliar, as if from another world. My mother stood there with a dozen long-stemmed yellow roses and an orchid for me.* She was smiling so happily at the sight of me. My father was plainly nervous, not knowing what to expect. As for my sister Vicki, she had changed completely. Seventeen when I had last seen her, a teenager with long straight hair, now she was a sophisticated-looking young woman of twenty, with a curly, frosted permanent. If I had passed her on the street, I would not have recognized her.

Nor would they have recognized me, I supposed, with my gaunt features and bizarre red hair. They hardly knew me, I thought, seeing me there in prison. We all sat down. I had no idea what to say. My mother kept telling me how happy they were to see me, how happy they all were that I was safe, how happy they were that it was all over and I would be coming home soon. The visit could have lasted ten minutes or an hour. I hardly remember what I said or did, but they told me later that I had curled up in a ball, like a fetus, and barely managed to mumble in a weak, disembodied tone of voice. My mother, bless her, asked over and over again if I weren't happy that it was all over now. She thought the charges would be "straightened out" and that I would be home in a day or two.

But I knew it was not over; it was just beginning. I was a prisoner again and I just knew that I would be beaten and tortured by the prison guards. They could not allow me to survive. Cinque had told me that. If I were not killed, he had said, I would be beaten and tortured, put on trial, and sent to jail. They would throw away the key. And I still believed him.

A dozen beautiful roses and an orchid. What would I do with them? There was no room for them in my cell. I gave them to the guard who led me back, asking her to put them in the dining area so that everyone could enjoy them. Instead, she put the roses in the guards' room and took the orchid home with her.

That first night I hardly slept. The fluorescent lights were on at all times and every half hour or so a guard would come by and stare in at me, presumably to see if I was still alive. I had not touched my dinner, which seemed to be mostly potatoes, and they had taken that away. I spent hours whispering to Emily Harris in the adjoining cell. She

---

* The roses were from a group of reporters covering the story outside my parents' apartment, and the orchid was from an FBI agent assigned to my case.

warned me against cooperating with the authorities or telling even my own lawyers or anybody anything at all. "You can't trust them," she warned me. I swore to her that I had not told the pigs anything. She lectured me on our defense: we had to position ourselves as defiant revolutionaries, refusing to cooperate in fascist, fixed trials, and we would make and issue statements to the people. We would get more publicity for our statements now than ever before, she said.

The next day I found out that I had two lawyers, not one. My father had also hired James Martin McInnes, who was reputed to be one of the most respected attorneys in San Francisco. Jim McInnes was well dressed, well spoken, capable, middle-aged, and very reserved. He was in sharp contrast to Terry Hallinan, who was young, eager, and volatile and told me to call him "Kayo," his nickname dating back to the days when he was the boxing champion of UCLA.

I had a very difficult time trying to explain to them what had happened to me. Despite all of Emily's warnings, my instinct was that the right thing to do in my circumstances was to tell my lawyers the whole truth.

Emotionlessly, I told them of my kidnapping, the time spent in the closet, being blindfolded and tied up. I told of the sex forced upon me by Cujo and Cinque and I was surprised to see tears come to the eyes of Kayo Hallinan. "I never dreamed that such things happened to you," he said softly. They did not square with his own preconceived notions of young student radicals fighting the establishment. But he sat there, taking notes. I told him about the Hibernia Bank robbery, the shooting at Mel's, the summer spent on the East Coast, the bank robberies in Sacramento, and the bombings in the San Francisco Bay Area. Actually, I skimmed the surface. Only bits and pieces of the story came out in disjointed whimpers as I responded to the lawyers' questions. It went on for hours. Little did I know then that that would be only the first of many times I would have to try to tell what had happened since my kidnapping.

Apparently the two lawyers did not get along with each other and had argued over the type of defense I should have. My father explained all this to me on one of his visits and it boiled down to my making the decision: Which one did I want for my defense attorney? I chose Kayo Hallinan.

A day or so later, I got into a fierce dispute with the attorney I had chosen. Kayo arrived with his father and demanded that I sign a six-

page affidavit which he said would support a motion that I be freed on
bail while awaiting trial. Having an innate fear of legal documents, I
read the affidavit warily. It was a rendition of what I had told him and
also, he said, what Wendy Yoshimura had told him about me. But it
seemed to be oversimplified in some places and exaggerated in others.
In essence, it stated that I had been kept in a closet "for several days,"
had been given liquids to drink that made me feel that I was on an
LSD trip, that afterward my mind became "confused and distorted,"
and finally that I realized I was becoming insane.

"I can't sign it because I don't remember it that way."

"Just sign the thing; it doesn't make any difference at this point,"
Vincent Hallinan insisted. "We have to get an affidavit on file if we're
going to get you out on bail."

Before I knew it, Vincent and Kayo both were hovering over me. I
felt browbeaten. I made them delete one or two obvious errors of fact
and then, in the presence of a notary, signed the thing and initialed
each page.

The next day the affidavit was blazoned in all the newspapers and
from the editorial comments I began to fear that my attorney was planning to have me plead insanity. That was the last thing I wanted. I felt
newly depressed, dispirited, exhausted, and humiliated. My father was
upset and worried.

The media was having an orgy of news and speculation every day,
the "Patty Hearst Show," as my family and I came to call it. The story
that startled us more than all the others, and which ultimately would
cause me the most harm, was a slanted version of my first meeting with
Trish Tobin two days after my arrest. Feeling euphoric, I talked and
talked in staccato sentences so rapidly that Trish could hardly get a
word in. At the other end of the long visiting table was Emily Harris,
talking with Teko's parents, and I was very much aware of her being in
the same room. So when Trish asked me about reports that I would
soon make a public statement of some sort, I told her that if I made
any public statement at all it would be from a "revolutionary feminist
perspective" because my politics obviously had changed since my kidnapping. I also remarked that I had been "pissed off" at having been
arrested, as opposed to her mother's reaction; she was "deliriously
happy" at the news of my arrest. Those published statements, coming
after my clenched-fist photo in the news, certainly did not help my
standing with the court, the public, or, later, the jury that weighed my

case. But they did tell us that my conversations with visitors at the jailhouse were being recorded and turned over to the FBI, which did not hesitate to release information to the press.

Bewildered, I did not know which way to turn. My mother and father were troubled, beseeching me silently with their mournful eyes to be their little girl once again. Back in my cell, Emily Harris still lectured, wanting me to continue as Tania, the defiant revolutionary. The lawyers kept pumping me for information, and I really did not know what they wanted. Or what I wanted.

I thought I wanted to be left alone, to be allowed to curl up, sleep, and wake up to find it had all been a dream. But I was the center of attention, a curiosity, a spectacle to gaze upon. Some of the women prisoners wandered into the isolation wing to catch a glimpse of me, and the jail guards dropped by to see me in person. One even asked me for my autograph. Emily's presence in the next cell disturbed my equilibrium. Even though I could not see her, I knew she was there. To the core of me, I still feared her. Why the authorities did not separate us by moving one or the other, I never could figure out. When my affidavit to the court became public, Emily became even more threatening. At the request of my lawyer, a guard was placed outside our cells to cut off our communication. When Emily found out about that she became murderously mad. She did manage to pass me one note warning me not to cooperate with the pigs.

"I was right," she hissed one night. "I knew we should have killed you way back when . . ."

Then the mail began to arrive by the bagfuls, hundreds of letters a day. There were letters from far-out radicals urging all sorts of actions upon me, mail from kooks and crazy people and some sympathetic letters too. One letter came from Charles Manson, the cult leader serving a life sentence for the bloody murders of Sharon Tate and others. "You write me," he said, promising to help me if I would do everything he told me to do. That was followed by letters from two of his followers, Squeaky Fromme and Sandra Good, saying, "Please write to Charlie— He's a beautiful person."

But by far most of the letters I received condemned me outright— not for robbing a bank, but for being so ungrateful and mean to my parents, for deserting my country and my heritage, for the unmentionable joys of sex with black men and hippies, and, in short, for being such a rich, spoiled bitch. I had thought that reading my mail would help pass the time. But those vituperative, angry epistles were hard to take. For the first time I realized how hated I had become. In fact, it had never dawned on me how much people seemed personally to care about my kidnapping and my days with the SLA. After a time, I agreed that the letters should be delivered to my lawyers: I did not want to see them anymore.

By the end of my first week in jail, my father was phoning around the country to find a new lawyer. Neither he nor my mother approved of the Hallinans. But choosing an attorney is like choosing one's surgeon: it must be done more on reputation and faith rather than on genuine knowledge. My father, upon the advice of Jim McInnes, contacted three of the most celebrated criminal lawyers in the nation: Edward Bennett Williams of Washington, D.C., Percy Foreman of Houston, Texas, and F. Lee Bailey of Boston. The first two were occupied and unavailable, and so F. Lee Bailey and his long-time associate, J. Albert Johnson, flew cross-country to see me. They seemed to me to be like the Lone Ranger and Tonto or Don Quixote and Sancho Panza. Lee Bailey appeared supremely self-confident and capable. While he was not at all tall or thin like the storybook image of Don Quixote, Al Johnson certainly was short, chubby, and cheerful as Sancho Panza, and happy in his role as the loyal sidekick of the top man. F. Lee Bailey's fame was spelled out for me by both of them. He had saved the Boston Strangler from an almost certain death penalty; he had won an acquittal for Dr. Sam Sheppard at a second trial for the murder of his wife; he had persuaded a jury that Dr. Carl Coppolino was not guilty of murdering his mistress's husband; and he had won an acquittal from a military tribunal for Marine captain Ernest Medina for his part in the infamous My Lai massacre. That I had never heard of F. Lee Bailey was due to my own ignorance, not to his lack of notoriety. In fact, Johnson told me, Bailey also wrote books.

Bailey and Johnson made certain things very clear before they would agree to accept my case. They had to be in complete charge of the defense; neither my father nor I would be on the defense team; if the Hallinans stayed on, they would merely assist in the defense. All the decisions in the case would be made by Bailey and Johnson; they were the experts. Furthermore, they would not undertake a defense which in any way supported the radical movement in this country.

Even with two famous attorneys, and all their assistants, acting on my behalf, my application to be set free on bail was denied in our first

On my way to court. (Photo credit: Wide World Photos)

The Ceremonial Courtroom in the San Francisco Federal Building. Note the press seats facing the jury box. (Photo credit: Wide World Photos)

By the end of the trial I weighed 87 pounds. (Photo credit: Wide World Photos)

The "clemency blanket" I crocheted to pass the time in prison. (Photo courtesy Francis Morgan)

Bernie wearing the "Pardon Patty" T-shirt sold by the committee to raise funds. (Photo courtesy Francis Morgan)

The grant of Executive Clemency. Behind me is Bernard Shaw. (Photo credit: San Francisco *Examiner*)

From left to right: Ingrid Martinez, George Martinez, me, and Bernard Shaw. The T-shirt was a present from my sisters. (Photo credit: San Francisco *Examiner*)

Bob Outman, himself a victim of terrorists, and me, running Arrow through an obstacle course. (Photo courtesy Ray de Aragon)

federal court hearing. That was hardly surprising. Not in my wildest fantasies had I expected the government to set me free. Instead, my lawyers pressed to have me transferred from jail to a government hospital, saying I needed psychiatric treatment to help prepare my defense. The judge denied that any transfer was necessary. He said he would appoint three psychiatrists to examine me in jail to determine my mental capacity to stand trial. My lawyers could then hardly object. In fact, when they looked into it, they were very pleased by the court's choice of doctors.

I was frightened. I did not want my mind probed by a bunch of headshrinkers. As far as I was concerned, it was all stupid and senseless: I was headed for a long term in prison, so why bother. The government had pictures of me in the act of robbing the bank and they had the tape recording of me bragging about it; witnesses were just icing on the cake. Kayo Hallinan advised me not to cooperate at all with the court-appointed psychiatrists. He said everything I told them would be used against me, against the Harrises, and against all SLA members in the future. He advised me to say that I could not remember anything that happened to me after I had emerged from the closet. That did not seem like much of a defense to me. But I hardly cared about anything anymore.

Bailey and Johnson were outraged when they found out that the Hallinans had advised anything so stupid as not cooperating with the psychiatrists. They advised the completely opposite tack. Once the psychiatrists heard my story, Bailey said, they could only help me. It would be apparent to the trained psychiatrists that I had been brainwashed and coerced into cooperating with the SLA. Everything that I told the psychiatrists, he added, would be sealed and kept confidential under the orders of the court. Only the doctors' official diagnosis of my condition would be presented in open court.

Moreover, it would be far better for my defense, Bailey said, for the impartial psychiatrists to explain to the jury what had happened to me than for me to testify about it myself. That was why I had to tell the court's doctors everything so that they could testify instead of me.

"Then I won't have to get up there on the witness stand?" I asked.

"No, you won't have to take the stand," he said, adding, "Unless it becomes absolutely necessary."

"Make sure that it's not necessary, then. I don't want to take the stand."

"Don't worry," he said.

"I'm too scared to get up there, in front of all those people," I admitted. "If I testify in public against them, the SLA will kill me."

"Everything will be fine," said Bailey.

Before he left, he gave me one important warning: I was being tried only for the Hibernia Bank robbery. Under no circumstances, he said, was I to tell the pyschiatrists anything about the more serious Carmichael bank robbery, in which the woman had been killed, or about the bombings. In fact, he said, I was to stop my story at the point where I had returned from the East Coast and had reached Nevada. "Tell them nothing about anything that happened in Sacramento or afterward in San Francisco," he ordered.

Bailey left the jail, to return to his office in Boston, and I was left with my own thoughts on the matter. The words that rang in my ears were not those of F. Lee Bailey. They were the words of Cinque, which he had repeated over and over to all of us after the Hibernia Bank robbery: "There is no such thing as a fair trial in this fascist state. We are all revolutionaries. And if the pigs don't shoot and kill us, like they'd like to, then they're going to put us in jail and throw away the key. We're revolutionaries, and they've got to put us down, if they can."

Public opinion was strongly against me. That was very evident from the news and feature stories appearing every day in the newspapers and in magazines. Four months earlier, before my arrest, the California Poll, by Mervin Field, the most respected in the state, found that most people did not favor any form of leniency for me. Of the people surveyed, 68 percent thought I should be sent to prison if found guilty; two thirds of the people believed I had joined the SLA voluntarily and had not been forced to make those tapes; nine out of every ten persons thought I was not being forced to remain underground with the SLA; and, worst of all, almost half of the people thought I had planned my own kidnapping. The publicity was continuing.

What kind of fair trial could I expect under those circumstances? I asked my lawyers what could be done and was told that Bailey was the foremost expert on publicity; I should leave such matters to him. What seemed to escape most people's attention was that if I had not been kidnapped I never in a million years would have been involved in robbing any bank, much less that of my best friend's father. The bitter irony of it all was that though I was the kidnap victim I was the one whom the Justice Department chose to prosecute. The Harrises were charged with neither the bank robbery nor my kidnapping. At this point they faced only state charges for their part in the shooting at Mel's Sporting Goods and the abduction of Tom Matthews and Frank Sutter. I would face those same charges *after* my trial in federal court.

Obviously, the government had a choice on how to proceed. They could have used me as a witness against the Harrises on my kidnapping. But then, having vouched for my credibility, they could hardly turn around and prosecute me. Or they could, as they did, prosecute me and worry about the Harrises and the others later. This decision was made in the Justice Department in Washington, apparently because the public and the media were more interested in me than in two unknown radicals named Harris. An "heiress" and a "celebrity"—could I ever hope for justice under such circumstances? I thought not.

The government had to prosecute me, it seemed, in order to prove that there was equal justice for all in America. The rich girl who had been kidnapped and who had robbed a bank had to be punished just as did the poor black man. How would it appear to the voters if the Ford administration, which had pardoned Richard Nixon for his complicity in the Watergate scandal, had chosen *not* to prosecute me? The Chief U. S. Attorney for Northern California, James R. Browning, Jr., had announced that he was going to conduct the case against me personally.

Even the crusty old judge assigned to my trial was caught up in the passion of the moment. Nor could he resist the publicity. A few days after the case was assigned to him, Judge Oliver Carter gave interviews to *Time* magazine and the New York *Times,* in which he said, among other things, that he knew me as a little girl, knew my father, had been a dinner guest at our home, but that none of that would influence him. "You can't be in public life and not know Randy Hearst," he declared. "But he doesn't scare me at all. I've got people, forebears, buried all around, at just as many places as he has. All their money and power falls off me like water off a duck's back." He went on to say, before the trial had even begun, that my guilt or innocence depended upon whether the jury would believe me or not. "The tales she tells are very horrible. It's kind of like—not to be facetious—you don't know whether to cry or to vomit."

It seemed a very strange thing for a judge to say. Besides, it was not true that Judge Carter knew my father or me or had ever been to our home. I asked Al Johnson if we couldn't request another judge for my trial. Judge Carter's remarks were certainly prejudicial and I had always thought a judge was forbidden to say anything at all to the press about a pending case. But Al said it would be too dangerous for us to try. First of all, such a motion probably would be denied and then Judge Carter certainly would be prejudiced against us, and beyond that, we must not even appear to be asking for special favors. I did not think that would be a special favor, but Al said that he and Bailey knew more about the law and about trials than I did. Again, he warned me not to try to conduct my own case.

I wanted my trial postponed until I felt stronger, but Al Johnson told me of the Speedy Trial Act, which required that I be brought to trial within three months. I again asked about the hostility and what could be done about all the publicity just before my trial. No juror could be unaffected by all of this, I said. Al gave me another lecture about leaving such matters to my attorneys. He made me feel stupid questioning the wisdom of F. Lee Bailey.

Al never ceased to extol the brilliance of his partner, with whom he had worked over the past eighteen years. Bailey was so capable, so smart, so energetic that he was more than just a courtroom tactician, Al said. He gave lectures all around the country. He was a pilot who flew his own jet; he owned a helicopter company and flew those too. He also was a best-selling author. In fact, Al had previously remarked, part of their fee for handling my case, as arranged with my father, was the right for Bailey to write a book. Al had said he would be giving me a paper to sign later on. Meanwhile, he said, I had to learn to trust my attorneys. I was to rest easy, assured that F. Lee Bailey, the "best damn lawyer in the whole country," was working full blast in my behalf back in Boston, while he, Al Johnson, Bailey's "legman," was gathering facts, information, and everything needed on the scene, which he was feeding to his partner. Al promised to remain at my side for the duration, advising me, protecting me, and helping me in every way he could. When he was not at the jailhouse, he always left a telephone number where I could reach him. He carried his own electronic portable telephone with him and sped to my aid on several occasions.

I hated the idea of having to reveal myself to these unknown doctors, who would probe my mind impersonally, stripping me of the last shreds of privacy. Cinque had done that to me in the SLA interrogations, and now I had to submit to basically the same thing at the hands of psychiatrists. My fear, no doubt, was based upon my family's disdain of psychiatry to resolve personal problems. My sisters and I had been brought up to believe that we were responsible for what we did and could not blame our transgressions on something being wrong inside our heads. I had joined the SLA because if I didn't they would have killed me. And I remained with them because I truly believed that the FBI would kill me if they could, and if not, the SLA would. In my mind now, I was a "bad girl" for doing all that and now would have to be punished.

When the first of the psychiatrists came to see me on September 30, just eleven days after my arrest, I simply crumpled under his scrutiny. I cried, murmuring and mumbling out replies that were not answers to his questions. He thought I was refusing to cooperate with him. This was Dr. Louis Joloyn West, Chairman of the Department of Psychiatry at UCLA, Director of the Neuropsychiatric Institute, Psychiatrist-in-Chief of UCLA Hospitals, a licensed M.D., Chairman of the Council on Research and Development of the American Psychiatric Association, psychiatric consultant to the Air Force, author of books and studies on prisoners of war, an internationally recognized expert in his field. I thought he had a creepy hypnotic voice. A tall, heavyset man who appeared to be kindly, I suspected "Jolly" of being too smooth, too soothing to be trusted.

After trying to deal with me for about an hour and a half, Dr. West left the consulting room, where we were meeting, and complained to Al Johnson about my refusing to cooperate fully with him. Al came in and spoke to me and after lunch Dr. West and I went at it for another two hours. He tried to be gentle and kind, I suppose, but his questions became more intimate and personal. It was one thing to explain things to the lawyers: their questions were for the most part factual and relatively superficial. I could answer them with a word, a short sentence, a nod of my head. But with Dr. West, and the other psychiatrists who followed him, the questions probed areas which brought me back to that closet and the abuse my comrades had meted out to me. It was astonishing how much had receded from my memory and how much of my ordeal had been altered by my acceptance of the SLA version of my status as a prisoner of war. But when Dr. West probed, I was forced to relive those moments again as they had happened. He would not allow me to gloss over events and repress my emotions any

further. And each time, I would break down in tears. I wept in these
sessions almost as much as I had wept in the SLA closet. It was the
first time since the closet that I had wept like that, the first time since
then that I allowed myself to truly *feel*. Dr. West, I thought, was inor-
dinately interested in the sex that went on within the SLA, particularly
in the lesbian relationships. He seemed to think free sex was an integral
part of the cell and I could sense that he simply did not believe me
when I told him the comrades were more devoted to combat drills and
training for the revolution than to sex. But then, even eminent psychiatrists have been conditioned to certain stereotypes which they take for
granted.

Despite all this and despite my own depression, Dr. West did get
through to me in time and I tried to tell him of Cinque's interrogations,
the threats, the metallic clicking of the rifles when I thought they were
going to kill me, the sex forced upon me in the closet, the offer to join
them or to die, the bank robbery, the criticism/self-criticism meetings,
the weapons, the combat drills, the political indoctrination, my fears,
my desire not to anger them, and my subsequent inability to escape or
even to telephone anyone for help.

All of this, or most of it, was extracted from me by the doctor very
slowly and painfully. I was amazed at how much I had repressed of
those early days of torture and torment. The mind, it seems, obliterates
the memory of pain. But I also suffered losses of memory of some periods of time before my kidnapping. I could not recall, for instance, a
single course I had been taking at Berkeley at the time I was kidnapped, or where my sisters had gone to school, or where I had spent
my last Christmas before the kidnapping. Dr. West, as he would later
tell the court, spent some thirty hours drawing out from me the information he needed for his psychiatric report.

Dr. West also ordered a complete physical checkup for me at Stanford University Hospital. I was physically, as well as mentally, in pretty
sad shape. For the trip outside the jail, I had to submit to a "pat-
down" by a young novice U.S. marshal named Janey Jimenez. She told
me right off that there were certain prescribed routines that had to be
followed, such as the pat-down, and that she had her job to do. I could
make things easy or difficult depending on my cooperation, but I had
to be moved at all times under maximum security. So I was waist-
chained and handcuffed and transported as a dangerous criminal to
Stanford Hospital. In a small examining room, I was kept anxiously

waiting for well over an hour for the examining doctors. I was refused permission to go to the bathroom and handed a bedpan. Janey, not allowed to leave me alone in the room, was obliged to use the same bedpan. It was the start of a rather special friendship between prisoner and guard.

When the examinations did begin, the doctors poked and probed and X-rayed with no concern for my personal feelings or any explanation of what they were doing. The gynecological examination was positively brutal and by the end of it I was in hysterics, sobbing, as I writhed in pain. When they led me to another room and attempted to sedate me in order to shove some electrodes up my nose for an electroenceph- alogram, fear overwhelmed me. I did not know what they were trying to do. I feared electric-shock treatment. I feared everything and everyone; I was helpless. But as if I were fighting for my life, I absolutely refused this test, screaming for my lawyers. It was put off and I was hustled back to jail.

Dr. West also called for a complete battery of psychological testing for me and brought in Dr. Margaret Singer, a renowned and respected clinical psychologist from UC-Berkeley, and she spent, according to her own calculations, some twenty hours with me, talking and testing. I was so apathetic it was difficult for her to get information out of me. But she was dauntless in giving me eight different psychological tests and several of them were a complex series of questionnaires within one test.* My ability to concentrate was so impaired that some of the tests had to be administered by flash cards.

I was quizzed and questioned by two other court-appointed psychi- atrists, Dr. Donald T. Lunde and Dr. Seymour Pollack, and out of all this came the consensus that I was not insane or psychotic, that I was mentally capable, in the legal sense of knowing right from wrong, of standing trial, but that I was indeed "emotionally and mentally im- paired to a significant degree."

Dr. Singer's testing showed that my cumulative IQ score had fallen from 130 at Santa Catalina School to 109, with the worst of the tests showing an IQ of 90. A variance of plus or minus 10 points on an IQ

---

* The tests were: the Wechsler Adult Intelligence Scale for my IQ, the Rhode Sentence Completion Test, the Draw-a-Person Test, the Gough Adjec- tive Checklist, the Murray Thematic Apperception Test (administered twice), the Sargent Insight Test, the Rorschach Procedure, and the lengthy Minnesota Multiphasic Personality Inventory (administered twice).

test is an acceptable result. However, a 20- to 40-point variance indicates that serious change has taken place. The other tests revealed me as "sad, hopeless . . . withdrawn, emotionally distressed and expressing a silent cry for help."

Dr. West, as the senior member of the team, diagnosed my condition as a "traumatic neurosis with dissociative features," which meant simply that I had been frightened out of my wits by the SLA, "subjected to powerfully effective coercive manipulation by her captors," and that I would need three or four months of psychiatric treatment before I would be "able with full competence to aid and assist counsel in her own defense." He recommended private, individual psychotherapy, preferably in a hospital setting and out of prison, to restore my mental health.

My trial was rescheduled to begin three months hence, on January 26, 1976, and I was allowed my own private therapist, but, because of government objections, my therapy would have to be conducted in jail, not in a hospital. Dr. West and Dr. Singer, who agreed to testify on my behalf at the trial, continued to work with me, but less intensively than before.

One day Dr. Singer said she wanted me to see another doctor. Since I had little choice in the matter, I was visited by a rather heavyset man who spoke in a thick Viennese accent straight out of Freud. This was Dr. Martin Orne, who was a psychiatrist *and* a psychologist, from the University of Pennsylvania. For hours over two separate visits I went over my whole story again for him, except that Dr. Orne frequently seemed to misunderstand me. He would leap to conclusions or suggest events that had not happened, and I would have to correct him. I thought him very strange. Some of his questions were most extraordinary. He acted or commented as though he was not believing a word I was saying, and at the same time he seemed unable to comprehend what I was trying to tell him in response to his questions.

Only at the end of the last session with him did the doctor reveal his thoughts. The doctor smiled at me in avuncular fashion, patted my hand, and said, "Miss Hearst, you really shouldn't feel embarrassed. Stronger men than you have cracked and cooperated with the enemy under less torturous conditions. The only thing surprising about all this is that you are here with us today. You suffered severe sensory deprivation being tied up and blindfolded in that closet for so long. Other people subjected to such sensory deprivation would have given up the will to live. They just curl up and die, deprived of their senses for so long. You survived and that is remarkable in itself. You are a survivor."

Dr. Orne's strange, off-center questioning was explained to me several days later. His particular field of expertise was lie detection and deception and he had been called in for his expert opinion on whether or not I was faking all or any part of my story. His questions had been designed to lead me into lying or into making my story more plausible than it actually was. Dr. Singer and Dr. West were happy to tell me that I had passed Dr. Orne's scrutiny with flying colors. In court, Dr. Orne would testify as to how he tested my truthfulness and reached his conclusion: "It was really quite remarkable. Miss Hearst simply did not lie." The prosecution objected vehemently to that! Judge Carter was obliged to instruct the jury that they and only they had to decide upon my credibility.

As the days in jail crept by, I grew more accustomed to this new environment which was a hundred times better for me than my days with the SLA. After a month, my solitary confinement ended and I was allowed to take my meals in the dining room with the other women inmates. I grew accustomed to the screams from the "drunk tank" and the steady banging on the door of the "padded cell" opposite my cell. Saturday nights were wild, with screaming, intoxicated women, some dressed in evening gowns, thrown into the drunk tank. Nights of the full moon were the wildest. Unfailingly, the crazies came out in force and the two drunk tanks were filled to overflowing.

I took up crocheting, puttered around the little cell, living in limbo, waiting. But the deputies and jail guards did not come to beat or torture me in the dead of night. As time went on they became more and more friendly. Nevertheless, there was no mistaking my condition: I was a prisoner again, helpless, undergoing repeated interrogations. I saw my family only during regular visiting hours, a half hour on Thursday and on Saturday, and then only through the bulletproof glass partition which separated us. We couldn't touch each other, and we could hardly communicate beyond superficialities, for we now knew the authorities were tape-recording everything we said over the telephones on either side of the glass partition. My mother anxiously wanted to know what she could do for me, what she could bring me, but she was not allowed to bring anything; my father tried to cheer me up with his wry jokes and funny stories, but I found it difficult to laugh. From the very start, they both firmly reassured me. "Hell, we knew those weren't your words or your thinking," my father said. "If you really wanted to give it to us, you would have been much more sarcastic. Don't forget, we know you, Pat. We knew you were being forced to say those things. Only the dumb public believed that garbage. People seemed to always forget that you'd been kidnapped. We were always happy to get those tapes and hear your voice. That's the only way we knew you were still alive. Believe me, we were relieved every time a new tape showed up."

The love and special knowledge we had of each other were still there. I felt that. But we were separated and kept apart by a wall of glass. And worse, despite their reassurances that they had not believed a word of the tapes, I was still not convinced that I had not hurt them terribly and that there was not some awful weakness in my character causing me to break under the strain of the SLA's people's prison.

My best moments in that jail, perhaps the only times I enjoyed a sense of normalcy in those surroundings, came with the regular pastoral visits of Ted Dumke. Ted was an old friend, albeit a casual one, from my pre-kidnap days at Berkeley, where he had been studying at a theological seminary. Now, as an Episcopal priest, he could make unlimited visits to me under prison regulations, which he did almost every day. He did no preaching, advising, or questioning of my motives and yet he was my greatest comfort at the time. We would sit for an hour or so in the attorneys' conference room, making small talk, playing cards, and just being with one another as friends.

Dr. West assured me that with some psychotherapeutic help I would make a complete recovery, finding my way back to the life I had known before. I had suffered a trauma, starting with my kidnapping, he told me, but I was not in any way chronically ill. To speed my recovery along, I agreed to see a therapist recommended by him and by Dr. Singer. Through their efforts, Dr. Elizabeth Richards, a psychiatrist in private practice in Palo Alto, came to see me for an hour, two times a week, on a regular basis. Through her, I came to understand my feelings of guilt and inadequacy over having been brainwashed and manipulated by the SLA, and we worked hard together on some of my newly developed phobias, such as my fear and inability to use the telephone for anything other than legal calls.

Not being psychologically oriented, I resisted for quite a while the explanations of brainwashing made by Dr. West and others. But in time, I came to understand brainwashing as an inexact, popular term for what psychologists have long known as coercive persuasion. In other words, anyone could be coerced to say or do anything by torture, beatings, abuse, and threats of death. In modern times, however, the Communists discovered that you did not have to put a man on a rack, twist his thumbs, or lash him to make him confess. The more sophisticated method was to weaken your prisoner gradually by depriving him of proper food, sleep, exercise, and then browbeating him through continual, unrelenting questioning until he agreed to what you wanted him to say or do and had, in fact, come to believe it himself.

In the 1930's the Western world was astonished when several of the top dissident leaders in the Soviet Union stood up in open court, without a mark of physical abuse on them, and confessed (apparently voluntarily) to crimes against the state and, in effect, condemned themselves to execution or exile in Siberia. In these famous purge trials, the condemned even accepted and agreed to their punishments as just.

In the cold war of the 1950's, Cardinal Mindzenty of Hungary, after only thirty-five days of imprisonment by the Communist regime, signed a written confession and admitted in open court, with impartial observers in attendance, to spying for the West and to various criminal acts against the state. People in the West were perplexed and confounded by such admissions from a cardinal of the Church. During the Korean War, not one of our servicemen who had been taken prisoner of war had tried to escape from the Communist Chinese prison camps; hundreds of our officers and enlisted men had appeared on Chinese television confessing to war crimes, condemning the United States, and some even embracing Communism. When the war ended, several of our men refused to return home, preferring to remain for years with the Chinese Communists. It had been a scandal of major proportions at the time, an embarrassment to American patriotism, and only after that had our Defense Department engaged psychologists to study the phenomenon of brainwashing.

During the Vietnam War, the same thing happened again: more televised false confessions by servicemen taken prisoner of war. This time, the Army hired Dr. West, Dr. Orne, and others to set up a program to train our pilots and soldiers in resisting the coercive persuasion of the Communist North Vietnamese. Dr. Orne organized an experiment in the Arizona desert in which one team of Air Force pilots acted as pris-

oners of war, with instructions on how to resist revealing the game's
military secrets; the other team was instructed on how to coerce those
simulated secrets out of their prisoners. The experiment was to last two
weeks and it was expected that perhaps 6 or 8 percent of the simulated
prisoners would break down, confess, and reveal secrets. These were
officers, trained combat pilots, and all the instructions and training
given to them beforehand did not help. Held prisoner in caged traps,
yelled at in a phony gibberish language, and interrogated unceasingly,
more than 25 percent of the prisoners broke down in three days. They
not only confessed their simulated secrets, they spilled out every bit of
confidential information they possessed. The other prisoners were in
such bad shape the whole experiment was called off after three days.
The results and the percentage of breakdowns were classified Top Secret.

In explaining all this, Dr. West repeatedly tried to reassure me that I
had no reason to feel guilty or humiliated. No one, including himself,
Dr. West said, could know beforehand whether they could withstand coercive persuasion. It depended upon how effective and adept
the captors were and how resistant the prisoner might be. Cinque and
the others had used a rather coarse, haphazard method, but then I had
been an easy subject for them. Because I was so young and apolitical, I
had no background experience or training with which to resist their
persuasion. Nevertheless, whether or not they knew really what they
were doing, they did employ the classic Maoist formula for thought
reform on me, which Dr. West called the three D's—Debility, Depend-
ency, and Dread.

I had been effectively weakened by my confinement in that closet,
deprived of sight, decent food, regular sleep and exercise, with a radio
blaring at me most of the time. I had grown fully dependent upon them
for the necessities of life as well as all the information I would receive
about the outside world. I could communicate with no one beyond
their own little group. And, finally, I certainly had learned to dread
them because of their own threats to kill me and their warnings that the
FBI would kill me if the agents could find me.

All this was reinforced on a daily basis by our criticism/self-criticism
meetings, in which I was obliged to renounce my former bourgeois life,
my family and friends, and all the values with which I had grown up.
All of this, Dr. West said, was based on the psychological theories underlying Chinese thought reform. Drawn from Pavlov's early experi-

ments in behavior modification, but much more sophisticated, Chinese thought reform holds that if a person is forced to recite certain ideas, even without believing them at first, he or she will come to in time. Psychologically, no one can long believe one thing and say or do another. In time, such a conflict would either make a person crack up or force him to adjust his actions to his thoughts, or his thoughts to his actions. Thus did Mao Tse-tung reform the thinking of hundreds of millions of Chinese who had lived their lives according to Confucius until the revolution. Then Mao set up schools to teach the children, meetings to instruct the adults, and in time when a whole nation's people recited over and over the quotations from Chairman Mao Tse-tung, the people came to believe what they had been reciting.

Thus did Cinque "reform" me into believing that a revolution was under way which in time would overthrow the government. At first, I remembered, I thought I was humoring Cin by telling him what he wanted to hear. But Cin had really been humoring me. I thought at first that they all were stark raving mad, crazy, out of their minds, but in time I came to accept what they believed because of the repetition of those daily criticism/self-criticism meetings. It is a difficult process to understand. We are raised to believe we enjoy freedom of thought. Cinque and the others told me that the people in America were all brainwashed in believing in bourgeois principles, ranging from family and monogamy to capitalism and two big cars in the garage. Cinque and the others were not alone in their beliefs. Many other radical groups of various persuasions throughout the United States still believe that the revolution is going on, a revolution which will in time topple bourgeois America and give the power to the people. It was all a question of who was brainwashing whom. But the single difference in my own case: I had been persuaded coercively—by force; no one had forced the Harrises or the others to adopt the SLA principles and Codes of War.

As the date of my trial approached, word came from F. Lee Bailey that I was to see one more psychiatrist, who was the expert's expert on Chinese thought reform and coercive persuasion used on prisoners of war in Korea, Communist China, and North Vietnam. So, over a four-day period in the second week of January, I spent fifteen hours going over my SLA experiences with Dr. Robert Jay Lifton of Yale University.

Dr. Lifton, author of several books on coercive persuasion and thought reform, and a consultant on the subjects to the Air Force, after taking what he called "a peek" at me, pronounced me a "classic case" which met all the psychological criteria of a coerced prisoner of war. He bemoaned the fact that he had not been able to see me during the first two weeks of my arrest, for then he could have observed the all-important transition from my coerced state of mind to my present state, when I had already shucked off a good deal of the "gunk" that had filled my mind.

The way I had acted immediately after my arrest—the clenched-fist salutes, giving my occupation as "urban guerrilla," the sentiments I expressed to Trish Tobin two days after my arrest—bolstered and confirmed his diagnosis of coercive persuasion. One does not revert back with the snap of the fingers upon being released. Dr. Lifton explained that many of the released POW's in Korea "spouted Communist gunk" for a full two weeks after being freed, until it finally dawned on them that the coercive pressure was off. If I had reacted differently, that would have been suspect, he said. In fact, he added, I was a rare phenomenon for psychiatrists studying coercive persuasion because I was the first and as far as he knew the only victim of a political kidnapping in the United States.

In his judgment, I had been "compliant" in going along with the SLA demands, but I had not been "converted" to their cause. Once freed from their power and control, I was realizing that I no longer had to comply with their thought reform and was, in fact, reverting to my former life and values. Dr. Lifton said he would be happy to testify on my behalf at the upcoming trial.

That was good news. However, if the defense used expert psychiatric testimony, the government was entitled to put its own experts on the stand in rebuttal. That meant that I would have to see two more doctors—for the government's side.

The first was Dr. Harry Kozol, an elderly, stout man with a high, squeaky voice and a strange accent. He was the Director of the Bridgewater, Massachusetts, Center for Criminally Dangerous Sex Offenders. I had five sessions with this man. At first, his questions were merely strange and sexually oriented:

Was Cinque black? Black black or light black?

What was the color of his eyes? The texture of his hair?

How did he caress you?

Tell me about the *seduction.* Did you kiss him?

Was he circumcised?

What did your *friends* do?

Tell me about your *lover,* William Wolfe . . .

The questions came at me like a full-scale cross-examination and I kept having to deny that anyone was my "friend" or my "lover" or that I had initiated any of the things that had been done to me. Then he began to ask me about the Harrises and what part they had played in various crimes. I refused point-blank to talk about the Harrises or anyone else still alive or say anything that could be used against them by the government. I told him I was still in fear of them. But he kept insisting. His provocative questions were beginning to make me ill, and within fifteen or twenty minutes he had me in hysterics. I ran out of the room, crying, looking for Al Johnson, whom I found standing by in another room. Then I came back and told Dr. Kozol that my lawyer said I did not have to answer such questions. He kept on. I ran out again. Came back. And on and on went those questions. In the end, Dr. Kozol and Al Johnson got into a furious argument and Al ended up taking him back to court for a hearing in an attempt to straighten out what the doctor could and could not ask me under the court order.

I was frankly surprised when I met the government's second expert. He turned out to be an M.D. and not a licensed psychiatrist at all. He was a bohemian type with a shaven head, wearing a turtleneck shirt with strands of beads around his neck. It seemed his specialty was treating runaway teenagers with drug and behavior problems and he had testified at more than two hundred trials in twenty-two states. This was Dr. Joel Fort, a "expert witness," who, according to Al Johnson, had volunteered to testify for the defense and then had gone over to the government's side when he was told that we could not use him.

Dr. Fort was easier on me than Dr. Kozol had been, but it was obvious that he had already made up his mind. He kept asking questions trying to pin down the notion that I had been a very unhappy girl before my kidnapping, that I was ashamed of my family's wealth and position, and that I wanted to break away from the family and be a rebel. None of that was true, which I tried to tell this doctor. My family life and upbringing had been a happy one and, in fact, I had always been thankful about the benefits and privileges of being a Hearst. But Dr. Fort clearly had his own stereotyped image of children of wealth. In four separate sessions, I went over the same story, the same facts of my

childhood, the kidnapping, the closet, the SLA, and the bank robbery.
Again I refused to talk about the Harrises or the others. The facts were
the same but the interpretations of those facts were different. Dr. Fort
seemed to have made up his mind that I had enjoyed being Tania, running around robbing banks and shooting up the streets of Los Angeles.
He thought I adored being "Queen of the SLA" (his phrase) and I
could not persuade him that he had it all wrong. Nor did I try very
hard. I wanted to get it over with, once and for all, and never talk of it
again.

When F. Lee Bailey returned to the jail, shortly before the trial was to
begin, I pleaded with him to keep me off the witness stand. I did not
think I could bear to go over all of this one more time. I felt shattered
by the ceaseless questioning. He again promised to keep me off the
stand.

My defense would be two-pronged, Bailey told me. First of all, I had
gone into the Hibernia Bank under clear duress. That part should be
easy. But the government, in order to convict me, would have to show
intent—that I had joined in the robbery voluntarily because I had
joined the SLA voluntarily. To prove that, the government would bring
in the shooting at Mel's and any and all events after the Hibernia Bank
robbery to try to prove that I had joined the SLA and cooperated with
them voluntarily. So our second line of defense would be diminished
capacity resulting from coercive persuasion—that I had been abused,
threatened, and scared out of my wits for so long that I was no longer
strong enough to resist. Legally, the defense would have to prove, he
said, that I had been reduced by the SLA to a state of diminished capacity and had not been mentally capable of resisting the SLA or of escaping. That was why the psychiatric testimony would be so important
—to link what had happened to me to what had happened to our
POW's in the Korean and Vietnam wars.

"If you were being tried in a military court, Patty," he told me, "I
could get you acquitted in one day."

CHAPTER

NINETEEN

"MAY IT PLEASE the Court, counsel, and ladies and gentlemen, I shall be somewhat more brief than Mr. Browning [the prosecutor], but I should say at the outset that ninety percent of what he told you in his opening about the manner in which the bank was robbed is not in dispute. And to save your time, we are hopeful that the evidence in support of those remarks is mercifully brief. The bank was robbed, it was robbed by the people described, except for Miss Hearst, but she was present, and she was carrying a weapon which was not operable. Before getting to that, however, I think that a short background may be helpful to you both as to the defendant and to those who took her from her home by force and against her will. In 1973, the Oakland School Superintendent, Marcus Foster, was assassinated. And the following day, the world heard for the first time, at least to my knowledge, of an organization of terrorists that called themselves the Symbionese Liberation Army . . ."

The famous F. Lee Bailey was outlining my defense to the seven women and five men sitting opposite me in the raised jury box. It was a jury from which blacks and college graduates had been systematically challenged by both the defense and the prosecution lawyers. In that stilled, tense, crowded courtroom, where everything looked so prim and proper, his voice was deep and resonant, the words simple and clear, the tone one of confidence and sincerity. . . . Marcus Foster

. . . Remiro and Little . . . the kidnapping . . . the closet . . . brain-washing . . . the bank robbery . . .

I sat there, numb, hearing that whole story one more time, trying to maintain control over my emotions. It seemed ominous that the testi-mony had begun on this day, February 4, 1976, exactly two years to the day that I had been dragged out of my Berkeley apartment.

Outside, the day was gray and overcast. Inside, on the nineteenth floor, the ceremonial courtroom was packed. I hardly dared to look up and around, lest I betray my fears to the horde of news reporters or media artists who filled spectator benches.

The news media, I was told, were furious with my family and me, as well as with the judge and court. More than three hundred of the top news people from all over the world had come to San Francisco to cover the "trial of the century" and most of them could not get into the courtroom. It was called the ceremonial courtroom because it was used for congressional hearings and swearing-in ceremonies, but the fifty-by-sixty-foot wood-paneled room could accommodate only one hundred eighty-three people. In the push-and-pull tug-of-war for seats, sixty-three were reserved for news organizations which represented many outlets; forty-eight unreserved seats were set aside for other news people, who would have to stand in line for them; sixteen seats went to the jury and four alternates. Six seats were reserved for my family, three in the front row and three in the rear. Those six seats were what infuriated the working press. Some of the press people were assigned seats in a jury box to the judge's left, facing the real jury, on the oppo-site side of the room. It was only later, after the trial, that we learned that several jurors had believed the press people had been positioned opposite them, at the request of my parents, in order to intimidate them. There were only fifty other seats left for the press and the gen-eral public and the waiting line was kept constant at one hundred and fifty, before marshals turned others away.

The press also was angry over being excluded from the *voir dire* questioning process in picking the jury panel while my family had been allowed to watch. For the first time in San Francisco history, a jury was going to be sequestered for the entire trial, from this first day to the day of the verdict. The necessity of locking up the jury at night had never been in doubt. The press was behaving like sharks in a feeding frenzy. Nothing was safe from their wild scavenging for "new angles" on the story—not even the potted plants in the halls of the Federal Building, which one day were headlined in the newspapers.

The jury selection had consumed four and a half days. Judge Carter had quizzed each one on his or her knowledge and interpretation of what he or she knew about Patty Hearst and the SLA. Of course, everyone on the jury panel had read stories or heard newscasts of the main events, but their own telling of what they thought they knew was supposed to reveal prejudice or preconceived notions on my guilt or innocence. It was evident that, unlike potential jurors at most other trials, just about everyone called *wanted* to serve on this jury. I was so nervous on the first day that my back muscles went into a spasm and knotted up. I could not move my neck. Someone had to find a doctor in the building, and she gave me two pills which not only relieved the spasm but just about knocked me out.

Al Johnson, acting as my legal mentor, explained what Bailey was doing. Al constantly tried to build up my confidence in the chief counsel and my certain acquittal. During the jury selection, he leaned over to me and explained seriously that "there are certain women who are 'Bailey types,' who just can't help going wacko over the guy—those are the types of women we are trying to select for your jury. . . . So don't worry about it . . . just relax."

But I could not relax. It was all I could do to keep from crying. Still, I liked Al Johnson; he seemed to mean well. During the *voir dire,* as the potential jurors answered the judge's questions, they kept referring to me in a most familiar fashion as "Patty," as if they had known me for years. I found this very distressing especially because of all the negative publicity given to my case. But Lee and Al both assured me that, on the contrary, this was a good sign. They said that it meant that these people felt they knew me and felt sympathetic toward me. I found this hard to believe.

Bailey was particularly interested in having on the jury men who had had military experience, because of the psychiatric testimony to come concerning coercive persuasion used on military POW's. He affected calling these men by their former rank in the armed services. He and Johnson, who were Marine veterans, also took to wearing their Marine Corps pins in their lapels.

In court, I looked at those seven women on the jury. They were so dissimilar in age, appearance, and background, and I wondered if any *one* of them was a "Bailey type." I could not tell; I could not read their minds. Would they understand what not even I had understood before about the process of coercive persuasion?

". . . And ultimately, finally, after exhaustive hours of psychological tests and psychiatric examinations and listening to all the tapes and examining all the evidence made available to them, the reports, running some 162 pages, the testimony will be from these people initially selected by this Court, and who will appear as defense witnesses—should the occasion arise—that Miss Hearst was a prisoner of war for twenty months, that she had every reason in her condition to believe that she had nowhere to go . . .."

Bailey's voice dropped to a low, intimate, personal tone as he reached the end of his opening statement. The jury was intent upon his every word. My mother and father, sitting in the front row of spectators, looked tense and tired.

". . . that her terror was real, that what she perceived any one of us would have perceived if so treated. And that it was impossible, due to what they have diagnosed her condition to have been, for her ever to have had any intent whatsoever to rob any bank or any person in the United States of America. The evidence, in sum, ladies and gentlemen, will show you that but for—this is the test—but for the kidnapping of Patty Hearst, there would have been no bank robbery including Patty Hearst, and she would not be here today. Thank you."

His opening was half the length and more than twice as effective as that of the U. S. Attorney for the Ninth District. Jim Browning, who had addressed the jury first, using sheafs of notes and diagrams of the bank, talked for almost two hours, summarizing what his witnesses would say. He managed to make the bank robbery dull! To convince the jury that I had robbed the bank voluntarily, he brought up the tape in which I had bragged about the robbery, and my shooting up the street outside of Mel's, as well as my "confession" to Tom Matthews and portions of the SLA book. In effect, he was telling the jury what the whole world already knew—that the government had pictures, witnesses, and several admissions in my own words which he said would prove that I was guilty of willingly robbing the Hibernia Bank.

When the prosecutor had finished and the jury filed out of the courtroom for a recess, Bailey dramatically demanded a mistrial, on the grounds that the prosecutor had brought in the post-robbery events in

Los Angeles, which "taints the jury so that it no longer can hear this case."

"Okay," said the judge. "The motion will be denied."

Al Johnson explained to me that we were asking for a hearing on a defense motion that all testimony relating to what had happened after the bank robbery, for which I had been charged, should be excluded from the trial. Our contention was that I was on trial for the bank robbery only and the jury should not be prejudiced by any other crimes I might have committed after the bank robbery. The government argued that those post-robbery events tended to show my true intent in robbing the bank and should be permitted in evidence. To convict me, the government had to show not only that I participated in robbing the bank; it had to prove that I had done so voluntarily and deliberately. Everything I had done from the time of my kidnapping to the events in Los Angeles, in the government's view, indicated my intent.

The government started the presentation of its case, taking two whole days, Thursday and Friday, to prove that the bank had, indeed, been robbed, that there were cameras in the bank, that I had been in the bank holding a sawed-off carbine along with a black man wearing a floppy hat named Donald DeFreeze and three other women, who were duly named. The government put on nineteen witnesses to testify to a ninety-second event, which the defense would have been happy to stipulate to. Instead, F. Lee Bailey cross-examined almost all of them, the U. S. Attorney re-examined them, and Bailey re-cross-examined. I could not tell what the jury made of it all. The witnesses—bank employees and customers—disagreed over what they saw and heard. By the second day, the most celebrated trial of the year, if not the decade, had become boring. At the defense table, we thought we saw the honorable Judge Oliver Carter catnapping.

For the hearing on the admissibility of the government's post-robbery evidence, Al Johnson told me that I would *have* to take the witness stand. I refused in protest. But Johnson insisted that I was the only one who could explain the circumstances under which I "confessed" to wanting to rob the bank—in the tape recording, to Tom Matthews in his van, and again in the SLA book manuscript. So, that Monday, I took the witness stand.

The media concluded that I had been coached, because of my careful answers, but all that Bailey and Johnson ever instructed me to do was to answer questions with a yes or no or with as short and direct a reply as possible, to volunteer no information, and to leave everything else, even if I did not understand it, to my lawyers. For some reason I could not fathom, Bailey added that I should never say on the witness stand, "I can't remember." If I could not remember something, he said, I should reply, "I don't recall."

What I recall mostly from my first day on the witness stand was the judge saying, "Would you speak up, Miss Hearst, so counsel can hear you?" The microphone, amplifying my weak voice, was no more than an inch from my mouth. I testified that Angela Atwood had written the tape about the bank robbery and I had merely read it; that I had told Tom Matthews about the bank robbery because Bill Harris had told me to recite my regular spiel for outsiders; that the Harrises had supervised the SLA manuscript which was *supposed* to show how great the SLA was and that not everything in it was true.

But under cross-examination by Browning, things were different. I tried to explain that I was in constant fear of being killed unless I did what I was told to do. But there was nothing clear-cut or logical to explain why I had helped the Harrises escape from Mel's, why I did not try to escape later when left alone for a few minutes with Tom Matthews in the van or when Jack Scott was driving me cross-country. For instance, on the shooting at Mel's the prosecutor put the questions this way:

"Now, can you explain to me, Miss Hearst, why you did that?"

With a deep sigh, I tried:

"From the time I took the blindfold off until that happened, there were classes every day and this was one of the particular ones on what to do if something like that happened, and when it happened I didn't even think. I just did it, and if I had not done it and if they had been able to get away, they would have killed me." I was thinking of the Codes of War.

"Did you prefer staying with the Harrises, who had threatened to kill you, to simply walking away?" he asked.

"Did I what?"

"You rescued the Harrises, did you not, when you could have walked away?"

"I couldn't have walked away."

"Why not?"

"Because if I walked away, the other members of the SLA would have come looking for me and I felt that the FBI was looking for me too."

And so it went. I tried to respond to the questions but I had the distinct feeling that here in court no one could understand or wanted to understand the situation I had been in. They had not been there. The crux of it was my state of mind at the time, what I had been thinking, my intent, and only I could know that.

The biggest and most important fight at this two-day hearing came when the U. S. Attorney tried to question me about two sheets of paper found in the Harrises' apartment, which contained my handwritten notations on the surveillance of a bank, one of the fifteen we had cased in the Sacramento area. Bailey objected violently. Judge Carter overruled his objection. Then Bailey instructed me not to answer the question. This area of questioning would lead to my having to tell them of the Carmichael bank robbery, in which Mrs. Opshal had been shot and killed. The judge ruled that he would allow the prosecutor's question "because there is a whole course of conduct here that has to be evaluated, rather than a single incident."

His face flushed a deep red, Bailey instructed me again not to answer the question on the constitutional grounds of self-incrimination. "You are requiring the defendant to answer questions on the subject matter now sought, fished out by the prosecutor, which would, or might, expose her to charges, State and Federal, for felonious crimes, which I will not further allow," he told the judge. On those grounds, the judge upheld Bailey's objection *for this particular hearing* and precluded Browning from asking me any more questions about events in Sacramento.

We won that one. But we lost on the overall motion to suppress the evidence that pertained to my actions after the bank robbery. Bailey had argued that I had been forced by the SLA to make the tape, talk to Matthews, and help write the SLA book manuscript; therefore my admissions were forced upon me and should not be put before the jury. The prosecutor argued that all my statements had been made voluntarily to third parties, not to any government or police officials, and the jury should be told about them because they showed my intent and state of mind. He declared that the prosecution intended to show that I had joined the SLA voluntarily, robbed the bank voluntarily, and had said as much in the tape, to Tom Matthews, and in the SLA book. It was the only way the government could present the material to the jury because, he declared, although the government had asked, the Harrises, through their attorney, had "notified the government that they do not wish to come in and testify."

I was outraged! How could that man say such a thing? How could the government even consider putting my *kidnappers* on the stand to testify against me? Why weren't the Harrises being tried for the Hibernia Bank robbery, not to mention my kidnapping?

In denying our motion to exclude the damaging testimony, Judge Carter ruled: "At this time, I will deny the motion to suppress. And I will find that by a preponderance of the evidence that the government has established that the statements made by the defendant after the happening of the bank robbery, whether by tape recording, or oral communication, or in writing, were made voluntarily."

That meant the government could introduce that evidence, and, it seemed to me from what he said, that the judge already thought I was guilty. If he believed that I had made the tape recording about the bank robbery on my own accord, then he would not believe I had been forced to do anything else connected with this case. It also seemed that the U.S. prosecutor would do or say anything to win his case. It was as though I were seeing a preview of the whole trial in this hearing and my hopes sank to a new low.

Given the green light, the government presented Anthony Shepard, the clerk at Mel's who had caught Bill Harris shoplifting, and Tom Matthews, the high school senior. Shepard described in detail the events at Mel's and then added a new wrinkle. He identified *me,* instead of Bill Harris, as the person who advanced upon him with a submachine gun when we were abandoning our van. On cross-examination, Bailey got him to admit that that was not what he had told the police on the day of the incident. At that time, he identified the person who forced him to back up his car as a man six feet tall. But Shepard said he changed his mind later on.

Tom Matthews, still irrepressibly happy, told the jury that in the van, while he was a prisoner, I had told him of joining the SLA, robbing the bank, and that "she said it was a good feeling to see her two comrades come running across the street." In cross-examination, Bailey tried to get young Matthews to admit that he too had been scared and had not tried to escape because of Bill Harris sitting there with a submachine gun cradled in his arms. But the ingenuous young man replied, "No, I was more excited than scared." He had in fact enjoyed the adventure of being with the fugitives, he said.

As a final question, Bailey asked Matthews what he had done with the piece of handcuff he had kept as a souvenir and the witness's face crumpled. He admitted that he still had it. As he left the witness stand, he was collared by two FBI agents and taken off for further grilling. Obviously, he had not told the FBI about keeping that souvenir.

Browning played the bank surveillance camera still photos, which had been run together to make a sort of jerky, old-time motion picture of the robbery in progress. There I was in the middle of the bank holding my semi-automatic carbine, pointing it this way and that way, then looking at my wrist as though checking the time (although I was not wearing a watch). It was awful, sitting there in court, seeing myself in the role of Tania and wondering what the jury would make of it all. Even with the movie, one could not quite be sure what was happening: Was I acting under my own free will? Or were Camilla Hall and DeFreeze pointing their guns at me? It did not make that much difference. Cinque could have shot anyone he wanted to shoot in the bank at the time, including me. . . . But would the jury understand that? I fought back tears.

The prosecution then put seven FBI agents on the stand, one after another, to pin down various aspects of the case, ending with Agent Padden, who gave his version of the circumstances of my arrest. And the prosecution rested, saving the remainder of its ammunition for rebuttal.

At the luncheon recess, I wished that we could just put up no defense, and get it all over with. But, Bailey said, that would have been tantamount to pleading guilty. The only way to exonerate myself was to win an acquittal. There had never been any inclination at all to plea-bargain with the government.

I had understood that I would not have to testify and be subjected to days of questioning by Jim Browning in front of a jury and the horde of newspaper people in the courtroom. I suppose I was the last to know, for Bailey and Johnson had told the press that I was likely to take the stand before the jury in order to refute the prosecution testimony. But they did not tell me until the beginning of the defense. Then they did not give me any choice. "You have to testify, Pat," said my lawyer.

The previous day, my former comrades had set off a bomb in one of the three guest houses at San Simeon. Apparently they had gone through the guest house on a guided tour and left a bomb there, timed to go off after they had left. No one was hurt, but a side wall was blown out, along with furniture and bric-a-brac, with damage estimated at close to one million dollars. And today, they had sent a covering communiqué, signed by the New World Liberation Front, taking credit for the bombing and demanding of my father $250,000 to pay for the legal defenses of the Harrises. The communiqué threatened further bombings and violence if their demands were not met within forty-eight hours. At the same time, the Harrises, from their jail cells in Los Angeles, were giving interviews to the press, saying that I had been a voluntary and loyal member of the SLA and only now was I becoming a turncoat to save my own hide.

The defense opened that afternoon, February 13, a Friday, with five of my Berkeley neighbors describing how they had seen me being dragged screaming from my apartment, the shots being fired and two cars screeching away. Yes, indeed, I had been kidnapped. Their testimony was brief. Then F. Lee Bailey led me gently by the arm to the witness stand.

I could hear the stir of anticipation in the courtroom and I hated F. Lee Bailey at that moment for misleading me about not putting me on the witness stand. That day and the following Monday and Tuesday I went over the whole thing, event by event. I listened to the SLA tape-recorded communiqués and was barely able to control the tears that threatened to flood my eyes as I heard Cinque's bombastic voice, raving in that courtroom as if he were alive again. With all my inner strength I fought off showing emotional reactions. It was bad enough to have to go over all of it again, but I was determined not to put on a "show" for the audience. Bailey and Johnson were not pleased. They wanted emotional outbursts, but they were not going to get them from me. Then I braced myself for what would become five full days of cross-examination by the U. S. Attorney of San Francisco.

There were no surprises for me in his questioning. I had gone over all of that material, in even greater detail, with the psychiatrists at the San Mateo jail. Nevertheless, my story did not come out in quite the same way in the courtroom. Giving short or one-word answers to lawyer's questions did not provide a straight, smooth narrative. Jim Browning, the prosecutor, skipped from subject to subject, intimating by the wording of his questions and his tone of voice his disbelief in what I was saying. It was as if he thought that the SLA was comprised of a small group of idealistic young people who really were not as cruel as I had made them out to be. They had taken me out of the closet from time to time to go to the bathroom, right? They had fed me. They had held conversations with me in the closet. Was sex *forced* upon me in the closet? Did I resist? Why not? Had I not been in love with William Wolfe (Cujo)? When I was offered a chance to stay with the SLA or go home, why didn't I choose to return home? Why didn't I try to escape? Why didn't I shoot them all when I was given a carbine to stand guard duty at night? Why didn't I shoot them in the bank? Why didn't I try to telephone my parents? Had I sent them any Christmas cards? Why not? Hadn't I written part of the SLA book manuscript? Hadn't I freed the Harrises from possible arrest at Mel's? Why didn't I just walk away from the van instead? Why hadn't I escaped from Jack Scott on those trips across the country? Didn't I have many opportunities to escape from the Harrises during the long year's time between the shootout and my arrest? What had happened all during that missing year? What was I concealing?

With the jury out of the courtroom, my lawyer persisted in his objection to my being questioned on that missing year, because it would force me to incriminate myself and if I pleaded the Fifth Amendment it would suggest to the jury that I wished to hide other crimes. Judge Carter ruled against us again, saying that the law held that "where a defendant takes the stand and testifies about a certain period of time [in my case from the time of my kidnapping to my arrest], the defendant has no right to plead the Fifth Amendment on a portion of that time frame." Bailey asked for a fifteen-minute recess.

During the recess, he told me that under no circumstance was I to answer any question about the so-called missing year, for that would open the questioning to the Carmichael bank robbery. Not only would that influence the jury, but it would leave me wide open to be prosecuted on that more serious crime. Newspaper stories already had linked me publicly to that bank robbery. In fact, one story even reported that the FBI had a positive identification of me having been inside the bank. I was sure that most if not all of the jurors knew about those press reports, which were current a few weeks after my arrest. I asked Bailey if it would not be better for me to tell my whole story about Carmichael than to leave it to the jury to imagine much worse than the truth about it. He told me I did not know what I was talking about. Very firmly, he instructed me on what to say, to follow his signals in the courtroom. Standing beside me, he would nod or shake his head to each question. It was the only course open to us, he said.

"Miss Hearst, you testified earlier, I believe, that you had come back across the United States with Jack Scott and they dropped you off in Las Vegas, please?" asked the U. S. Attorney. My attorney, standing off to one side, shook his head.

"I refuse to answer on the grounds that it may tend to incriminate me and cause extreme danger to myself and my family." This was the melodramatic answer which Bailey had told me to give. I was prepared to tell about the bombings and the threats against my family and myself if I testified against my former comrades. I believed those threats.

". . . extreme danger to herself and her family is not a legal basis for refusing to answer the question," declared Browning.

"Well, I instruct this witness to answer the question," said Judge Carter from his bench. "I've already ruled under the circumstance of her testimony she's not entitled to raise the Fifth Amendment in these circumstances."

"What is the answer to the question?" asked the prosecutor.

"I refuse to answer."

The judge threatened to cite me for contempt of court. I looked over at Bailey and he shook his head. "I refuse to answer," I repeated. What could Judge Carter do to me? Put me in jail? It was an idle threat.

"Who met you in Las Vegas?"

"I refuse to answer."

And on and on it went. Jim Browning had a fine time asking questions laden with innuendo. Was James Kilgore a member of the NWLF? What was your relationship with Steven Soliah? With Kathleen Soliah? Were you and those persons, as allies, not in fact engaged in a program of armed struggle?

"I refuse to answer."

Forty-two times Bailey instructed me to refuse to answer the prosecutor's questions, and the effect upon the seven women and five men in the jury box was devastating. The questions themselves, without my answers, told the jury what the prosecutor wanted them to hear. Further, they implied that there was much more beneath the surface that the jury was not being told about my criminal activities with the SLA, including the well-publicized Carmichael bank robbery.

Afterward, in the various analyses of the trial, there was a consensus in the legal community that my taking the witness stand and being forced to plead the Fifth Amendment against self-incrimination had dealt a deathblow to the defense. Many attorneys held that Bailey never should have put me on the witness stand in view of the risk of this happening.

Ironically, while I was refusing to respond in open court, I was telling all about the Carmichael bank robbery to another U. S. Attorney in secret. After my court day was over, I would go to another room in the Federal Building and meet with the chief federal prosecutor of Sacramento and his assistants, who were preparing their case against Steve Soliah for the Carmichael bank robbery. I told them everything I knew, answering all their questions. In exchange, I was granted "use immunity," that is, the government could not use anything I told them myself against me in any further proceeding.

My trial was still going on when Steve's began on March 10. The government could hardly prosecute me in San Francisco and also use me as their witness in Sacramento, vouching for my credibility. Instead of presenting the truth, the government tried to prove that Steve had been one of the robbers *inside* the bank, despite the fact that I had told them repeatedly that Steve had participated in the robbery but as a backup, outside the bank with Bill Harris. The prosecutors chose to rely on several witnesses who identified Steve as having been inside the bank. But when the defense in that trial showed that the witnesses were mistaken, Steve Soliah was acquitted. Emily Harris, who had shot Mrs. Opshal while leading the others in that robbery, was not prosecuted, or even indicted.

After seven full days on the witness stand, the worst part of my current ordeal was finished. I stumbled, blind-eyed, back to the defense table and sank down into the chair, thoroughly exhausted. Many in the courtroom had thought that I had responded listlessly, like a robot. It seemed as though my energy became depleted somewhere around midday. I had trouble concentrating. In truth, I had virtually given up eating any of the starch-laden, soggy jail food. I subsisted on bags of potato chips and packages of beef jerky, bought twice a week from the jail commissary. During the luncheon break on court days, my mother would smuggle sandwiches in for me via Al Johnson's briefcase. It was all I could do to keep alert at the defense table, listening to my own trial. That may have been due to my low level of energy or, more likely, to the high incidence of protracted, droning testimony.

Dr. West, Dr. Orne, and Dr. Lifton testified for the defense, describing and diagnosing my condition, explaining coercive persuasion and brainwashing, comparing my situation as a prisoner of war of the SLA to the POW's who had cooperated with *their* Communist jailers. Then they defended what they said under the convoluted cross-examination of Assistant U. S. Attorney David P. Bancroft, who was handling the psychiatric testimony for the government. The three psychiatrists were on the witness stand for two weeks, explaining, explaining, and explaining. It was too much. Each of them seemed to be going over the same material, saying the same things, and putting almost everyone to sleep. First one juror, then another, and then still another would seem to be dozing off, eyes closed, head nodding. Judge Carter now appeared to be asleep almost all the time, his eyes closed, head cupped in his hand, his elbow on the desk in front of him. The judge, a thin, sickly-looking old man, was obviously in frail health, having been hospitalized before the trial, but he did keep order in the court, rapping his gavel at the instant of a rare outbreak of laughter or noise in the courtroom. As the trial went into its second month, one of the newspaper artists, Joe Papin, captured the courtroom atmosphere with a wry cartoon, showing everyone in the courtroom fast asleep, including the eagle in the Great Seal of the United States, which hung on the wall high above Judge Carter's head.

The boredom quotient was relieved with the rebuttal testimony of the government's two expert witnesses. First Dr. Fort appeared in court with his own attorney with the plea that the court prevent his name from being reported in newspapers. That ridiculous request was denied by the judge but it did guarantee the doctor a good measure of publicity. Dr. Fort went over all of the events and psychological reports and testified that in his opinion I had joined the SLA and robbed the bank with them voluntarily because I had been bored and a rebel before my kidnapping.

"Doctor," asked Browning, "in your opinion was the defendant a private in an army of generals?"

"No, I think she was a queen in their army. She brought them international recognition. It was an exciting thing for her, and for the rest of them, that the media responded to the group the way it did."

Bailey, on lengthy cross-examination, attacked Dr. Fort's credentials and his credibility, and it went on for days. Dr. Fort was not a psychiatrist or a psychologist; he was an M.D. who described himself as a specialist in social and health problems. Bailey charged that Dr. Fort had offered his services to the defense, implying that if we had agreed to pay him, Dr. Fort would have testified on my behalf. The cross-examination became a personal, vitriolic battle between an "expert lawyer" and an "expert witness." Bailey clearly lost his cool during this fierce cross-examination, and perhaps the jury's sympathy as well, in going so far afield as to attempt to establish a seamy side of Dr. Fort's career. Dr. Fort was on the witness stand for a full week.

There also was considerable public speculation that my lawyer was overextending himself. For the first week in March he would rush from the courtroom at the end of the day, usually before the court adjourned, to fly in his private plane to Las Vegas, where he was conducting a paid legal seminar for trial lawyers, returning to San Francisco at midnight or afterward and appearing in court early the next morning. Some people in the press, and my parents as well, began wondering when he found time to prepare or develop his case.

Dr. Kozol gave more of the same. Describing me as a "rebel in search of a cause" before my kidnapping, he concluded that I had joined the SLA voluntarily because I could have left when Cinque had offered me the choice. "I would take the word of that black man," he declared.

Each time any of the expert witnesses gave their opinion, the judge would remind the jury that it was only an opinion and it was for the jury alone to decide the key issue of my intent. It would be up to the jury to decide whether to believe Drs. West, Orne, and Lifton, with all their academic honors, books, and impeccable credentials, who concluded that I was a victim, not a criminal, or to believe Drs. Fort and Kozol, who interviewed the same defendant, read the same psychological reports, and reached exactly the opposite conclusion.

In my estimation, the whole trial was a farce. The Hibernia Bank robbery seemed to have been forgotten. It was not mentioned for days and for weeks at a time. It was the media image of me on trial. I was portrayed as the symbol of the rebellious, radical youth movement of the sixties—the *ultimate* child of the sixties. But it was all so farfetched. I was not a child of the sixties; I was but a child, literally, *in* the sixties. In 1960, I was six years old.

My whole family was indignant hearing both Dr. Fort and Dr. Kozol
cite two or three insignificant peccadillos of my youth as examples of
my so-called rebellious nature. Anne was particularly resentful, commenting, "I'm glad it wasn't me who was kidnapped. With all the
pranks that I pulled growing up, I'd probably get the gas chamber."

Much of the public and the press seemed to want me punished not so
much for the crime of robbing the Hibernia Bank of $10,000 but rather
for supposedly turning upon my parents and upon middle-class morality and "thumbing my nose" at everybody. But how could anyone
who had the facts, and stopped to think for more than a minute, believe that someone kept bound and blindfolded in a closet for fifty-
seven days would *voluntarily* join forces with his or her tormentors?
How could anyone believe it had been *fun* to live in filth and privation
and paralyzing fear? I could not believe that Dr. Fort or Dr. Kozol or
even Jim Browning, the prosecutor, really believed what they were
telling the jury. Everyone seemed caught up in the adversary proceeding, and each side wanted to win.

F. Lee Bailey never expressed to me any doubt at all that we would
win an acquittal and Al Johnson kept reassuring me that while the
court proceedings might not make much sense to me as we went along,
Bailey would wrap it all up in one of his typically brilliant summations
to the jury. It was in the summation that Bailey could argue the facts of
the case and persuade the jury, Al Johnson told me with complete faith
in his colleague.

Still, for me it was all like a three-ring circus. Jim Browning was
constantly getting the dates of events mixed up, and from time to time
Judge Carter would appear confused about who was on trial. He would
call me Patricia Harris and refer at times to Bill and Emily Hearst. The
main arena might well have been the courtroom, but a full-scale
sideshow was being carried on throughout the trial in the special press
room on the seventh floor, where Bailey and Johnson and Browning
and Bancroft staged a daily performance after court for the ever-eager
press. Bailey would often slip out during testimony in order to talk to
some of his buddies in the press out in the corridor. Al Johnson would
always tell me that Bailey was doing more important work out in the
corridor swinging media opinion to our side than he would be able to
accomplish listening to dull periods of testimony. On one occasion,
when Dr. Kozol began testifying, the defense lawyers thought his voice

and manner of speaking so hilarious that they had to slip out of the courtroom to laugh in the corridor with their reporter friends. Bailey and Johnson looked at one another and one of them asked, "But who's in there with Pat?" Al was sent back to keep me company.

Meanwhile, my former comrades Bill and Emily Harris appeared from jail on the *Today* show, gave out interviews frequently to one and all, and from the sidelines were denying that any force was used on me, other than in the kidnapping itself. I had no reason to fear them, they declared. At the same time some NWLF groups were carrying out bombing raids on the Hearst Corporation. After sending threatening notes and bombing San Simeon, a bomb was planted and went off outside the Hearst headquarters building in New York City. One of the chalets at Wyntoon was bombed. My father hired a bodyguard to accompany my mother and him to the courtroom every day.

In the third ring of the circus, I had to contend almost every day with all sorts of kooks, cranks, and criminals who were being processed and filtered through the marshal's office on the top floor of the courthouse. Rising every day at 6 A.M. in the San Mateo jail, I would get dressed, drink a cup of coffee, and leave at 6:30 for the twenty-five-mile drive to San Francisco. Usually I had an hour and a half or almost two hours to spend in the marshal's holding cell until my trial began at 9:30. In that time, other prisoners—either those just arrested or those there awaiting their own trials—would parade by the cell. At times, another prisoner would be put in with me. One was a pretty Swiss girl who told me she could not understand the uptight Americans who had arrested her at customs for coming in with "a little marijuana."

"How much did you have on you?" Based on what she said, I was thinking in terms of a couple of joints.

"Oh, only two hundred and fifty kilos," she said nonchalantly. "It's nothing . . . everybody knows a little grass never hurt anyone. It's all so stupid and unfair."

Another time, a radical group had been rounded up and arrested on possession of illegal weapons and explosives. They were never put in the same cage with me, but I could hear them singing and calling out to me: "You snitch bitch, I wouldn't want to be you. . . . I'm high on the revolution and I've never been so happy . . ." It all sounded like so much claptrap to me now. They heaped verbal abuse on me

daily until one of their comrades turned government witness and
testified against them. Suddenly they were no longer the happy revolutionaries or so smart-alecky with me or with the U.S. marshals.

There were also repeated threats on my life. On my twenty-second
birthday the marshals considered one threat serious enough to transport
me in a different unmarked car, which took a completely different
route to the courthouse. I knew that there were radicals out there
who might very well seek instant fame by taking a shot at me. For a
while, Sara Jane Moore, who had tried to redeem her radical credentials by attempting to assassinate President Gerald Ford, was in
the San Mateo County Jail and was constantly seeking me out. I was
just as constantly dodging her and slamming my cell door shut in her
face. I was really too far gone in my own depression to take these
threats too seriously, but my parents were very concerned about my
safety and Bailey and Johnson always insisted that I was much safer in
jail than being out on bail.

The prosecution saved its one surprise witness for the end of its rebuttal case against me. Throughout the trial, we had an inside, secret
pipeline into the prosecutor's own home, something he never suspected.
At the dinner table every night he would tell his family all about the
case and his daughter would tell her friend at school and her friend
would call Al Johnson and tell *him* all about it. When we learned that
the prosecutor had a surprise witness in store for us by the name of Mr.
McMonkey, we could not figure out who that could possibly be. There
was no McMonkey in any of the area's telephone directories.

We found out near the end of the trial when Browning put three FBI
agents on the the stand. One described an enlargement of the group
SLA photograph we had taken, showing the Olmec monkey talisman I
wore around my neck. Another identified the Olmec monkey found in
my purse when I had been arrested. Another showed the jury another
Olmec monkey that had been taken from Cujo's body after his death in
the fire. At the defense table, we looked at one another in astonishment
—so that was Mr. McMonkey! It was a very clever move by the prosecution. The implication was clear: I had preserved that talisman because I had loved Willie Wolfe so deeply that I could not bear to part
with it. On the witness stand, I had told them that I could not stand
William Wolfe, much less love him, and now, in the closing days of the
trial, I could not explain to the jury that I had kept that little stone

figure only because I had believed it might have some value as an archaeological find. Browning also produced an "expert witness" who testified that my Olmec monkey was not old at all, but could be purchased at any roadside stand in Latin America. . . . We underestimated the impact of this evidence, but to almost everyone else the conclusion was that I had lied when I testified that I had believed Cujo when he told me the figurines were 2,500 years old. No one considered that Cujo had lied to me.

That Olmec monkey figurine, turning up as my long trial was coming to its end, had a strange, personal effect upon me. Sitting there in the courtroom and seeing the two little stone figures dangling from the hand of the prosecutor, I was suddenly struck with the piercing reality of it all: For the first time, I realized with absolute certainty that Cujo was dead . . . Cinque was dead . . . the others were gone . . . they could not hurt me anymore . . .

With all the testimony in, the trial almost over, Al told me about preparing for the summation to the jury. "Tomorrow, for the closing arguments, Pat, I want you to wear that blue pants suit of yours. It's very important."

I thought he must be mad. How could something like that be important? I asked him.

"It's tradition," he declared. "Everyone wears their sincere blues for final arguments. Now don't argue with me, just take my word for it; it's important, so do what I say!"

In the courtroom the next day, the prosecution table, which usually was crowded with attorneys and FBI agents, was nearly empty. Jim Browning sat there with only one assistant at his side. No one could miss the contrast with the defense table. Every lawyer associated with the defense team was crowded around the table and they all were wearing "sincere" dark blue suits. I felt like a fool in my navy pants suit. "It looks like a goddamn board of directors meeting," I overheard my father grumble.

In winding up his laborious, point-by-point summation of the case to the jury, the U.S. prosecutor held up the little stone monkey figure that had been found in my purse. Dangling the necklace from his outstretched hand, he told the jury:

"I ask you also to consider Miss Hearst's testimony when I asked her what her strong feeling was about Willie Wolfe; do you remember that?

She says, 'I couldn't stand him.' . . . On the occasion of her arrest, she
had this little stone face in her purse that Willie Wolfe gave her over a
year and a half after he had raped her, according to her. She couldn't
stand him and yet there is the little stone face that can't say anything,
but I submit to you, can tell us a lot. . . .

"In short, ladies and gentlemen, we ask you to reject the defendant's
entire testimony as not credible. She asks us to believe she didn't mean
what she said on the tapes. She didn't mean what she wrote in the documents. She didn't mean it when she gave this power salute, this
clenched-fist salute, after her arrest. That was out of fear of the Harrises, she tells us. She didn't mean it when she told the San Mateo
County deputy sheriff that she was an urban guerrilla. She says the
Tobin conversation wasn't the real Patricia Hearst. The Mel's shooting
incident was simply a reflex, ladies and gentlemen; the untruths in the
affidavits were simply some attorney's idea. She was in such fear she
couldn't escape in nineteen months, while she was crisscrossing the
country, or even get word to her parents or someone else. The confession to Matthews was recited out of fear. She couldn't stand Willie
Wolfe, yet she carried that stone face with her until the day she was
arrested.

"It's too big a pill to swallow, ladies and gentlemen. It just does not
wash. I ask whether you would accept this incredible story from anyone but Patricia Hearst. And if you wouldn't, don't accept it from her
either."

Jim Browning's summation was not brilliant or dazzling, but it was
well prepared and very thorough. He spoke for two hours, covering
just about every major point at issue during the seven-week trial, quoting excerpts from the testimony in such a way that even some of the
words of defense witnesses were used against me.

F. Lee Bailey's turn came directly after the luncheon recess. There
was a tension, an anticipation in the courtroom. I think everyone, including myself, relished the climax of the trial—the summation of evidence by the famous and brilliant attorney from Boston. I expected him
to demolish the prosecutor's carefully twisted tapestry of evidence. I
expected him to bring together and to make sense of that great mass of
evidence so that the seven women and five men of the jury—as well
as the media people in the back of the courtroom—could see and understand once and for all what had happened to me in those months I
had spent with Cinque and the Harrises.

The judge said, "You may proceed, Mr. Bailey." He rose from the defense table, grabbing an unruly stack of notes, and I could see that his hands were shaking. His hair was slightly mussed and his face was flushed. I wondered if he had been drinking at lunch. He detached the microphone from its stand at the attorney's podium and began to address the jury without referring to his notes. Soon, he was talking of people eating each other in the Andes, of G. Gordon Liddy, of the plot of a book called *A Covenant with Death*, and he talked at length about himself and the difficult tasks of lawyers. It was not easy to follow his train of thought.

He seemed to be talking more about his difficulty in handling this case than about the specific evidence, more about what had appeared in the press than about what was said in the courtroom. And then disaster struck. As he swept his arm up in a gesture, he knocked a glass of water off the podium. The water dribbled down the front of his pants. Several members of the jury tittered. The judge smiled. But F. Lee Bailey went on talking, disregarding the ignobility of having wet his pants. (The jury had a good laugh about this later in the jury room.) It was, to say the least, distracting.

He spoke for less than forty-five minutes, but as I cringed in my seat, trying to follow his disjointed discourse, it seemed like a lifetime. He skipped from one point to another, never to my mind quite putting it all together.

"Patricia Hearst was not a bad girl. She is not famous for anything she did before February 4. She's famous for what happened to her afterward. And what did happen is up to you to decide. . . .

"This case is riddled with doubt. It always will be. Perry Mason brings perfect solutions to all cases. Real life doesn't work that way. No one is ever going to be sure. But there is not anything close to proof beyond a reasonable doubt that Patty Hearst wanted to be a bank robber. What you know, and you know in your hearts to be true, is beyond dispute. There was talk about her dying, and she wanted to survive. Thank God, so far she has. Thank you very much."

After we had left the courtroom, I accosted Al Johnson. What had happened to Bailey in the courtroom? Bailey was not with us, for he had gone immediately to the press room, and I doubt if I would have had the nerve to attack the great man. Al hung his head. "I honestly don't know, Pat," he said. "We rehearsed the closing arguments for hours last night and it was great. But he didn't use any of it.

I just don't know why he did it that way, but I'm sure he had a good reason. He doesn't believe that a closing argument should take more than twenty minutes. . . . I just don't know."

The next morning, Wednesday, March 10, 1976, Judge Carter instructed the jury on the law applicable to the case. As he droned on with the technicalities of the law, I kept hearing him imply to the jury that legally, technically, and in fact I was guilty. I knew that both the defense and government attorneys submitted the points of law they wanted included in the judge's charges to the jury. I could hear the judge give both sides, but it always seemed to come out to my ear as a request for a guilty verdict.

"The fact that a witness refuses to answer a question after being instructed by the Court to answer may be considered by the jury in determining the credibility of the witness and the weight her testimony deserves. . . .

"That the defendant may have been kidnapped by others prior to the commission of the crimes charged is not alone sufficient to absolve her of responsibility for any subsequent criminal acts. . . . The compulsion must be present, and immediate, and of such a nature as to induce a well-founded fear of impending death or serious bodily injury. . . ."

Hearing the judge's charge, my mother, who had attended every day of the trial, was crying. I looked over at her, marveling at her strength, and thought that there is only so much a person can endure.

The jury filed out of the courtroom to begin its deliberations at 10:48 and I was taken up to the marshal's holding cell on the top floor. The arrangements were that as long as the jury was in deliberation, I would wait upstairs in the courthouse; when the jury retired for the night, I would be taken back to the San Mateo County Jail. At 5 P.M. I was transported back to jail. Everyone speculated that the jury would be out a long time. Almost everyone around me, including the U.S. marshals, told me to expect an acquittal. Al Johnson thought at the least I would get a hung jury. Janey Jimenez joked about what we would have to drink together when I was set free, probably at the end of the weekend. I was the only one who was not the least bit optimistic about the outcome, for while I had not felt that the case was lost during the testimony, I thought it had certainly been lost, or thrown away, during the closing arguments.

Back at the courthouse early the next morning, arrangements were made for me to meet with my parents and sisters in one of the jury rooms. Our meeting was very emotional. It was, with the exception of the night of my arrest, the first time that I had been able to touch and hug them in two years. The prospect of returning home with them, free at last and done with it all, in a day or two or three, was just too much for any of us. We attempted our usual family jokes and gibes, but the tears flowed pretty freely. "Don't get your hopes up," I tried to warn my sisters. "You never can tell what a jury will do."

The jury sent word out that they did not want to break for lunch. A couple of hours later the word came that they had reached a verdict. The brevity of the deliberations came as a great surprise. Speculation abounded. The U.S. marshals, who had grown close to me, promised me a party immediately after the acquittal. They even started taking drink orders, jokingly.

"What'll you have, Janey?"

"A margarita."

"What'll you have, Pat?"

"Bread and water," I replied.

It took another two hours to round up all the principals and allow the press people and spectators to pass through the electronic search device at the door. So it was past four in the afternoon when all were in their assigned places and the jury filed into the courtroom.

As usual, all eyes in the press corps were on me . . . I could sense that they were watching to catch some emotion, some nuance of feeling, some hint of reaction that they could play up. In a final desperate attempt at showmanship, one of the defense team whispered to me, "No matter what the verdict, Pat, I want you to jump up and throw your arms around your mother. It'll look great!" But I was determined to show no emotion whatever, no matter what the outcome. Bailey looked at the somber faces and leaned over. "It's bad," he said, stating the obvious. They were all staring straight ahead, not at me. The foreman handed the slip of paper to a court crier, who handed it to the court clerk, a kindly man who had slipped pieces of candy to me during the trial. The clerk opened the paper and his face sagged as he read it. The judge read the verdict to himself, nodded, and handed the paper back to the clerk to be read to the open court:

"We, the jury, find the defendant *guilty* on the first count and *guilty* on the second count."

Janey Jimenez, standing behind me, burst into tears.

"I never had a chance," I said to Bailey in a daze. If he heard me, he did not bother to answer.

CHAPTER

TWENTY

AT FIRST I had been terrified of the San Mateo County Jail. Now it was as familiar as home. There were never-changing surroundings, the same faces, a steady routine, and very little pressure as long as you coasted along with the bureaucracy. After the verdict, the guards searched my cell and removed every conceivable object with which they thought I might kill myself. I laughed at them. I had survived the SLA and I could live through any incarceration. I had learned how to get along in the jailhouse: Mind your own business, but be prepared to fight if you have to. There were a few inmates who tried to provoke me with insults but I had been well toughened in the long months with the SLA. The county jail was a hundred times better than being a POW or a private in the SLA.

I spent most of the time alone in my small cell, crocheting or reading. But I also got out and walked around the cell area, listening to the stories of other inmates, discovering how heroin, marijuana, and other drugs were smuggled into the jail, and learning generally how to get along in this special world. Bailey and Johnson said they would appeal my conviction on grounds that the judge had erred in allowing testimony on other, post-robbery crimes, which adversely influenced the jury. But what I wanted most was to get out, however temporarily, on bail so that I could be with my family. I had little hope of avoiding a prison sentence. Speculation focused on the idea that because I was a Hearst I would be treated lightly, and it appeared that much of the press and the public were clamoring for a long sentence as just punishment. They seemed to have forgotten that I had been the victim of a violent kidnapping and prolonged abuse.

I readily agreed to cooperate with the authorities and to testify, if need be, against the Harrises. I hated them for what they'd done to me. But it was only after my arrest and the hours spent with the psychiatrists that I had come to understand just how cruel and inhuman they had been to me, beyond any political or revolutionary theory. My sister Gina had asked Dr. Singer, the Berkeley psychologist, what made Bill and Emily Harris the way they were. She had replied, "Some people are just evil."

Toward the others, the Soliahs, Kilgore, Bortin, Bonnie Wilder, I felt no animosity. They had nothing to do with my kidnapping. However, Bailey and Johnson told me that if I cooperated with the authorities, I would have to answer their questions about all the people and events of which I had knowledge. And while there was no "deal" or guarantee that cooperation would lessen my sentence, it would be a fundamental aspect of proving to the government that I was not a revolutionary. After all, Johnson told me, I had been convicted and in the minds of many, including Judge Carter, there was no assurance that I was not an adherent of the SLA. The public was never aware of my cooperation with the authorities during and after my trial. All my meetings with the FBI and prosecutors were kept secret to protect me from retribution by terrorists or fellow inmates. Johnson assured me that Bailey and his staff, plus a Harvard Law professor, would begin work on an appeal to overturn my conviction. "Don't worry," he said, adding, "You're safer here in jail than out on the street where anyone could get you."

Vincent Hallinan, my former attorney, publicly denounced the Bailey-Johnson handling of my case. "No amount of mischance, negligence, stupidity, or idiocy could have loused up the case worse than the way it was loused up . . ." Al advised me to pay no attention to such Monday-morning quarterbacking. I did not know what to think. After the verdict a new wave of depression engulfed me. I did not seem able to connect with anyone or take an active interest in anything pertaining to my legal situation. Crocheting helped pass the time while I waited for the date when Judge Carter would sentence me. The press started anew its clamor for interviews but I turned down all such requests. Family visits still were limited to twice a week and there seemed nothing more I could do but wait.

About two days after my conviction, Al came to me with a letter.

"Remember the paper I told you I would be bringing you to sign one day? Well, here it is." The letter was to a publisher. It stated that I agreed to F. Lee Bailey writing a book about me and the trial and pledged that I would cooperate with him and not compete with a book of my own for at least eighteen months after his was published. I couldn't argue. I signed it for him, confused as to the necessity for it.

A week after being convicted in San Francisco, I was flown down to Los Angeles, hustled through a raving mob of television and newspaper cameramen, and brought before a judge of the Los Angeles County court. There I was arraigned on the same charges lodged against the Harrises—eleven counts of assault, robbery, and kidnapping resulting from the events surrounding the shoot-out at Mel's.

Al Johnson told me not to worry about it. He always said that. I was beyond worrying. I had reached the point where I believed that I could have been convicted of *any* crime anywhere in California simply because I was "Patty Hearst."

Finally, on April 12, I was brought before Judge Carter for sentencing. I did not like what had apparently been worked out beforehand with the attorneys involved. Judge Carter imposed the maximum sentence upon me—twenty-five years for the bank robbery plus ten more years for the use of a firearm in the commission of a felony. The maximum sentence was a necessary formality that would enable the court to commit me to a ninety-day psychiatric study by the Bureau of Prisons. On the basis of its report, the judge would pass final sentence. I pleaded with Al Johnson to get me out of this internment for psychological study. It would be like waiting in limbo. I wanted to be sentenced so that I could be released on bail and wait in freedom until my conviction was overturned. Bailey and Johnson had assured me that there had been enough errors in law at my trial to ensure a reversal in the Court of Appeals. But there was a "Catch-22": I could not appeal until after being sentenced by the trial judge following the ninety-day evaluation. Or so I was told. I later learned that my conviction could have been appealed any time after the judgment. As for the sentence, this ninety-day study was a means by which Judge Carter could give me a lighter sentence than ordinary or perhaps even sentence me to time already served. Al Johnson could outargue me every time. But after each of his visits, I could not help but think that once again I had been given the runaround. It seemed ridiculous for the court to want more psychological tests or reports on me; I had seen all those psychiatrists and psychologists in San Mateo before my trial and they had written hundreds of pages. What more could they want from me? Further, in my heart, I knew that Judge Carter was not going to give me a light sentence: I sensed that all during the trial. All this, as far as I was concerned, was for naught.

From the courtroom I was led, not back to jail, but down to the U. S. Attorney's office and seated at a large square table. There I faced at least twenty federal, state, and local prosecutors and FBI agents, while my lawyers negotiated the arrangements under which I would cooperate with them. I felt like a pawn in a master chess tournament. The FBI wasted no time at all; the debriefing started immediately and continued the next morning in a jury room of the San Mateo courthouse. I began from the beginning, telling three FBI men all about that missing year. . . .

It was the same three almost all the time: Charles Bates, agent-in-charge of the San Francisco office; Lawrence Lawler, the assistant agent-in-charge; and a special agent, a bald man named Monte Hall. I saw them so many times that I nicknamed them "the Three Stooges" and sometimes called them "Mo, Larry, and Curly." I was just amusing myself, with no malice intended, and they took it all in stride, although "Curly" was less than flattered. As my protector, Al Johnson sat in on all the sessions. It was exhausting, hour after hour answering their questions, going over the whole thing again. There was a major irony —while the jury had rejected my story, these federal agents had no trouble believing me.

It was after the third or fourth session with them, late in the afternoon, that I was returned to my jail cell feeling particularly tired and weak. I lay down in my bunk bed and knew I could not sleep. My body craved rest yet my mind raced on, alive and active with thought. I got up to walk the cell area. Then I coughed and felt a sharp, piercing pain in my chest and a sort of sound from within me, as though a balloon were deflating. Pain shot down my right arm. My first thought was "collapsed lung," and I said to myself, "That's all I need at this point."

The pain subsided and I was still alive, but feeling depleted. I made my way to the deputy sheriff's office on the floor. "I don't feel well at all," I told her. "Something's wrong . . . I've got to see the doctor . . ."

After she finished what she was writing at her desk she looked up at me. The expression on her face suddenly changed. She picked up the phone and called the jail doctor and then told me to go back and wait in my cell. The doctor would get to me just as soon as he finished his rounds in the men's wing.

I was so sleepy but every time I closed my eyes I felt the room spin and the last bit of vital energy slipping out of my body. It reminded me of the weakness I had felt in the SLA's people's prison. I was beginning to die. I knew that if I fell asleep in my cell, I would never wake up. So I sat up and began slapping my face to stay awake and conscious. Every time I moved, my body hurt.

It was a full hour and a half before I was summoned to the doctor's office. I walked in and heard him ask, "So what's wrong with you?" He put a stethoscope to my chest and listened and after a bit of thought announced, "You might have a slight pneumothorax . . . nothing that a little chicken soup wouldn't cure."

Not knowing what a pneumothorax was, I told him, "I think my lung's collapsed . . . I heard this pop and air going out of it, like a balloon." A woman paramedic in the office agreed. While the doctor and deputies wondered what to do, I asked if I could call my lawyer. Al had left for the airport to go to Los Angeles, where I was due in court the next day. Knowing I could not reach him, I phoned my mother and asked her to try to trace him. But I did not tell her what had happened to me. From the sound of my voice, however, she knew something was *very* wrong.

The jail doctor decided I needed hospitalization, but no one could locate a U.S. marshal and only federal marshals are empowered to take a federal prisoner out of a county jail. The sheriff could not be reached. Tensions rose as they all disputed what to do with me: There was a danger of my dying and they could not risk that with the most famous prisoner in the country. . . . Then, the Duty Officer declared that he would take full responsibility for moving me to nearby Sequoia Hospital in Redwood City, a private hospital which had a special trauma unit in its emergency room. Phone calls were made, I was waist-chained and handcuffed according to regulations, and with two deputies supporting me by the arms, I was walked out of the San Mateo County Jail for the last time.

When I got to Sequoia Hospital, the emergency room had been sealed off and made secure and a young doctor was there, waiting for me. "Take those chains off her," he ordered upon seeing me.

The X-ray photograph showed it clearly: my left lung appeared large, white, and whole; my right lung had collapsed and showed up as a small, shriveled, ugly mass. "Spontaneous pneumothorax," the doctor pronounced. The X-ray also revealed that my heart had gone into trauma and had moved precariously toward my left lung.

By that time, Al Johnson was in the emergency room with me, along with the deputy sheriffs and several deputy U.S. marshals. But the young doctor, who was in his early thirties, was clearly in charge. No, I could not be moved. Yes, I needed to be operated on immediately. A tube had to be inserted into my chest to suction out the air and to re-create a vacuum in the chest cavity. That would allow the lung to reinflate and repair itself.

"What happens if you don't operate?" I asked.

The doctor replied, "You'll die."

All this was being discussed over my prone body on the emergency table and I must have reacted, for a nurse standing there exclaimed, "What's the matter with all of you? Can't you go off and talk about this somewhere else? This poor girl has gone into shock."

The marshals wanted me moved to a government hospital. The doctor vetoed that. My blood pressure had dipped to a systolic reading of 60. They could not get any reading on diastolic pressure. I was shivering under a heap of warm blankets. The doctor could not find an un-collapsed vein for an intravenous anesthetic, so he administered a local. As a female deputy sheriff held my hand, the doctor cut a small incision in my chest and inserted a tube into the cavity. It seemed to me he would never stop pushing that tube into me. It felt as though he intended to push me through the emergency operating table. The tube was attached to the suction machine. My upper torso was taped heavily with white surgical adhesive, and with the machine trailing behind, I was wheeled upstairs to a private room.

I had survived again. Janey Jimenez came to visit me late that night, accompanied by Deputy Marshal Glen Robinson. Janey took one look at me and burst into tears. She told me later that I looked grayish, wasted away, and near death, with the machine gurgling constantly at my side. All I knew at the time was that I was in pain. In her consternation, Janey left her purse lying on the foot of my bed and got a dressing down for that from Glen. "You can't leave your purse, with your weapon in it, that close to a prisoner! What's the matter with you?"

"Oh, hell, what can she do in that condition?" Janey answered back. But she took her purse away.

The federal marshals and deputy sheriffs from San Mateo, who were responsible for my safety but were prevented from moving me by the hospital doctors, got into some sort of jurisdictional dispute. Angry and frustrated over their dilemma, they finally had to go to a great deal of trouble and expense to guard me at this hospital. The window blinds in my room were always drawn, a closed-circuit television sentry system was set up in the hall, and U.S. marshals and San Mateo deputy sheriffs armed with handguns and Mace were posted outside my room around the clock. Every day the marshal's office, under pressure from Judge Carter, asked if I could be moved. Every day the hospital authorities refused permission. My parents were angry and bitter. How could it be, they continually asked, that I could live through being kidnapped by a band of terrorists and then almost die in the hands of the United States government? No one had a satisfactory answer. Nor could my parents do anything about it. I was a convicted felon now; I belonged to the government.

While recovering from the chest surgery, I was given a complete physical and it was discovered that I was afflicted with a classic case of malnutrition. My mother came into her element when she was given permission to bring me my "fourth meal" of the day every afternoon. I was down to eighty-seven pounds when my mother started to visit me with pizzas, fresh cracked crab, lox and cream cheese on bagels, and pints of ice cream.

On the tenth day, the hospital doctor pronounced my lung healed and completely reinflated. The deputy marshals were in my room within ten minutes of the pronouncement. "Get your clothes on right now or we'll throw a blanket over you and drag you out of here," one of them said.

The news that I was moving came as a surprise. My right arm and just about all of my right side were stiff and sore. I struggled to get out of bed, but could hardly move. Al Johnson was there but his protests were useless. Nor would they tell him where I was being taken. As we were leaving, three FBI agents arrived to interview me. A fierce jurisdictional argument erupted between the two independent arms of our nation's law enforcement system. Each accused the other of obstruction of justice. The FBI wanted to gather information from me about other crimes; the U.S. marshals insisted that they had to get me back into prison. Both sides telephoned their home offices for instructions. It turned out that the FBI was not as all-powerful as they had thought. The marshal's office had custody of my body. When the FBI asked where I was being taken so that they could interview me there, the marshals refused to tell them.

We sped off in the marshals' car, destination unknown, with the FBI trailing. It was a wild thirty-three-mile ride eastward across the San Mateo Bridge to the Federal Correctional Institution in Pleasanton. The newspapers the next day headlined: "Patty Kidnapped Again."

I was booked, fingerprinted, and photographed, but I refused to sign myself in (in any event, I couldn't use my right arm). The prison guards, unaware of my condition, escorted me to a room in the hospital wing, handed me some sheets and blankets, and commanded, "Make your own bed." That was next to impossible using one hand and I struggled along until a guard came in and helped me. Then the FBI agents entered for their rescheduled debriefing.

There was little love or cooperation between the prisoner and her jailers, who apparently thought they had to bend over backward to avoid giving me *any* special treatment. After a few days in the hospital wing, I was moved to a bleak cell in the isolation wing of the prison, supposedly for my own safety. The one window was boarded up, making the bare room virtually airless. I woke up each morning at 6:30, gagging on the fumes of pine-scented disinfectant used in the morning scrub-down.

It was not long before I began to go stir crazy in that little room. Excused from any work detail because of my operation and prohibited from mixing with other prisoners for security reasons, I became more and more upset, frustrated, and nervous. My only assignment, given by the doctors at Sequoia Hospital, was "finger climbing on the wall." I "walked" my fingers up the wall to restore mobility and muscle tone to my right arm. I did that with such fierceness that I was soon scraping my knuckles raw on the wall. The prison authorities listed it in their reports as "self-abuse."

Pleasanton was supposed to be the place where I would receive my ninety-day psychological evaluation, but it seemed to me that the authorities just did not know how to handle me as a prisoner because of my celebrity and the fear that I might be hurt if they put me in the general prison population.

The press began to run stories of my being pampered by the prison system. Pleasanton, a co-correctional institution, was described as a "luxury prison" with a "campus-like atmosphere." Those descriptions were based largely on the modern structure and the landscaping of lawns and flower beds in front of the prison. The reporters never looked past surface appearances and into the bleak reality of prison life. The cells in the women's section were small rooms, equipped with doors rather than bars, and to those who were not confined there, that might have seemed luxurious. But not to me or any of the other prisoners I encountered behind the double twelve-foot barbed-wire fences.

After about two weeks, I was moved out of the isolation wing and into the women's drugs section and given a room containing a bed, a small desk, a small chest for my clothes, and toilet facilities. The manager of the section gave me an extremely friendly and enthusiastic welcoming lecture, saying that he wanted me to think of him as my friend and confidant.

"You're not my friend," I declared. "As far as I am concerned, you are no different from Cinque. I'm your prisoner and all I want to do is to get these ninety days over with."

The doors of the housing units were open from 6:30 A.M. to 9 P.M., and while they were not allowed in each other's units, men and women could meet in all other areas. In theory, that might sound fine. In practice, it meant that the women were little more than "meat on the hoof." The men continually harassed women who were unwilling to "coed" with them. The women fought among themselves over selected men, and there was constant fighting among the men over favored women. The television room in the men's wing was called "The Forum," after the boxing arena in New York, for that was the prisoner-designated area for men to fight out their differences. The casual acceptance by staff members of transsexuals and transvestites surprised me, for I had assumed that these inmates would meet with particular prejudice.

Most of the women in the prison were convicted of drug-related crimes and they were not necessarily harmless. Whenever I ventured out of my cell into one of the common areas, I was pointed out and accosted. Sometimes the inmates were merely curious, but often enough I was taunted, jostled, bumped, pinched, or challenged to a fight. I walked about warily; most of the time I kept to myself in my cell. Al Johnson was frantic with worry that I would be hurt or killed. "I've got to get you out of here," he would tell me on each of his visits.

The evaluation sessions had barely got started when Al succeeded in his efforts to have me transferred to a safer facility. He did it by threats and bravado, warning the prison authorities that they would be held strictly accountable for my safety. After all, I had not yet been given a final sentence, he told them, and my life and state of mind were being endangered for the sake of a ninety-day study. So early one morning I was moved to the Federal Metropolitan Correction Center, a high-rise prison in downtown San Diego.

It was a ten-hour automobile ride and news of the transfer traveled faster than I did. So I had to run the gauntlet of the San Diego press before I could get into what the press this time called "a luxury hotel of a prison." I was tucked away in an eight-by-ten room in the hospital section on the third floor. The whole section was deserted except for a diabetic Indian in his forties. My evaluation study was to begin all over again and this time a number of young, seemingly inexperienced personnel came to interview me, each of them trying to delve into the supposed secrets of my days with the SLA. They sounded like voyeurs, with the same old questions I had answered before my trial, giving the same old tests I had taken before. As they kept insisting upon my cooperation, I grew more recalcitrant and disdainful. I told them what I thought: This whole evaluation study was stupid, useless, and a waste of time. I took the Wechsler IQ test again and this time scored 140. As they gave me more and more psychological tests, I put less and less time and thought into each of them. Finally I just ran my pencil down the sheets of multiple choices and marked them at random. The doctors never seemed to catch on.

When the doctors there probed into my early life and upbringing, I would angrily repeat, "I told all this to eleven doctors already and I don't see what this has got to do with how I should be treated for sentencing or in jail." They wanted, for that report, an expression of remorse over the bank robbery. "I don't feel any remorse," I would insist. "Yes, I would do it again," I would tell each of them. "It saved my life. If someone put a gun to my head and told me to rob a bank, I would rob a bank."

They kept trying to explain the necessity for me to repent, and, in effect, to ask the court for mercy. But that meant admitting guilt, admitting that I had acted willingly and not under duress, and that I refused to do. I was confident that my conviction would be overturned. I would be found innocent of any crime. I believed that. And believing that, all this psychological evaluation seemed a complete waste of time. What difference did Judge Carter's sentence make?

To avoid the doctors and the peekaboo games so many other people on the staff played in order to catch a glimpse of me, I took to reading all night long and sleeping through as much of the day as possible. I took up embroidery. I faithfully practiced climbing the wall with the fingers of my right hand until I had restored freedom of movement in my arm. I looked upon all of this as a ninety-day period of cooling my heels, recognizing that my worst enemy was boredom, and after what I had been through, this was not too bad. I even got used to the nightmares in which I found myself running from Bill and Emily Harris, stumbling around in masses of blood, and waking up screaming.

My family and Ted Dumke made frequent trips down to San Diego to bolster my morale and it was during this period that I joined the Episcopal Church, something I had long intended to do. Ted brought Bishop Robert Woltersdorff of San Diego to the prison to receive me into the Church. My mother accepted my decision graciously, saying that she preferred me to be a practicing Episcopalian rather than a lapsed Catholic. My father too was pleased, for his side of the family were almost all Episcopalians. After my conversion, I could take communion whenever Ted visited me, and it helped to make my days easier.

I had been in the San Diego prison for about two months when Judge Carter died suddenly of a heart attack. My case was reassigned to William H. Orrick, Jr., a federal judge who had been on the bench for only two years. So that he would have time to study and review the enormous trial transcript and legal briefs, Judge Orrick ordered that my evaluation study be extended for an additional ninety days. Then he thought he would be ready to pass sentence upon me.

Bailey and Johnson flew out to reassure me that I had a better chance for a light sentence from Judge Orrick than I had had with Judge Carter. Bailey said that Judge Orrick was widely known as a political liberal and could be expected to be more sympathetic upon sentencing. I disagreed vehemently, wondering why these supposedly sophisticated lawyers could not understand the politics involved.

"I don't want a liberal judge," I told them. "Get me the most conservative, hanging judge you can find, and I'll take my chances with him."

"Why do you say that?" asked Johnson.

"Because that's the only kind of judge who might understand just

how horrible the SLA really was and will have no sympathy for them,"
I explained. My parents also disagreed with Bailey and Johnson. But
they refused to risk the supposed dangers inherent in challenging a
judge over bias.

Distraught, I pleaded with my attorneys to get me sentenced. I
wanted it done right away so that I could apply for bail. I did not want
to spend another ninety days incarcerated during a make-believe psychological study. Bailey lectured me once again against trying to be my
own lawyer. Leave it to them, he said, adding that I was much safer in
prison than I would be out on bail where the remnants of the SLA
could get at me. I cried that it was my life and I was willing to take my
chances. They told me to keep calm, leave it all to them.

When they left, I pleaded with my father and mother to hire another
lawyer, to consult with someone else, to do something. But all they did
was tell me that I did not understand the difficulties involved and only
Bailey and Johnson knew the intricacies of my case well enough to
handle my appeal. I tried to explain why I had lost my confidence in
them, but my father insisted that they were two of the finest lawyers in
the country. "Besides, it's too late to bring a new lawyer into the case,"
he said. When my parents left, I found a telephone directory and
thumbed through the Yellow Pages, fantasizing about calling another
lawyer.

A few days later, the Harrises' trial began in Los Angeles and I was
appalled to read in the newspapers that their line of defense was that *I*
was responsible for everything that had happened at Mel's. All they
would "admit" was that Bill Harris was *accused* of shoplifting. It was
Patty Hearst who had shot up the street and forced them to run and to
commandeer the vehicles of Tom Matthews and Frank Sutter. As a
matter of fact, their defense lawyer told the jury, Patty Hearst had endangered the lives of the Harrises, not the other way around, and if
Patty Hearst had not opened fire with a submachine gun, none of this
would have happened at Mel's. I began to wonder: Was it possible that
they could be acquitted?

By now, I had lost much of my old fear of Teko and Yolanda. The
first time I had appeared in a court hearing with them, I was trembling
with fear, but the second time, when my Los Angeles trial was severed
from theirs, I decided to get my own sweet revenge. It was a little
thing, but important to me. I dressed to the hilt for that hearing and
carefully painted my fingernails with a bright red polish. It was as

"bourgeois" as I could be, and from their glares at my polished finger-nails, I knew that they got the message.

The Harrises' trial was into its third week when I was taken to the Los Angeles Superior Court on July 26 for a hearing on the eleven-count indictment over the Mel's shoot-out. My trial there was post-poned to January 10, 1977. After the court appearance I sat down to talk with several assistant district attorneys concerning the Harrises. I think I surprised them when I readily agreed to testify for the prosecu-tion.

The next day, the government, which had just rested its case, asked the court for permission to reopen the prosecution so that I could ap-pear as a witness. The court ruled that the government could present its witness, in rebuttal, following the defense presentation. The Harrises took a quick recess with their attorneys and then announced they would present no defense. That meant no rebuttal. They were con-victed of multiple counts of robbery, felonious assault, and kidnapping and a month later they were both sentenced to eleven years to life in prison. The Harrises showed their disdain for the court by refusing to stand for the sentencing.

The community at large must have heaved a great sigh of relief, along with me, at the heavy sentence meted out. What we did not know was that once the Harrises were sent to state prison, their sentences were modified—not by any court but by a Community Release Board, which had recently been established in California to review prison sen-tences in relation to the needs of the community. The Community Release Board, composed of political appointees, saw fit to reduce the sentences of the Harrises to three years. That meant they would be free in September 1978, three years after their arrest.

I did not know about that sentence modification until Lowell Jensen, the district attorney of Alameda County, came to see me in San Diego. He asked if I would be willing to testify against the Harrises, if Alameda County brought them up on charges of having kidnapped me. Without my testimony, he said, there would be little chance of convict-ing them. There were no other witnesses available, except my old neighbors in Berkeley, and they had not been close enough to identify either of the Harrises. The D.A. promised that if convicted in Oakland, the Harrises would receive the stiff sentence they deserved. He ex-pressed his personal sympathy for my having been tried and convicted of the Hibernia Bank robbery instead of the Harrises. But he could not explain why the *federal* prosecutors had made no move against the Harrises.

I came up for sentencing before Judge Orrick in San Francisco, in the same courtroom in which I had been tried, on September 24, 1976. I had already served more than one year in jail. U. S. Attorney Jim Browning recommended that I be made to serve more time because I had shown no remorse and to demonstrate that "rebellious young people who become revolutionaries, for whatever reason, and voluntarily commit criminal acts, will be punished."

Al Johnson asked for leniency to be shown by the court, saying that I had already been "brutalized, vilified, tortured, molested . . . punished, convicted, and incarcerated."

Judge Orrick, who had brought his entire family to court for the occasion, rejected any idea that I be sentenced under the Youthful Offender Act because, he said, I was in no need of rehabilitation. He said the purpose of his sentence was for punishment and deterrence because "violence is unacceptable and cannot be tolerated."

I was not surprised when he sentenced me to seven years.

That was the *average* sentence meted out for armed bank robbery, the judge explained, as if that proved his evenhandedness in treating the rich and poor alike.

Three days later I was testifying before the Alameda County grand jury in Oakland about the circumstances of my kidnapping. The Harrises were indicted for kidnapping two days later, the twenty-ninth of September.

Meanwhile, I was again committed to the federal prison in Pleasanton. Al Johnson got busy all over again, demanding this time that I be transferred to a safer facility for my own protection under the Witness Protection Program: I was testifying now for the government and, under federal regulations, was entitled to government protection. So I was ferried back to San Diego and this time given a room in the contagious ward of the hospital section. Now that I had been sentenced, Al Johnson promised that Lee Bailey would appeal my conviction and I would then be entitled to ask for bail while awaiting a decision from the Ninth Circuit Court of Appeals. All Bailey had to do, Al said, was to convince the court that if set free on bail I would not run away. I sat in that room doing embroidery for another two months, enduring anxiety attacks: Would I get bail or not? It was not at all certain. Al Johnson kept telling me, "You're really safer in prison than out on the street, Pat. People want to kill you out there. They hate you. . . ."

"I'll take my chances," I said.

"Well, it's a problem because the judge wants to be assured of good security for you out there. . . . He wants to be sure nothing will happen to you . . . and we're trying to arrange it. . . . Be patient."

On November 19, the marshals drove me in a van from San Diego to San Francisco for a hearing. They tried to reassure me that bail would be granted; otherwise the court would not have had me make the long trip. I was not convinced. During a stop, one of the marshals telephoned ahead and received word that the judge was vacillating. He returned to the van with an ashen face. "I just don't know," he said.

Not knowing was excruciating. I learned nothing more until I arrived at the courthouse, and then things moved swiftly. I was granted bail! One million dollars to guarantee my appearance in San Francisco; another $250,000 to guarantee my showing up to face charges in Los Angeles. I was being released in the custody of my parents. And there was a proviso: My parents agreed to provide round-the-clock protection for me with four bodyguards on duty at all times.

CHAPTER

TWENTY-ONE

HOME HAD CHANGED since I had been away. The big, old house in Hillsborough, where I had grown up, had been sold, and my parents had moved to an elegant apartment on California Street, atop Nob Hill, in San Francisco. While most of the furniture was familiar, the rooms, the floor plan, the ambience were quite different. But that did not matter; it felt good to be surrounded by happy, loving people. Aunts, uncles, cousins, and family friends all came by to renew old ties. Janey Jimenez, who had quit the Marshals Service to pursue an advanced college degree, came up from San Diego to stay with us. For the first time in almost three years, I enjoyed laughter all around me. It was a time to tell jokes, drink and eat, and not look back. It was the first time in a long while for my parents, too, to forget the past and enjoy the moment. We celebrated, almost nonstop, for four days.

I met the twelve men who were to be my bodyguards as they showed up for their three eight-hour shifts, almost all of them San Francisco policemen moonlighting on their off hours. They had accepted the jobs to act as bodyguards to a private person, not knowing whom they would be guarding. But in fairly short order, they became close friends of the family, often joining in our parties and upon occasion filling in as instant dates for my sisters and me.

On my third night at home, I suggested that we all go out somewhere so I could see a bit of the town. Al Johnson protested that it was "too dangerous," and my mother and father, clearly worried, begged me to stay at home. But I insisted that I did not want to be a prisoner in my own house. I wanted some freedom. We compromised by agreeing to venture across the street to the Top of the Mark, the famous cocktail lounge on the top floor of the Mark Hopkins Hotel. Janey, Al Johnson, and I sat at one table; three of the bodyguards sat at the next table. The hotel sent over a bottle of champagne to toast my freedom. Al Johnson in typical fashion promised, "Pat, you'll never see another day in jail; we're going to get that conviction overturned and that will be it."

The manager came to the table, greeted me, and summoned Al away for a private talk. When Al returned he told us that the hotel had received a telephoned bomb threat because I was there. Al was so disturbed I thought he would carry me off if I refused to go. We beat a hasty retreat back to the family apartment.

I stayed in after that, trying to regain my strength and a bit more weight. I busied myself in the kitchen trying my hand at some gourmet cooking. Most of the time I spent with the family, receiving guests. Then gradually I began to accept invitations to a few parties and dinners given by old friends and after a while I began dating. It was difficult adjusting to what had been my old way of life. I was different, changed and hardened and grown street-wise from my days with the SLA. I had been through too much to revert to the naïve, innocent girl I had been as a teenager. It amused me to think back at how grown-up I had thought myself when I enrolled in Menlo College and then UC-Berkeley. I had thought I knew it all then. And I had known nothing. Now, after two years with the SLA and one year behind bars, I began to realize how much I had to reappraise just about everything around me. I was moved by the poignancy of seeing the havoc those three years had wrought upon my parents.

We tried, as was the family custom, to make light of it all. But it was difficult. My father told me how in desperation he had hired swamis and psychics to help find me after I had been kidnapped. Mom spoke of their anguish in not knowing whether I was dead or alive. They told me of the FBI virtually camping in the family house in Hillsborough and how Charles Bates had assured them that I had been "brainwashed" by the SLA and might have to be hospitalized and given psychiatric help upon my return. The chief FBI agent also told them that I would not be prosecuted. In the meantime, FBI agents were going about questioning my parents, relatives, and friends about my childhood, gathering evidence that the U. S. Attorney would later use at my trial.

Hounded by the FBI on one side and by the press on the other, my parents had lived through those years on public display. They could not hope to clear up all the distorted and mistaken stories written about me and the family. They were exasperated by what my father called misplaced sympathy from people who approached them. To them, my father would always say: "You shouldn't feel sorry for us; you should feel sorry for my daughter—she's the one who was kidnapped." Worst of all, my father told me, were those misguided well-wishers who would tell him: "Oh, I know how you must be feeling . . . I've got a rotten, no-good, etc., daughter too." To that he would retort, "Really? Was your daughter kidnapped?" and then storm off. They could laugh it off after it was all over, but at the time it hurt.

They had not been hurt by what I had been forced to say on those tapes and they kept reassuring me that they understood why I had not tried to contact them. I explained my fear that they had abandoned me because of what I had said on the tapes and we delved deeply into the complex process of brainwashing.

My kidnapping had been a tidal wave that engulfed the entire family. Everyone feared that the SLA might make a new attack upon the family. My sisters had changed their names and taken new identities while attending school or working and for a time were accompanied by bodyguards. They found out who their true friends were. Some refused point-blank to see them or have them at parties in fear of the SLA bursting in. Others merely shied away with no explanation. At times, they knew they were being kept under surveillance by FBI agents. On one trip to Canada, Anne had been arrested by the FBI as she crossed the border back into the United States at Niagara Falls. She was taken into custody, handcuffed, and accused of having three marijuana *seeds* on the floor of her car. But in custody she was grilled unmercifully by the federal agents, who accused her of making contact with me somewhere in Canada.

Doubt and anxiety swept my father into entirely new areas, different from those he had known before. He visited various community, social, church, and radical groups trying to make contact with someone who could reach the SLA. He went into the prisons seeking inmates who had known Cinque. He oversaw the food distribution program, handled the FBI and the press, read the thousands of letters from the public which poured into his office and were sifted for his inspection by his secretary, Helen Mehawk. He had Charles Gould at his side, publisher of the *Examiner* and long-time friend and colleague, who could and did share the agony.

But my mother had no one, except my father, to give her solace. My mother, who had been such a vital, active, positive person, was swept off the course of the life she had always known and believed in. The kidnapping and government prosecution had rendered her helpless: there was nothing she could do, and that was a special agony she had never known before. In the relentless glare of publicity, she retreated into seclusion. She gave up her position on the California Board of Regents; she withdrew from the various civic and social organizations in which she had been so active. She had held herself together and put up a fine front throughout those three years of my absence, and then when I returned home on bail, she fell apart. Bewildered and depressed, she temporarily became an emotional disaster. Rather than I, it was my mother who needed help to regain her equilibrium.

With seven months of therapy behind me, aside from an overall lack of energy, I felt fine and thoroughly in control of myself and growing stronger by the day. I got through the days and evenings fairly well. But those nightmares of violence and pursuit did not cease. Several times a week, I would wake up in the middle of the night, screaming. In my dreams, I was still struggling with Bill and Emily Harris. Nor could I hide those screams of terror from my family. They all heard me; they knew.

As a comfort and as further protection, knowing my love for animals, my father decided to make me a present of a trained guard dog. One of the bodyguards inquired at the Prion Animal Institute in nearby San Carlos. "I don't train dogs for terrorists" was the retort of Robert Outman, the proprietor and trainer. Bob, a former deputy sheriff in San Mateo, had been shot by an NWLF terrorist lying in ambush. His life was saved by his German shepherd, who attacked and drove off the gunman. Bob was forced to retire on a disability pension from the force and had opened a training center for "companion dogs," trained to defend one person, and "attack dogs," trained for police work. After the facts of my case were explained to him, Bob agreed to meet me and

only then decided to take me on. I spent two weeks at his institute,
learning the proper commands and how to handle a companion dog
named Arrow, a two-and-a-half-year-old German shepherd that my father had selected for me.

Those were two of the happiest weeks for me. Finally, I was *doing*
something, rather than having something done to me. I was in command. Arrow was simply magnificent, a large, strong, intelligent, well-
behaved dog. The transition from handler to owner took two weeks
and then I took Arrow home, but I like to think it was love at first
sight. He made me feel secure, being there at my side, sleeping in the
same room with me. Even the nightmares subsided with Arrow there.
But more than that, those two weeks during the third month of my new
freedom laid the foundation for a new, lasting friendship with Bob
Outman and an interest on my part in training German shepherds.

In January 1977, the family and I moved back to Hillsborough, into
a modest ranch house, which my mother loved for its grounds and garden. The press persisted in calling this three-bedroom house a mansion.
They hounded us almost every day, camping outside, misinterpreting or
deliberately distorting any small comment we made while dashing by
them. My parents seemed to live in fear, not only of violence but also
of the press reporting negative stories about me. They virtually stopped
going out at all and they tried to double-check every party I attended
for fear of the publicity that might be involved. Oftentimes, they
telephoned Al Johnson in Boston to ask *his* permission for my going
somewhere.

Gradually, I came to see that I could not return to my former circle
with any satisfaction. The young men I grew up with now seemed too
naïve. They had different interests and we had little to talk about. I
found myself spending more time at home, talking with my sisters and
with the bodyguards. These police officers understood the SLA and
what had happened to me better than any of my old Hillsborough
friends.

I spent a lot of time at the home of Mrs. Virginia Blight, the grandmother of a friend of my sister Anne. The matriarch of her large Greek
family, an accomplished artist, small and vivacious, she was "Nana" to
a large group of young people who gravitated to her home for its ever-
present warmth, good cheer, and just plain fun. So my sisters and I had
what we called double holidays. We celebrated Thanksgiving at our

home and again at Nana's; we ate Christmas dinner at our home and another Christmas dinner the next night at Nana's.

When my trial date for the Mel's shoot-out rolled around on April 18, I went to the Los Angeles Superior Court and pleaded *nolo contendere**—I would not contest the felony assault and robbery charges against me. Besides, what could I say about Mel's that I had not already said at the previous trial? It was with a good deal of apprehension that I showed up in court on May 9 to be sentenced. The judge, E. Talbot Callister, could give me anything from probation to fifteen and one half years in jail. No deals had been made and I did not know what he would do. When my sisters and I and four bodyguards flew down to Los Angeles the day before sentencing, I packed a small bag, with family photos and a toothbrush, just in case I was dispatched immediately to prison. I did not know what to expect, nor did I trust anyone's opinion. Al Johnson always told me not to worry and I had learned to discount his opinion just about one hundred percent. We had a quiet "farewell party" that night in a hotel room.

Both Anne and Gina were too upset to go to the sentencing, but I dragged myself off to the courthouse, with my parents and bodyguards. We met with Bailey and Johnson in a private room before our scheduled court appearance. We did not get along very well, and F. Lee Bailey excused himself from the conversation and sat down at a table and began to write something down.

He was just then and there scribbling some notes for his pre-sentencing arguments, only about five minutes before court time. I told him I did not think he should be delivering the sentencing arguments in court and that he should leave it to Sydney Irmas, the local counsel in Los Angeles. Bailey fumed and raged at me and I became equally furious with him.

In court, I was so nervous I barely heard the chief deputy district at-

---

* *Nolo contendere* means, literally, "no contest." The accused does not admit the charges but neither does he contest them. Upon the entry of such a plea the judge almost always finds the defendant guilty and sentences him accordingly. If he is sentenced to probation he is entitled to request that the record be expunged at a later date. The judgment of guilty is then set aside, as is the plea of *nolo*. A finding of not guilty is substituted and the conviction is overturned. My convictions on the charges in Los Angeles were overturned on May 9, 1980.

torney of Los Angeles, Samuel Mayerson, recommend that I be given probation because of the unusual aspects of the case, because of the time I had already served, and because I posed no threat to the community.

"No matter what this court does, some will cry 'too lenient' and others will say 'too harsh.' I can only say to your Honor that the voices I have heard pressing for the harshest sentence have been from those with the least knowledge of the facts or with the greatest personal animosity. My own reaction has been that the inclination to appear not to show favoritism to this defendant because of her alleged social status has created too great a possibility that she could be treated more harshly than would someone else."

Bailey, who refused to surrender his right to speak for me as chief counsel, pleaded for probation on the grounds that I had been punished enough by the SLA as well as by the government. Judge Callister, saying that this was the most difficult decision he had had to make out of all the thousands of sentences he had passed upon defendants while on the bench, cited all the reasons—my being kidnapped, "subjected to fifty-seven days of horrible torture by her abductors," no prior criminal record, no risk to society, the plight and anguish of my parents, the time I had already served in prison, the lack of any need for further confinement—and he sentenced me to five years' probation.

I never saw or spoke to F. Lee Bailey again. But then I had not seen him during the seven months since my sentencing in federal court. In the press and public opinion polls, the battle of right and wrong raged on: Was I being treated too leniently because of the Hearst name; or was I being treated too harshly because of the Hearst name? In the opinion polls, the public was beginning to change its mind: Now only half the people responding thought I should be made to serve the remainder of my seven-year sentence; slightly less than half thought I had served enough time already. Underlying public opinion there was a palpable note of cynicism in the press that somehow, with all my supposed privileges and pull, I would never return to prison—that my flamboyant lawyer from Boston would think of some way to get me off.

When my appeal to overturn the San Francisco conviction was denied on November 3, 1977, the first word I got of it was over the radio. Al Johnson called later that day and asked to speak to my father, not me. When I got on the phone he assured me that I still had a chance because Bailey would rewrite the appeal and submit it to the Supreme Court of the United States.

As the months passed, I despaired. I had lawyers who refused to discuss my case with me, preferring to talk only with Dad. My parents, and particularly my father, still had complete faith in the two Boston attorneys, but I was becoming exasperated with them. I had no contact at all with F. Lee Bailey and no control over Al Johnson. On the other hand, Al seemed to have complete control over me, and I did not like it. Again I begged my parents to find another attorney, but all they did was try to calm me down.

Finally, Bernard Shaw, a bodyguard whom I had begun dating, suggested that I talk with his attorney, George C. Martinez, about my appeal. I was more impressed with George Martinez at that first meeting than he was with me. He was low-key, cautious, and very different from Lee or Al.

He told me later his first impression was that my complaints and fears were just a case of sour grapes. However, he soon changed his mind. Afterward, when I asked him to look over my appeal papers, he held out little hope of success. He warned me to prepare myself to return to prison. But once I was inside, he advised, the impact of my being incarcerated might help him convince the judge to exercise his absolute right to reduce the sentence he imposed. "The fastest way to get you out is to get you back in." That was not particularly good news, but it made sense and I understood and trusted his explanation. George, in his quiet manner, also persuaded me not to fire Bailey and Johnson publicly but rather to allow him to work out an amicable parting.

On April 24, when the Supreme Court declined to hear argument on my appeal, I was prepared and was not at all surprised when Judge Orrick ordered me to report back to prison at Pleasanton to complete serving my seven-year sentence. The date set was May 15 by 4 P.M.

For my final week of freedom, Bernie Shaw, my sisters, and I and a group of friends went on a whirlwind tour of just about all the best and worst night spots that San Francisco had to offer. On May 15, we drove out to Pleasanton in three cars, arriving at the old army base about 3 P.M. We parked there to say our goodbyes—my sisters, Bernie, George Martinez and his wife, Ingrid, Janey Jimenez, Trish Tobin, Ted

Dumke, Nana, Bob and Cathy Outman, four of my bodyguards, and several other friends. And, of course, Arrow. My mother and father stayed behind, deciding it was wiser not to accompany me and make a public display of their emotions.

We expected the press to be there at the prison gate. In fact, we had learned that some reporters had camped out there for two weeks, suspecting that I might try to sneak past them by surrendering myself earlier than scheduled.

Timing our arrival at the prison for exactly five minutes before the four o'clock deadline, we could see the press crowd as we drove up. Leaving our cars, we walked in a group toward the entrance and for a few moments everything seemed calm and almost solemn. Then the overeager reporters, photographers, and television camera crews— about fifty in all—began to run at us, a real stampede. All hell broke loose. In the wild free-for-all, there was more shoving, kicking, and punching than picture taking. Janey Jimenez got a black eye and was thrown to the ground. Trish's leg was bloodied. Bernie and the other bodyguards had me well protected but at the door into the prison the crush was so great that I could not get in to the guardhouse. Finally, a prison official reached out into the melee, grabbed my hand, lifted me up, and pulled me over the bodies that were blocking my way. The press was locked out, screaming to get in for more pictures. I was shaken but otherwise unharmed.

It was a wild end and a new beginning: I had had to fight my way into prison.

Fingerprinted, photographed, strip-searched, I was booked and given the same number assigned to me on my last stay at Pleasanton, Prisoner 00077-181. The last three numbers designated the facility, FCI Pleasanton. The first row of digits gave me the status of an old-timer. When I had been brought there after the collapse of my lung, I had been only the seventy-seventh prisoner booked into Pleasanton since the prison had been changed from a Youthful Offender Facility to a Federal Correctional Institution (adult prison).

The prison had changed considerably. It had been a co-correctional, minimum security prison. Now it was classified as a medium security institution; the men were gone, and the prison held approximately four hundred women. More than one hundred inmates who were disciplinary problems had been transferred from the maximum security women's prison in Alderson, West Virginia. With these incorrigibles came all the ensuing problems of mixing different categories of inmates. There was a real concern over the possibility of an inmate attempting to kill me in order to become famous or to prevent me from testifying at the upcoming trial of the Harrises for my kidnapping. In a long meeting with Jay Allman, the associate warden, it was explained that the prison could not provide me with any special security, but I was instructed to report any and all incidents to him. Explaining the prison's rules and regulations, Jay Allman suggested that I follow the regulations to the letter and that I also try to make friends in the prison.

Assigned to cell G-133, I flopped down on my unmade bed in complete exhaustion. I had been up since four o'clock that morning, unable to sleep in nervous anticipation of this moment. Before long, several inmates came by to say hello and get a look at the famous new prisoner. At 10:15, a guard summoned me to the warden's office and ordered me to get busy and clean it up.

I asked to be excused, explaining that I had been up since four and felt too weak to do any work. "You don't want to start out here with a shot, do you?" she challenged me. "That won't look very good on your prison record." I didn't know what to tell her. I didn't care what went on my prison record. All I wanted to do was to lie down and go to sleep. Fortunately, George Martinez returned an earlier call and was put through to the warden's office. He straightened it out. I would clean the warden's office the next night, so that the guards could show that I was not being treated differently from any other prisoner. I felt faint and had to put my head down between my knees. When I was finally led back to my cell, I vomited.

When my family visited the next day, they explained what had been started on my behalf. The unhappy entourage which accompanied me to Pleasanton had returned to Hillsborough to comfort my mother and father. As conversation faltered, Nana challenged them all:

"What's the matter with you people? We can't just sit around; we've got to do something."

"What can we possibly do?" someone asked.

"We have to go right to the top; forget the middlemen. We have to go to the President. He's the only one who can do anything for Patty now."

Everyone stared at her, but this energetic seventy-five-year-old woman started in right there in naming things that could be done, people to be contacted, procedures to be followed. The others began to join in the planning, more to humor her than anything else. My father sat through it all silently, thinking that these well-meaning people were on a fool's errand. He could not conceive that with public opinion so against me the President of the United States would find it politically advantageous to notice a few well-intentioned friends. My mother held out little hope. Nevertheless, the Campaign to Free Patty, which later was given the very respectable name of the Committee for the Release of Patricia Hearst, was organized on the day I returned to prison. It was headed by the indomitable Mrs. Virginia Blight and the indefatigable Reverend Edward Dumke.

My part in this campaign was to start giving interviews to the press, to meet with influential people who agreed to see me. Frankly, the idea was to try to change public opinion. So much had been written by people who had never met me and who had no conception of what I was really like. The idea appealed to me. I did not want to be tucked away in prison and forgotten.

After checking prison regulations, I began to give two interviews to the press every month, the maximum allowed. I started with the local San Mateo *Times, People* magazine, *McCall's, Look, Redbook, The Ladies' Home Journal*. I saw a number of well-known columnists, including William F. Buckley, Jr., and Bob Greene. I met with Barbara Walters, Jane Pauley, and David Hartman. And there were others. All of them, without exception, helped to reverse public opinion. I made friends among the press because it was only at first hand and with personal conversation that I was able to get across to all these journalists that I was not a terrorist or a mixed-up kid or a spoiled brat. The press interviews focused on human-interest stories of my life in prison and my hopes for the future, rather than upon my past with the SLA or the trial. The positive tone of these stories certainly helped me with the outside world. However, they had the reverse effect inside the prison, where many of the inmates became envious and hostile because of the tremendous public attention given to me.

Under the circumstances, I got along with most of the inmates in my unit. I had a small circle of friends, a somewhat larger group of acquaintances, and others whom I carefully avoided. Among the latter were the Manson girls, Squeaky Fromme and Sandra Good, who were as crazy as ever. Now they would respond only to the names "Red" and "Blue," after the color of the flowing caftans they wore. Many of the women in my unit were drug addicts and prostitutes involved in drug-related crimes. Narcotics were always around in the prison, although it was difficult to know the extent of their distribution. Several of my new friends, who had been "working" in Alaska, still managed to keep themselves supplied with drugs by sleeping with certain of the prison guards. Sexual favors were sold for two to five "joints" per session in a bathroom, storeroom, or empty cell. One girl "O.D.'d" on cocaine; another gave birth in the prison without anyone, including herself, having suspected that she was pregnant.

Ironically, my fame as a gun-toting revolutionary and bank robber gave pause to a good many of the women who might have thought of harassing me or taking me on. However, I steered clear of the Alderson group of incorrigibles who were led by a revoltingly crude old woman. She had run a big-time drug-distribution ring with her sons somewhere on the East Coast, engaging in a wide assortment of crimes; in prison she held sway over a sizable group of girls who would run and fetch for her.

There were prisoners of all sorts at Pleasanton. One dowdy, middle-aged woman, who puttered around in a flowered housedress and looked as though she could not have done anything worse than steal food stamps, had led a string of prostitutes in Arizona who lured servicemen into the desert, where they would be murdered and robbed of their pocket money. She was serving life.

Another matronly woman had embezzled enough money from the bank in which she worked to put her three children through college. After nine years of stealing, she turned herself in, expecting probation. She was serving five years. A third woman, who was a Constitutional Conservative and refused to pay taxes, was serving six months. One young woman from Oklahoma had been sentenced to six years for "criminal trespass." She had been arrested for camping overnight on federal reserve land. Her real crime, it seemed, was being a white woman married to an Indian.

All inmates had to work and everyone had to put in one hundred eighty hours in the kitchen, starting out in the "dish room." Almost everyone hated it with a passion. Yet I found that I rather enjoyed working in the dish room. The place was hot and steamy but I could work like a robot on the assembly line where the dishes were scraped, rinsed, and put into the giant washing machines for sterilization. When my required time in the dish room was up, I was offered a job clerking in the warden's office, but I declined. I did not want to be put on display for the visitors who regularly toured the prison. Instead, I chose to stay on in the kitchen, requesting a transfer to a cook's job. There, with three other girls, I prepared meals for nearly four hundred inmates. Not too much culinary art was involved or possible. We cooked in forty-gallon steam kettles. The bonus for cooks was that we could prepare our own meals from the food on hand.

It took nearly six months, but the Committee for the Release of Patricia Hearst was in full swing. It was not unlike a political campaign. We had committees in every state of the Union and as far off as Puerto Rico and the Philippines. We had city leaders and state leaders, and a truly grass-roots movement in which more and more people gave their time and their efforts freely in my behalf. John Sweeney, who owned a computer company in Los Angeles, provided us with the free use of his computers for our mailing lists. A printer in Los Angeles produced our pamphlets and flyers without charge. My sisters and Ted Dumke appeared regularly on radio and television talk shows. FREE PATTY bumper stickers, pins, and T-shirts were distributed widely. I had a special T-shirt which said in the front: PARDON ME, and on the back: BEING KIDNAPPED MEANS ALWAYS HAVING TO SAY YOU'RE SORRY. I received as many as two hundred letters a day and answered each one. These names and addresses were fed into the computer and added to our list of supporters. The whole campaign was aimed at getting people to write letters and send petitions to President Carter or to his Pardon Attorney, John R. Stanish. Although some people believed that my family was bankrolling the campaign, the truth was that my parents were so fearful of being accused of seeking special treatment for me that they deliberately stayed out of the committee's way.

It was about this time that my father came to me and said that he and Mom had decided to separate after forty years of marriage. "Do you think this will hurt your clemency application?" he asked. "If you do, we'll wait." They had been through so much in the past five years and now, in their own personal unhappiness, their primary concern was still me. I was saddened by their decision, but I told them, "This time, you've got to think of yourselves first, not the press, the public, or anyone else."

My father never thought much of the Free Patty campaign, but he thought it might help change public opinion.

The amateur campaign, as my father called it, was tied in with the legal efforts of my lawyer. George was so cautious that not until the letter-writing campaign was well under way did he tell me that I had some reason to hope for Presidential clemency. George had spoken to an aide in the Pardon Attorney's office who had been unexpectedly encouraging. But there were two essential ingredients in any successful application. I had to file a formal petition asking for executive clemency and there had to be a substantial expression of public support for my release.

That was all the committee needed to hear; they doubled their efforts in my behalf. Tens of thousands of letters reached the Pardon Attorney in what was to become one of the largest campaigns for clemency in the history of this country.

On another front, George had prepared a series of motions to win my release from prison. He went to see Judge Orrick in chambers in June and then again in July. With the new U. S. Attorney in San Francisco, William Hunter, in attendance, Judge Orrick indicated in the first meeting that he might act on his own to reduce my sentence after I testified at the Harris trial. In the second meeting, again with the U. S. Attorney present, George pointed out that time was running out, and my motions must be filed soon or not at all.

The judge said, "I told you I have my own motion to modify her sentence in my drawer." George then advised the judge he had already consulted me on this and, in accordance with my wishes, he would soon be filing formal motions not only for a reduction of sentence but also to vacate my conviction. Judge Orrick pondered this for a moment and then commented, "I don't know what that motion could be based upon unless you are thinking of alleging insufficiency of counsel." George, startled, did not enlighten him. That was precisely the motion he had in his briefcase.

Family and friends were not the only ones who wanted me freed. In early August, before the expected start of the Harris trial, Lowell Jensen, the district attorney of Alameda County, feared that his case would be severely weakened by my imprisonment. He urged Judge Or-

rick to cut my sentence to time already served so that I could testify at
the Harris trial as a free woman and not as a prisoner testifying in the
hope of earning her freedom. The U. S. Attorney for San Francisco advised the judge that he had no objections to my release. Still Judge Orrick did not respond. George visited me in prison two and three times a
week, faithfully reporting what was happening with my case, and I told
him I wanted him to file both motions. I did not trust Judge Orrick to
act on his own. Moreover, I did not believe that justice was possible in
his court. So in the first week of August my attorney filed two motions
in federal court: one, to modify my sentence to time already served,
and two, to overturn my conviction alleging that my former attorneys
did not defend me adequately.

As time went on, more and more people rallied to my cause. One of
the prime movers in my clemency campaign was Congressman Leo
Ryan, who represented the San Mateo congressional district where my
family lived. The first time he made the trip to Pleasanton to visit me,
he was told by a guard that I did not want to see him. Before he left,
however, the congressman shrewdly gave his card to someone else to
be delivered to me, asking if there was any way he could be of help. I
replied with a letter explaining that I was sorry I had missed him but I
had not known he was at the prison. Leo Ryan was a straightforward,
no-nonsense man. He called a press conference and publicly accused
the prison of "a deliberate deception." Nor did he stop there. He wrote
letters to the Bureau of Prisons and to just about every congressman
and senator who had any interest at all in the prison system, demanding a full-scale investigation.

After that, Leo Ryan came to visit me fairly often. At first, we found
ourselves at counter-purposes. He was engaged in trying to find a program of alternative punishment, by which I could be released to work
in the community. I told him in no uncertain terms that that was not
what I was seeking. I wanted clemency and/or a reversal on my conviction. Once we understood each other we became friends and my
clemency campaign became one of two top priorities in his office. The
other was the investigation of the People's Temple in Guyana. Leo circulated a petition in Congress urging the Justice Department to recommend to the President that I be freed from prison:

"Never before in the history of our country has such a bizarre set of
circumstances led to such a tragic result: a victim of a violent kidnap-

ping participated in a bank robbery under the direction and motivation of her abductors."

Forty-eight members of the House of Representatives, covering a broad spectrum of political opinion, signed that petition. On the day he left for Guyana, Leo sent me a short letter: "Off to Guyana. See you when I return. Hang in there." In Guyana, Leo Ryan was shot and killed, a tragic loss to this country, while trying to help the brainwashed unfortunates in the People's Temple there.

On August 31, 1978, after delaying the start of their kidnapping trial by legal maneuvers for two years, Bill and Emily Harris surprised everyone by pleading guilty in Oakland to four of the thirteen counts against them. The other nine counts were dropped, including the most serious, kidnapping with bodily harm, which could have sent them to jail for life without possibility of parole. Before the plea bargain was negotiated, an assistant D.A. came to see me in prison to explain that it would be "easier all around" to accept their plea to four counts. They would get at least ten years *added on* to their Los Angeles sentence, he said. But in court, given permission to address a crowd of about forty supporters, Bill Harris was unrepentant: "The plea does not mean we have feelings of remorse. Instead we feel pride in what these actions were able to accomplish." He boasted that he and Emily would be "back on the streets" by 1983.

The Harrises were sentenced on October 3, under California's indeterminate-sentence law, to one to twenty-five years in prison. That sentence was later modified by the Community Release Board, which scheduled their release for early 1984. If my sentence was not shortened by the President of the United States, I would not get out of prison until *after* the Harrises. I did not see a single editorial in any newspaper or magazine commenting upon the Harrises' sentence in comparison to mine.

There was still no word or sign from Judge Orrick. As the Free Patty letter-writing campaign continued, John Stanish wrote to Judge Orrick asking his intentions in the case before the Pardon Attorney proceeded any further. No answer from the judge. Stanish then wrote on behalf of the President asking that the judge, on or before November 7, inform him of what action, if any, he intended to take in my case. On that date, Judge Orrick gave his answer. He denied all motions to reduce my sentence or to set aside the verdict on grounds of insufficiency of counsel.*

John Stanish came to see me in prison that same day. He questioned me for hours about my captivity with the SLA, what had happened at my trial, and what my intentions were for the future. I was surprised to find a federal official so warm and personable and so genuinely interested. I told him I had no intention of asking for parole ever. I did not want to be set free as a paroled convict who had been shown mercy, thereby legitimizing the government's proceedings against me. I was innocent.

He returned the next day with U. S. Attorney William Hunter, an attractive former professional football player. He exuded that intimidating air of supreme self-confidence of a star athlete. The two of them asked my attorney to leave the room, because they wanted to see me alone. The U. S. Attorney who succeeded Jim Browning remarked at one point that he had been surprised when the government decided to bring me to trial instead of the Harrises and was even more surprised when the government won a conviction. Toward the end of the interview, they both asked me if I would accept Presidential clemency, which would reduce my sentence to time served. Yes, I would. Would I then drop my legal efforts?

No, I told them, clemency only stops the punishment; I would continue to try to overturn the conviction and wipe the record clean. That troubled them. They did not want me to embarrass the President or themselves by appearing ungrateful for executive clemency. I assured them that I would not be ungrateful for any clemency granted, but that clemency was not enough. They were not mutually exclusive. The two men left without making any promises; but they were clearly supportive.

California's U. S. Senator S. I. Hayakawa came to see me and joined in the public cry that I be freed. Former Governor Ronald Reagan called for my release. Lieutenant Governor Mervin Dymally called for a full pardon. Cesar Chavez, the farm union leader, supported my release. Charles Bates, the FBI agent-in-charge in San Francisco, wrote the Attorney General recommending my being set

---

* In 1981, the U. S. Court of Appeals in the Ninth Circuit overruled Judge Orrick's decision and granted me an evidentiary hearing on my claim that my conviction should be set aside.

free. Seventy-five San Francisco policemen signed Bernie's petition. Six jurors at my trial said I should not have been given such a long sentence. San Francisco's Board of Supervisors voted a unanimous resolution demanding that I be freed. John Wayne spoke out forcefully and rallied the troops in my behalf. He said, "It seems quite odd to me that the American people have immediately accepted the fact that one man can brainwash nine hundred human beings into mass suicide [referring to the Guyana tragedy] but will not accept the fact that a ruthless group, the Symbionese Liberation Army, could brainwash a little girl by torture, degradation and confinement." Editorials across the country urged the President to set me free. Letters poured into the office of the Pardon Attorney. By the last week in January 1979, rumors were flying. On January 28, the President's sister, Ruth Carter Stapleton, came to visit me.

The next day, George greeted me in the visiting room and announced, "I've got good news for you . . . But let me explain the whole thing to you before you say anything . . . Your sentence has been commuted, but there are conditions."

He read me the long "Conditional Commutation of Sentence," which bore the Presidential Gold Seal and the signature of Jimmy Carter. In effect, the President was saying that he was commuting my sentence for humanitarian reasons. Then a long string of conditions was attached, such as not consorting with known criminals, not being around weapons of any kind, and having to report to the probation department for a year.

He then read the White House's press announcement on commuting my sentence:

> It is the consensus of all of those most familiar with this case that but for the extraordinary criminal and degrading experiences that the petitioner suffered as a victim of the SLA she would not have become a participant in the criminal acts for which she stands convicted and sentenced and would not have suffered the punishment and other consequences she has endured.

The President had postdated the commutation to February 1 to allow for arrangements for my release. I was immediately moved from the general prison area to a secluded section of the hospital wing and locked in a room for which only two officials had the key. Meanwhile, they planned my release as if it were a military operation. Maximum security was arranged. No one wanted me assassinated on prison grounds.

For the better part of three days I sat in isolation, too excited and too nervous to do anything but pace up and down that small room and think. It was all over; I was going home.

Allowed the use of a telephone, I talked with my family and friends and helped plan the homecoming party for about fifty family and committee members. I don't know how I got through those three days of waiting, but at 8 A.M. on February 1, 1979, almost five years from the day of my kidnapping, having spent almost two years in prison, I walked out of Pleasanton.

I waved the gold-sealed commutation paper at the television cameras, and called out: "Here it is—the commutation."

At home, I hugged my parents at the doorstep, greeted and kissed relatives, and then gave one more interview to a crowd of smiling journalists and cameramen. The questions put to me were all friendly in tone and pretty much what I expected. But at one point, when I was saying that I might go on a vacation to get away from it all, Jane Pauley, of the *Today* show, asked: "But where can you go where you wouldn't be known as Patricia Hearst?"

My response was immediate and from the heart: "I don't see anything wrong with being Patricia Hearst."

INDEX